Microsoft®

Administrator's Pocket Consultant

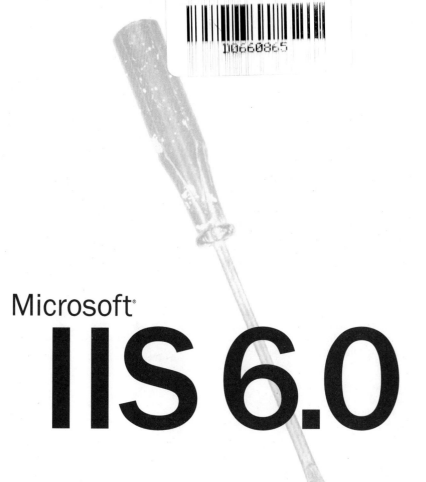

Microsoft®
IIS 6.0

William R. Stanek

PUBLISHED BY
Microsoft Press
A Division of Microsoft Corporation
One Microsoft Way
Redmond, Washington 98052-6399

Copyright © 2003 by William R. Stanek

Library of Congress Cataloging-in-Publication Data pending.

Printed and bound in the United States of America.

1 2 3 4 5 6 7 8 9   QWE   8 7 6 5 4 3

Distributed in Canada by H.B. Fenn and Company Ltd.

A CIP catalogue record for this book is available from the British Library.

Microsoft Press books are available through booksellers and distributors worldwide. For further information about international editions, contact your local Microsoft Corporation office or contact Microsoft Press International directly at fax (425) 936-7329. Visit our Web site at www.microsoft.com/mspress. Send comments to *mspinput@microsoft.com*.

Acquisitions Editor: Jeff Koch
Project Editors: Valerie Woolley, Julie Miller
Technical Editor: Bob Hogan

Body Part No. X08-64090

Contents at a Glance

Table of Contents

Part II
Web Server Administration

Part III
Essential Services Administration

Part IV
Performance, Optimization, and Maintenance

Tables

Acknowledgments

Writing *Microsoft IIS 6.0 Administrator's Pocket Consultant* was a lot of fun—and a lot of work. As you'll see, IIS 6.0 is very different from its predecessors, and that meant a lot of research to ensure the book was as accurate as it could be. It is gratifying to see techniques I've used time and again to solve problems put into a printed book so that others may benefit from them. But no man is an island and this book couldn't have been written without help from some very special people.

As I've stated in *Microsoft Windows XP Administrator's Pocket Consultant* and in *Microsoft Windows Server 2003 Administrator's Pocket Consultant*, the team at Microsoft Press is top-notch. Julie Miller and Valerie Woolley were instrumental throughout the writing process. They helped me stay on track and get the tools I needed to write this book. Completing and publishing the book wouldn't have been possible without their help! Susan McClung headed up the editorial process for nSight, Inc. As the Project Manager, she wore many hats and helped out in many ways. Thank you!

Unfortunately for the writer (but fortunately for readers), writing is only one part of the publishing process. Next came editing and author review. I must say, Microsoft Press has the most thorough editorial and technical review process I've seen anywhere—and I've written a lot of books for many different publishers. Bob Hogan was the technical editor for the book. Once again, it was a great pleasure working with Bob. I'd also like to thank Joseph Gustaitis for his careful copy editing of this book. I believe Joe has been the copy editor for every Pocket Consultant that I've written. His work is always top-notch!

I would also like to thank Michael Bolinger, Jeff Koch, and Juliana Aldous Atkinson. Thank you for being flexible when it came to the writing and the schedule. Thank you also for shepherding this project through the publishing process!

Hopefully, I haven't forgotten anyone, but if I have, it was an oversight. *Honest.*;-)

Introduction

Microsoft IIS 6.0 Administrator's Pocket Consultant is designed to be a concise and easy-to-use resource for managing Web servers running Internet Information Services (IIS), Indexing Service, File Transfer Protocol (FTP), Simple Mail Transfer Protocol (SMTP), Post Office Protocol 3 (POP3) Service, and Web Service Extensions, including ASP, ASP.NET, Background Intelligent Transfer Service, and Microsoft Windows .NET Framework. This is the readable resource guide that you'll want on your desktop at all times. The book covers everything you need to perform core Web administration tasks for IIS, Indexing Services, ASP, ASP.NET, FTP, SMTP, POP3 Service, and Web Service Extensions. Because the focus is on giving you maximum value in a pocket-sized guide, you don't have to wade through hundreds of pages of extraneous information to find what you're looking for. Instead, you'll find exactly what you need to get the job done.

In short, the book is designed to be the one resource you turn to whenever you have questions regarding Web server administration. To this end, the book zeroes in on daily administration procedures, frequently used tasks, documented examples, and options that are representative while not necessarily inclusive. One of the key goals is to keep content so concise that the book remains compact and easy to navigate and yet to ensure that the book is packed with as much information as possible—making it a valuable resource. Thus, rather than a hefty 1000-page tome or a lightweight 100-page quick reference, you get a valuable resource guide that can help you quickly and easily perform common tasks, solve problems, and implement advanced IIS techniques, such as customized redirection, metabase optimization, and automation scripts.

Who Is This Book For?

Microsoft IIS 6.0 Administrator's Pocket Consultant covers IIS, Indexing Service, FTP, SMTP, POP3 Service, and Web Service Extensions, including ASP, ASP.NET, Background Intelligent Transfer Service, and Windows .NET Framework. The book is designed for:

- Current Microsoft Web administrators
- Intranet / extranet administrators
- Administrators migrating to Microsoft Web-based solutions
- Programmers, engineers, and QA personnel who manage internal or test servers running any of these services

To pack in as much information as possible, I had to assume that you already have basic networking skills and a basic understanding of Web servers and that both IIS and Indexing Services are successfully installed on your systems. With this in mind, I don't devote entire chapters to understanding the Web services, using name services, building Web sites, or installing IIS. I do, however, cover configuration, enterprise-wide server management, performance tuning, optimization, automation, and much more.

I also assume that you're fairly familiar with the standard Windows user interface and that if you plan to use the scripting techniques outlined in the book, you know scripting. If you need help learning Windows or scripting, you should read other resources (many of which are available from Microsoft Press).

How Is This Book Organized?

Microsoft IIS 6.0 Administrator's Pocket Consultant is designed to be used in the daily administration of IIS, Indexing Service, FTP, SMTP, POP3 Service, and Web Service Extensions, and, as such, the book is organized according to job-related tasks rather than service features. If you're reading this book, you should be aware of the relationship between Pocket Consultants and Administrator's Companions. Both books are designed to be a part of an overall administrator's library. While Pocket Consultants are the down-and-dirty, in-the-trenches books, Administrator's Companions are the comprehensive tutorials and references that cover every aspect of deploying a product or technology in the enterprise.

Speed and ease of reference is an essential part of this hands-on guide. The book has an expanded table of contents and an extensive index for finding answers to problems quickly. Many other quick reference features have been added to the book as well. These features include quick step-by-steps, lists, tables with fast facts, and extensive cross-references. The book is broken down into both parts and chapters. The parts contain a part-opener paragraph or two about the chapters grouped in that part.

Part I, "Web Administration Fundamentals," covers the fundamental tasks you need for IIS administration. Chapter 1 provides an overview of IIS administration tools, techniques, and concepts. Chapter 2 explores core IIS administration. You'll learn about administration components, Windows services, Internet Services Manager, and server configurations.

In Part II, "Web Server Administration," you'll find the essential tasks for administering Web servers running IIS. Chapter 3 details management techniques for Web sites and servers. You'll also learn how to create and manage virtual directories. Customizing IIS is the focus of Chapter 4. In this chapter you'll learn about managing individual pages, browser redirection techniques, custom headers and footers, server error messages, and more. Chapter 5 discusses techniques and procedures you'll use to run IIS applications on your Web servers. Chapter 6 extends this discussion to cover ASP.NET, worker processes, and application pools.

Chapter 7 covers Web site and server security. To manage server security, you'll create user logins, configure directory permissions, and assign operators. The permissions and operator privileges you assign determine the actions users can perform as well as what areas of the Web site they can access. The final chapter in this section explores server certificates and Secure Sockets Layer (SSL). You use certificates to enable secure Web communications. SSL is used to protect sensitive information by encrypting the data sent between client browsers and your server.

Essential services administration is the subject of Part III. Chapter 9 covers techniques for managing File Transfer Protocol (FTP) servers. You'll find information on configuring FTP servers, controlling access to directories, enabling anonymous uploads and downloads, and more. Chapter 10 focuses on key issues related to working with SMTP and POP3 e-mail services. Chapter 11 continues this discussion with a look at advanced configuration issues. The final chapter in this part examines indexing services. You'll learn all about the latest indexing techniques, creating and managing catalogs, tuning performance, and creating index service query forms.

Part IV, "Performance, Optimization, and Maintenance," covers administration tasks you'll use to enhance and maintain IIS. Chapter 13 provides the essentials for monitoring Web server performance and solving performance problems. Chapter 14 starts with a look at common tasks for tracking user access and then dives into configuring server logs. Chapter 15 explores IIS optimization, and Chapter 16 covers IIS backup and recovery. You'll learn how to update registry settings for IIS and how to work with the IIS metabase.

Conventions Used in This Book

I've used a variety of elements to help keep the text clear and easy to follow. You'll find code terms and listings in monospace type, except when I tell you to actually type a command. In that case the command, as well as anything else you should type in, appear in **bold** type. When I introduce and define a new term, I put it in *italics*.

Other conventions include the following:

Note To provide additional details on a particular point that needs emphasis.

Best Practices To examine the best technique to use when working with advanced configuration and administration concepts.

Caution To warn you when there are potential problems you should look out for.

More Info To offer pointers to more information on the subject.

Real World To provide real-world advice when discussing advanced topics.

Security Alert To point out important Microsoft Windows Server 2003 and IIS security issues.

 Tip To offer helpful hints or additional information.

I truly hope you find that *Microsoft IIS 6.0 Administrator's Pocket Consultant* provides everything you need to perform essential administrative tasks on IIS as quickly and efficiently as possible. Your thoughts are welcome; please send them to me at *williamstanek@aol.com*. Thank you.

Support

Every effort has been made to ensure the accuracy of this book and the contents of the companion disc. Microsoft Press provides corrections for books through the World Wide Web at the following address:

http://mspress.microsoft.com/support/

If you have comments, questions, or ideas regarding this book or the companion disc, please send them to Microsoft Press using either of the following methods:

Postal Mail:

> Microsoft Press
> Attn: Editor, *Microsoft IIS 6.0 Administrator's Pocket Consultant*
> One Microsoft Way
> Redmond, WA 98052-6399

E-mail:

> *mspinput@microsoft.com*

Please note that product support isn't offered through the above mail addresses. For support information, visit Microsoft's Web site at *http://support.microsoft.com/*.

Part I

Microsoft Windows Server 2003 Web Administration Fundamentals

The goal of Part I of this book is to introduce you to IIS 6.0, focusing on the fundamentals you need for Web administration. Chapter 1 provides an overview of Web administration tools, techniques, and concepts. Chapter 2 explores core Web administration using Microsoft Internet Information Services (IIS). You'll learn about administration components, Internet Information Services (IIS) Manager, and server configurations.

Chapter 1

Overview of Microsoft Web Services

Each new version of Microsoft Internet Information Services (IIS) has represented a major advance in Web server technology. The changes have been dramatic, and they've improved reliability, availability, scalability, manageability, and security. However, no version of IIS has brought the kinds of changes you'll find in IIS 6.0—so if you think you know IIS 6 because you knew a previous version, think again.

Microsoft's entire .NET strategy is tied to IIS 6., so much so that you can think of IIS as the heart of Web application services within the Microsoft Windows .NET Framework. IIS is no longer a simple bundle of services for putting up a Web site—it's a complete solution for hosting Web servers and Web applications, and the Web application architecture is one of the most versatile you'll find anywhere.

IIS 6 has been redesigned from the bottom up. For starters, ASP.NET and the Windows .NET Framework are fully integrated into IIS 6, which significantly changes the way you use IIS. Further, unlike IIS 5, where the main Web server process was often a major choke point that severely affected performance, IIS 6 has a redesigned request processing architecture that allows the server to perform better, to reserve fewer resources, to handle more virtual servers, to detect failures and resolve them, and much more.

IIS 6 has many other new and enhanced features. Few are more important than the changes to the security architecture. IIS 6 has multiple levels of security, and it adds authentication mechanisms (including .NET Passport authentication and delegated authentication),improves Secure Sockets Layer (SSL) by enhancing performance and adding support for crypto service providers, and supports Uniform Resource Locator (URL) authorization whereby administrators can control access according to applications and URLs.

Because of the many changes, a lot of what you know about IIS is obsolete or irrelevant. But it's not all bad news. There's a light at the end of the tunnel—well, it's more like a freight train coming right at you—but it's there. The changes in IIS 6 are well worth the time and effort you'll spend learning the new architecture and the new techniques required to manage Web servers. Our dependence on ASP.NET and Windows .NET Framework will only grow over time, and the more you learn about the heart of the .NET architecture—IIS 6—the better prepared you'll be for now and for the future.

Note Throughout this book I'll refer to administration of IIS, Web applications, and the Indexing Service as *Microsoft Web administration* or simply *Web administration*. Microsoft Indexing Service is used to create text indexes of the contents and properties of files so that the files can be searched using standard queries.

As you get started with Microsoft Web administration, you should concentrate on these key areas:

- What's new or changed in IIS 6
- How IIS works with your hardware
- How IIS works with Microsoft Windows–based operating systems
- Which administration tools are available
- Which administration techniques you can use to manage and maintain IIS

 Note In this book, the term *Windows Server 2003* refers to these members of the Microsoft Windows Server 2003 family: Windows Server 2003, Standard Edition; Windows Server 2003, Enterprise Edition; Windows Server 2003, Datacenter Edition; and Windows Server 2003, Web Edition. In addition, all procedures described in this book are based on the default version of Windows Server 2003; if you are using the Classic Start menu, some of the steps will be slightly different.

Introducing IIS 6

Internet Information Services (IIS) is designed to provide secure, scalable solutions for creating and managing World Wide Web sites and servers. You can use IIS to publish information on intranets, extranets, and the Internet. Because today's Web sites use related services, like File Transfer Protocol (FTP), Simple Mail Transfer Protocol (SMTP), ASP.NET, and Windows .NET Framework, IIS bundles these services as part of a comprehensive offering. A separate but related service is the Indexing Service, which is used to build catalogs of documents that can be searched. When you add this capability to a Web site, it allows users to search for topics of interest using a standard Hypertext Markup Language (HTML) form.

IIS 6 Request Processing Architecture

Unlike IIS 5, where the main Web server process was often a major choke point that severely affected performance, IIS 6 has a redesigned request processing architecture that allows the server to perform better, to reserve fewer resources, to handle more virtual servers, to detect failures and resolve them, and much more. This architecture has several key features:

- **HTTP listener process** In IIS 6, the main Web server process is a kernel-mode driver called Http.sys. It's used for Hypertext Transfer Protocol (HTTP) parsing and caching. It's responsible for listening for requests and passing them off to worker processes.

- **Worker processes**   Worker processes run in an isolated mode that allows administrators to group different Web applications. Worker processes are isolated by application pool and can be allocated on demand, meaning they're allocated system resources when they become active and don't use system resources when they're inactive. This architecture improvement, along with others, ensures that IIS 6 can support many more concurrent processes than previous versions.

- **Application pools**   Groups of Web applications are called *application pools*. Application pools are separated from one another by process boundaries and are serviced by one or more worker processes, which applications in the pool share. All Web sites and applications on a server are assigned to an application pool. Settings for application pools allow you to monitor worker processes and to recover automatically from any problems that might occur.

- **Application pool request queue**   When requests are passed off from Http.sys to worker processes, the requests are placed in the appropriate application pool request queue. Each application pool has a separate request queue. Worker processes assigned to the application pool handle the request in first in, first out (FIFO) order. You can assign worker processes a processor affinity so that specific processors handle their workload.

Although you'll learn even more about the request processing architecture in Chapter 2, "Core IIS Administration," these two chapters only scratch the surface of the dramatic change the new architecture represents. To understand the architecture completely, you'll need to read the chapters in Part II, "Web Server Administration." These chapters discuss site, server, and application configuration; worker process assignment; and application pool configuration.

IIS 6 Security Architecture

The security architecture is another major area where IIS 6 has been redesigned. The new security architecture has several important features that you should know about right now:

- **Capability lockdown**   IIS isn't installed by default on Windows Server 2003. When you install IIS, the default installation allows only static content (HTML files) to be served, and all other functions and types of content must be specifically enabled. Nonstatic content is managed through the Web Service Extensions settings. See Chapter 4, "Customizing Web Server Content," for details. Further, if you upgraded the operating system on a server that was previously running IIS, the IIS service might be disabled. To reenable IIS, you might need to enable the IIS service as well as the associated services.

- **Privilege changes**   By default, many IIS 6 features run using the built-in account NetworkService. This account has very few privileges and is designed to ensure that IIS and related processes have very few privileges on the server. Although good for security and reducing potential vulnerabilities, it might change the way you use IIS, and some applications or features might work differently than you expect. Be sure to take a look at this account's privileges.

- **Tool and file restrictions** IIS won't serve requests for invalid files. It verifies all file requests before serving them, checking file extensions and for the existence of the requested content. IIS won't run command-line tools or other command-line executables.

- **Authentication enhancements** IIS has a number of enhancements for authenticating requests, including URL authorization and delegated authentication, but the most important change is without doubt the support for .NET Passport authentication. Through their .NET Passport identification, users can be validated and authorized access according to the access controls in their corresponding Active Directory service user account.

 Real World There's a way to run Web applications in IIS 5 mode. It's called IIS 5 isolation mode. Although operating in this mode might solve problems with applications that won't run under the new IIS 6 architecture, security restrictions might also be affecting the way applications are running. Be sure to read Chapter 7, "Enhancing Web Server Security," so that you understand the changes to the security architecture.

Additional IIS 6 Features

IIS 6 has many additional features. Some that you'll want to learn about include:

- **FTP restart** FTP restart allows clients to resume FTP downloads without having to download the entire file again if an interruption occurs during transfer. When a connection is broken during a download, compliant clients (such as Microsoft Internet Explorer 5) can reestablish their file transfer using the REST command, and the file transfer will resume where it left off.

- **FTP user isolation** IIS 6 allows you to isolate users to their own directories so that they can't view or overwrite other users' content.

- **Health monitoring** Just as Windows Server 2003 monitors the health of its running processes, so does IIS 6. IIS 6 takes this monitoring a few steps further, though. It can detect and recover from memory leaks, problems in code, and blocking calls. IIS can also check for nonresponsive processes and then recycle or restart processes as necessary.

- **Host headers** Host headers allow you to host multiple Web sites on a single computer with only one Internet Protocol (IP) address. Here, IIS uses the host name passed in the HTTP header to determine the site that a client is requesting.

- **HTTP 1.1 and HTTP compression** IIS fully supports the HTTP 1.1 protocol and the compression enhancements it defines. Using HTTP compression, you can compress both static and dynamic results of HTTP queries for transmission to HTTP 1.1–compliant clients. Unlike IIS 5, where compression was implemented using an Internet Server Application Programming Interface (ISAPI) filter and could only be enabled for an entire server, IIS 6 builds in compression as a feature that you can control precisely to the file level.

- **Kernel-mode cache** Http.sys runs in kernel mode and passes requests directly to the worker processes without intermediaries. Previously requested static content can be cached, and unlike previous versions of IIS, dynamic content can be cached in kernel mode as well to improve performance. To better support Active Server Pages (ASP), ASP templates are stored in memory and deallocated from memory to free space for new templates. Unlike previous versions, IIS 6 uses a persistent ASP template cache. Here, deallocated templates are written to disk, where they can be accessed and reallocated. IIS 6 also has a heuristics-based caching policy. This policy is designed to ensure that files are cached when it makes sense and aren't cached otherwise.

- **On-demand starting and time-out** You can configure application pools so that worker processes start on demand and time out when they're no longer needed. By starting on demand, the process uses resources only when it's active. By timing out, the resources used by the worker process can be freed up when the process has been idle for a certain amount of time.

- **Process accounting and process throttling** Process accounting provides information about how individual Web sites use CPU resources. Process throttling allows you to limit CPU usage for out-of-process applications and thereby potentially reduce performance problems on the server as a whole.

- **Rapid-fail protection** Rapid-fail protection allows IIS to monitor worker processes for failure. If IIS detects failure, IIS can take actions to record and recover, such as logging a related event in the event logs and restarting the worker process.

- **SSL 3 and TLS** SSL 3 and Transport Layer Security (TLS) provide secure methods of exchanging information between clients and servers. SSL 3 and TLS also enable the use of client certificates that can be read by Internet Server Application Programming Interface (ISAPI) server pages. Client certificates are used to authenticate users and control access by mapping the client certificate to a Windows user account.

- **WebDAV** Web Distributed Authoring and Versioning (WebDAV) extends the HTTP 1.1 protocol and is integrated into IIS. Using WebDAV, remote users can publish, lock, and manage resources on a Web server using an HTTP connection.

- **XML metabase** The IIS metabase is now formatted using Extensible Markup Language (XML) and stored in plaintext files. XML's structure makes it easier to search and maintain the metabase and also improves performance when working with the metabase. The XML metabase can be edited while IIS is running. It can be used to save configurations at the server, site, or application level so they can be used on other servers, which can help ensure that configurations across server farms are exact copies of each other. The metabase also supports automatic versioning and history. This means that IIS automatically tracks changes to the metabase and changes that are made can be rolled back to restore a previous configuration.

Choosing Appropriate Web Server Hardware

Guidelines for choosing hardware for Internet servers are much different from those for choosing other types of servers. A Web hosting provider might host multiple sites on the same computer and might also have service level agreements that determine the level of availability and performance required. On the other hand, a busy e-commerce site might have a dedicated Web server or even multiple load-balanced servers. Given that Internet servers are used in a wide variety of circumstances and might be either shared or dedicated, here are some guidelines for choosing server hardware:

- **Memory** The amount of memory that's required depends on many factors, including the requirements of other services, the size of frequently accessed content files, and the random access memory (RAM) requirements of the Web applications. High-volume servers should have a minimum of 512 MB of RAM. More RAM will allow more files to be cached, reducing disk requests.

 Note Don't forget that as you add physical memory, virtual paging to disk grows as well. With this in mind, you might want to ensure that the Pagefile.sys file is on the appropriate disk drive.

More Info For detailed information on memory management and performance tuning, see Chapter 13, "Performance Tuning and Monitoring."

- **CPU** The CPU processes the instructions received by the computer. The clock speed of the CPU and the size of the data bus determine how quickly information moves among the CPU, RAM, and system buses. Static content, such as HTML and images, place very little burden on the processor, and standard Windows Server 2003 recommended configurations should suffice. Faster clock speeds and multiple processors increase the upper capacity of a Web server, particularly for sites that rely on dynamic content.

- **SMP** IIS supports symmetric multiprocessors (SMPs) and can use additional processors to improve performance. If the system is running only IIS and doesn't rely on dynamic content or encryption, a single processor might suffice. You should always use multiple processors if IIS is running alongside other services, such as Microsoft SQL Server or Microsoft Exchange Server.

- **Disk drives** The amount of data storage capacity you need depends entirely on the size of content files and the number of sites supported. You need enough disk space to store all your data plus workspace, system files, and virtual memory. Input/output (I/O) throughput is just as important as drive capacity. However, disk I/O is rarely a bottleneck for Web sites on the public Internet—generally, bandwidth limits throughput. High-bandwidth sites should consider hardware-based redundant array of independent disks (RAID) solutions using copper or fiber channel–based small computer system interfaces (SCSIs).

- **Data protection** Unless you can tolerate hours of downtime, you should add protection against unexpected drive failures by using RAID. RAID 0 (disk striping without parity) offers optimal read/write performance, but if a drive fails, IIS won't be able to continue operation until the drive is replaced. Because of this, RAID 0 isn't the recommended choice. RAID 1 (disk mirroring) creates duplicate copies of data on separate drives, but recovery from drive failure might interrupt operations while you restore the failed drive from backups. RAID 5 (disk striping with parity) offers good protection against single-drive failure but has poor write performance. Keep in mind that if you've configured redundant load-balanced servers, you might not need RAID. With load balancing, the additional servers might offer the necessary fault tolerance.

- **UPS** Sudden power loss and power spikes can seriously damage hardware. To prevent this, get an uninterruptible power supply (UPS). A UPS system gives you time to shut down the system properly in the event of a power outage, and it's also important in maintaining system integrity when the server uses write-back caching controllers that do not have on-board battery backups. Professional hosting providers often offer UPS systems that can maintain power indefinitely during extended power outages.

If you follow these hardware guidelines, you'll be well on your way to success with IIS.

Choosing the Server Operating System

IIS 6, Web applications, and the Indexing Service are designed to run on Windows-based operating systems. Four versions of Windows Server 2003 are available. Each server edition has different features:

- **Windows Server 2003, Web Edition** This version of the software is designed to provide Web services for deploying Web sites and Web-based applications. As such, this server edition includes Windows .NET Framework, IIS, ASP.NET and network load balancing features but lacks many other features, including Active Directory. In fact, the only other key Windows features in this edition are the Distributed File System (DFS), Encrypting File System (EFS), and Remote Desktop for administration. Windows Server 2003, Web Edition, supports up to 2 GB of RAM and two central processing units (CPUs).

- **Windows Server 2003, Standard Edition** This version is designed to provide services and resources to other systems on a network. It's a direct replacement for Windows NT 4 Server and Windows 2000 Server. The operating system has a rich set of features and configuration options. Windows Server 2003, Standard Edition, supports up to 4 GB of RAM and four CPUs.

- **Windows Server 2003, Enterprise Edition** This version extends the features provided in Windows Server 2003, Standard Edition to include support for Cluster Service, Metadirectory services, and Services for Macintosh. It also supports 64-bit Intel Itanium-based computers, hot-swappable RAM, and Non-Uniform Memory Access (NUMA). Enterprise servers can have up to 32 GB of RAM on x86, 64 GB of RAM on Itanium, and eight CPUs.

- **Windows Server 2003, Datacenter Edition** This version is the most robust Windows server. It has enhanced clustering features and supports very large memory configurations with up to 64 GB of RAM on x86 and 512 GB of RAM on Itanium. It has a minimum CPU requirement of 8 and can support up 32 CPUs in all.

Note The various server editions support the same core features and administration tools. This means you can use the techniques discussed in this book regardless of which edition of Windows Server 2003 you're using.

Most of the time you'll want to consider using Windows Server 2003, Web Edition, for your Web server and Web application server needs. However, as mentioned above, the Web edition has specific feature limitations. If you need Active Directory to be installed on the server (which usually isn't the case), you'll want to install a different version. If you need Cluster Service or other high availability features, you'll need to install Windows Server 2003, Enterprise Edition, or Windows Server 2003, Datacenter Edition.

Other feature limitations of the Web Edition will affect your decision as well. The Web Edition doesn't support the following Windows features: 64-bit Support for Intel Itanium-Based Computers, Cluster Service, Enterprise Universal Description, Discovery and Integration (UDDI) Services, Fax Service, Hot Add Memory, Internet Authentication Service (IAS), Internet Connection Firewall (ICF), Metadirectory Services (MMS) Support, Network Bridge, Internet Connection Sharing (ICS), NUMA, Remote Installation Services (RIS), Removable and Remote Storage, Services for Macintosh, Terminal Server, Terminal Server Session Directory, and Windows Media Services. Check the Windows Server documentation for any changes.

Working with IIS 6: What You Need to Know Right Now

As you've seen, IIS 6 is very different from its predecessors. IIS 6 has a new processing architecture, a new security architecture, and many other enhancements. As you might expect with all these changes, there are many things you should know right away about IIS 6 components, configuration, and services.

Installing Web and Application Server Components and Default Sites

IIS and Indexing Service are no longer installed during the installation of the operating system. You install these and other Web server components through the Windows Components Wizard, accessible through Add Or Remove Programs on the Control Panel. The key Web server components you might want to use include:

- **Certificate Services** Installs a certificate authority to issue public key certificates for use in authentication.

- **E-mail Services** Provides basic Post Office Protocol 3 (POP3) services so that POP3 mail clients can send and receive mail in the domain. Once you install this service, you define a default domain for mail exchange and then create and manage mailboxes. This basic service works well for datacenters and remote locations where e-mail exchange is needed but you don't need the power and versatility of Exchange Server.

- **Indexing Service** Installs indexing service for fast full-text searching of Web documents.

- **Web Application Server** Provides IIS and ASP.NET services. You can install ASP.NET, COM+, Distributed Transaction Coordinator (DTC), IIS, Message Queuing, Microsoft Data Engine, and the Web Application Server Console.

By default, all subcomponents of certificate services, e-mail services, and indexing services are installed when the related option is selected in the Windows Components Wizard. For the Application Server component this isn't the case. You'll want to select this component and then click Details. Then, add components as necessary by selecting them. Some of these subcomponents have subcomponents of their own as well. The one you'll want to check is IIS. In the Application Server dialog box, select Internet Information Services (IIS) and then click Details.

The IIS application server components include:

- **Background Intelligent Transfer Service (BITS) Server Extensions** Installs an extension that allows Web clients to use available bandwidth for data transfers and restart incomplete transfers.

- **Common Files** Installs common files required by IIS programs and documentation that covers server administration and publishing site content.

- **File Transfer Protocol (FTP) Service** Installs the FTP server service used to transfer files using FTP.

- **FrontPage 2002 Server Extensions** Installs extensions that allow Web site authoring and administration using Microsoft FrontPage and Microsoft Visual InterDev. If you elect to install these extensions, the Administration Web site isn't installed. IIS is configured so that you can manage servers and applications using FrontPage or the Microsoft SharePoint Team Services.

- **Internet Information Services (IIS) Manager** Installs the MMC snap-in for the IIS administration tools.

Note Throughout this book, we will refer to the Internet Information Services (IIS) Manager server component as the *IIS snap-in*.

- **Internet Printing** Installs extensions that allow Web-based printer management and printing to shared printers over the Internet, an extranet, or an intranet.

- **NNTP Service** Installs the Network News Transfer Protocol (NNTP) service used to create and manage newsgroups.

- **SMTP Service** Installs the Simple Mail Transfer Protocol (SMTP) service used for outgoing mail from a Web server.

- **World Wide Web Server** Installs the Web service used to publish and manage Web sites.

When you install Internet services, default sites are created on the computer. In most instances these default sites are active by default. If the default sites aren't active, you can start them using the IIS snap-in. To start the snap-in, click Start, choose All Programs, Administrative Tools, and then Internet Information Services (IIS) Manager. Default sites you see might include:

- **Default FTP Site** The default site for FTP services—which is installed only when you elect to install this option as part of the IIS installation. By default, anonymous connections are allowed access to FTP sites. Disable this service if you don't intend to use FTP for file transfers.

- **Default Web Site** The default site for Web services. By default, anonymous connections are allowed access to Web sites. Disable anonymous connections unless your site is ready to go public.

- **Administration Web Site** The default site for browser-based administration. By default, this site is only accessible from the local system. If you wish to use this service for remote administration, change the default IP filtering.

 Note When the administration Web site is stopped, you can't manage sites using the Remote Administration tools. These tools are Web-based and depend on the administration Web site. This Web site isn't enabled by default. You must enable ASP as a valid Web Server Extension, as discussed in Chapter 3, "Configuring Web Sites and Servers," and also start the site. If you install the FrontPage Server Extensions on a Web server, you use the SharePoint tools for Web-based administration.

- **Default SMTP Virtual Server** The default site for SMTP services. If you don't use pages that generate e-mail messages, don't start SMTP services. By default, only servers that authenticate themselves in the domain can relay mail on the server. This denies permission to relay e-mail through the server and protects the server from being used to deliver unsolicited e-mail messages.

- **Default NNTP Virtual Server** The default site for NNTP services. The default configuration allows client posting and updates from news feeds and grants permission to other servers to pull articles from the server. If necessary, change these settings before starting an NNTP server.

If an IIS feature you want to use isn't available in the IIS snap-in, you can install it using the Windows Components Wizard. To access and use this wizard, follow these steps:

1. Log on to the computer using an account with administrator privileges.

2. Click Add Or Remove Programs in the Control Panel. This displays the Add Or Remove Programs dialog box.

Note   Throughout this book, I refer to clicking or double-clicking, the most common techniques used for accessing folders and running programs. Through the Taskbar And Start Menu Properties dialog box, you can change the look and feel of the graphical interface. Some options, such as the Control Panel, can appear as menus with clickable menu items that run programs or as menu items that open dialog boxes. You can also change the mouse click options with the Folder Options utility in the Control Panel to allow either single-click open/run or double-click to open. Because of this, when I say click, you might actually have to double-click, or vice versa.

3. Click Add/Remove Windows Components to start the Windows Components Wizard, shown in Figure 1-1.

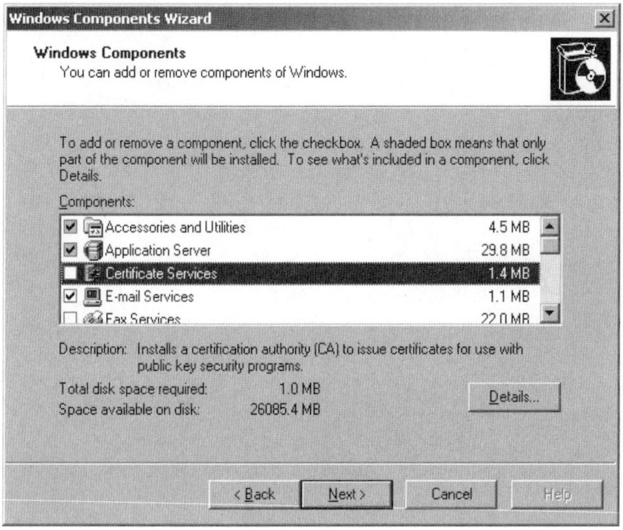

Figure 1-1. *Use the Windows Component Wizard to select components to add or remove.*

4. Select Certificate Services, E-Mail Services, or Indexing Service as necessary.

5. Select Application Server. Click Details to add and remove individual components. You can now select subcomponents to install or uninstall them.

6. Select Internet Information Services (IIS). Click Details to add and remove individual components. You can now select subcomponents to install or uninstall them.

7. When ready to continue, click OK twice and then Next. The selected components are then installed (or uninstalled).

8. Click Finish when prompted.

Installing Internet Services and Service-Related Accounts

When you install Web and application server components, several services are installed on the computer. You can check for these services using the Services utility or Computer Management. Both utilities are found on the Administrative Tools menu. Services you might see include:

- **ASP.NET State Service**   Provides support for out-of-process session states when using ASP.NET

- **Background Intelligent Transfer Service**   Transfers files in the background using idle network bandwidth

- **Certificate Services**   Provides services for creating, managing, and removing X.509 certificates

- **COM+ Event System**   Provides system event notification services for COM components

- **COM+ System Application**   Provides configuration and tracking for COM components

- **Cryptographic Services**   Provides management services for certificate authorities

- **Distributed Transaction Coordinator**   Coordinates transactions for Microsoft Distributed Transaction Coordinator (DTC)

- **FTP Publishing Service**   Provides services for transferring files using FTP and also allows administration of an FTP server through the IIS snap-in

- **HTTP SSL**   Enables SSL by providing the necessary services for Hypertext Transfer Protocol Secure (HTTPS)

- **IIS Admin Service**   Allows administration of IIS through the IIS snap-in

- **Indexing Service**   Indexes the contents and properties of files, providing quick access to files through a flexible query language

- **Message Queuing**   Provides the necessary services for distributed messaging and message queuing

- **Microsoft POP3 Service**   Provides POP3 service for mail transfer and retrieval

- **MSSQL$UDDI** Provides Web database services for the Microsoft Data Engine

- **MSSQLServerADHelper** Provides Active Directory helper services for the Microsoft Data Engine

- **Network News Transport Protocol (NNTP)** Provides network news services and allows administration of NNTP servers through the IIS snap-in

- **Simple Mail Transport Protocol (SMTP)** Provides mail transfer services and allows administration of SMTP sites through the IIS snap-in

- **SQLAgent$UDDI** Provides SQL Server Agent services for the Microsoft Data Engine

- **Web Element Manager** Provides access to user interface elements needed for the Remote Administration Web tools

- **World Wide Web Publishing Service** Provides services for transferring files using HTTP and also allows administration of an HTTP server

By default, most Web-related services run as the Local Service account. This allows the services to interact with the operating system. To tighten security, some services, such as the Microsoft POP3 service and the World Wide Web Publishing Service, run as the NetworkService account. This account has fewer privileges than the Local Service account.

Note You might find that the World Wide Web Publishing Service and other services normally running under the NetworkService account are running under the Local Service account on your system. This can happen if you install components, such as Certificate Services, that require more interaction with the operating system than a standard IIS installation.

When you install IIS, several accounts are created as well. These accounts are:

- **IIS_WPG** The IIS Worker Process Group account. All worker processes running under IIS use this group account. If this account is disabled or locked out, IIS won't function normally.

- **IUSR_*ComputerName*** The Internet guest account used by anonymous users to access Internet sites. If this account is disabled or locked out, anonymous users can't access Internet services. In a domain, this account is a member of the Domain Users and Guests groups. Otherwise, it's only a member of the Guests group.

- **IWAM_*ComputerName*** An account used by IIS to run out-of-process applications. If this account is disabled or locked out, out-of-process applications can't start. As all applications and sites configured under IIS 6 are technically out-of-process, IIS might not work properly if this account isn't available. In a domain, this account is a member of the Domain Users and IIS_WPG groups. Otherwise, it's only a member of the IIS_WPG groups.

Tip The IUSR and IWAM accounts have a password that never expires and can't be changed by users. You can, however, set and manage the password for these accounts as you would for any other account.

Other Web server and application components might cause additional accounts to be created, including the following:

- **ASPNET** An account used to run ASP.NET worker processes. This account is a member of the Domain Users group.
- **Cert Publishers** A group account that allows member users to publish X.509 public key certificates.

Web Administration Tools and Techniques

Web administrators will find that there are many ways to manage Web and application servers. The key administration tools and techniques are covered in the following sections.

Managing Resources with Key Administration Tools

Many tools are available for managing Web resources. Key tools you'll use are shown in Table 1-1. Most of these tools are available on the Administrative Tools menu. Click Start and choose All Programs, Administrative Tools, and then the tool you want to use. You can use all the tools listed in the table to manage local and remote resources. For example, you can connect to a new computer in the IIS snap-in and then, afterward, you can remotely manage all its sites and services from your system.

Table 1-1.   Quick Reference for Key Web Administration Tools

Administration Tool	Purpose
Active Directory Users and Computers	Manages domain user, group, and computer accounts.
Certification Authority	Manages certificate services for public key X.509 certificates.
Computer Management	Manages services, storage, and applications. The Services And Applications node provides quick access to Indexing Service catalogs and IIS sites and servers.
Data Sources	Configures and manages Open Database Connectivity (ODBC) data sources and drivers. Data sources link Web front ends with database back ends.
DNS	Public Internet sites must have fully qualified domain names (FQDNs) to resolve properly in browsers. Use the Domain Name System (DNS) administrative snap-in to manage the DNS configuration of your Windows Server DNS servers.

Table 1-1.   Quick Reference for Key Web Administration Tools

Administration Tool	Purpose
Event Viewer	Manages events and system logs.
Internet Information Services Snap-In	Manages Web and application server resources using a Microsoft Management Console (MMC) snap-in.
Remote Administration	Manages Web and application server resources using a browser-based interface. Formerly called Internet Services Manager.
Performance	Tracks system performance, pinpoints performance problems, and configures system event logs and alerts.
POP3 Service	Used to view and manage POP3 e-mail domains and mailboxes.
Services	Views service information; starts and stops system services; configures service logons and automated recoveries.

Installing Administration Tools

When you add services to a server, the tools needed to manage those services are automatically installed. If you want to manage these servers remotely, you might not have these tools installed on your workstation. In this case you need to install the administration tools on the workstation you're using.

To install the Windows administration tools, follow these steps:

1. Log on to the workstation using an account with administrator privileges.
2. Insert the Windows Server CD-ROM into the CD-ROM drive.
3. When the Autorun screen appears, click Perform Additional Tasks, and then click Browse This CD. This starts Windows Explorer.
4. Double-click the I386 folder, and then double-click Adminpak.msi. The complete set of Windows Server management tools is installed on your workstation or server.

Real World   The Windows 2000 Administration tools are incompatible with Windows XP Professional and Windows Server 2003. If you upgrade to Windows XP Professional from Windows 2000 Professional, you'll find that many of the Windows 2000 administration tools won't work and you'll encounter errors frequently. You should uninstall these tools and instead install the Windows Server Administration Tools Pack (Adminpak.msi) on the Windows XP Professional systems that administrators use. The Windows Server administration tools are compatible with both Windows 2000 and Windows Server 2003.

While you're working with the distribution CD-ROM, you might want to install the Windows Support Tools. The support tools are a collection of utilities for handling everything from system diagnostics to network monitoring. You can install the support tools by completing the following steps:

1. Insert the Windows Server CD-ROM into the CD-ROM drive.

2. When the Autorun screen appears, click Perform Additional Tasks, and then click Browse This CD. This starts Windows Explorer.

3. In Windows Explorer, double-click Support and then double-click Tools.

4. Double-click Suptools.msi. This starts the Windows Support Tools Setup Wizard. Click Next.

5. Read the End User License Agreement, and then, if you agree and want to continue, click I Agree and then click Next.

6. Enter your user information and then click Next.

7. Select the destination directory for the support tools. The default location is %ProgramFiles%\System Tools. If you don't want to use the default location, type a new directory path or click Browse to search for a location. The tools use about 23 MB of disk space.

8. Click Install Now.

 Note   %ProgramFiles% refers to the ProgramFiles environment variable. The Windows operating system has many environment variables, which are used to refer to user-specific and system-specific values. I'll often refer to environment variables using this syntax: %*Variable Name%*.

Web Administration Techniques

Web administrators have many options for managing IIS. The key administration tools are:

- Internet Information Services snap-in

- Remote Administration (formerly Internet Services Manager)

- IIS Administration objects (which are manipulated by the administration scripts)

- Administration scripts

The IIS snap-in provides the standard administration interface for IIS. Figure 1-2 shows the main window for the IIS snap-in. To start the IIS snap-in, click Start and choose All Programs, Administrative Tools, and then Internet Information Services (IIS) Manager.

When started, the IIS snap-in automatically connects to the local IIS installation, if it's available. Once you connect to remote IIS installations, the IIS snap-in automatically connects to these installations upon startup as well. You can change this behavior by disconnecting from the remote server while in the snap-in. See Chapter 3 for more information on using the IIS snap-in.

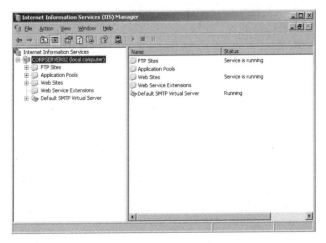

Figure 1-2. *Use the IIS snap-in to manage local and remote IIS installations.*

Remote Administration uses the administration Web site to access remote IIS installations using a secure HTTP connection. You can allow or disallow remote browser-based administration by starting or stopping the Administration Web site. When installed, IIS randomly selects two Transmission Control Protocol (TCP) port numbers from 2000 to 9999 and assigns these port numbers to the administration Web site. One TCP port is used for standard, not secure, connections and the other for secure connections to the administration Web site. The default configuration is to allow only secure connections for administration.

The site responds to browser requests for all permitted domains, but the administrator must specify the port number because it differs from the default HTTPS port 443. For example, if the server's domain name is primary.microsoft.com and the administrative port is 9394, you can connect to the administration Web site by typing the following URL into your browser window: *https://primary. microsoft.com:9394/.*

Figure 1-3 shows the main window for Remote Administration. By default, basic authentication is configured. Since you're required to use a secure connection (HTTPS), this setting is adequate, but you might want to consider using another authentication technique. With basic authentication, you're prompted for a user name and password when the site is accessed. If you provide the proper logon information and are a member of the Windows Administrators group, you'll be permitted to administer IIS remotely through the administration Web site.

Figure 1-3. *Use Remote Administration to manage remote IIS installations.*

In previous versions of IIS, you could designate Web site operators who could remotely administer IIS. Web site operators were a special group of users who had elevated privileges on individual Web sites. IIS 6 doesn't allow you to designate operators. But that's okay because most of the time operator accounts weren't used.

You can also manage IIS settings and configuration through Windows Script Host (WSH)—and you'll be happy to know that you no longer need to use Active Directory Service Interface (ADSI) to manage the metabase. Because the metabase is now formatted as XML and stored in plaintext files, you can say goodbye to complex key paths and all that other stuff that went along with it!

The IIS Windows scripts are stored in the %SystemRoot%\System32 directory. Table 1-2 provides an overview of each of the scripts. These scripts are all written using VBScript.

Table 1-2. **Quick Reference for Key IIS Administration Scripts**

Administration Script	Purpose
Iisapp.vbs	Reports process IDs and application pool IDs for currently running worker processes. These processes run as W3wp.exe.
Iisback.vbs	Allows you to back up or restore the IIS configuration. You can also list backups or delete individual backups.
Iiscnfg.vbs	Imports, exports, or copies the IIS configuration.
Iisext.vbs	Configures the Web Server Extensions.
Iisftp.vbs	Manages and lists available FTP sites.
Iisftpdr.vbs	Manages and lists virtual directories for an FTP site under a given root.
Iisvdir.vbs	Manages and lists virtual directories for a Web site under a given root.
Iisweb.vbs	Manages and lists available Web sites.

The scripts are designed to work with the command-line Windows Script Host, Cscript.exe. This host must be registered as the default scripting host on the computer you're using to execute the scripts. You can ensure that Cscript.exe is registered as the default host by entering the following command in a command prompt:

```
cscript //H:cscript
```

Because the IIS scripts are stored in the %SystemRoot%\System32 directory, you can run a script from any directory on the server by typing the script name on the command-line, such as:

```
iisweb /query
```

Type the script name followed by /? on the command-line to display basic help information.

Chapter 2
Core IIS Administration

Core Internet Information Services (IIS) administration tasks revolve around connecting to servers, managing services, and saving metabase configurations. In IIS you connect to individual servers and manage their IIS components through the IIS snap-in, the Application Server snap-in, or the Remote Administration tool. You can use a single IIS server to host multiple resources. Web and File Transfer Protocol (FTP) resources are referred to as Web sites and FTP sites, respectively. Simple Mail Transfer Protocol (SMTP) and Network News Transfer Protocol (NNTP) resources are referred to as SMTP virtual servers and NNTP virtual servers, respectively.

Sites and virtual servers are server processes that have their own configuration information, which can include Internet Protocol (IP) addresses, port numbers, and authentication settings. To perform most administration tasks with sites and servers, you'll need to log in to the IIS server using an account that has administrator privileges. You can find detailed information on security in Chapter 7, "Enhancing Web Server Security."

Understanding the IIS Architecture

Most administrators don't understand the actual underpinnings of IIS. Yet to really understand how IIS works, you have to understand the architecture. You can think of IIS as a layer over the operating system where, in most cases, you might need to perform an operating system level task before you perform an IIS task. This is true in several key areas:

- **Directories** Sites, virtual servers, and other resources use the Microsoft Windows Server 2003 file and directory structure. Before you create IIS resources, such as sites or virtual servers, you should ensure that any necessary directories have been created.

- **Permissions** Windows Server 2003 permissions ultimately determine whether users can access files and directories. Before users can access files and directories, you must ensure that the appropriate users and groups have access at the operating system level. After you set operating system (OS)– level permissions, you must set IIS-specific security permissions.

Windows services and processes are other areas where Windows Server 2003 and IIS are tightly integrated. IIS has two operating modes that affect services and processes. These operating modes are:

- **IIS 5 isolation mode** The standard processing mode of IIS 5
- **Worker Process isolation mode** The default processing mode of IIS 6.0 on a clean install

The IIS 5 isolation mode and worker process isolation mode are mutually exclusive. The World Wide Web Service can operate only in one mode or the other, which means that all Web sites configured on a server use the same operating mode.

The sections that follow examine each operating mode, providing a discussion of how, why, and when the modes are used, as well as providing details of what the components of each mode are. IIS application and application pools are discussed in detail in Chapter 5, "Running IIS Applications," and Chapter 6, "Managing ASP.NET, Application Pools, and Worker Processes."

Understanding and Using IIS 5 Isolation Mode

You use IIS 5 isolation mode to run Web applications that were developed for older versions of IIS. Using this operating mode affects how IIS is used and how IIS interacts with other components.

IIS 5 Isolation Mode Overview

IIS 5 isolation mode operates nearly the same as the standard mode of IIS 5 depicted in Figure 2-1. Service Host processes control all resources of the same type running on a server. Because of this, Windows Server 2003 uses the Service Host to manage all instances of a specific resource, such as Web or FTP sites, running on a server. For example, if you start or stop the World Wide Web Publishing Service, you're controlling all Web sites running on the server through the related Service Host process.

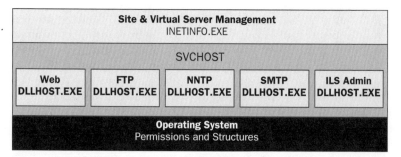

Figure 2-1. *Here is a conceptual view of the IIS 5 isolation mode.*

Because of the layered structure of IIS, starting or stopping an Internet Information Service doesn't directly affect the Service Host. Instead, Windows Server 2003 uses an intermediary to control the Service Host for you. This intermediary is the

InetInfo process. A single instance of Inetinfo.exe is used to manage the Service Hosts as well as Internet Server Application Programming Interface (ISAPI) applications that run within the IIS process context. When you control IIS individually, Windows Server 2003 controls the Service Host through InetInfo. InetInfo also makes it possible to manage all IIS resources running on a server. You can, for example, issue a restart command in the IIS snap-in that restarts IIS completely. See the section entitled "Starting, Stopping, and Restarting All Internet Services," later in this chapter, for more details.

ISAPI applications are a key part of the IIS 5 architecture. ISAPI applications are server-based applications that run on IIS Web sites. As Figure 2-2 shows, you use DLL Host (Dllhost.exe) to manage out-of-process ISAPI applications. Any pooled ISAPI applications running on the server run within the context of a single instance of Dllhost.exe. In contrast, isolated ISAPI applications run within the context of separate DLL Host processes.

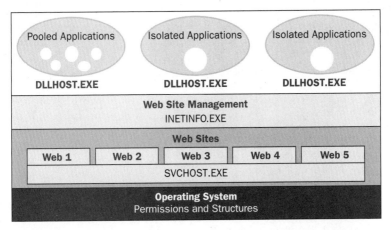

Figure 2-2. *Use DLL Host (Dllhost.exe) to manage out-of-process ISAPI applications.*

Understanding Application Incompatibilities and Consequences

You must use IIS 5 isolation mode for Web applications that aren't compatible with the IIS 6 worker process model. Characteristics that might make an application written for IIS 5 incompatible with worker process mode include:

- **Session states that are managed in-process** You can configure IIS 6 to recycle worker processes periodically, on demand, or when a specific criterion is met. When a worker process is recycled, session state data might be lost.

- **Code that sends out requests to other worker processes** IIS 6 worker processes can't communicate or send out requests to other processes. Worker processes are completely isolated to prevent applications or sites in one application pool from stopping applications or sites in another application pool.

- **Components that don't support loading by multiple processes** Multiple IIS 6 worker processes might load and run ISAPI and COM components concurrently. If concurrent instances of an ISAPI or COM component can't run simultaneously, the components are incompatible for worker process isolation mode.

If you have incompatible applications, you have several choices:

- Switch to IIS 5 isolation mode, forcing all applications to run in this mode and losing all the benefits of IIS 6 worker process isolation mode. To switch to IIS 5 isolation mode in IIS Manager, right-click Web Sites and then click Properties. In the Service tab, select Run WWW Service In IIS 5 isolation mode, and then click OK. Afterward, when prompted to restart the World Wide Web Service, click Yes. The reconfiguration process can take several minutes, so be patient.

- Configure separate Web application servers, each running in a different mode. Run IIS 5–compatible applications on servers running IIS 5 isolation mode. Run IIS 6–compatible applications on servers running worker process isolation mode.

- Migrate incompatible applications to IIS 6 architecture. If you do this, be sure to look at these server support functions: CustomError (to use IIS custom errors), ExecuteUrl (to replace read raw data filters), ReportUnhealthy (to force recycle unstable or questionable process), and VectorSend (to manage multiple buffer and file handles). The IIS 6 architecture also supports Unicode Uniform Resource Locators (URLs), COM+ partitions, dynamic-link library (DLL) runtime versioning (fusion), and poolable objects using the multithreaded apartment model.

Switching to IIS 5 mode also affects the way ASP.NET is used on the server. In IIS 5 isolation mode, ASP.NET uses its own processing model. This processing model is similar to worker process isolation mode and has similar capabilities. Process model configurations for ASP.NET applications are taken from the Windows .NET Framework XML file, which is called Machine.config.

In contrast, under the default configuration, ASP.NET and IIS are directly integrated. ASP.NET uses the worker process model architecture of IIS 6. ASP.NET applications can take advantage of IIS 6 features, and applications are configured through the application pool settings. The only exception is that if you've configured maximum input/output (I/O) threads or maximum worker threads in a Machine.config file, these settings will still be read and used. All other configuration settings in the Machine.config file are ignored.

Switching to IIS 5 Isolation Mode

To switch to IIS 5 isolation mode, follow these steps:

1. Expand the Internet Information Services node in the IIS or the Application Server snap-in.

Note   If the server you want to work with isn't listed, right-click Internet Information Services, select Connect, and then type the server name or click Browse to find a server. If necessary, select Connect As and provide your logon credentials for the remote server. Click OK.

2. Expand the server node. Right-click Web Sites and then click Properties.

3. In the Service tab, select Run WWW Service In IIS 5 Isolation Mode, and then click OK.

4. When prompted to restart the World Wide Web Service, click Yes. Windows Server 2003 then reconfigures processing and restarts the Web service. This process can take several minutes, so be patient.

Understanding and Using Worker Process Isolation Mode

Worker process isolation mode is the default mode of IIS. This mode allows sites and applications to:

- Recycle worker threads
- Monitor process health
- Use advanced application pooling configurations
- Take advantage of other IIS 6 features

From a high level, worker process isolation mode is similar to IIS 5 isolation mode. Service Host processes control all resources of the same type running on a server. Starting, pausing, or stopping a service affects all sites of the same type on the server. It doesn't directly affect the Service Host. Instead, Windows Server 2003 uses an intermediary to control the Service Host for you. For non-Web services, this intermediary is the InetInfo process. A single instance of Inetinfo.exe is used to manage the FTP, SMTP, and NNTP Service Hosts.

Management of the Web service and Web applications is internalized. The Web Administration Service component of the Web Service Host is used to manage the service itself. Worker processes are used to control applications, and no ISAPI applications run within the IIS process context.

Worker processes are used in several ways:

- **Single worker process—single application**   Here, a single worker process running in its own context (isolated) handles requests for a single application, as well as instances of any ISAPI extensions, and filters the application needs. The application is the only one assigned to the related application pool.

- **Single worker process—multiple applications** Here, a single worker process running in its own context (isolated) handles requests for multiple applications assigned to the same application pool, as well as instances of any ISAPI extensions, and filters the application needs.

- **Multiple worker processes—single application** Here, multiple worker processes running in their own context (isolated) share responsibility for handling requests for a single application, as well as instances of any ISAPI extensions, and filter the application needs. The application is the only one in the related application pool.

- **Multiple worker processes—multiple applications** Here, multiple worker processes running in their own context (isolated) share responsibility for handling requests for multiple applications assigned to the same application pool, as well as instances of any ISAPI extensions, and filter the application needs.

Benefits of Using Worker Processing Mode

Running IIS in worker processing mode has many benefits. In this mode, all sites run within an application context and have an associated application pool. The default application pool is DefaultAppPool. You can also assign sites and applications to custom application pools.

Each application or site in an application pool can have one or more worker processes associated with it. The worker processes handle requests for the site or application.

You can configure application pools to manage worker processes in many ways. You can configure automatic recycling of worker threads based on a set of criteria, such as when the process has been running for a certain amount of time or uses a specific amount of memory. You can also have IIS monitor the health of worker threads and take actions to recover automatically from failure. These features might eliminate or reduce your dependence on third-party monitoring tools or services.

In worker processing mode, you can also create a Web garden where you configure multiple worker processes to handle the workload. Applications configured using this technique are more responsive, more scalable, and less prone to failure. Why? A Hypertext Transfer Protocol (HTTP) listener, called Http.sys, listens for incoming requests and places them in the appropriate application pool request queue. When a request is placed in the queue, an available worker process assigned to the application can take the request and begin processing it. Idle worker processes handle requests in first in, first out (FIFO) order.

Worker processes can also be started on demand. If there are unallocated worker processes and no current idle worker processes, IIS can start a new worker process to handle the request. In this way, resources aren't allocated until they're needed, and IIS can handle many more sites than it could if all processes were allocated on startup.

Switching to Worker Processing Mode

To switch to worker processing mode, follow these steps:

1. Expand the Internet Information Services node in the IIS or the Application Server snap-in.

Note   If the server you want to work with isn't listed, right-click Internet Information Services, select Connect, and then type the server name or click Browse to find a server. If necessary, select Connect As and provide your logon credentials for the remote server. Click OK.

2. Expand the server node. Right-click Web Sites and then click Properties.

3. In the Service tab, clear Run WWW Service In IIS 5 Isolation Mode, and then click OK.

4. When prompted to restart the World Wide Web Service, click Yes. Windows Server 2003 then reconfigures processing and restarts the Web service. When the process is finished, you'll have an Application Pools node that you can use to manage the default application pool and any other pools you create on the server.

Working with IIS and URLs

To retrieve files from IIS servers, clients must know three things: the server's address, where on the server the file is located, and which protocol to use to access and retrieve the file. Normally, this information is specified as a URL. URLs provide a uniform way of identifying resources that are available using IPs. The basic mechanism that makes URLs so versatile is their standard naming scheme.

URL schemes name the protocol the client will use to access and transfer the file. Clients use the name of the protocol to determine the format for the information that follows the protocol name. The protocol name is generally followed by a colon and two forward slashes. The information after the double slash marks follows a format that depends on the protocol type referenced in the URL. Here are two general formats:

protocol://hostname:port/path_to_resource

protocol://username:password@hostname:port/path_to_resource

Host name information used in URLs identifies the address to a host and is broken down into two or more parts separated by periods. The periods are used to separate domain information from the host name. Common domain names for Web servers begin with *www*, such as *www.microsoft.com*, which identifies the Microsoft WWW server in the commercial domain. Domains you can specify in your URLs include:

- **com**   Commercial sites
- **edu**   Education sites

- **gov**   Nonmilitary government sites
- **mil**   Military sites
- **net**   Network sites
- **org**   Organizational sites

Port information used in URLs identifies the port number to be used for the connection. Generally, you don't have to specify port numbers in your URLs unless the connection will be made to a port other than the default. As shown in Table 2-1, port 80 is the default port for HTTP. If you request a URL on a server using the URL *http://www.microsoft.com/docs/my-yoyo.htm,* port 80 is assumed to be the default port value. On the other hand, if you wanted to make a connection to port 8080, you'd need to type in the port value, such as *http://www.microsoft.com:8080/docs/my-yoyo.htm.*

Port values that fall between zero and 1023, referred to as *well-known ports,* are reserved for specific data type uses on the Internet. Port values between 1024 and 49151 are considered registered ports, and those between 49152 and 65535 are considered dynamic ports.

Table 2-1.   Default Ports for IIS Resources

Protocol	Default Port
FTP	21
SMTP	25
HTTP	80
NNTP	119

The final part of a URL is the path to the resource. This path generally follows the directory structure from the server's home directory to the resource specified in the URL.

URLs for FTP can also contain a user name and password. User name and password information allow users to log in to an FTP server using a specific user account. For example, the following URL establishes a connection to the Microsoft FTP server and logs on using a named account: *ftp://sysadmin:rad$4 @ftp.microsoft.com/public/download.doc.*

In this instance, the account logon is *sysadmin,* the password is *rad$4,* the server is *ftp.microsoft.com,* and the requested resource is *public/download.doc.*

If a connection is made to an FTP server without specifying the user name and password, you can configure the server to assume that the user wants to establish an anonymous session. In this case the following default values are assumed: *anonymous* for user name and the user's e-mail address as the password.

URLs can use uppercase and lowercase letters, the numerals 0-9, and a few special characters, including:

- Asterisks (*)
- Dollar signs ($)
- Exclamation points (!)

- Hyphens (-)
- Parentheses (left and right)
- Periods (.)
- Plus signs (+)
- Single quotation marks (')
- Underscores (_)

You're limited to these characters because other characters used in URLs have specific meanings, as shown in Table 2-2.

Table 2-2.   Reserved Characters in URLs

Character	Meaning
:	The colon is a separator that separates protocol from the rest of the URL scheme; separates host name from the port number; and separates user name from the password.
//	The double slash marks indicate that the protocol uses the format defined by the Common Internet Scheme Syntax (see RFC 1738 for more information).
/	The slash is a separator and is used to separate the path from host name and port. The slash is also used to denote the directory path to the resource named in the URL.
~	The tilde is generally used at the beginning of the path to indicate that the resource is in the specified user's public Hypertext Markup Language (HTML) directory.
%	Identifies an escape code. Escape codes are used to specify special characters in URLs that otherwise have a special meaning or aren't allowed.
@	The at symbol is used to separate user name and/or password information from the host name in the URL.
?	The question mark is used in the URL path to specify the beginning of a query string. Query strings are passed to Common Gateway Interface (CGI) scripts. All the information following the question mark is data the user submitted and isn't interpreted as part of the file path.
+	The plus sign is used in query strings as a placeholder between words. Instead of using spaces to separate words that the user has entered in the query, the browser substitutes the plus sign.
=	The equal sign is used in query strings to separate the key assigned by the publisher from the value entered by the user.
&	The ampersand is used in query strings to separate multiple sets of keys and values.
^	The caret is reserved for future use.
{}	Braces are reserved for future use.
[]	Brackets are reserved for future use.

To make URLs even more versatile, you can use escape codes to specify characters in URLs that are either reserved or otherwise not allowed. Escape codes have two components: a percent sign and a numeric value. The percent sign identifies the start of an escape code. The number following the percent sign identifies the character being escaped. The escape code for a space is a percent sign followed by the number 20 (%20). You could use this escape code in a URL such as this one:

http://www.microsoft.com/docs/my%20party%20hat.htm

IIS and Application Server Snap-In Essentials

The IIS snap-in is a Microsoft Management Console (MMC) snap-in for managing IIS resources in Windows domains. You'll use this tool to perform administration routine tasks, such as starting Internet services, starting individual sites, and rebooting servers remotely.

If you work with ASP.NET, Windows .NET Framework, or Component Services, you can also use the Application Server snap-in. Application Server has three primary nodes:

- **.NET Configuration** Configure and manage Windows .NET Framework assemblies, assembly caches, remoting services, runtime security, and ASP.NET applications

- **Internet Information Services (IIS) Manager** Configure and manage Web, FTP, SMTP, and NNTP services

- **Component Services** Configure and manage COM components and COM+ applications

Other than the fact that there are additional administration nodes, you manage IIS in the Application Services snap-in using the same techniques as those with the IIS snap-in. Because of this, I won't provide a separate discussion on using the Application Services snap-in. If you prefer the Application Services snap-in, start from this tool rather than the IIS snap-in, as specified.

 Note The Remote Administration tool provides a browser-based interface for managing Web and FTP resources. This tool has many of the same features as the IIS snap-in. For details on starting and using this tool, see the section entitled "Web Administration Techniques" in Chapter 1, "Overview of Microsoft Web Services."

Starting and Using the Internet Information Services (IIS) Manager Snap-In

The IIS snap-in is accessible in several locations. You can access the snap-in through a preconfigured console by clicking Start and choosing All Programs, Administrative Tools, and then Internet Information Services (IIS) Manager. Or you can access the snap-in through Manage Your Server, which can also be started from the Administrative Tools menu. Once you start Manage Your Server, click Open The Web Interface For Remote Administration Of Web Servers.

Figure 2-3 shows the main window for the IIS snap-in. The snap-in automatically connects to local IIS installations (if available). You can connect to one or more remote computers as well. Each additional computer to which you connect has a separate node that you can use to manage its resources.

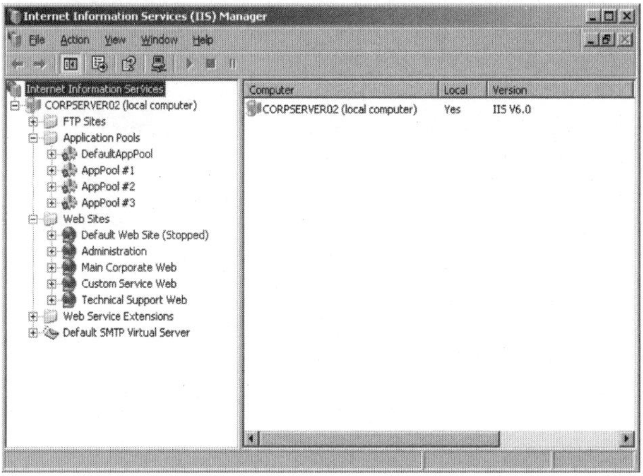

Figure 2-3. *Use the IIS snap-in to manage Web, FTP, SMTP, and NNTP resources.*

When you select the Internet Information Services node in the left pane, the right pane displays a summary of current computer connections. The connection summary provides:

- **Computer**   Name of the computer to which you're connected.

- **Local**   States whether you're connected to a local IIS installation. If the field value is set to Yes, you're connected to a local IIS installation. Otherwise, you're connected to a remote installation.

- **Version**   Version of IIS installed on the computer.

- **Status**   Status of the computer, such as unavailable or restarting.

If you expand the computer node, you'll find individual nodes for each service configured, application pools (if running in worker processing mode) and Web Service Extensions. When you select Web Sites or FTP Sites under a computer node in the left pane, the right pane displays an overview of these resources on the computer. The resource overview provides:

- **Description**   Basic description of site or virtual server assigned through the Properties dialog box.

- **Identifier**   Unique numeric value associated with the site.

- **State**   Status of the site or virtual server, such as running, stopped, paused or unknown.

- **Host Header Value**   Host name passed in the HTTP header to clients (if applicable).

- **IP Address**   IP address of the site or virtual server. Incoming IP traffic is mapped by port and IP address to a specific site or virtual server instance. The value All Unassigned allows the HTTP, FTP, SMTP, or NNTP protocol to respond on all unassigned IP addresses that are configured on the server.

- **Port**   Port number the site or virtual server listens on. Default ports for FTP and HTTP are 21 and 80, respectively.

- **SSL Port**   Secure port number the site or virtual server listens on. Default port for HTTP is 443.

- **Status**   Additional status information for the site or virtual server.

When first accessed, the IIS snap-in automatically connects to local IIS installations (if available). You can connect to other computers. If you do this, each computer will have its own node.

Connecting to Other Servers

Most of the time you'll manage IIS installations from your desktop system. When you do this, you'll need to establish a remote connection to the server you want to manage. The steps for establishing remote connections are:

1. Start the IIS snap-in.

2. In the left pane, right-click Internet Information Services and then select Connect. The Connect To Computer dialog box is displayed.

3. In the Computer Name field, type the name of the computer to which you want to connect. You can also type the server's IP address or fully qualified domain name (FQDN). Click Browse to search for a computer.

4. If you need to authenticate yourself on the computer, select Connect As and then provide the user name and password for an account with the appropriate privileges.

5. Click OK.

 Real World   Firewalls and proxy servers might affect your ability to connect to systems at remote locations. If you need to connect regularly to servers through firewalls or proxies, you'll need to consider the administration techniques you might want to use and then consult your company's network or security administrator to determine what steps need to be taken to allow those administration techniques. Typically, the network/security administrator will have to open TCP or UDP ports to allow remote communications between your computer or network and the remote computer or network. Each type of tool you want to use might require you to open different ports. For example, if you want to remotely administer a Web site using the Web tool, you'll need to open the standard and secure TCP port for the administration Web site. However, corporate policy might not allow the administrator to perform these tasks or might require prior approval from an information technology (IT) manager.

Starting, Stopping, and Restarting All Internet Services

As discussed earlier in the chapter, Window Server 2003 uses the Inetinfo.exe process to manage all Internet Information Services. InetInfo is able to do this because it tracks all IIS resources running on a computer and can issue commands to these resources. As an administrator, you can control InetInfo through the IIS snap-in or the Iisreset.exe command-line utility.

If you want to start, stop, or restart all of your Internet services from within the IIS snap-in, follow these steps:

1. In the IIS snap-in, select the icon for the computer you want to work with. If the computer isn't shown, connect to it, as discussed in the section of this chapter entitled "Connecting to Other Servers," and then select it.

2. Choose All Tasks from the Action menu and then select Restart IIS. This displays the Stop/Start/Restart dialog box shown in Figure 2-4.

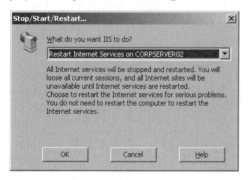

Figure 2-4. *Stop, start, and restart all Internet Services.*

3. Use the drop-down menu to perform the following tasks:
   * Start Internet Services on *computername*.
   * Stop Internet Services on *computername*.
   * Restart *computername*.
   * Restart Internet Services on *computername*.

4. Click OK.

With the Restart Internet Services command, the sequence of tasks is important to understand. This command performs the following tasks:

1. Stops all Internet Information Services running on the computer, including World Wide Web Publishing Service, FTP Publishing Service, Network News Transport Protocol Service, Simple Mail Transport Protocol Service, and IIS Admin Service.

2. Attempts to resolve potential problems with runaway processes or hung applications by stopping all Dr. Watson (Drwtsn32.exe), MTX (Mtx.exe), and DLL Host (Dllhost.exe) processes.

3. Starts all Internet Information Services and then starts DLL Hosts as necessary.

You can also use the Iisreset.exe command-line utility to start, stop, and restart Internet Services. To start any Internet Information Services that are stopped on the local computer, type the following command:

iisreset /start

To stop all Internet Information Services that are running, paused, or in an unknown state on the local computer, type the following command:

iisreset /stop

To stop and then restart Internet Information Services on the local computer, type the following command:

iisreset /restart

You can also control Internet Information Services on remote computers. To do this, use the following syntax:

iisreset *computername command*

such as:

iisreset engsvr01 /restart

Table 2-3 provides a listing of all switches for the Iisreset.exe command-line utility. Rebooting computers is covered in the section of this chapter entitled "Rebooting IIS Servers."

Table 2-3. IISRESET Switches Defined

Switch	Definition
/DISABLE	Disable restarting of Internet Services on the local system.
/ENABLE	Enable restarting of Internet Services on the local system.
/NOFORCE	Don't forcefully terminate Internet services if attempting to stop them gracefully fails.
/REBOOT	Reboot the local or designated remote computer.
/REBOOTONERROR	Reboot the computer if an error occurs when starting, stopping, or restarting Internet services.
/RESTART	Stop and then restart all Internet services. Attempt to resolve potential problems with runaway processes or hung applications.
/START	Start all Internet services that are stopped.
/STATUS	Display the status of all Internet services.

Table 2-3.   IISRESET Switches Defined

Switch	Definition
/STOP	Stop all Internet services that are running, paused, or in an unknown state.
/TIMEOUT:*val*	Specify the time-out value (in seconds) to wait for a successful stop of Internet services. On expiration of this time-out, the computer can be rebooted if the /REBOOTONERROR parameter is specified. With /STOP and /RESTART, an error is issued. The default value is 20 seconds for restart, 60 seconds for stop, and 0 seconds for reboot.

Starting, Stopping, and Pausing Individual Resources

Sites and virtual servers that use the same Internet Service can be controlled individually or as a group. You can control individual sites and virtual servers much like you do other server resources. For example, if you're changing the configuration of a site or performing other maintenance tasks, you might need to stop the site, make the changes, and then restart it. When a site is stopped, the site doesn't accept connections from users and can't be used.

An alternative to stopping a site or virtual server is to pause it. Pausing a resource prevents new client connections but doesn't disconnect current connections. When you pause a site or virtual server, active clients can continue to retrieve documents, work with messages, and perform other tasks. No new connections are accepted, however.

You can start, stop, or pause a site or virtual server by completing the following steps:

1. Start the IIS snap-in.
2. In the left pane, select the icon for the computer you want to work with. If the computer isn't shown, connect to it as discussed in the section of this chapter entitled "Connecting to Other Servers," and then select it.
3. Select FTP Sites or Web Sites as necessary, and then right-click the site or virtual server you want to manage. You can now:

   * Select Start to start the site or virtual server.
   * Select Stop to stop the site or virtual server.
   * Select Pause to pause the site or virtual server. After you pause a site or virtual server, click Pause again when you want to resume normal operations.

Note Groups of sites or virtual servers running under the same Internet Service are controlled through their master process. For example, the master process for all Web sites running on a computer is the World Wide Web Publishing service. Stopping this service stops all Web sites using the process and all connections to these sites are disconnected immediately. Starting this service restarts all Web sites that were running when the World Wide Web Publishing service was stopped. To learn how to control Internet Services, see the section of this chapter entitled "Managing IIS Services."

Rebooting IIS Servers

The IIS snap-in and Iisreset.exe utility have extensions that allow you to reboot local and remote computers. In order to use these extensions, you must have installed IIS on the computer and you must be a member of a group that has the appropriate user rights. To reboot a local system, you must have the right to shut down the system. To reboot a remote system, you must have the right to force shutdown from a remote system. You should only reboot an IIS server if the restart IIS procedure fails.

You reboot an IIS server with the snap-in by completing the following tasks:

1. In the IIS snap-in, select the icon for the computer you want to work with. If the computer isn't shown, connect to it as discussed in the section of this chapter entitled "Connecting to Other Servers," and then select it.

2. Click Action and then select Restart IIS. This displays the Stop/Start/Restart dialog box shown previously in Figure 2-4.

3. Select Restart *computername* on the drop-down list and then click OK.

4. A system shutdown message is sent to the target computer. This message explains that the computer is being shut down in 5 minutes. After completing the shutdown process, the system will reboot.

To reboot a computer using Iisreset.exe, type the following command:

iisreset *computername* /reboot

such as the following example:

iisreset engsvr01 /reboot

If users are working on files or performing other tasks that need to be exited gracefully, you should set a time-out value for services and processes to be stopped. By default the time-out is zero seconds, which forces immediate shutdown and tells Windows Server 2003 not to wait for services to be shut down gracefully. You could set a time-out value of 60 seconds when rebooting engsvr01 as follows:

iisreset engsvr01 /reboot /timeout:60

Managing IIS Services

Each IIS server in the organization relies on a set of services for publishing pages, transferring files, and more. To manage IIS services, you'll use the Services node in the Computer Management console, which you start by doing the following:

1. Click Start and choose All Programs, Administrative Tools, and then Computer Management. Or select Computer Management in the Administrative Tools folder in Control Panel.

2. Right-click the Computer Management entry in the console tree and select Connect To Another Computer on the shortcut menu. You can now choose the IIS server whose services you want to manage.

3. Expand the Services And Applications node by clicking the plus sign (+) next to it and then choose Services.

Figure 2-5 shows the Services view in the Computer Management console.

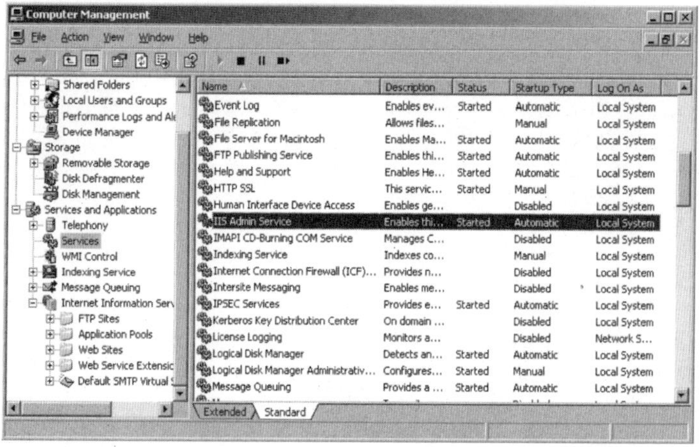

Figure 2-5. *Use the Services node to manage IIS services.*

The key fields of this dialog box are used as follows:

- **Name** The name of the service.

- **Description** A short description of the service and its purpose.

- **Status** The status of the service as started, paused, or stopped. (Stopped is indicated by a blank entry.)

- **Startup Type** The startup setting for the service.

Note Automatic services are started when the system boots up. Manual services are started by users or other services. Disabled services are turned off and can't be started.

- **Log On As** The account the service logs on as. The default in most cases is the local system account.

Key IIS Services

Table 2-4 provides a summary of key services that IIS uses or depends on. Note that the services available on a particular IIS server depend on its configuration. Still, this is the core set of services that you'll find on most IIS servers.

Table 2-4. Key IIS Services

Name	Description
Event Log	Logs event informational, warning and error messages issued by IIS and other applications
FTP Publishing Service	Provides services for transferring files using FTP and also allows administration of an FTP server
IIS Admin Service	Allows administration of IIS through the IIS snap-in
Indexing Service	Indexes the contents and properties of files, providing quick access to files through a flexible query language
Network News Transport Protocol (NNTP)	Provides network news services and allows administration of NTTP servers through the IIS snap-in
Simple Mail Transport Protocol (SMTP)	Provides mail transfer services and allows administration of SMTP sites through the IIS snap-in
World Wide Web Publishing Service	Provides services for transferring files using HTTP and also allows administration of an HTTP server

Starting, Stopping, and Pausing IIS Services

As an administrator, you'll often have to start, stop, or pause IIS services. You manage IIS services through the Computer Management console or through the Services utility. When you manage IIS services at this level, you're controlling all sites or virtual servers that use the service. For example, if a computer publishes three Web sites and you stop the World Wide Web Publishing Service, all three Web sites are stopped and are inaccessible.

To start, stop, or pause services in the Computer Management console, follow these steps:

1. In the left-hand pane, right-click the Computer Management entry in the console tree and select Connect to Another Computer on the shortcut menu. You can now choose the IIS server whose services you want to manage.

2. Expand the Services And Applications node by clicking the plus sign (+) next to it, and then choose Services.

3. In the right-hand pane, right-click the service you want to manipulate, and then select Start, Stop, or Pause as appropriate. You can also choose Restart to have Windows stop and then start the service after a brief pause. In addition, if you pause a service, you can use the Resume option to resume normal operation.

Tip   When services that are set to start automatically fail, the status is listed as Blank and you'll usually receive notification in a dialog box. Service failures can also be logged to the system's event logs. In Windows Server 2003, you can configure actions to handle service failure automatically. For example, you could have Windows Server 2003 attempt to restart the service for you. For details, see the section of this chapter entitled "Configuring Service Recovery."

Configuring Service Startup

Essential IIS services are configured to start automatically, and normally they shouldn't be configured with another startup option. That said, if you're troubleshooting a problem, you might want a service to start manually. You might also want to disable a service so that its related virtual servers don't start. For example, if you move an SMTP virtual server to a new server, you might want to disable the SMTP service on the original IIS server. In this way the SMTP service isn't used, but you could turn it on if you need to (without your having to reinstall SMTP support).

You configure service startup as follows:

1. In the left-hand pane of the Computer Management console, connect to the IIS server whose services you want to manage.

2. Expand the Services And Applications node by clicking the plus sign (+) next to it, and then choose Services.

3. In the right-hand pane, right-click the service you want to configure and then choose Properties.

4. On the General tab, use the Startup Type drop-down list to choose a startup option as shown in Figure 2-6. Select Automatic to start the service when the system boots up. Select Manual to allow the service to be started manually. Select Disabled to turn off the service.

5. Click OK.

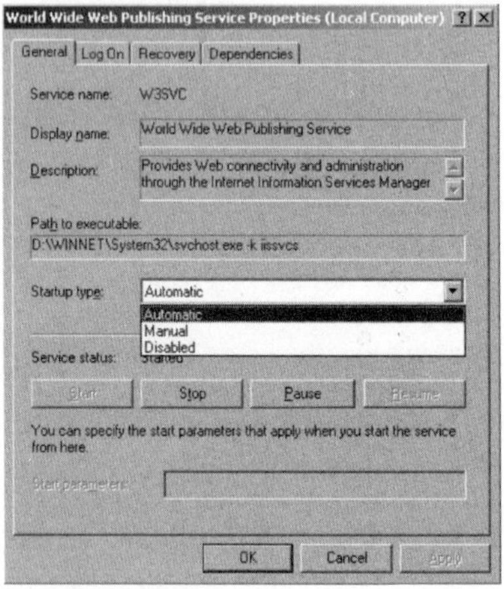

Figure 2-6. *For troubleshooting, you might want to change the service startup option.*

Configuring Service Recovery

You can configure Windows services to take specific actions when a service fails. For example, you could attempt to restart the service or reboot the server. To configure recovery options for a service, follow these steps:

1. In the left-hand pane of the Computer Management console, connect to the computer whose services you want to manage.

2. Expand the Services And Applications node by clicking the plus sign (+) next to it and then choose Services.

3. In the right-hand pane, right-click the service you want to configure and then choose Properties.

4. Select the Recovery tab, shown in Figure 2-7. You can now configure recovery options for the first, second, and subsequent recovery attempts. The available options are:

   • Take No Action

   • Restart The Service

   • Run A Program

   • Restart The Computer

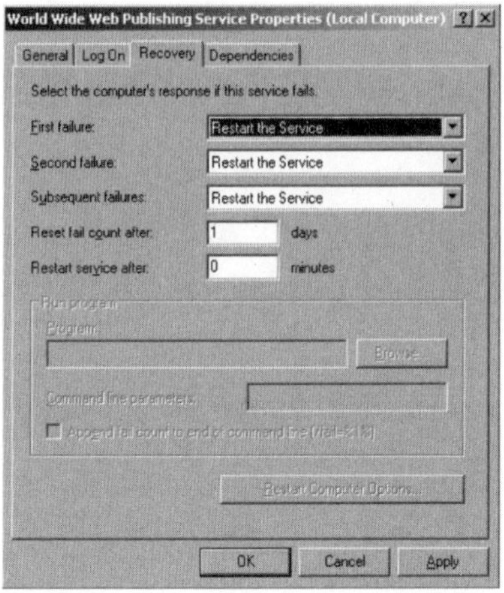

Figure 2-7. *You can configure services to recover automatically in case of failure.*

5. Configure other options based on your previously selected recovery options. If you elected to restart the service, you'll need to specify the restart delay. After stopping the service, Windows Server 2003 waits for the specified delay before trying to start the service. In most cases a delay of 1–2 minutes should be sufficient.

6. Click OK.

When you configure recovery options for critical services, you *might* want Windows Server 2003 to try to restart the service on the first and second attempts and then reboot the server on the third attempt.

Part II
Web Server Administration

In this part you'll find the essential tasks for administering World Wide Web servers running Internet Information Services (IIS). Chapter 3 details management techniques for Web sites and servers. There, you'll also learn how to create and manage virtual directories. Shaping the content of your Web server to suit your particular needs is the focus of Chapter 4, where you'll also learn about managing individual pages, browser redirection techniques, custom headers and footers, server error messages, and Multipurpose Internet Mail Extensions (MIME) types. In Chapter 5, you'll learn about IIS application options and how to configure essential application components. In Chapter 6, you'll learn how to manage worker processes and application pools. Chapter 7 covers Web site and server security. To manage server security, you'll create user logins, configure directory permissions, and assign operators. Chapter 8, the final chapter in this section, explores server certificates and server extensions.

Chapter 3

Configuring Web Sites and Servers

Tasks for configuring Web sites and servers are broken down into several categories. You'll find sections in this chapter on Web site naming and identification, managing master Web service properties, creating Web sites, and other topics.

Web site properties are a key part of Web site management and configuration. Web site properties identify the site, set its configuration values, and determine where and how documents are accessed. You can set Web site properties at several levels:

- As global defaults
- As site defaults
- As directory defaults

You set global defaults through the Web Sites node, and all Web sites on the server can inherit them. You set individual defaults through the Web Site Properties dialog box, and they apply only to the selected Web site. You set directory defaults through the Directory Properties dialog box, and they apply only to the selected directory.

Web Site Naming and Identification

This section discusses Web site naming and identification techniques. Each Web site deployed in the organization has unique characteristics. Different types of Web sites can have different characteristics. Intranet Web sites typically use computer names that resolve locally and have private Internet Protocol (IP) addresses. Internet Web sites typically use fully qualified domain names (FQDNs) and public IP addresses. Intranet and Internet Web sites can also use host header names, allowing single IP address and port assignments to serve multiple Web sites.

Understanding IP Addresses and Name Resolution

Whether you're configuring an intranet or Internet site, your Web server must be assigned a unique IP address that identifies the computer on the network. An IP address is a numeric identifier for the computer. IP addressing schemes vary depending on how your network is configured, but they're normally assigned from a range of addresses for a particular network segment (also known as a *subnet*). For example, if you're working with a computer on the network segment 192.168.10.0, the address range you have available for computers is usually from 192.168.10.1 to 192.168.10.254.

Although numeric addresses are easy for machines to remember, they aren't easy for human beings to remember. Because of this, computers are assigned text names that are easy for users to remember. Text names have two basic forms:

- Standard computer names, which are used on private networks
- Internet names, which are used on public networks

Private networks are networks that are either indirectly connected to the Internet or completely disconnected from the Internet. Private networks use IP addresses that are reserved for private use and aren't accessible to the public Internet. Private network addresses fall into the following ranges:

- 10.0.0.0–10.255.255.255
- 172.16.0.0–172.31.255.255
- 192.168.0.0–192.168.255.255

Private networks that use Internet technologies are called *intranets*. Information is delivered on intranets by mapping a computer's IP address to its text name, which is the NetBIOS name assigned to the computer. Although Microsoft Windows components use the NetBIOS naming convention for name resolution, Transmission Control Protocol/Internet Protocol (TCP/IP) components use the Domain Name System (DNS). Under Windows, the DNS host name defaults to the same name as the NetBIOS computer name. For example, if you install a server with a computer name of CorpServer, this name is assigned as the NetBIOS computer name and the default DNS host name.

In contrast, public networks are networks that are connected directly to the Internet. Public networks use IP addresses that are purchased or leased for public use. Typically, you'll obtain IP address assignments for your public servers from the provider of your organization's Internet services. Internet service providers (ISPs) obtain blocks of IP addresses from the American Registry for Internet Numbers. Other types of organizations can purchase blocks of IP addresses as well.

On the Internet, DNS is used to resolve text names to IP addresses. A hypothetical DNS name is *www.microsoft.com*. Here, *www* identifies a server name and *microsoft.com* identifies a domain name. As with public IP addresses, domain names must be leased or purchased. You purchase domain names from name registrars, such as Internet Network Information Center (InterNIC). When a client computer requests a connection to a site using a domain name, the request is transmitted to a DNS server. The DNS server returns the IP address that corresponds to the requested host name, and then the client request is routed to the appropriate site.

Don't confuse the public DNS naming system used on the Internet with the private naming system used on intranets. DNS names are configured on DNS servers and resolved to IP addresses before contacting a server. This fact makes it possible for a server to have multiple IP addresses, each with a different DNS name. For example, a server with an internal computer name of Gandolf could be configured with IP addresses of 207.46.230.210, 207.46.230.211, and 207.46.230.212. If these IP addresses are configured as *www.microsoft.com*, *services.microsoft.com*, and *products.microsoft.com*, respectively, in the DNS server, the server can respond to requests for each of these domain names.

Understanding Web Site Identifiers

Each Web site deployed in your organization has a unique identity it uses to receive and to respond to requests. The identity includes the following:

- A computer or DNS name
- An IP address
- A port number
- An optional host header name

The way these identifiers are combined to identify a Web site depends on whether the host server is on a private or public network. On a private network, a computer called CorpIntranet could have an IP address of 10.0.0.52. If so, the Web site on the server could be accessed in the following ways:

- Using the Universal Naming Convention (UNC) path name: \\CorpIntranet or \\10.0.0.52
- Using a Uniform Resource Locator (URL): *http://CorpIntranet/* or *http://10.0.0.52/*
- Using a URL and port number: *http://CorpIntranet:80/* or *http://10.0.0.52:80/*

On a public network, a computer called Dingo could be registered to use the DNS name *www.microsoft.com* and the IP address of 207.46.230.210. If so, the Web site on the server could be accessed in either of the following ways:

- Using a URL: *http://www.microsoft.com/* or *http://207.46.230.210/*
- Using a URL and port number: *http://www.microsoft.com:80/* or *http://207.46.230.210:80/*

Hosting Multiple Sites on a Single Server

Using different combinations of IP addresses, port numbers, and host header names, one can host multiple sites on a single computer. Hosting multiple sites on a single server has definite advantages. For example, rather than installing three different Web servers, one could host *www.microsoft.com*, *support.microsoft.com*, and *service.microsoft.com* on the same Web server.

One of the most efficient ways to host multiple sites on the same server is to assign multiple IP addresses to the server. Figure 3-1 shows an example of this configuration.

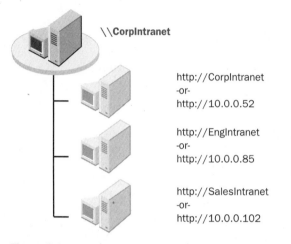

\\CorpIntranet

http://CorpIntranet
-or-
http://10.0.0.52

http://EngIntranet
-or-
http://10.0.0.85

http://SalesIntranet
-or-
http://10.0.0.102

Figure 3-1. *You can use multiple IP addresses to host multiple Web sites on a single server.*

To use this technique, you must follow these steps:

1. Configure the TCP/IP settings on the server so that there is one IP address for each site that you want to host.

2. Configure DNS so that the host names and corresponding IP addresses can be resolved.

3. Configure each Web site so that it uses a specific IP address.

With this technique, users can access the sites individually by typing the unique domain name or IP address in a browser. Following the example shown in Figure 3-1, you can access the Sales intranet by typing **http://SalesIntranet/** or **http://10.0.0.102/**.

Another technique you can use to host multiple sites on a single server is to assign each site a unique port number while keeping the same IP address, as shown in Figure 3-2. Users will then be able to do the following:

- Access the main site by typing the DNS server name or IP address in a browser, such as **http://Intranet/** or **http://10.0.0.52/**

- Access other virtual servers by typing the domain name and port assignment or IP address and port assignment, such as **http://Intranet:88/** or **http://10.0.0.52:88/**

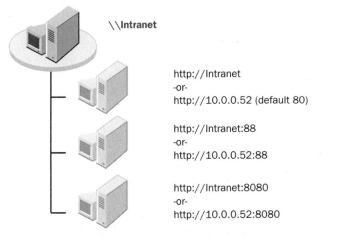

Figure 3-2. *Another technique is to use multiple port numbers to host multiple Web sites on a single server.*

The final method you can use to host multiple sites on a single server is to use host header names. Host headers allow you to host multiple sites on the same IP address and port number. The key to host headers is a DNS name assignment that's configured in DNS and assigned to the site in its configuration.

An example of host header assignment is shown in Figure 3-3. Here, a single server hosts the sites CorpIntranet, EngIntranet, and SalesIntranet. The three sites use the same IP address and port number assignment but have different DNS names.

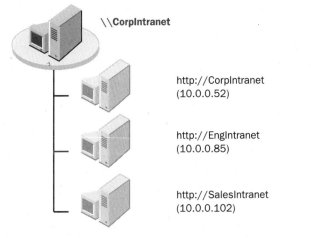

Figure 3-3. *You can use host headers to support multiple Web sites on a single server, with a single IP address.*

To use host headers, you must do the following:

1. Configure DNS so that the host header names and corresponding IP addresses can be resolved.

2. Configure the primary Web site so that it responds to requests on the IP address and port number you've assigned.

3. Configure additional Web sites so that they use the same IP address and port number and also assign a host header name.

Host headers have specific drawbacks. Earlier versions of browsers that don't support Hypertext Transfer Protocol (HTTP) 1.1 are unable to pass host header names back to IIS. Although Microsoft Internet Explorer 3, Netscape Navigator 2, and later versions of these browsers support the use of host header names, earlier versions of these browsers don't. Visitors using earlier browsers will reach the default Web site for the IP address.

Another drawback to host headers is that you can't use host headers with Secure Sockets Layer (SSL). With SSL, HTTP requests are encrypted, and the host header name within the encrypted request can't be used to determine the correct site to which the request must be routed.

Checking the Computer Name and IP Address of Servers

Before you configure Web sites, you should check the server's computer name and IP address. You can view the computer name by completing the following steps:

1. Start the System utility in Control Panel.

2. Select the Computer Name tab. The tab displays the FQDN of the server and the domain or workgroup membership. The FQDN is the DNS name of the computer.

3. The DNS name is the name that you normally use to access the IIS resources on the server. For example, if the DNS name of the computer is www.microsoft.com and you've configured a Web site on port 80, the URL you use to access the computer from the Internet is *http://www.microsoft.com/*.

You can view the IP address and other TCP/IP settings for the computer by completing the following steps:

1. Access Network Connections by clicking Start and selecting Control Panel and Network Connections. Or double-click Network Connections in the Control Panel dialog box.

2. Right-click Local Area Connection and then select Properties. This opens the Local Area Connection Properties dialog box.

3. Open the Internet Protocol (TCP/IP) Properties dialog box by double-clicking Internet Protocol (TCP/IP). Or you could select Internet Protocol (TCP/IP) and then click Properties.

4. The IP Address and other TCP/IP settings for the computer are displayed, as shown in Figure 3-4.

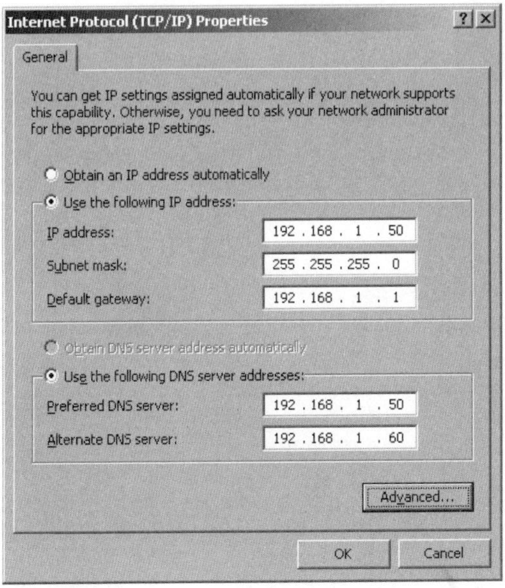

Internet Protocol (TCP/IP) Properties   ? X

| General |

You can get IP settings assigned automatically if your network supports this capability. Otherwise, you need to ask your network administrator for the appropriate IP settings.

  ○ Obtain an IP address automatically
  ◉ Use the following IP address:

    IP address: 192 . 168 . 1 . 50
    Subnet mask: 255 . 255 . 255 . 0
    Default gateway: 192 . 168 . 1 . 1

  ○ Obtain DNS server address automatically
  ◉ Use the following DNS server addresses:

    Preferred DNS server: 192 . 168 . 1 . 50
    Alternate DNS server: 192 . 168 . 1 . 60

                                Advanced...

                    OK   Cancel

Figure 3-4. *Use the Internet Protocol (TCP/IP) Properties dialog box to view and configure TCP/IP settings.*

Real World   IIS servers should use static IP addresses. If the computer is obtaining an IP address automatically, you'll need to reconfigure
the TCP/IP settings. See Chapter 16, "Managing TCP/IP Networking,"
in *Microsoft Windows Server 2003 Administrator's Pocket Consultant*
(Microsoft Press, 2003), for details.

Managing Global Web Site Properties

You use global Web site properties to set default property values for new Web sites created on a server. Anytime you change global properties, existing Web sites might inherit the changes as well. In some cases you'll have the opportunity to specify which sites and directories within sites inherit changes. In other cases the changes are applied automatically to all existing Web sites and you aren't prompted to either accept or decline.

To change global Web site properties for a server, follow these steps:

1. In the IIS snap-in, double-click the icon for the computer you want to work with. If the computer isn't shown, connect to it as discussed in the section entitled "Connecting to Other Servers" in Chapter 2, "Core IIS Administration," and then perform the remaining steps.

2. Right-click Web Sites and then select Properties. This opens the Web Sites Properties dialog box for the computer.

3. Use the tabs and fields of the Web Sites Properties dialog box to configure the default property values. When you're finished making changes, click OK.

4. Before applying changes for permissions and authentications, made in the Security tab of the Web Sites Properties dialog box, IIS checks the existing settings in use for all child nodes of the selected resource (if any). If a Web site or directory within a Web site uses a different value, an Inheritance Overrides dialog box is displayed. Use this dialog box to select the site and directory nodes that should use the new setting, and then click OK.

Creating Web Sites

When you install the World Wide Web Publishing Service for IIS, a default Web site is created. In most cases you don't need to change any network options to allow users access to the default Web site. You simply tell users the URL path that they need to type into their browser's Address field. For example, if the DNS name for the computer is *www.microsoft.com* and the site is configured for access on port 80, a user can access the Web site by typing **http://www.microsoft.com/** in the browser's Address field.

Unlike previous editions of IIS, IIS 6.0 installs with minimum functionality and as a result, IIS is configured to serve static content only. To serve dynamic content, you must enable Web Service Extensions as discussed in Chapter 4, "Customizing Web Server Content." In IIS 5, the following virtual directories were created automatically:

- **IISHelp**   Contains online help documentation and is located in %SystemRoot%\Help\IisHelp by default. This directory is set up as a pooled Internet Server Application Programming Interface (ISAPI) application called IIS Help Application.

- **IISAdmin**   Contains operator administration pages for the Web site. This directory must be configured for any Web site that you want operators to be able to control remotely. By default, the directory is located in %SystemRoot%\System32\Inetsrv\Iisadmin and is configured as a pooled ISAPI application called Administration Application.

- **IISSamples**   Contains sample documents that can be helpful for administrators and developers. By default, the directory is located in the \Iissamples directory within the IIS installation and is configured as a pooled ISAPI application called Sample Application.

In IIS 6, these directories are no longer available. All IIS help and administration functions are moved to the Administration Web site. You can no longer access these directories. Instead, you use the Remote Administration Tool as discussed in the section entitled "Web Administration Techniques" in Chapter 1, "Overview of Microsoft Web Services." Further, if you install Microsoft FrontPage Server Extensions, the Administration Web site isn't installed and Remote Administration is unavailable. You can only manage the Web server through FrontPage and the FrontPage Server Extensions components.

Anytime you install additional components or services, the base installation might be modified to allow serving related content. Here are some examples:

- **Install ASP.NET and the .NET Framework** IIS is configured to allow ASP.NET applications.

- **Install Microsoft Certificate Services** IIS is configured to allow Active Server Pages (ASP), and virtual directories are created for managing certificate enrollment and the certificates themselves.

- **Install Internet Printing** IIS creates a Printers virtual directory on the default Web site. This directory is located in %SystemRoot%\Web\Printers. However, Internet Printing isn't enabled by default. You must enable Internet Printing through the Web Service Extensions.

- **Install Background Intelligent Transfer Service (BITS)** IIS is updated to allow background intelligent transfers. Web site and directory dialog boxes will have an additional tab for configuring BITS. BITS, however, after its installation, won't be enabled by default. You must do this through Web Service Extensions.

- **Install E-Mail Services** IIS is updated so that e-mail services can be remotely administrated through the Remote Administration tools.

Real World With previous installations of IIS, I recommended that you delete the default Web site. Simply put, there were too many security holes in the base installation. With the improvements to IIS 6, however, the default Web site is inherently secure.

You can create additional Web sites by completing the following steps:

1. If you're installing the Web site on a new server, ensure that the World Wide Web Publishing Service has been installed on the server.

2. If you want the Web site to use a new IP address, you must configure the IP address before installing the site. For details, refer to the "Assigning a Static IP Address" section of Chapter 16, "Managing TCP/IP Networking," in *Microsoft Windows Server 2003 Administrator's Pocket Consultant.*

3. In the IIS snap-in, double-click the icon for the computer you want to work with, and then right-click Web Sites. From the shortcut menu, choose New and then select Web Site. If the computer isn't shown, connect to it as discussed in the "Connecting to Other Servers" section of Chapter 2, and then perform this task.

Tip If you want to create a Web site with the exact same configuration and directory structure as another Web site, you can create the Web site from a metabase configuration file. Create a backup of the Web site configuration as discussed in the section entitled "Creating IIS Backup Configurations" in Chapter 16, "IIS Backup and Recovery." Then restore the configuration using a new Web site name as discussed in the section of Chapter 16 entitled "Restoring Site Configurations."

4. The Web Site Creation Wizard is started. Click Next. In the Description text box, type a descriptive name for the Web site, such as **Corporate WWW Server**. Click Next.

5. As shown in Figure 3-5, use the IP address drop-down list to select an available IP address. Choose (All Unassigned) to allow HTTP to respond on all unassigned IP addresses that are configured on the server. Multiple Web sites can use the same IP address, provided that the sites are configured to use different port numbers or host header names.

```
Web Site Creation Wizard                                    [x]

IP Address and Port Settings
   Specify an IP address, port setting, and host header for the new Web site.


   Enter the IP address to use for this Web site:
   ┌──────────────────────────────────┬──┐
   │192.168.1.50                      │▼ │
   └──────────────────────────────────┴──┘

   TCP port this Web site should use: (Default: 80)
   ┌──────┐
   │80    │
   └──────┘

   Host Header for this Web site: (Default: None)
   ┌──────────────────────────────────┐
   │                                  │
   └──────────────────────────────────┘



   For more information, read the IIS product documentation.

                         < Back    [  Next >  ]    Cancel
```

Figure 3-5. *Set the IP address and port values for the new site in the Web Site Creation Wizard.*

6. The TCP port for the Web site is assigned automatically as port 80. If necessary, type a new port number in the TCP Port field. Multiple sites can use the same port, provided that the sites are configured to use different IP addresses or host header names.

7. If you plan to use host headers for the site, type the host header name in the field provided. On a private network, the host header can be a computer name, such as EngIntranet. On a public network, the host header must be a DNS name, such as services.microsoft.com. The host header name must be unique. Click Next.

8. Set the home directory for the Web site. Click Browse to search for a folder. The Browse For Folder dialog box opens. Select the folder you want to use as the home directory.

 Note This folder must be created before you can select it. If necessary, click Make New Folder in the Browse For Folder dialog box to create the directory.

9. If you want to create a secure or private Web site, clear Allow Anonymous Access To This Web Site. By default, new Web sites are configured for anonymous access. This means that users can access the Web site without needing to authenticate themselves. Click Next.

10. You can set access permissions for the Web site in the Web Site Creation Wizard. Normally, you'll want to set Read and Run Scripts permissions only, as shown in Figure 3-6. The standard permissions are the following:

   - **Read** Allows users to read documents, such as Hypertext Markup Language (HTML) files

   - **Run Scripts** Allows users to run scripts, such as ASP files or Perl scripts

   - **Execute** Allows users to execute programs, such as ISAPI applications or CGI executable files

   - **Write** Allows users to upload files to the site, such as with FrontPage

   - **Browse** Allows users to view a list of files if they enter the name of a valid directory that doesn't have a default file

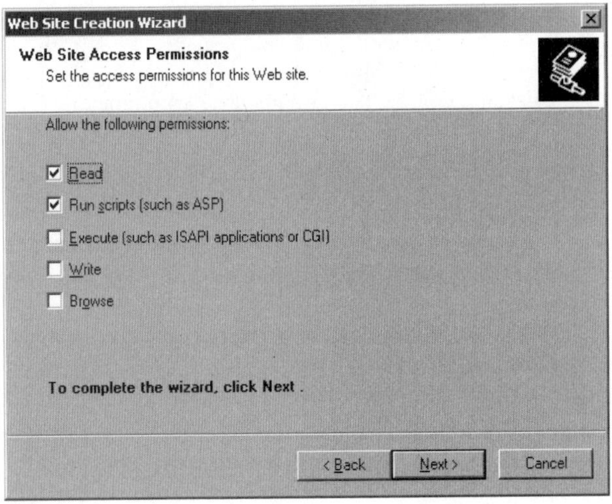

Figure 3-6. *Set access permissions for the Web site in the Web Site Creation Wizard.*

11. Click Next and then click Finish. The Web site is created but isn't started. You should finish setting the site's properties before you start the site and make it accessible to users.

Real World I recommend that you create a top-level directory for storing the home directories and then create subdirectories for each site. The default top-level directory is C:\Inetpub. If you use this directory, you could create subdirectories called CorpWWW, CorpServices, and CorpProducts to store the files for *www.microsoft.com*, *services.microsoft.com*, and *products.microsoft.com*, respectively.

Managing Web Site Properties

The sections that follow examine key tasks for managing Web site properties. You configure most Web site properties through the Web site's Properties dialog box.

Configuring a Site's Home Directory

Each Web site on a server has a home directory. The home directory is the base directory for all documents that the site publishes. It contains a home page that links to other pages in your site. The home directory is mapped to your site's domain name or to the server name. For example, if the site's DNS name is *www.microsoft.com* and the home directory is C:\Inetpub\Wwwroot, then browsers use the URL *http://www.microsoft.com/* to access files in the home directory. On an intranet, the server name can be used to access documents in the home directory. For example, if the server name is CorpIntranet, then browsers use the URL *http://CorpIntranet/* to access files in the home directory.

You can view or change a site's home directory by completing the following steps:

1. Start the IIS snap-in and then, in the left pane (Console Root), click the plus sign (+) next to the computer you want to work with. If the computer isn't shown, connect to it as discussed in the "Connecting to Other Servers" section of Chapter 2.

2. Double-click Web Sites. Right-click the Web site you want to manage and then choose Properties.

3. Select the Home Directory tab, as shown in Figure 3-7.

4. If the directory you want to use is on the local computer, select A Directory Located On This Computer, and then type the directory path in the Local Path text box, such as C:\Inetpub\Wwwroot. To browse for the folder, click Browse.

5. If the directory you want to use is on another computer and is accessible as a shared folder, select A Share Located On Another Computer, and then type the UNC path to the share in the Network Directory field. The path should be in the form \\ServerName\SharedFolder, such as \\Gandolf\CorpWWW. Then click Connect As and type the user name and password that should be used to connect to the shared folder.

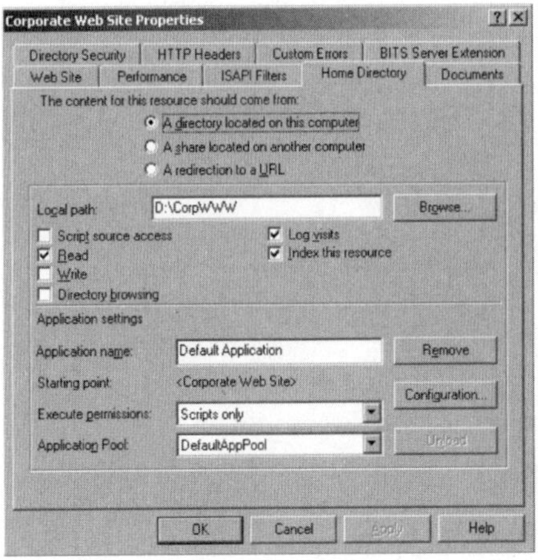

Figure 3-7. *You can change a site's home directory at any time.*

Note If you don't specify a user name and password, the user's Windows credentials are authenticated before allowing access. If this is an anonymous access site, the Users group should have access to the shared folder. Otherwise, the network connection to the folder will fail. See the section entitled "Working with File and Folder Permissions" in Chapter 7, "Enhancing Web Server Security," for more details on access permissions.

6. If you want to redirect users to another URL, select A Redirection To A URL, and then follow the techniques outlined in the "Redirecting Browser Requests" section of Chapter 4.

7. Click OK.

Configuring Ports, IP Addresses, and Host Names Used by Web Sites

Each Web site has a unique identity. The identity includes TCP port, SSL port, IP address, and host name settings. The default TCP port is 80. The default SSL port is 443. The default IP address setting is to use any available IP address.

To change the identity of a Web site, complete the following steps:

1. If you want the Web site to respond to a specific IP address, you must configure the IP address before updating the site. For details, refer to the "Configuring Static IP Addresses" section of Chapter 16, "Managing TCP/IP Networking," in *Microsoft Windows Server 2003 Administrator's Pocket Consultant.*

2. Start the IIS snap-in and then, in the left pane (Console Root), click the plus sign (+) next to the computer you want to work with. If the computer isn't

shown, connect to it as discussed in the "Connecting to Other Servers" section of Chapter 2.

3. Double-click Web Sites. Right-click the Web site you want to manage and then choose Properties. The dialog box shown in Figure 3-8 is displayed.

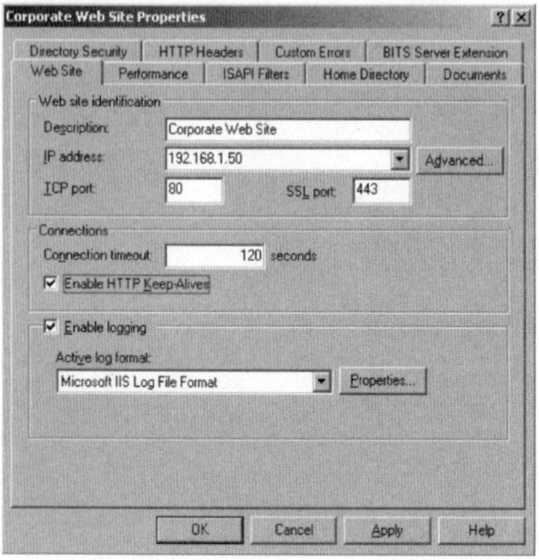

Figure 3-8. *You modify a site's identity through the Web Site tab in the Properties dialog box.*

4. The Description text box shows the descriptive name for the Web site. The descriptive name is displayed in the IIS snap-in and isn't used for other purposes. You can change the current value by typing a new name in the Description text box.

5. The IP address drop-down list shows the current IP address for the Web site. If you want to change the IP address, use the drop-down list to select an available IP address or choose (All Unassigned) to allow HTTP to respond on all unassigned IP addresses. Multiple Web sites can use the same IP address, provided that the sites are configured to use different port numbers or host header names.

6. The TCP port for the Web site is assigned to port 80 automatically. If necessary, type a new port number in the TCP Port field. Multiple Web sites can use the same TCP port, provided that the sites are configured to use different IP addresses or host header names.

7. If you plan to use host headers for the site, click Advanced, then Add, and finally type the host header name in the Host Header Value text box. On a private network, the host header can be a computer name, such as EngIntranet. On a public network, the host header must be a DNS name, such as *services.microsoft.com*. The host header name must be unique.

8. By default, Web servers use port 443 for SSL. If you've installed an SSL certificate on the server as discussed in Chapter 8, "Managing Microsoft Certificate Services and SSL," SSL is enabled for use, and you can change the SSL port by typing a new value in the SSL Port field. Multiple sites can use the same SSL port, provided that the sites are configured to use different IP addresses.

9. Click OK.

Configuring Multiple Identities for a Single Web Site

Throughout this chapter I've discussed techniques you can use to configure multiple Web sites on a single server. The focus of the discussion has been on configuring unique identities for each site. In some instances you might want a single Web site to have multiple domain names associated with it. A Web site with multiple domain names publishes the same content for different sets of users. For example, your company might have registered *example.com, example.org*, and *example.net* with a domain registrar to protect your company or domain name. Rather than publishing the same content to each of these sites separately, you can publish the content to a single site that accepts requests for each of these identities.

The rules regarding unique combinations of ports, IP addresses, and host names still apply to sites with multiple identities. This means that each identity for a site must be unique. You accomplish this by assigning each identity unique IP address, port, or host header name combinations.

To assign multiple identities to a Web site, complete the following steps:

1. If you want the Web site to use multiple IP addresses, you must configure the additional IP addresses before modifying the site properties. For details, refer to the "Configuring Static IP Addresses" section of Chapter 16, "Managing TCP/IP Networking," in *Microsoft Windows Server 2003 Administrator's Pocket Consultant*.

2. Start the IIS snap-in and then, in the left pane (Console Root), click the plus sign (+) next to the computer you want to work with. If the computer isn't shown, connect to it as discussed in the "Connecting to Other Servers" section of Chapter 2.

3. Double-click Web Sites. Right-click the Web site you want to manage and then choose Properties. The dialog box shown previously in Figure 3-8 is displayed.

4. In the Web Site tab, click Advanced. As Figure 3-9 shows, you can now use the Advanced Web Site Configuration dialog box to configure multiple identities for the site.

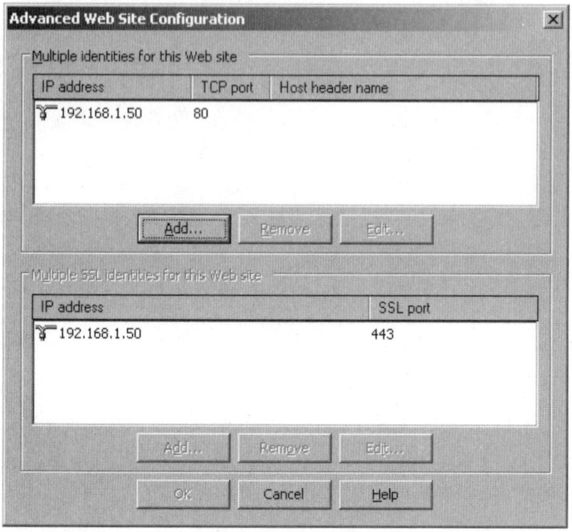

Figure 3-9. *Web sites can have multiple identities.*

5. Use the Multiple Identities For This Web Site frame to manage the following TCP port settings:

- **Add** Adds a new identity. Click Add, select the IP address you want to use, and then type a TCP port and optional host header name. Click OK when you're finished.

- **Edit** Allows you to edit the currently selected entry in the identities frame.

- **Remove** Allows you to remove the currently selected entry from the identities frame.

6. Use the Multiple SSL Identities For This Web Site frame to manage SSL port settings. Click Add to create new entries. Use Edit or Remove to modify or delete existing entries.

7. Click OK twice to return to the IIS snap-in.

Restricting Incoming Connections and Setting Time-Out Values

You control incoming connections to a Web site in two key ways. You can set a limit on the number of simultaneous connections, and you can set a connection time-out value.

Normally, Web sites accept an unlimited number of connections, and this is an optimal setting in most environments. However, a large number of connections will cause the Web site to slow down—sometimes so severely that nobody can access the site. To avoid this situation, you might want to limit the number of simultaneous connections. Once the limit is reached, no other clients are permitted to access the server. New clients must wait until the connection load on the server decreases; however, currently connected users are allowed to continue browsing the site.

The connection time-out value determines when idle user sessions are disconnected. With the default Web site, sessions time out after they've been idle for 120 seconds (2 minutes). This prevents connections from remaining open indefinitely if browsers don't close them correctly.

You can modify connection limits and time-outs by completing the following steps:

1. Start the IIS snap-in and then, in the left pane (Console Root), click the plus sign (+) next to the computer you want to work with. If the computer isn't shown, connect to it as discussed in the "Connecting to Other Servers" section of Chapter 2.

2. Double-click Web Sites. Right-click the Web site you want to manage and then choose Properties.

3. The Connection Timeout field, located in the Web Site tab of the Properties dialog box, controls the connection time-out. Type a new value to change the current time-out.

4. Select the Performance tab. To remove connection limits, select Unlimited in the Web Site Connections frame. To set a connection limit, select Connections Limited To, and then type a limit.

5. Click OK.

Configuring HTTP Keep-Alives

The original design of HTTP opened a new connection for every file retrieved from a Web server. Because a connection isn't maintained, no system resources are used after the transaction is completed. The drawback to this design is that when the same client requests additional data, the connection must be reestablished, and this means additional traffic and delays.

Consider a standard Web page that contains a main HTML document and 10 images. With standard HTTP, a Web client requests each file through a separate connection. The client connects to the server, requests the document file, gets a response, and then disconnects. The client repeats this process for each image file in the document.

Web servers compliant with HTTP 1.1 support a feature called HTTP Keep-Alives. With this feature enabled, clients maintain an open connection with the Web server rather than reopening a connection with each request. HTTP Keep-Alives are enabled by default for new Web sites. In most situations clients will see greatly improved performance with HTTP Keep-Alives enabled. Keep in mind, however, that maintaining connections requires system resources. The more open connections there are, the more system resources that are used. To prevent a busy server from getting bogged down by a large number of open connections, you might want to limit the number of connections, reduce the connection time-out for client sessions, or both. For more information on managing connections, see the "Restricting Incoming Connections and Setting Time-Out Values" section of this chapter.

To enable or disable HTTP Keep-Alives, follow these steps:

1. Start the IIS snap-in and then, in the left pane (Console Root), click the plus sign (+) next to the computer you want to work with. If the computer isn't shown, connect to it as discussed in the "Connecting to Other Servers" section of Chapter 2.

2. Double-click Web Sites. Right-click the Web site you want to manage and then choose Properties.

3. In the Web Site tab of the Properties dialog box, select Enable HTTP Keep-Alives to enable HTTP Keep-Alives. Clear this check box to disable HTTP Keep-Alives.

4. Click OK.

Managing Directories

The directory structure of IIS is based primarily on the Windows Server 2003 file system, but it also provides additional functionality and flexibility. Understanding these complexities is critical to successfully managing IIS Web sites.

Understanding Physical and Virtual Directory Structures

Earlier in this chapter, I discussed home directories and how they were used. Beyond home directories, Microsoft Web sites also use the following:

- Physical directories
- Virtual directories

The difference between physical and virtual directories is important. A physical directory is part of the file system and to be available through IIS, it must exist as a subdirectory within the home directory. A virtual directory is a directory that isn't necessarily contained in the home directory but is available to clients through an alias. Physical directories and virtual directories are configured and managed with the IIS snap-in, but they're displayed differently. Physical directories are indicated with a standard folder icon. Virtual directories are indicated using a folder icon with a globe in the corner.

Both physical and virtual directories have permissions and properties that you can set at the operating system level and the IIS level. You set operating system permissions and properties in Windows Explorer. You set IIS permissions and properties in the IIS snap-in.

You create physical directories by creating subdirectories within the home directory using Windows Explorer. You access these subdirectories by appending the directory name to the DNS name for the Web site. For example, you create a Web site with the DNS name *products.microsoft.com*. Users are able to access the Web site using the URL *http://www.microsoft.com/*. You then create a subdirectory within the home directory called "search." Users are able to access the subdirectory using the URL path *http://www.microsoft.com/search/*.

Even though locating your content files and directories within the home directory makes it easier to manage a Web site, you can also use virtual directories. Virtual directories act as pointers to directories that aren't located in the home directory. You access virtual directories by appending the directory alias to the DNS name for the site. If, for example, your home directory is D:\Inetpub\Wwwroot and you store Microsoft Word documents in E:\Worddocs, you would need to create a virtual directory that points to the actual directory location. If the alias is *docs* for the E:\Worddocs directory, visitors to the *www.microsoft.com* Web site could access the directory using the URL path *http://www.microsoft.com/docs/*.

Creating Physical Directories

Within the home directory, you can create subdirectories to help organize your site's documents. You can create subdirectories within the home directory by completing the following steps:

1. Start Windows Explorer. Click Start, choose All Programs, Accessories, and finally Windows Explorer.

2. In the Folders pane, select the home directory for the Web site.

3. In the Contents pane, right-click a blank area and select New, then Folder from the shortcut menu. A new folder is added to the Contents pane. The default name is initialized to New Folder and selected for editing.

4. Edit the name of the folder and press Enter. The best directory names are short but descriptive, such as Images, WordDocs, or Downloads.

Tip   If possible, avoid using spaces as part of IIS directory names. Officially, spaces are illegal characters in URLs and must be replaced with an escape code. The escape code for a space is %20. Although most current browsers will replace spaces with %20 for you, earlier versions of browsers might not, and won't be able to access the page.

5. The new folder inherits the default file permissions of the home directory and the default IIS permissions of the Web site. For details on viewing or changing permissions, see Chapter 7, "Enhancing Web Server Security."

Tip   The IIS snap-in doesn't automatically display new folders. You might need to click the Refresh button on the toolbar (or press F5) to display the folder.

Creating Virtual Directories

A *virtual directory* is a directory available to Internet users through an alias for an actual physical directory. In previous versions of IIS, you had to create the physical directory prior to assigning the virtual directory alias. In IIS 6, you can create the physical directory if one is needed when you create the virtual directory.

To create a virtual directory, follow these steps:

1. Start the IIS snap-in, and then, in the left pane (Console Root), click the plus sign (+) next to the computer you want to work with. If the computer isn't shown, connect to it as discussed in the "Connecting to Other Servers" section of Chapter 2.

2. Double-click Web Sites. Right-click the Web site on which you want to create the virtual directory, choose New from the shortcut menu, and then select Virtual Directory. This starts the Virtual Directory Creation Wizard. Click Next.

More Info If you want to create a virtual directory with the exact same configuration as a directory in another Web site, you can create the virtual directory from a metabase configuration file. Create a backup of the virtual directory configuration as discussed in the section entitled "Creating IIS Backup Configurations" in Chapter 16. Then restore the configuration using a new alias as discussed in the section of Chapter 16 entitled "Restoring Virtual Directory Configurations."

3. In the Alias text box, type the name you want to use to access the virtual directory. As with directory names, the best alias names are short but descriptive. Click Next.

4. Set the path to the physical directory where your content is stored. Type the directory path or click Browse to search for a directory. The directory must be created before you can select it. If necessary, click Make New Folder in the Browse For Folder dialog box to create the directory before you select it. However, don't forget about checking and setting permissions at the operating system level as discussed in Chapter 7.

5. Set access permissions for the virtual directory. Normally, you'll want to set Read and Run Scripts permissions only. The standard permissions are these:

   - **Read** Allows users to read documents, such as HTML files
   - **Run Scripts** Allows users to run scripts, such as ASP files or Perl scripts
   - **Execute** Allows users to execute programs, such as ISAPI applications or CGI executable files

- **Write**   Allows users to upload files to the site, such as with FrontPage

- **Browse**   Allows users to view a list of files if they enter the name of a valid directory that doesn't have a default document

6. Click Next and then click Finish. The virtual directory is created.

Note   A virtual directory that is created as an application is indicated with an icon that shows an assembly cog. If, however, the virtual directory is part of the default application pool, the virtual directory is indicated with an icon that shows a globe. For more information on pooled applications, see Chapter 6, "Managing ASP.NET, Application Pools, and Worker Processes."

Modifying Directory Properties

You can modify the settings for a physical or virtual directory at any time. You set directory permissions and general directory properties in Windows Explorer. You set IIS permissions and properties in the directory properties dialog box. In the IIS snap-in, right-click the directory and then select Properties.

Renaming Directories

You can rename physical and virtual directories in the IIS snap-in. When you rename a physical directory, the actual folder name of the directory is changed. When you rename a virtual directory, the alias to the directory is changed. The name of the related physical directory isn't changed.

To rename a physical directory, follow these steps:

1. In the IIS snap-in, click the plus sign (+) next to the Web site you want to work with.

2. Right-click the directory you want to rename and select Rename from the shortcut menu. The directory name is selected for editing.

3. Edit the name of the folder and then press Enter.

Caution   Browsers store file and directory paths in bookmarks. When you change a directory name, you invalidate any URL that references the directory in its path string. Because of this, renaming a directory might cause a return visitor to experience the 404 File Or Directory Not Found error. To resolve this problem, you might want to redirect browser requests to the new location using the technique discussed in the "Redirecting Browser Requests" section of Chapter 4.

In previous versions of IIS, you could rename virtual directories by right-clicking the virtual directory in the IIS snap-in and selecting Rename. In IIS 6, you can no longer rename virtual directories through the IIS snap-in. The reason for this is that virtual directories are now created as applications automatically and renaming would require several instance changes in the running IIS configuration.

To rename a virtual directory, you could delete the existing virtual directory and then create a new one using the desired name. This won't preserve the original directory settings, however. If you want to preserve the settings of the current virtual directory, you will need to perform the following steps:

1. Create a backup of the virtual directory configuration as discussed in the section entitled "Creating IIS Configuration Backups" in Chapter 16.

2. Restore the virtual directory with a new alias as discussed in the section of Chapter 16 entitled "Restoring Virtual Directory Configurations."

Deleting Directories

You can delete physical and virtual directories in the IIS snap-in. When you delete a physical directory, the directory and its contents are removed and placed in the Recycle Bin. When you delete a virtual directory, only the alias to the directory is removed. The actual contents of the related physical directory aren't changed.

To delete a physical or virtual directory in the IIS snap-in, follow these steps:

1. In the IIS snap-in, click the plus sign (+) next to the Web site you want to work with.

2. Right-click the directory you want to delete and select Delete from the shortcut menu. When asked to confirm the action, click Yes.

Chapter 4

Customizing Web Server Content

Most Web administrators don't need to create Web server content. Typically, content creation is the job of Web designers and content management is the job of Web administrators. Designers and administrators often work closely together to ensure that corporate sites, intranets, and extranets have the exact look and feel that management wants. A large part of this is customizing the way the Web server uses content. You might need to configure the server to redirect browser requests to other directories or Web sites. You might need to create custom headers and footers or assign specific types of default documents to be used.

You can customize the content in many other ways as well. Rather than use generic error messages, you might want to create custom error messages that are specific to your company's Web pages. Custom error messages can contain menus, graphics, links, and text that help lost users find their way. If your organization uses unique types of content, you might need to configure servers to use additional content types. To help track advertising, you might want to create jump pages. To better manage outages, you might want to create an update site. These techniques and more are discussed in this chapter.

Don't worry. You don't have to master every technique in this chapter, but the more you know about customizing content and the options available, the better you'll be as an administrator.

Configuring Web Service Extensions

Unlike previous versions, Microsoft Internet Information Services (IIS) 6.0 is configured by default to serve only static content. This means the standard default configuration serves only static Hypertext Markup Language (HTML) documents. Before a Web server can serve any other type of document, the appropriate Web Service extension must be enabled.

Using Web Service Extensions

A *Web Service extension* is any type of nonstatic document or functionality that requires special processing. Web Service extensions that can be configured on IIS include:

- **Active Server Pages** Controls whether server-side scripts written as Active Server Pages (ASP) can be used. This extension is always installed.

- **ASP.NET** Controls whether ASP.NET applications can be used. This extension is made available when you install ASP.NET as a Web Application Server component.

- **BITS Server Extensions** Controls whether background Internet transfers can be used. This extension is made available when you install the Background Intelligent Transfer Service (BITS) server extension as an IIS component.

- **Indexing Service** Controls whether Web server content can be indexed and then searched. This extension is made available when you install Indexing Service as a Microsoft Windows component.

- **Internet Data Connector** Controls whether pages can use the Internet Data Connector. This extension is always installed.

- **Internet Printing** Controls whether the server can be used for Internet printing. This extension is made available when you install Internet Printing as an IIS component.

- **Server Side Includes** Controls whether pages can use Server Side Includes. This extension is always installed.

- **WebDAV** Controls whether pages can use Web Distributed Authoring and Versioning (WebDAV). This extension is always installed.

IIS also makes use of Common Gateway Interface (CGI) and Internet Server Application Programming Interface (ISAPI) extensions. Generally speaking, CGI is enabled through a processing engine for a specific scripting language, such as Perl, that's implemented as an ISAPI filter. IIS also makes use of ISAPI filters when processing some types of requests. ASP.NET requests are in fact handled by an ISAPI filter. You can configure ISAPI filters globally for all sites on a server through Web Sites properties or for individual Web sites through the individual site properties.

To enhance security, IIS 6 makes a distinction between known and unknown CGI/ISAPI extensions. By default, all unknown CGI and ISAPI extensions are prohibited, and you must specifically add and configure a CGI/ISAPI filter before it can be used. If you remove this restriction by allowing unknown CGI and ISAPI extensions to be used, filters that haven't been specifically added and configured might be used.

You configure Web Service extensions globally for all sites on a Web server using the Web Service Extensions node in the IIS snap-in. When you access the Web Service Extensions node, each extension that's installed on the server is listed along with the status of the extension, as shown in Figure 4-1.

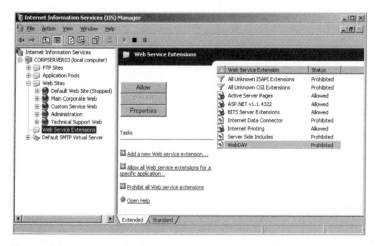

Figure 4-1. *Use the Web Service Extensions node to allow or prohibit IIS to process various types of nonstatic content.*

Allowing and Prohibiting Web Service Extensions

Web Service extensions can be individually allowed or prohibited. Allowing an extension tells IIS that requests for related content can be served and that the server can process the requests. Prohibiting an extension tells IIS that requests for related content shouldn't be handled; instead, they should be rejected, as IIS does with requests for file extensions that it doesn't recognize.

Allowing and prohibiting extensions is fairly straightforward using any of the following options:

- **Allow Extension**   To allow an extension to be serviced, select it and then click Allow.

- **Prohibit Extension**   To prohibit an extension, select it and then click Prohibit. Afterward, confirm the action by clicking Yes when prompted.

- **Prohibit All Extensions**   To prohibit all extensions and lock down a server so that only static content can be served, click Prohibit All Web Service Extensions and then confirm the action by clicking Yes when prompted.

Managing Web Content

As discussed in Chapter 3, "Configuring Web Sites and Servers," every Web site on a server has a home directory. The home directory is the base directory for all documents that the site publishes. Copying files into the home directory, a virtual directory, or any subdirectory of these directories is, in fact, how you publish documents on a Web site.

Documents inherit the default properties of the site and the default permissions of the Windows folder in which they're placed. You can change these properties and permissions for each individual document or for all documents within a directory.

 Caution Browsers can cache file and directory paths in bookmarks. To prevent errors when renaming or deleting files, you might want to redirect browser requests to the new location using the technique discussed in the "Redirecting Browser Requests" section of this chapter.

Opening and Browsing Files

You can open files in a browser from within the IIS snap-in. To do this, right-click the file and then select Open from the shortcut menu. This opens the file using a directory path, such as D:\Inetpub\Wwwroot\Default.htm.

You can display most types of files in the default browser by opening them. However, if the file is an .asp document or other type of dynamic content and the Web site is running, the file won't be displayed. You must be browsing the file to view it in Microsoft Internet Explorer. To browse a file, right-click the file and then select Browse from the shortcut menu.

Modifying the IIS Properties of Files

You can modify the settings for a Web file at any time. You set file permissions and general file properties in Windows Explorer. You set IIS permissions and properties in the file's Properties dialog box. In the IIS snap-in, right-click the file, and then select Properties.

Renaming Files

You can rename Web files in the IIS snap-in. To do that, follow these steps:

1. Start the IIS snap-in and then click the plus sign (+) next to the Web site you want to work with.
2. Navigate within the site, click the file you want to rename, pause for a moment, and then click the file name. The file name is selected for editing.
3. Edit the name of the file and then press Enter.

 Note Using the "click, pause, click" technique for renaming a file can take a bit of practice. Remember to click on the file's name and not its icon. If you find it just isn't working, right-click the file you want to rename and then select Rename.

Deleting Files

You can delete physical and virtual directories in the IIS snap-in. When you delete a physical directory, the directory and its contents are removed and placed in the Recycle Bin. When you delete a virtual directory, only the alias to the directory is removed. The actual contents of the related physical directory aren't deleted.

To delete a physical or virtual directory in the IIS snap-in, follow these steps:

1. In the IIS snap-in, click the plus sign (+) next to the Web site you want to work with.

2. Right-click the directory you want to delete and then select Delete from the shortcut menu. When asked to confirm the action, click OK.

Redirecting Browser Requests

Browser redirection is a useful technique to prevent errors when you rename or delete content within a Web site. When you redirect requests, you tell a browser to take the following actions:

- Look for files in another directory
- Look for files on a different Web site
- Look for files on another computer
- Look for a specific file instead of a set of files
- Run an ISAPI application instead of accessing the requested files

Each of these redirection techniques is examined in the sections that follow. Tips for creating customized redirection routines are examined in the "Customizing Browser Redirection" section of this chapter.

Redirecting Requests to Other Directories or Web Sites

If you rename or delete a directory, you can redirect requests for files in the old directory to the new directory, another directory, or even another Web site. When a browser requests the file at the original location, the Web server instructs the browser to request the page using the new location. You redirect requests to other directories or Web sites as follows:

1. In the IIS snap-in, click the plus sign (+) next to the Web site you want to work with.

2. Right-click the directory you want to redirect and then select Properties.

3. Select the Virtual Directory or Directory tab as appropriate, and then select A Redirection To A URL, as shown in Figure 4-2.

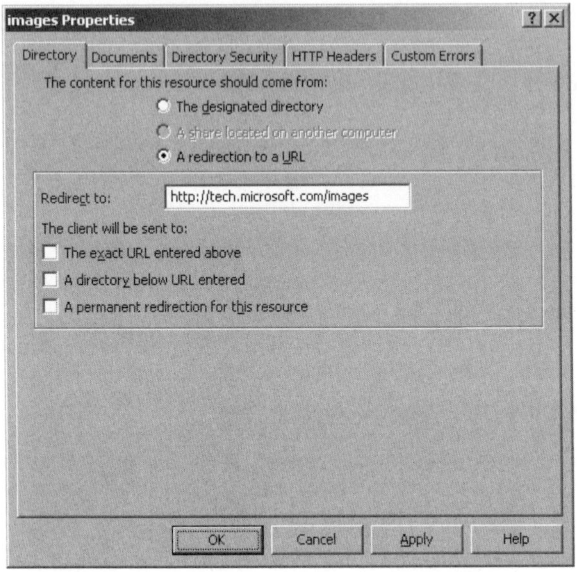

Figure 4-2. *You can redirect requests for files in one directory to another directory.*

4. In the Redirect To field, type the Uniform Resource Locator (URL) of the destination directory or Web site. For example, to redirect all requests for files in the /Docs directory to the /CorpDocs directory, type **/CorpDocs**. To redirect all requests for files located at *http://www.microsoft.com/Docs* to *techsupport.microsoft.com/CorpDocs*, type **http://techsupport.microsoft.com/CorpDocs**.

5. Click OK. Now all requests for files in the old directory are mapped to files in the new directory. For example, if the browser requested *http://www.microsoft.com/Docs/adminguide.doc/* and you redirected requests to *http://techsupport.microsoft.com/CorpDocs/*, the browser would request *http://techsupport.microsoft.com/CorpDocs/adminguide.doc/*.

Redirecting All Requests to Another Web Site

If you stop publishing a Web site but don't want users to reach a dead end if they visit, you should redirect requests for the old Web site to a specific page at the new site. You redirect requests to a specific page at another site by completing the following steps:

1. In the IIS snap-in, right-click the Web site you want to work with and then select Properties.

2. Select the Home Directory tab and then select A Redirection To A URL, as shown in Figure 4-3.

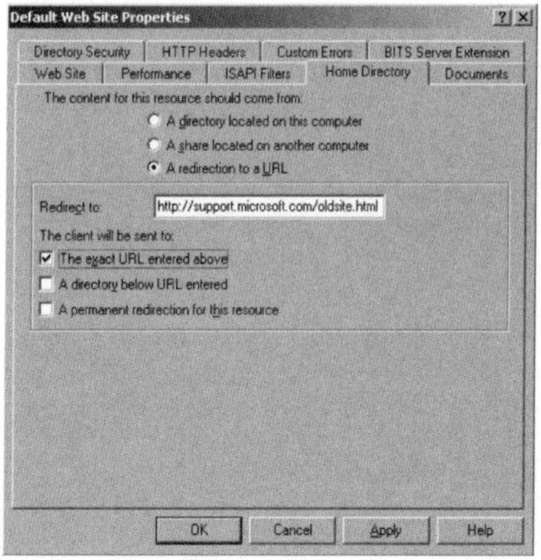

Figure 4-3. *Another redirection technique is to redirect all requests for files to a specific location at another Web site.*

3. In the Redirect To field, type the complete URL path to the page at the new site, such as **http://www.microsoft.com/oldsite.html**.

4. In The Client Will Be Sent To section, select The Exact URL Entered Above, and then click OK. Now all requests for files at the old site are mapped to a specific page at the new site.

Retrieving Files from a Network Share

IIS can retrieve files from a network share instead of the local hard disk drive. To configure this, complete the following steps:

1. In the IIS snap-in, right-click the Web site you want to work with and then select Properties.

2. Select the Home Directory tab and then select A Share Located On Another Computer, as shown in Figure 4-4.

3. Type the Universal Naming Convention (UNC) path to the network share in the Network Directory field. The path should be in the form \\ServerName\ SharedFolder, such as \\Gandolf\CorpWWW. Afterward, click Connect As.

4. In the Network Directory Service Credentials dialog box that appears, clear the Always Use The Authenticated User's Credentials When Validating Access To The Network Directory check box, and then type the user name and password that should be used to connect to the shared folder.

5. Click OK. Now all requests for files on the Web site are mapped to files on the specified network share.

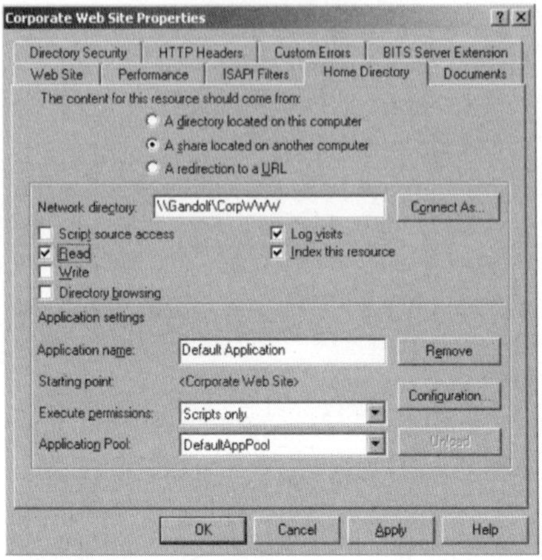

Figure 4-4. *Network shares can be used as source directories for content. To map to a share, you must use redirection.*

Redirecting Requests to Applications

If your organization's development team has created a custom application for the Web site, you can redirect all requests for files in a particular directory (or for the entire site, for that matter) to an application. Parameters passed in the URL can also be passed to the application; the technique you use to do this is as follows:

1. In the IIS snap-in, click the plus sign (+) next to the Web site you want to work with.

2. Right-click the directory you want to redirect and then select Properties. If you want to redirect all requests for the site, right-click the Web site entry and then select Properties.

3. Select the Home Directory, Virtual Directory, or Directory tab as appropriate, and then select A Redirection To A URL.

4. In the Redirection To field, type the application's URL, including any variables needed to pass parameters to the program, such as /CorpApps/ Login.exe?URL =V+PARAMS=P, where V and P are redirection variables. A complete list of redirect variables is provided in Table 4-1.

5. In The Client Will Be Sent To section, select The Exact URL Entered Above and then click OK. Now all requests for files in the directory or site are mapped to the application.

Customizing Browser Redirection

The previous sections looked at basic redirection techniques. Now it's time to break out the power tools and customize the redirection process. You can customize redirection anytime you select the A Redirection To A URL option.

In all of the previous discussions, when you selected A Redirection To A URL, additional options were displayed in The Client Will Be Sent To section. Without selecting additional options, all requests for files in the old location were mapped automatically to files in the new location. You can change this behavior by selecting any of the following options in The Client Will Be Sent To section:

- **The Exact URL Entered Above**   Redirects requests to the destination URL without adding any other portions of the original URL. You can use this option to redirect an entire site or directory to one file. For example, to redirect all requests for the /Downloads directory to the file Download.htm in the home directory, select this option and then type **/Download.htm** in the Redirect To field.

- **A Directory Below URL Entered**   Redirects a parent directory to a child directory. For example, to redirect your home directory (designated by /) to a subdirectory named /Current, select this option and then type **/Current** in the Redirect To field.

- **A Permanent Redirection For This Resource**   Sends a 301—Permanent Redirect message to the client. Without using this option, redirections are considered temporary, and the client browser receives the 302—Temporary Redirect message. Some browsers can use the 301—Permanent Redirect message as the signal to permanently change a URL stored in cache or in a bookmark.

You can customize redirection using redirect variables as well. As Table 4-1 shows, you can use redirect variables to pass portions of the original URL to a destination path or to prevent redirection of a specific file or subdirectory.

Table 4-1.   Redirect Variables for IIS

Variable	Description	Example
$S	Passes the matched suffix of the requested URL. The server automatically performs this suffix substitution; you use the $S variable only in combination with other variables.	If /Corpapps is redirected to /Apps and the original request is for /Corpapps/Login.exe, then /Login.exe is the suffix.
$P	Passes the parameters in the original URL, omitting the question mark used to specify the beginning of a query string.	If the original URL is /Scripts /Count.asp?valA=1&valB=2, then the string "valA=1&valB=2" is mapped into the destination URL.

(continued)

Table 4-1. **Redirect Variables for IIS**   *(continued)*

Variable	Description	Example
$Q	Passes the full query string to the destination.	If the original URL is /Scripts / Count.asp?valA=1&valB=2, then the string "?valA=1&valB=2" is mapped into the destination URL.
$V	Passes the requested path without the server name.	If the original URL is //Gandolf /Apps/ Count.asp, then the string "/Apps/ Count.asp" is mapped into the destination URL.
$0 through *$9*	Passes the portion of the requested URL that matches the indicated wildcard character.	If the original URL is //Gandolf/Apps/ Data.htm, $0 would be Gandolf, $1 would be Apps, and $2 would be Data.htm.
!	Use this variable to prevent redirecting a subdirectory or an individual file.	

The final way you can customize redirection is to use redirect wildcard characters. Use redirect wildcard characters to redirect particular types of files to a specific file at the destination. For example, you can use redirect wildcard characters to redirect all .htm files to Default.htm and all .asp files to Default.asp. The syntax for wildcard character redirection is

```
*;*.EXT;FILENAME.EXT[;*.EXT;FILENAME.EXT...]
```

where *.EXT* is the file extension you want to redirect and *FILENAME.EXT* is the name of the file to use at the destination. As shown, begin the destination URL with an asterisk and a semicolon and separate pairs of wildcard characters and destination URLs with a semicolon. Be sure to account for all document types that users might request directly, such as .htm, .html, and .asp documents.

You can use wildcard character redirection by completing the following steps:

1. In the IIS snap-in, click the plus sign (+) next to the Web site you want to work with.

2. Right-click the directory you want to redirect and then select Properties. If you want to redirect all requests for the site, right-click the Web site entry, and then select Properties.

3. Select the Home Directory, Virtual Directory, or Directory tab as appropriate, and then select A Redirection To A URL.

4. In the Redirection To field, type the wildcard character redirection values. For example, if you want to redirect wildcards to redirect all .htm files to Default.htm and all .asp files to Default.asp, you'd enter:

   ```
   *;*.HTM;DEFAULT.HTM;*.ASP;DEFAULT.ASP
   ```

5. In The Client Will Be Sent To section, select The Exact URL Entered Above and then click OK. Now all requests for files in the directory or site are mapped using wildcard characters, if possible.

Customizing Web Site Content and HTTP Headers

IIS sets default values for documents and Hypertext Transfer Protocol (HTTP) headers. You can modify these default values at the site, directory, and file level.

Configuring Default Documents

Default document settings determine how IIS handles requests that don't specify a document name. If a user makes a request using a directory path that ends in a directory name or forward slash (/) rather than a file name, IIS uses the default document settings to determine how to handle the request.

When default document handling is enabled, IIS searches for default documents in the order in which their names appear in the default document list and returns the first document it finds. If a match isn't found, IIS checks to see if directory browsing is enabled and, if so, returns a directory listing. Otherwise, IIS returns a 404—File Not Found error.

You can configure default document settings at the site or directory level. This means that individual directories can have default document settings that are different from the site as a whole. Standard default document names include Default.htm, Default.asp, Index.htm, and Index.html.

You can view current default document settings or make changes by following these steps:

1. In the IIS snap-in, right-click the Web site, virtual directory, or directory you want to work with and then choose Properties.

2. Select the Documents tab. The Enable Default Content Page check box determines whether default documents are used. To turn on default document handling, select this check box. To turn off default document handling, clear this check box.

3. To add a new default document, click Add. Next, type the name of the default document, such as **Index.html**, and then click OK.

4. To remove a default document, select it in the list provided, and then click Remove.

5. To change the search order, select a document, and then click either Move Up or Move Down.

6. Click OK.

Configuring Document Footers

You can configure IIS to automatically insert an HTML-formatted footer document on the bottom of every document it sends. The footer can contain copyright information, logos, or other important information. As with default documents, you can configure document footers at the site or directory level.

This means that individual directories can have different footer settings from the site as a whole.

Enabling Automatic Footers

To configure automatic footers, follow these steps:

1. Create an HTML-formatted document and save it to a folder on a Web server's local hard disk drive. The footer document shouldn't be a complete HTML page. Instead, it should include only the HTML tags necessary for content that's to be displayed in the footer.

2. In the IIS snap-in, right-click the Web site, virtual directory, or directory you want to work with and then choose Properties.

3. Select the Documents tab and then select the Enable Document Footer check box.

4. In the field provided, type the path to the footer file or click Browse to display the Open dialog box, which you can use to find the file.

5. Click OK.

Disabling Automatic Footers

To disable automatic footers, follow these steps:

1. In the IIS snap-in, right-click the Web site, virtual directory, or directory you want to work with and then choose Properties.

2. Select the Documents tab and then clear the Enable Document Footer check box.

3. Click OK.

Using Content Expiration and Preventing Browser Caching

Most browsers store documents that users have viewed in cache so that the documents can be displayed later without having to retrieve the entire page from a Web server. You can control browser caching using content expiration. When content expiration is enabled, IIS includes document expiration information when sending HTTP results to a user. This enables the browser to determine if future requests for the same document need to be retrieved from the server or whether a locally cached copy is still valid.

You can configure content expiration at the site, directory, or file level. Site level settings affect all pages in the site. Directory level settings affect all files in the directory and subdirectories of the directory. File level settings affect the currently selected file only. Three content expiration settings are available:

- **Expire Immediately** Forces cached pages to expire immediately, preventing the browser from displaying the file from cache. Use this setting when you need to make sure that the browser displays the most recent version of a dynamically generated page.

- **Expire After** Sets a specific number of minutes, hours, or days during which the file can be displayed from cache. Use this setting when you want to ensure that the browser will retrieve a file after a certain period.

- **Expire On** Sets a specific expiration date and time. The file can be displayed from cache until the expiration date. Use this setting for time-sensitive material that's no longer valid after a specific date, such as a special offer or event announcement.

Tip In ASP pages you can control content expiration by putting a Response.Expires entry in the HTTP header. Use the value Response.Expires = 0 to force immediate expiration. Keep in mind that HTTP headers must be sent to the browser before any page content is sent.

Enabling Content Expiration

You set content expiration on site, directory, and file levels. Keep in mind that individual file and directory settings override site settings. So if you don't get the behavior you expect, check for file or directory settings that might be causing a conflict.

You can configure content expiration for a site, directory, or file by completing the following steps:

1. In the IIS snap-in, right-click the site, directory, or file you want to work with and then choose Properties.

2. Choose the HTTP Headers tab, and then select the Enable Content Expiration check box.

3. To force cached pages to expire immediately, select Expire Immediately.

4. To set a specific number of minutes, hours, or days before expiration, select Expire After, and then configure the expiration information using the fields provided.

5. To set specific expiration date and time, select Expire On, and then configure the expiration information using the fields provided.

6. Click OK.

Disabling Content Expiration

You set content expiration on site, directory, and file levels. Keep in mind that individual file and directory settings override site settings. So if you don't get the behavior you expect, check for file or directory settings that might be causing a conflict.

You can disable content expiration for a site, directory, or file by completing the following steps:

1. In the IIS snap-in, right-click the site, directory, or file you want to work with and then choose Properties.

2. Select the HTTP Headers tab and then clear the Enable Content Expiration check box.

3. Click OK.

Using Custom HTTP Headers

When a browser requests a document on a Web site handled by IIS, IIS normally passes the document with a response header prepended. Sometimes you might want to modify the standard header or create your own header for special situations. For example, you could take advantage of HTTP headers that are provided for by the HTTP standards, but for which IIS provides no interface. Other times you might want to provide information to the client that you couldn't pass using standard HTML elements. To do this, you can use custom HTTP headers.

Custom HTTP headers contain information that you want to include in a document's response header. Entries in a custom header are entered as name value pairs. The Name portion of the entry identifies the value you're referencing. The Value portion of the entry identifies the actual content you're sending.

Custom HTTP headers typically provide instructions for handling the document or supplemental information. For example, the Cache-Control HTTP header field is used to control how proxy servers cache pages. A field value of Public tells the proxy server that caching is allowed. A field value of Private tells the proxy server that caching isn't allowed.

To view or manage custom HTTP headers for a site, directory, or file, follow these steps:

1. In the IIS snap-in, right-click the site, directory, or file you want to manage and then choose Properties.

2. Select the HTTP Headers tab. The Custom HTTP Headers frame shows currently configured headers in *name: value* format.

3. Use the following options to manage existing headers or create new headers:

   - **Add**   Adds a custom HTTP header. To add a header, click Add. Type a header name and then type a header value. Complete the process by clicking OK.

   - **Edit**   Edits a custom HTTP header. To edit a header, select it, and then click Edit. Use the Properties dialog box provided to change the header information, and then click OK.

   - **Remove**   Removes a custom HTTP header. To remove a header, select it and then click Remove.

4. Click OK to close the Properties dialog box for the site, directory, or file you're working with.

Using Content Ratings

IIS has a built-in content rating system based on the Platform for Internet Content Selection (PICS) system. PICS was developed by the Recreational Software Advisory Council (RSAC), now called the Internet Content Rating Association (ICRA), and it's based on the work of Dr. Donald Roberts of Stanford University. Under the PICS rating system, content can be rated according to levels of violence, sex, nudity, and offensive language. Each rating has a separate threshold level that goes from level 0, in which no elements of the designated category are found, to level 4, in which explicit materials are used.

You can set content ratings for an entire site, individual directories, and individual files. Before setting content ratings, you should fill out an ICRA questionnaire to obtain the recommended content ratings for the type of content.

Enabling Content Ratings

To set content ratings for a site, directory, or file, follow these steps:

1. In the IIS snap-in, right-click a site, directory, or file and then select Properties.
2. Select the HTTP Headers tab and then, under Content Rating, click Edit Ratings.
3. On the Ratings tab select the Enable Ratings For This Content check box.
4. In the Category list box, click a ratings category and then use the rating slider to set the level of potentially objectionable material for the category. Each setting displays a description of the rating level.
5. Type your e-mail address in the E-Mail Address Of Person Rating This Content field, and then use the Expire On selection list to choose a ratings expiration date.
6. Click OK twice.

Disabling Content Ratings

To disable content ratings for a site, directory, or file, follow these steps:

1. In the IIS snap-in, right-click a site, directory, or file and then select Properties.
2. Select the HTTP Headers tab and then, under Content Rating, click Edit Ratings.
3. On the Ratings tab clear the Enable Ratings For This Content check box.
4. Click OK twice.

Customizing Web Server Error Messages

IIS generates HTTP error messages when Web server errors occur. These errors typically pertain to bad client requests, authentication problems, or internal server errors. As the administrator, you have complete control over how error messages are sent back to clients. You can configure IIS to send generic HTTP errors or default custom error files, or you can create your own custom error files.

Understanding Status Codes and Error Messages

Status codes and error messages go hand in hand. Every time a user requests a file on a server, the server generates a status code. The status code indicates the status of the user's request. If the request succeeds, the status code indicates this, and the requested file is returned to the browser. If the request fails, the status code indicates why, and the server generates an appropriate error message based on this error code. This error message is returned to the browser in place of the requested file.

A status code is a three-digit number that might include a numeric suffix. The first digit of the status code indicates the code's class. The next two digits indicate the error category, and the suffix (if used) indicates the specific error that occurred. For example, the status code 403 indicates an access forbidden problem, and within this access category a number of specific errors can occur: 403.1 indicates that execute access is denied, 403.2 indicates that read access is denied, and 403.3 indicates that write access is denied.

If you examine the Web server logs or receive an error code while trying to troubleshoot a problem, you'll see status codes. Table 4-2 shows the general classes for status codes. As you can see from the table, the first digit of the status code provides the key indicator as to what has actually happened. Status codes beginning with 1, 2, or 3 are common and generally don't indicate a problem. Status codes beginning with 4 or 5 indicate an error and a potential problem that you need to resolve.

Table 4-2. General Classes of Status Codes

Code Class	Description
1XX	Continue/protocol change
2XX	Success
3XX	Redirection
4XX	Client error/failure
5XX	Server error

Knowing the general problem is helpful when you're searching through log files or compiling statistics. When you're troubleshooting or debugging, you need to know the exact error that occurred. Look up that error code in Table 4-3, which provides a listing of the HTTP 1.1 error codes and a brief description of the error.

Tip Because of security concerns about providing complete details on errors, the HTTP substatus code is no longer passed to clients (in most instances). Instead, clients should see a general status code, such as 401 or 402. If you're trying to troubleshoot a problem, you might want to configure access logging so that the substatus codes are recorded in the server logs temporarily. That way you can view the logs to get detailed information on any errors.

Table 4-3.   HTTP 1.1 Error Codes and Error Messages

Error Code	Error Text
400	Cannot resolve the request
401.1	Unauthorized: Access is denied due to invalid credentials
401.2	Unauthorized: Access is denied due to server configuration favoring an alternate authentication method
401.3	Unauthorized: Access is denied due to an ACL set on the requested resource
401.4	Unauthorized: Authorization failed by a filter installed on the Web server
401.5	Unauthorized: Authorization failed by an ISAPI/CGI application
401.7	Unauthorized: Access denied by URL authorization policy on the Web server
403.1	Forbidden: Execute access is denied
403.2	Forbidden: Read access is denied
403.3	Forbidden: Write access is denied
403.4	Forbidden: SSL is required to view this resource
403.5	Forbidden: SSL 128 is required to view this resource
403.6	Forbidden: IP address of the client has been rejected
403.7	Forbidden: SSL client certificate is required
403.8	Forbidden: DNS name of the client is rejected
403.9	Forbidden: Too many clients are trying to connect to the Web server
403.10	Forbidden: Web server is configured to deny Execute access
403.11	Forbidden: Password has been changed
403.12	Forbidden: Client certificate is denied access by the server certificate mapper
403.13	Forbidden: Client certificate has been revoked on the Web server
403.14	Forbidden: Directory listing is denied on the Web server
403.15	Forbidden: Client access licenses have exceeded limits on the Web server
403.16	Forbidden: Client certificate is ill-formed or is not trusted by the Web server
403.17	Forbidden: Client certificate has expired or is not yet valid
403.18	Forbidden: Cannot execute requested URL in the current application pool
403.19	Forbidden: Cannot execute CGIs for the client in this application pool
403.20	Forbidden: Passport logon failed
404	File or directory not found
404.1	File or directory not found: Web site not accessible on the requested port
404.2	File or directory not found: Lockdown policy prevents this request
404.3	File or directory not found: MIME map policy prevents this request

(continued)

Table 4-3. HTTP 1.1 Error Codes and Error Messages   *(continued)*

Error Code	Error Text
405	HTTP verb used to access this page is not allowed
406	Client browser does not accept the MIME type of the requested page
407	Initial proxy authentication required by the Web server
410	File has been removed
412	Precondition set by the client failed when evaluated on the Web server
414	Request URL is too large and therefore unacceptable on the Web server
500	Internal server error
500.11	Server error: Application is shutting down on the Web server
500.12	Server error: Application is busy restarting on the Web server
500.13	Server error: Web server is too busy
500.14	Server error: Invalid application configuration on the server
500.15	Server error: Direct requests for GLOBAL.ASA are not allowed
500.16	Server error: UNC authorization credentials incorrect
500.17	Server error: URL authorization store cannot be found
500.18	Server error: URL authorization store cannot be opened
500.19	Server error: Data for this file is configured improperly in the metabase
500.20	Server error: URL authorization scope cannot be found
500-100	Internal server error: ASP error
501	Header values specify a configuration that is not implemented
502	Web server received an invalid response while acting as a gateway or proxy server

Note In some cases Internet Explorer might replace custom errors with its own HTTP error message. Typically, this is done when the error message is considered to be too small to be useful to the user. Internet Explorer attempts to determine message usefulness based on message size. When 403, 405, or 410 error messages are smaller than 256 bytes or when 400, 404, 406, 500, 500.12, 500.13, 500.15, or 501 error messages are smaller than 512 bytes, the custom error message sent by IIS is replaced by a message generated by Internet Explorer.

Managing Custom Error Settings

For each of the standard errors, you can specify how the error is handled. Individual files can have different settings from their parent directory and sites, which means that file settings override directory settings and directory settings override site-wide settings. The following error handling options are available:

- **Default** Sends a standard IIS error message to the client.
- **File** Sends a customized error file to the client. This option is used with static content.
- **URL** Sends a message that redirects the client to a specific URL. This option is used with dynamic content.

Custom files supplied in the standard IIS installation handle most HTTP errors. These files are located in the %SystemRoot%\Help\Iishelp\Common directory. You can edit the default error files directly, or you can create your own files. Be sure to use the File error handling option with static content, such as HTML pages, and the URL type handler with dynamic content, such as .asp pages. If you don't do this, you might get unexpected results.

The following sections examine how you can view and edit error settings.

Real World When you use an .asp file to handle custom errors, the error code and the original URL are passed to the ASP page as query parameters. You must configure the ASP page to read the parameters from the URL and set the status code appropriately. For example, if Notfound.asp is designed to handle 404 errors and the user accesses a page using the URL *http://www.microsoft.com/data.htm/*, then the ASP page is invoked using the URL *http://www.microsoft.com/NotFound.asp?404; http://www.microsoft.com/data.htm/*, and your ASP page must extract the 404 and *http://www.microsoft.com/data.htm/* parameters from the URL.

Viewing Custom Error Settings

You can view custom error settings by following these steps:

1. In the IIS snap-in, right-click the site, directory, or file you want to manage, and then choose Properties.

2. Click the Custom Errors tab. As shown in Figure 4-5, you should now see a list of the standard HTTP errors and how they're handled. Entries are organized by the following categories:

   - **HTTP Error** The HTTP status code for the error, which might include a suffix
   - **Type** The method used to handle the error (default, file, or URL)
   - **Contents** The error text, file path, or URL path associated with the error

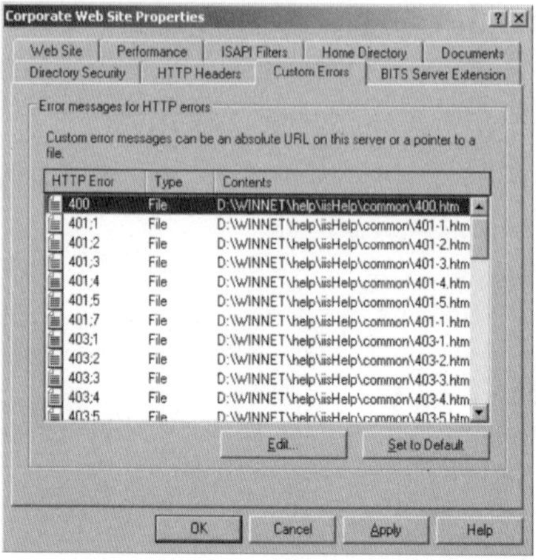

Figure 4-5. *The Custom Errors tab shows the error settings for the site, directory, or file you've selected for editing.*

3. Click OK when you're finished viewing the error settings.

Editing Custom Error Settings

You can edit custom error settings by completing these steps:

1. In the IIS snap-in, right-click the site, directory, or file you want to manage and then choose Properties.

2. Click the Custom Errors tab. You should now see a list of the standard HTTP errors and how they're handled.

3. Double-click the entry for the error you want to edit or select the entry and then click Edit. The Edit Custom Error Properties dialog box is displayed, as shown in Figure 4-6.

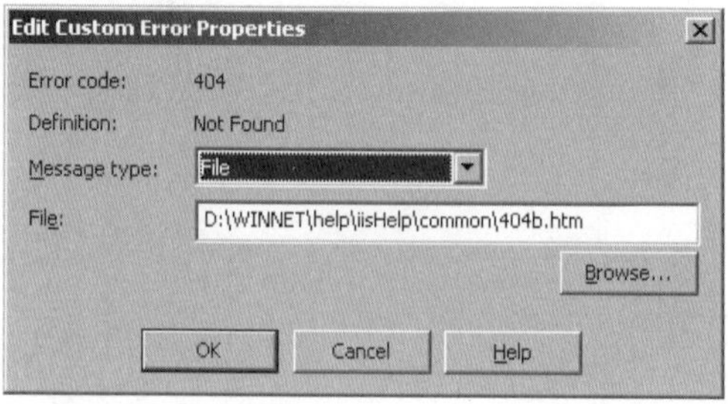

Figure 4-6. *The Edit Custom Error Properties dialog box provides an overview of the error and how it's handled.*

4. Use the Message Type drop-down list to choose the error handling technique. The options available depend on the type of error and generally include the following:

- **Default**   Uses the default error information shown in the Error Code, Sub Error Code, and Definition fields when returning an error message.

- **File**   Returns the file specified when the error occurs. Type the complete file path or click Browse to search for the file.

- **URL**   Returns the URL specified to the client. Type an absolute URL path for resources on other servers or use a relative URL path for resources on the current server.

5. Click OK twice.

Using MIME and Configuring Custom File Types

Every file that's transferred between IIS and a client browser has a data type designator, which is expressed as a Multipurpose Internet Mail Extensions (MIME) type. IIS fully supports MIME.

Understanding MIME

To understand MIME, you need to know how servers transfer files using HTTP. HTTP is a multipurpose protocol that you can use to transfer many types of files, including full-motion video sequences, stereo sound tracks, high-resolution images, and other types of media. The transfer of media files wouldn't be possible without the MIME standard. Web servers use MIME to identify the type of object being transferred. Object types are identified in an HTTP header field that comes before the actual data, and this allows a Web client to handle the object file appropriately.

Web servers set the MIME type using the Content_Type directive, which is part of the HTTP header sent to client browsers. MIME types are broken down into categories, with each category having a primary subtype associated with it. Basic MIME types are summarized in Table 4-4.

Table 4-4.   Basic MIME Types

Type	Description
Application	Binary data that can be executed or used with another application
Audio	A sound file that requires an output device to preview
Image	A picture that requires an output device to preview
Message	An encapsulated mail message
Multipart	Data consisting of multiple parts and possibly many data types

(continued)

Table 4-4. **Basic MIME Types** *(continued)*

Type	Description
Text	Textual data that can be represented in any character set or formatting language
Video	A video file that requires an output device to preview
X-world	Experimental data type for world files

MIME subtypes are defined in three categories:

- **Primary**   Primary type of data adopted for use as a MIME content type
- **Additional**   Additional subtypes that have been officially adopted as MIME content types
- **Extended**   Experimental subtypes that haven't been officially adopted as MIME content types

You can easily identify extended subtypes because they begin with the letter x followed by a hyphen. Table 4-5 lists common MIME types and their descriptions.

Table 4-5. **Common MIME Types**

Type/Subtype	Description
Application/ mac-binhex40	Macintosh binary-formatted data
Application/msword	Microsoft Word document
Application/ octet-stream	Binary data that can be executed or used with another application
Application/pdf	Acrobat Portable Document Format (PDF) document
Application/postscript	Postscript-formatted data
Application/rtf	Rich Text Format (RTF) document
Application/ x-compress	Data that has been compressed using UNIX compress
Application/x-gzip	Data that has been compressed using UNIX gzip
Application/x-tar	Data that has been archived using UNIX tar
Application/ x-zip-compressed	Data that has been compressed using PKZip or WinZip
Audio/basic	Audio in a nondescript format
Audio/x-aiff	Audio in Apple Audio Interchange File Format (AIFF)
Audio/x-wav	Audio in Microsoft WAV format
Image/gif	Image in Graphics Interchange Format (GIF)
Image/jpeg	Image in Joint Photographic Experts Group (JPEG) format
Image/tiff	Image in Tagged Image File Format (TIFF)
Text/html	HTML-formatted text

Table 4-5. Common MIME Types

Type/Subtype	Description
Text/plain	Plain text with no HTML formatting included
Video/mpeg	Video in the Moving Picture Experts Group (MPEG) format
Video/quicktime	Video in the Apple QuickTime format
Video/x-msvideo	Video in the Microsoft Audio Video Interleaved (AVI) format
X-world/x-vrml	Virtual Reality Modeling Language (VRML) world file

Hundreds of MIME types are configured using file extension to file type mappings. These mappings allow IIS to support just about any type of file that applications or utilities on the destination computer might expect. If a file doesn't end with a known extension, the file is sent as the default MIME type, which indicates that the file contains application data. In most cases use of the default MIME type means that the client is unable to handle the file or to trigger other utilities that handle the file. If you expect the client to handle a new file type appropriately, you'll need to create a file extension to file type mapping.

MIME type mappings set in Web Sites Properties apply to all Web sites on the server. In the Properties dialog box for a specific site, you can edit existing MIME types, configure additional MIME types, or delete unwanted MIME types. These changes are applied to all Web sites the next time you start IIS. You can also create additional MIME type mappings for individual sites and directories. When you do this, the MIME type mappings are available only in the site or directory in which they're configured.

Viewing and Configuring MIME Types for All Web Sites on a Server

You can create new MIME types for all Web sites on a server by completing the following steps:

1. In the IIS snap-in, right-click the computer node for the IIS server you want to work with and then select Properties.

2. Click MIME Types. As shown in Figure 4-7, you should see a list of the computer MIME types. Computer MIME types are active for all Web sites on the server.

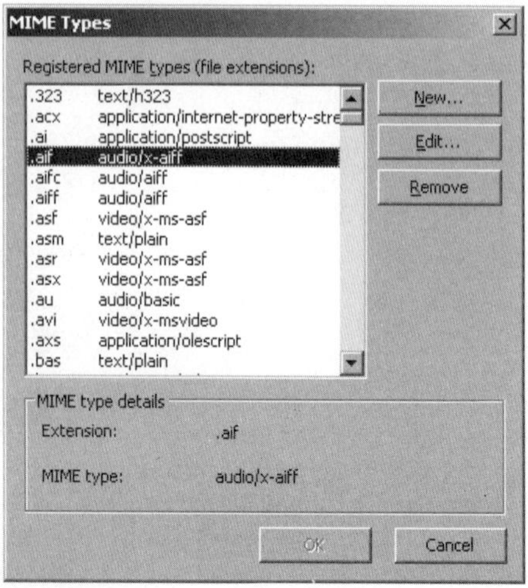

Figure 4-7. *Use the MIME Types dialog box to view and configure computer MIME types.*

3. Use the following options to configure new computer MIME types:

- **New**   Adds a new MIME type. Type a file extension in the Extension field, such as **.html**, and then type a MIME type in the MIME Type field, such as **text/html**. Complete the process by clicking OK.

- **Remove**   Removes a MIME type mapping. To remove a MIME type, select it and then click Remove.

- **Edit**   Edits a MIME type mapping. To edit a MIME type, select it and then click Edit. Use the MIME Type dialog box provided to change the file extension and the content MIME type.

4. Click OK twice.

Viewing and Configuring MIME Types for Individual Sites and Directories

You can limit the availability of custom MIME types by adding MIME types at the site or directory level. When you work with MIME settings at this level, the only values displayed are those you've defined.

To view or configure site or directory MIME settings, follow these steps:

1. In the IIS snap-in, right-click the Web site you want to manage and then choose Properties.

2. On the HTTP Headers tab, click MIME Types. This displays the MIME Types dialog box.

3. Use the following options to register new MIME types:

   - **New** Adds a new MIME type. Type a file extension in the Extension field, such as .html, and then type a MIME type in the MIME Type field, such as text/html. Complete the process by clicking OK.

   - **Remove** Removes a MIME type mapping. To remove a MIME type, select it and then click Remove.

   - **Edit** Edits a MIME type mapping. To edit a MIME type, select it and then click Edit. Use the MIME Type dialog box provided to change the file extension and the content MIME type.

4. Click OK twice.

Note You won't see any computer MIME types inherited from the Web server's master properties. You'll see only the MIME types registered for the currently selected Web site or directory, even though both sets of MIME types apply.

Additional Customization Tips

Update sites, jump pages, and error forwarding are three additional techniques you can use to customize your IIS Web sites. Each of these techniques is discussed in the sections that follow.

Using Update Sites to Manage Outages

An update site allows you to handle outages in a way that's customer-friendly. Use the update sites function to display alternate content when your primary sites are offline. So rather than seeing an error message where the user expects to find content, the user sees a message that provides information regarding the outage as well as additional helpful information.

Each Web site you publish should have an update site. You create update sites by completing the following steps:

1. Have your Web development department create a Web page that can be displayed during outages. The page should explain that you're performing maintenance on the Web site and that the site will be back online shortly. The page can also provide links to other sites that your organization publishes so that the user has somewhere else to visit during the maintenance.

2. Use Windows Explorer to create a directory for the update site. The best location for this directory is on the Web server's local drive. Afterward, copy the content files created by the Web development team into this directory.

Tip I recommend that you create a top-level directory for storing the home directories and then create subdirectories for each update site. For example, you can create a top-level directory D:\UpdateSites and then use subdirectories called WWWUpdate, ServicesUpdate, and ProductsUpdate to store the files for *www.microsoft.com*, *services.microsoft.com*, and *products.microsoft.com*, respectively.

3. Start the IIS snap-in and then, in the left pane (Console Root), click the plus sign (+) next to the computer you want to work with. If the computer isn't shown, connect to it.

4. Click the Web Sites node. You should now see a list of Web sites already configured on the server. You should note the host header, IP address, and port configuration of the primary site you want to mimic during outages. To view this information, right-click the desired Web site, choose Properties, and click the Web Site tab. Click Advanced to view host header values.

5. Create a new site using the configuration settings you just noted. Name the site so that it clearly identifies the site as an update site. Don't start the update site.

6. You need to edit the site's properties. Right-click the site entry and then select Properties.

7. Use the fields in the Documents tab to perform the following tasks:
   * Enable default content pages
   * Remove the existing default documents
   * Add a default document and set the document name to the name of the outage page created by your Web development department

8. Select the Custom Errors tab. Edit the properties for 400, 404, and 500 errors. These errors should have the Message Type set to File and have a File path that points to the outage page created by your Web development department.

9. Update other site properties as necessary and then close the Properties dialog box by clicking OK.

Once you create the update site, you can activate it as follows:

1. Use the IIS snap-in to stop the primary site prior to performing maintenance, and then start the related update site.

2. Confirm that the update site is running by visiting the Web site in your browser. If the site is properly configured, you should be able to append a file name to the URL and be directed to the outage page.

3. Perform the necessary maintenance on the primary site. When you're finished, stop the update site and then start the primary site.

4. Confirm that the primary site is running by visiting the Web site in your browser.

Using Jump Pages for Advertising

A jump page is an intermediate page that redirects a user to another location. You can use jump pages to track click-throughs on banner advertisements or inbound requests from advertising done by the company.

With banner ads, jump pages ensure that users visit a page within your site before moving off to a page at an advertiser's site. This allows you to track the success of advertising on your site. Here's how it works:

1. A page in your site has a banner ad that is linked to a jump page on your site.
2. A user clicks on the ad and is directed to the jump page. The Web server tracks the page access and records it in the log file.
3. The jump page is configured to redirect the user to a page on the advertiser's Web site.

With corporate advertising, jump pages ensure that you can track the source of a visit to advertising done by the company. This allows you to track the success of your company's advertising efforts. Here's how it works:

1. The marketing department develops a piece of advertising collateral—for instance, a product brochure. Somewhere in the brochure, there's a reference to a URL on your site. This is the URL for the jump page you've configured.
2. A user types in the URL to the jump page as it was listed in the ad. The Web server tracks the page access and records it in the log file.
3. The jump page is configured to redirect the user to a page on your Web site where the advertised product or service is covered.

Each jump page you create should be unique, or you should create a dynamic page that reads an embedded code within the URL and then redirects the user. For example, you can create a page called Jump.asp that reads the first parameter passed to the script as the advertising code. Then you can create a link in the banner ad that specifies the URL and the code, such as Jump.asp?4408.

Handling 404 Errors and Preventing Dead Ends

Users hate dead ends, and that's just what a 404 error represents. Rather than having the browser display an apparently meaningless 404—File Or Directory Not Found error, you should throw the user a lifeline by doing one of two things:

- Replacing the default error file with a file that provides helpful information and links
- Redirecting all 404 errors to your site's home page

Either technique makes your Web site a better place to visit. This feature could be the one thing that separates your Web site from the pack.

Chapter 5
Running IIS Applications

Not long ago, when Web sites were primarily static Hypertext Markup Language (HTML) pages, the most serious problems facing Web administrators were configuring multiple sites on the same server and keeping the server running without failure. With the growing importance of Web servers not just on the Internet but also everywhere within the organization, different issues have emerged. Web servers have to do more—and not just with respect to handling and responding to requests. Web servers must provide services, host applications, and serve dynamic content; but more services and functions can't come at a sacrifice to performance, availability, or reliability. Web servers have to do more with less.

To address the issues of availability, reliability, and performance, Internet Information Services (IIS) 6.0 has been reengineered and given a new request processing and application-handling architecture. This redesigned architecture offers an exponential increase in the number of sites that can be hosted on the same server and in responsiveness. It also boosts availability by reducing outages from routine maintenance and service failure.

Because a thorough understanding of these changes is essential to your success as a Web administrator, the discussion of these architecture changes has been covered over several chapters. Chapter 2, "Core IIS Administration," introduced the two processing modes of the IIS 6 architecture: IIS 5 isolation mode and IIS 6 worker process isolation mode.

This chapter extends that discussion and focuses on the top-level functionality— the functionality that's available for all sites and applications configured on sites whether the server is running in IIS 5 isolation mode or IIS 6 worker process isolation mode. The next chapter, Chapter 6, "Managing ASP.NET, Application Pools, and Worker Processes," builds on this discussion, focusing on the additional features and configuration options available only when running a server in IIS 6 worker process isolation mode.

Note As you read these chapters, don't forget that the definition of a Web application is quite different from what it used to be. Every site and virtual directory you configure on an IIS 6 server runs in an application context. Technically speaking, the sites and virtual directories are applications and you can manage them as such.

Essentials for Working with IIS Applications

The Internet Server Application Programming Interface (ISAPI) provides the core functionality for the application architecture. As depicted in Figure 5-1, ISAPI acts as a layer over IIS that can be extended using ISAPI applications, Active Server Pages (ASP), ASP.NET, and third-party extensions. The following sections provide an overview of ISAPI applications, ASP, and ASP.NET. Because third-party IIS extensions behave much like ISAPI applications, they aren't examined separately.

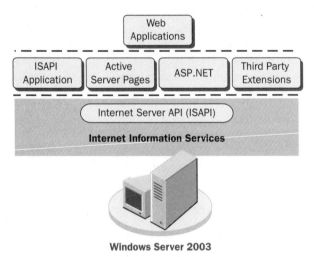

Figure 5-1. *ISAPI acts as a layer over IIS.*

Understanding ISAPI Applications

ISAPI applications fall into two categories:

- ISAPI filters
- ISAPI extensions

You use both filters and extensions to modify the behavior of IIS. ISAPI filters are dynamic-link libraries (DLLs), or executables, that are loaded into memory when the World Wide Web Publishing Service is started and remain in memory until the IIS server is shut down. ISAPI filters are triggered when a Web server event occurs on the IIS server. For example, you could create a filter that responds to Read events by logging the client's browser type in a database.

You can apply ISAPI filters globally or locally. Global filters affect all IIS Web sites running on a server and are loaded into memory when the World Wide Web Publishing Service is started. Anytime you add new global filters or modify existing global filters, you must stop and then restart the World Wide Web Publishing Service. Local filters are called site filters. Site filters affect a single IIS Web site and can be dynamically loaded into memory when a request that uses such a filter is made to the site.

When several filters are configured to respond to the same events, they're executed sequentially. Administrators can control the sequence by assigning priority levels to filters. Filters with higher priority are executed before filters with lower priority. Filters with the same priority are executed at the global level, as specified in the master World Wide Web properties, and then at the site level, as specified in the Web site properties. Filters with the same priority at the same level within IIS are executed according to the order in which they were loaded into memory. If you discover a conflict, you can change the filter load order as necessary.

ISAPI filters aren't ideal choices when you need to perform long-running operations, such as database queries, or when you want to process the entire body of requests. In these instances ISAPI extensions work better.

Like ISAPI filters, ISAPI extensions are defined as DLLs or executables. Unlike global filters, which are loaded with the World Wide Web Publishing Service, extensions are loaded on demand and are executed in response to client requests. Normally, ISAPI extensions are used to process the data received in requests for specific types of files. For example, when a client makes a request for a file using the .asp extension, IIS uses the Asp.dll ISAPI extension to process the contents of ASP and return the results to the client for display.

When you install IIS, default ISAPI extensions are configured for use on the Web server. ISAPI extensions are configured to respond to specific types of Hypertext Transfer Protocol (HTTP) requests or all HTTP requests for files with a specific file extension. The key types of HTTP requests are summarized in Table 5-1.

Table 5-1.   HTTP Request Types Used with ISAPI Extensions

Request Type	Description
DELETE	A request to delete a resource. This request normally isn't allowed unless the user has specific privileges on the Web site.
GET	A request to retrieve a resource. The standard request for retrieving files.
HEAD	A request for an HTTP header. The return request doesn't contain a message body.
OPTIONS	A request for information about communications options.
POST	A request to submit data as a new subordinate of a resource. Typically used for posting data from fill-out forms.

(continued)

Table 5-1. HTTP Request Types Used with ISAPI Extensions   *(continued)*

Request Type	Description
PUT	A request to store the enclosed data with the resource identifier specified. Typically used when uploading files through HTTP.
TRACE	A request to trace the client's submission (for testing or debugging).

Because ISAPI extensions are loaded on demand, you can add extensions at any time without having to restart IIS. However, if you modify an ISAPI extension that's already loaded into memory, you must stop and then restart the World Wide Web Publishing Service to apply the new configuration settings. As with ISAPI filters, ISAPI extensions have global and local context. If you set an ISAPI extension in the master World Wide Web properties, the extension is available to all Web sites on the server. On the other hand, if you set an ISAPI extension in a site's properties, the extension is available only on that site.

ISAPI extensions don't have priorities and you shouldn't configure multiple ISAPI extensions to handle the same type of content. In addition, ISAPI extensions always run in a single server process. This process can be the same server process as the one used by IIS, a pooled process shared by multiple applications, or an isolated process.

Understanding ASP Applications

ASP is a server-side scripting environment used to create dynamic Web applications. An ASP application is a collection of resource files and components that are grouped logically. Logically grouping files and components as an application allows IIS to share data within the application and to run the application as a shared, pooled, or isolated process. You can have multiple applications per Web site, and you can configure each application differently.

IIS resource files include ASP pages, HTML pages, GIF images, JPEG images, and other types of Web documents. An ASP page is a file that ends with the .asp extension that includes HTML, a combination of HTML and scripting, or only scripting. Scripts within ASP pages can be intended for processing by a client browser or the server itself. Scripts designed to be processed on the server are called server-side scripts and can be written using Microsoft Visual Basic Scripting Edition (VBScript), Microsoft JScript, or any other scripting language available on the server.

ASP provides an object-based scripting environment. Server-side scripts use the built-in objects to perform common tasks, such as tracking session state, managing errors, and reading HTTP requests sent by clients. A list of built-in objects is provided in Table 5-2.

Table 5-2. Built-In ASP Objects

Built-In Object	Description
Application	Used to share information among all users of an ASP application.
ASPError	Tracks information about error conditions that have occurred in scripts on ASP pages.
ObjectContext	Maintains information on application component instances and provides access to the built-in ASP objects. Also provides methods and events used to commit or abort transactions.
Request	Obtains the values sent in the HTTP request by the client browser.
Response	Sends the HTTP response to the client browser.
Scripting Context	Provides access to built-in objects. Supported for backward compatibility only. Use ObjectContext instead.
Server	Used to perform server-related tasks, such as executing files and transferring state information to another ASP page, and to instantiate server components.
Session	Stores information about a specific user session (provided the user's browser supports cookies and cookies are enabled).

ASP scripts can also use IIS components. IIS components are executable programs that use the Component Object Model (COM) and Component Services to communicate with IIS. Prebuilt components are available in the standard IIS 6 installation and as part of the IIS 6 Resource Kit. Table 5-3 summarizes the available components. Components marked with an asterisk can be found in the %SystemRoot%\System32\Inetsrv directory on the IIS server. The other components must be obtained from the resource kit. If you remove the components from the %SystemRoot%\System32\Inetsrv directory, they'll no longer be available to your ASP applications.

Table 5-3. Prebuilt Components for ASP Applications

Prebuilt Component	Description
Ad Rotator (Adrot.dll)*	Rotates banner ads displayed on a Web page according to a specified schedule.
Browser Capabilities (Browsercap.dll)*	Determines the capabilities, type, and version of each browser that accesses your Web site.
Content Linking (Nextlink.dll)*	Creates tables of contents for Web pages and provides navigational links to previous and subsequent pages.
Content Rotator (Controt.dll)*	Rotates HTML content on a Web page according to a specified schedule.
Counters (Counters.dll)*	Creates a counter that tracks page hits for an entire Web site and access to individual pages.

(continued)

Table 5-3. **Prebuilt Components for ASP Applications** *(continued)*

Prebuilt Component	Description
Logging Utility (Logscrpt.dll)	Allows applications to read the HTTP activity log files generated by IIS.
MyInfo (Myinfo.dll)	Tracks personal information pertaining to the site or its creator.
Page Counter (Pagecnt.dll)	Counts and displays the number of times a Web page has been accessed.
Status (Status.dll)	Returns server status information when running Personal Web Server for Macintosh.
Tools (Tools.dll)	Provides utility functions that check file existence, match site ownership, look for plug-ins (Macintosh only), process HTML form data, and generate random integers.

Understanding ASP.NET Applications

ASP.NET moves away from the reliance on ISAPI and ASP to provide a reliable framework for Web applications that takes advantage of the Microsoft .NET Framework. ASP.NET is, in fact, a set of .NET technologies for creating Web applications. With ASP.NET, developers can write the executable parts of their pages using any .NET-compliant language, including Microsoft Visual C# .NET, Visual Basic .NET, and JScript .NET.

Unlike ASP, ASP.NET has components that are precompiled prior to runtime. These precompiled components are called *assemblies*. Compiled assemblies not only load and run faster than ASP pages, but also are more secure. Requests for ASP.NET assemblies are handled quite differently from other requests. The basic request handling process looks like this:

Request → IIS → aspnet_isapi.dll → HttpApplication → HttpHandler → HttpModule

A global ISAPI filter provides the hooks into ASP.NET. This filter, aspnet_filter.dll, is loaded into memory automatically when run on an IIS 6 Web server that's configured to use ASP.NET. IIS maps ASP.NET file extensions to this ISAPI filter. This filter's job is to forward requests to the correct worker process.

> **Note** As you might recall from the discussion in Chapter 2, ASP.NET uses its own processing model when IIS runs in IIS 5 isolation mode. This processing model is similar to worker process isolation mode and has similar capabilities. On the other hand, when running a server in IIS 6 worker process mode, ASP.NET and IIS are directly integrated. Here, ASP.NET uses the worker process model architecture of IIS 6, and ASP.NET applications can take advantage of IIS 6 features.

The ASP.NET worker process wraps the request into an instance of the Http-Context class, which is used to represent the request as an object that the current instance of the ASP.NET application can view and manipulate. The HttpContext object is then passed off to an instance of the HttpApplication class, which maintains information on application scope, data, and events. A specific HttpHandler is then chosen based on the original request's file extension, and one or more HttpModule objects processes the request. HttpModule has many event classes, such as BeginRequest, AuthenticateRequest, and AuthorizeRequest, which are used to process the request.

As shown in Figure 5-2, you configure and manage ASP.NET assemblies using the .NET Configuration snap-in for the Microsoft Management Console (MMC). The .NET configuration has five key components:

- **Assembly Cache**   Contains sets of assemblies that are available to all .NET applications running on the server. The default installation includes a large number of predefined assemblies, which provide the core functions that can be accessed from .NET applications.

- **Configured Assemblies**   Contains sets of assemblies that you've configured with additional policies. Assemblies can have policies for version binding or assembly codebases, or both. Binding policies are useful when you need to redirect requests for particular versions of an assembly to new versions of the assembly. Codebase policies allow you to specify the codebase location for various assembly versions.

- **Remoting Services**   Configures the communications channels that applications use. Each channel, such as HTTP client or Transmission Control Protocol (TCP) client, can have different properties to configure.

- **Runtime Security Policy**   Configures assemblies permissions to access protected resources. You can adjust the level of trust for individual assemblies or all assemblies according to security zone (My Computer, Local Intranet, Internet, Trusted Sites, Untrusted Sites). You can also view permissions granted to specific assemblies.

- **Applications**   Allows you to view and configure .NET applications. You can check assembly dependencies, configured assemblies, and remoting services configurations.

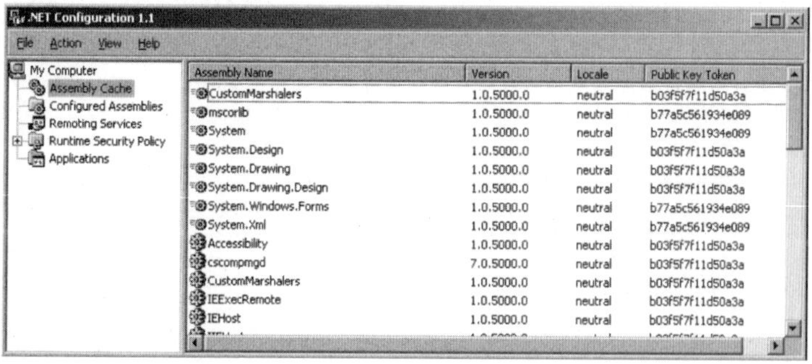

Figure 5-2.   *Use .NET Configuration to view and manage ASP.NET assemblies.*

Defining Custom Applications

You use the IIS snap-in to configure custom applications, .NET Configuration to manage .NET assemblies, and the Component Services snap-in to manage COM components. As part of the standard installation, Web sites have a predefined application that allows you to run custom programs without making changes to the environment. You could, for example, copy your ASP files to a site's base directory and run them without creating a separate application. Here, the ASP application you've defined runs as a default application within the context of the default application pool.

 Real World Novice administrators who don't understand its purpose often accidentally or purposefully remove the default application pool. If this happens, application behavior might change. For example, you suddenly might be unable to share session states between ASP pages. The reason for this is that ASP pages and other types of files that were using the default application pool no longer have an application context, and all associated application pool settings are no longer available.

To be clear, the default application pool allows you to run IIS applications regardless of where they might be located within the site's directory structure, as long as the directories in which those files are located have the appropriate execute permissions (either Scripts Only or Scripts And Executables). If you want to delete the default application pool, you should create specific application pool contexts for each application that you want to run.

To get better control over applications, you should configure separate contexts for key applications. Application contexts are defined using basic and advanced application settings. Basic application settings include the following:

- **Application Name** A descriptive name for the application.
- **Starting Point** Sets the base directory for the application. All files in all subdirectories of the base directory are considered to be part of the application.
- **Execute Permissions** Sets the level of program execution that's allowed.
- **Application Protection** Determines how the application runs and which application resources are shared with IIS and other applications (only used with IIS 5 isolation mode).
- **Application Pool** Determines which application pool is used with the application. You can configure multiple application pools, and each can have a different worker process configuration (only used with IIS 6 worker process mode).

Advanced application settings include:

- **Application Mappings**   Sets application caching and maps file extensions to DLLs for execution
- **Application Options**   Sets configuration options that control how the application runs, including time-outs, buffering, and the default scripting language
- **Application Debugging**   Enables or disables debugging and script error messages

Application settings create application contexts within which your application runs. Without an application context, your customized pages run as separate files and are unable to take advantage of key IIS features. Application contexts are defined at the directory level. All files in all subdirectories of the application's base directory are considered to be part of the application. Because of this, the best way to create applications is to follow these steps:

1. In Windows Explorer, create a folder that will act as the application's starting point and then set appropriate access Windows permissions on the folder.

2. Use the IIS snap-in to create a virtual directory that maps to the directory.

3. Configure application settings for the directory as defined in the "Creating Applications" section of this chapter.

Using and Running Applications

Each application has a starting point. The starting point sets the logical namespace for the application. That is, the starting point determines the files and folders that are included in the application. Every file and folder in the starting point is considered part of the application.

You can define application starting points for the following:

- An entire site
- A directory
- A virtual directory

When you define a sitewide application, all files in all the Web site's subdirectories are considered to be a part of the application. When you define an application for a standard or virtual directory, all files in all subdirectories in this directory are considered part of the application.

As stated earlier, the application starting point sets the namespace for an application. A namespace is a way of associating an area of memory with an easily recognized name that associates a group of files and components. The memory area used by an application determines its protection setting.

Application Protection Settings in IIS 5 Isolation Mode

In IIS 5 isolation mode, there are three application protection settings:

- **Low (IIS Process)**   Low protection allows applications to run in process and share resources with IIS. Low protection provides the best performance but makes it possible for a stray application to crash IIS.

- **Medium (Pooled)**   Medium protection allows applications to run as a pooled process, which means that all applications with this priority share the same IIS process instance but don't run in process with normal IIS resources. If a single application fails, it will affect all other applications running at medium protection—but it won't affect IIS itself.

- **High (Isolated)**   High protection allows applications to run completely out of process (or *isolated*), which means that the application doesn't share processes with other applications and the failure of other applications doesn't affect this high-priority application.

If you use medium or high protection settings, you allow IIS to isolate the application to a specific process. Process isolation protects the server's World Wide Web Publishing Service from application problems that could otherwise cause the Web server to crash or freeze. Process isolation also allows you to configure scheduled application restarts and automatic termination of application processes in case of a fatal error.

Application protection settings affect memory access. Applications that share the same process as IIS share the same memory area and are able to call each other with little overhead. Applications that share a pooled process or are isolated must use a process called *marshaling* to make requests across process boundaries. Marshalling is required whenever an application needs to interact with IIS or other applications. Because marshaled calls are slower than calls within a single process, pooled and isolated applications don't perform as well as applications sharing the IIS process.

Out-of-process applications and components, including ISAPI extensions, aren't able to access metabase properties by default. This restriction is designed to prevent unauthorized changes to the metabase. If you want to allow out-of-process applications to access the metabase, you should change the identity for out-of-process applications to a specific user account and give that account access to the metabase.

Tip   You use the Component Services snap-in to manage authentication for application components. In the Component Services snap-in, expand Component Services, then Computers, then My Computer, and then COM+ Applications. Right-click IIS Out-Of-Process Pooled Applications, select Properties, and then select the Identity tab. The user context to which you assign the application must have file permissions to access the metabase. To check file permissions, right-click the metabase file (%SystemRoot%\System32\Inetsrv\MetaBase.xml) in Windows Explorer, select Properties, and then select the Security tab.

In IIS 5 isolation mode, application protection and caching settings change the way memory is used on your IIS server. The operating system incurs additional overhead every time a new application is started and every time new programs are loaded into memory. The amount of overhead depends on the application configuration settings. To obtain a basic understanding of the overhead for applications, consider the following scenario:

An IIS server is configured with three Web sites: a corporate Web site, a service Web site, and an administration Web site. The server is also running a Simple Mail Transfer Protocol (SMTP) server. In the baseline configuration, the server runs the following IIS processes:

- **Inetinfo.exe**   This process is used to manage the service hosts and ISAPI applications that run within the IIS process context.

- **Svchost.exe**   These three processes control Web resources, SMTP resources, and the baseline installation.

- **Dllhost.exe**   This process is used to manage IIS processes (and any in-process applications that might be defined). No pooled or out-of-process applications are defined initially.

As Table 5-4 shows, these baseline processes use 27,848 KB of memory on the server. To determine how application processing affects the server, I defined additional applications:

- **Pooled Application 1**   An application running with medium application protection

- **Pooled Application 2**   An application running with medium application protection

- **Isolated Application 1**   An application running with high application protection

- **Isolated Application 2**   An application running with high application protection

Table 5-4.   IIS Application Overhead Baselines for Sample Server

Process	Baseline IIS	Pooled Application 1	Pooled Application 2	Isolated Application 1	Isolated Application 2
Inetinfo.exe	7568	8360	8388	8440	8472
Dllhost.exe	4968	4968	4968	4960	4960
Dllhost.exe	NA	5436	5492	5080	5080
Dllhost.exe	NA	NA	NA	5460	5460
Dllhost.exe	NA	NA	NA	NA	5248
Svchost.exe	3060	3080	3080	3084	3100

(continued)

Table 5-4. IIS Application Overhead Baselines for Sample Server   *(continued)*

Process	Baseline IIS	Pooled Application 1	Pooled Application 2	Isolated Application 1	Isolated Application 2
Svchost.exe	9908	9920	9920	9920	9920
Svchost.exe	2344	2344	2344	2344	2344
Total Memory Usage (KB)	**27,848**	**34,108**	**34,192**	**39,288**	**44,584**

Although the process of defining applications doesn't really affect the baseline configuration, running the applications does affect memory usage. When I use Pooled Application 1, a new Dllhost.exe process is started and the base memory usage changes to 34,108 KB. Because the additional Dllhost.exe process is used to manage all pooled applications, starting the second pooled application (Pooled Application 2) doesn't spawn any new processes and the additional memory usage is minimal. On the other hand, each time I start a new isolated application, a new Dllhost.exe process is started, and an incremental amount of memory is used. Running Isolated Application 1 causes a third Dllhost.exe process to start, and the baseline memory usage goes to 39,288 KB. Running Isolated Application 2 causes a fourth Dllhost.exe process to start, and the baseline memory usage goes to 44,584 KB.

As you can see from the example, each new Dllhost.exe host process used about 5000 KB of additional memory, and, in the end, IIS used about 45,000 KB of memory on the server. Although this isn't a lot of memory, a server with more complex applications could use considerably more memory, especially as additional ISAPI extensions and Common Gateway Interface (CGI) programs are loaded into memory. Servers also cache Web documents, and a portion of memory is always reserved for this file cache.

Application Protection Settings in IIS 6 Worker Process Isolation Mode

In IIS 6 worker process isolation mode, all applications run completely out of process with IIS. There are no longer any in-process applications. Because applications don't share processes or files with other applications, the failure of one application shouldn't affect other applications.

Request processing in this mode is a bit different from what you might be used to. First of all, IIS 6 uses a kernel mode HTTP listener (Http.sys) to watch for incoming requests. As requests come in, the listener queues requests in the appropriate application pool request queue. Although application pools can have multiple applications associated with them, each application pool has one and only one request queue.

The queue is managed in first in, first out (FIFO) fashion with dedicated worker processes monitoring the queue for incoming requests. Each application can have one or more dedicated worker processes. Worker processes are said to be dedicated because no other application pool can use another application pool's worker process. If a process dedicated to the application pool for which the request has been made is available, the worker process retrieves the request from the queue and processes it. When it's finished, the process returns to an idle state and waits for the next request to come into the queue.

Unlike IIS 5 isolation mode, where the operating system incurs additional overhead based on whether applications are in process or out of process, applications in IIS 6 worker process mode always operate out of process. This means memory is allocated every time a new application is started and every time new programs are loaded into memory. The good news, however, is that IIS 6 is much smarter in the way memory is allocated.

Memory is allocated on demand (rather than automatically at startup) when the first request for a resource serviced by the application arrives in the request queue. Further, in the IIS 6 mode, idle processes can time out, thereby returning the resources they use. Errant (or orphan) processes can also be automatically recycled to free resources and recover resources that might have been lost due to a memory leak or hung process.

The new model is best understood when you compare the IIS 5 model to the IIS 6 model. If you go back to the example described in the previous section and refer to Table 5-4, you see that applications configured on a Web server can use up memory quickly, especially when you consider that I've created a single site, single server example. Now imagine a more typical scenario where a single Web server is hosting multiple sites. IIS 5 pre-allocates memory at startup for each site, and then, when applications are started, additional memory is allocated. The pages served by those applications in turn could have static and dynamic components that are cached. On a busy server with lots of dynamic sites, several gigabytes of memory can get used up quickly this way.

In contrast, on the same server running IIS 6, where memory is allocated on demand to processes and application components and then returned when idle or otherwise recycled, the resource usage is very different. The same server that was previously bogged down can handle many more sites and applications.

Managing Custom IIS Applications

You configure and manage custom IIS applications through the Web Site Properties dialog box. As part of the standard installation, all Web sites created in IIS have a default application that's set as a sitewide application, meaning its starting point is the base directory for the Web site. The default application allows you to run custom applications that use the preconfigured application settings. You don't need to make any changes to the environment. You can, however, achieve better control by defining applications with smaller scope, and the sections that follow tell you how to do this.

Creating Applications

IIS applications are collections of resource files and components that are grouped together to take advantage of key IIS features. In IIS 5 isolation mode, those features include file buffering, session state tracking, and component caching. In IIS 6 mode, those features include worker process recycling, health monitoring, and rapid fail protection.

You can create an application by completing the following steps:

1. In the IIS snap-in, right-click the site, directory, or virtual directory that you want to use as the starting point for the application and then select Properties. Select the Home Directory, Directory, or Virtual Directory tab as appropriate. This displays the dialog box shown in Figure 5-3.

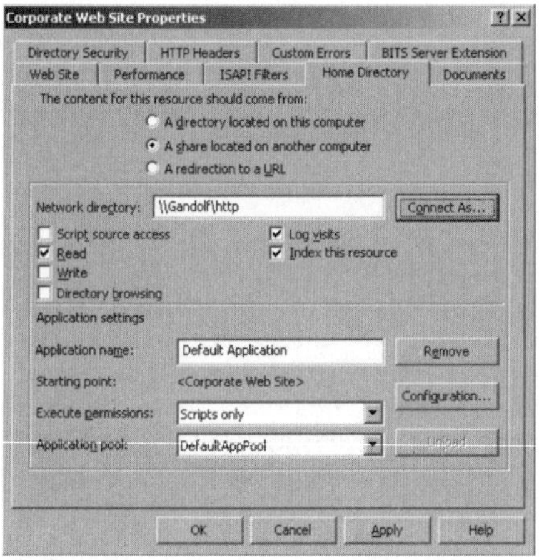

Figure 5-3. *Use the Properties dialog box to configure custom applications.*

2. You use the fields in the Application Settings frame to configure the application. If the Application Name and Application Pool fields appear dimmed, it means that the directory is already within the context of another application. This is all right; you can still create your application. However, keep in mind that by doing so, you remove the directory and all its subdirectories from the current application context.

3. Click Create to start the application definition process. If an application was created by default, you might need to click Remove first.

4. The Application Name field sets a descriptive name for the application. By default, this field is set to the directory name. You can change this value by typing a new name.

5. Use the Execute Permissions selection drop-down list to set the level of program execution that's allowed for an application. Three execute permissions levels are defined:

- **None**   Only static files, such as HTML or GIF files, can be accessed.
- **Scripts**   Only scripts, such as ASP scripts, can be run.
- **Scripts And Executables**   All file types can be accessed and executed.

6. If running in IIS 5 isolation mode, use the Application Protection selection list to specify the memory area used by the application as one of the following:

- **Low (IIS Process)**   Low protection allows applications to run in process and share resources with IIS. All applications with this priority share the IIS process instance.

- **Medium (Pooled)**   Medium protection allows applications to run as a pooled process. All applications with this priority share the same IIS process instance but don't run in process with normal IIS resources.

- **High (Isolated)**   High protection allows applications to run completely out of process. Isolated applications don't share processes with other applications, and the failure of other applications doesn't affect this high-priority application.

7. If running in IIS 6 worker process mode, select the application pool to use. Although you can use the default application pool (DefaultAppPool), it's better to create pools for specific types of applications and sites as discussed in Chapter 6.

8. Create the application by clicking Apply. You then have the option to click Configuration to configure advanced settings. Advanced settings are discussed in the sections that follow.

Configuring Application Mappings and Caching

Application mappings are used to specify the ISAPI extensions and CGI programs that are available to applications. Application mappings for Web sites are inherited from the WWW Service master properties at the time the site is created. Application mappings for individual directories are inherited from the site properties at the time the directory is created and made available to IIS. Each application mapping has three components:

- **Extension**   The file extension that's associated with the ISAPI extension or CGI program. File extensions don't have to have file type associations at the operating system level and can be more than three characters.

- **Executable Path**   The file path to the ISAPI extension or CGI program. IIS uses the executable path to determine which ISAPI extension or CGI program should be loaded. The associated DLL or executable must be in a directory that's accessible to IIS. Typically, this means placing the DLL or executable in the %SystemRoot%\System32 or %SystemRoot%\ System32\Inetsrv directory. If you're using extensions included with the .NET Framework, the DDL or executable would be located within the %SystemRoot%\Microsoft.NET\ Framework\ directory structure.

- **Verbs** The HTTP request types that are used with the ISAPI extension or CGI program. For a detailed list of HTTP request types, refer to Table 5-1.

ISAPI extensions and CGI programs with mappings are loaded dynamically into memory when IIS receives a request for a file with the designated extension, and they're unloaded when IIS is finished processing the request. You can change this behavior by enabling application caching. With caching enabled, IIS doesn't unload the associated DLL or executable but instead maintains it in memory.

You control ISAPI extension caching at the site level of the Web site you are working with. This setting is inherited by all applications configured on the site and cannot be set differently for individual applications within the site. To view or manage ISAPI extension caching, follow these steps:

1. In the IIS snap-in, right-click the site that you want to work with and then select Properties.
2. On the Home Directory tab, click Configuration.
3. Enable application caching by selecting Cache ISAPI Extensions. Clear this check box to disable caching.
4. Click OK twice.

Note In most instances, you'll want IIS to use extension caching. The exception is when you are doing debugging or troubleshooting and want to force IIS to reload components each time they're used.

Unlike ISAPI extension caching, you have granular control over application mappings and can set mappings for individual directories differently from the mappings used for the site as a whole. You control application mappings through the Application Configuration property sheet shown in Figure 5-4. To access this property sheet, follow these steps:

1. In the IIS snap-in, right-click the site, directory, or virtual directory that's used as the starting point for the application and then select Properties.
2. Select the Home Directory, Directory, or Virtual Directory tab as appropriate and then click Configuration.
3. The Application Extensions frame shows the current mappings for ISAPI extensions and CGI programs. As shown in Figure 5-4, each application mapping has an associated file extension, executable path, and verb list.

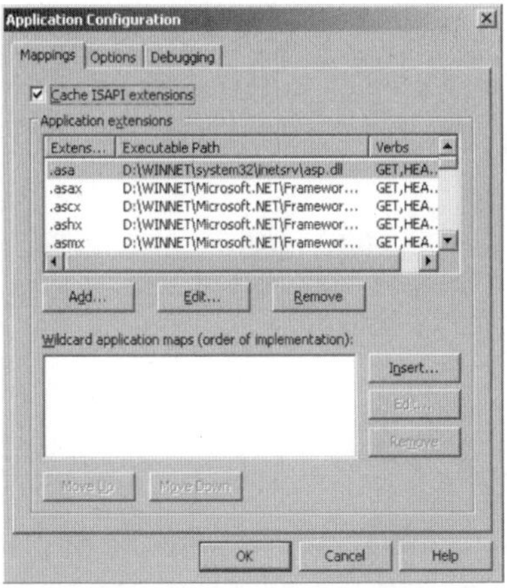

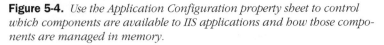

Figure 5-4. *Use the Application Configuration property sheet to control which components are available to IIS applications and how those components are managed in memory.*

Once the Application Configuration property sheet is displayed, you can manage existing component mappings or create new component mappings. The techniques for doing this are examined in the following sections.

Adding Application Mappings

To add application mappings, follow these steps:

1. Access the Application Configuration property sheet for the application and then click Add. This displays the Add/Edit Application Extension Mapping dialog box, as shown in Figure 5-5.

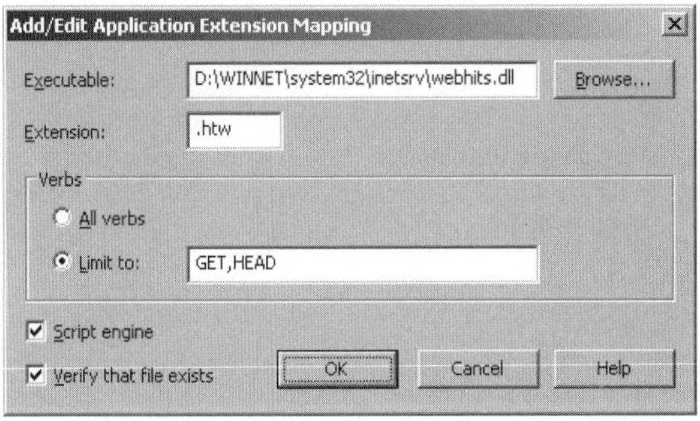

Figure 5-5. *Add new application mappings using the Add/Edit Application Extension Mapping dialog box.*

2. In the Executable field, type the file path to the ISAPI extension or CGI program that you want to use. The file path should end in .exe or .dll, such as C:\Windows\System32\Inetsrv\Asp.dll. If you don't know the file path, click Browse to display the Open dialog box, which you can use to find the executable.

 Note The DLL or executable must be located on a local hard disk. In most cases, DLL or executables should be placed in the %SystemRoot%\System32 or %SystemRoot%\System32\Inetsrv directory.

3. In the Extension field, type the file name extension that should be associated with the ISAPI extension or CGI program. Be sure to include the period (.) with the extension designator, such as *.html*.

 Tip If you want the ISAPI extension or CGI program to handle requests for all file types, place an asterisk (*) in the Extension field. From then on, requests for files within the application scope are sent to the component you've specified regardless of the file extension. Keep in mind that file requests also must match the parameters set for the verb list.

4. Use the options in the Verbs frame to set the verb list for the application mapping. Select All Verbs to pass all requests with the defined extension to the application or select Limit To and then enter request types in a comma-separated list.

 Note The verb list controls the types of requests that are passed to an application. For example, you could configure one mapping to handle GET, HEAD, and POST requests for .htm files and another mapping to handle PUT, TRACE, and DELETE requests for .htm files.

5. Applications can run in directories with Scripts Only or Scripts And Executable permissions. If you want the ISAPI extension or CGI program to run in directories designated as Scripts Only, select the Script Engine check box. Otherwise, clear this check box and the component will run only in directories designated with Scripts And Executable permissions.

6. Select Verify That File Exists to have IIS check the existence of a requested file and to ensure that the user making the request has appropriate access permissions before running the associated ISAPI extension or CGI program. If the file doesn't exist or if the user doesn't have access permissions, a warning message is returned to the browser and the component isn't executed.

Note   Verify That File Exists is useful when you use scripts mapped to executables that don't send a CGI response if a script is inaccessible. One such example is Perl, which doesn't return a CGI response in this instance. Using this option can cause a performance hit on a busy server. The reason for this is that the file is opened twice—once by IIS and once by the associated component.

7. Click OK three times to return to the IIS snap-in.

Editing Application Mappings

You can edit existing application mappings by completing the following steps:

1. Access the Application Configuration property sheet for the application, select the desired mapping, and then click Edit. This displays the Add/Edit Application Extension Mapping dialog box previously shown in Figure 5-5.

2. Make the necessary adjustments to the mapping and then click OK three times to return to the IIS snap-in.

3. The new settings are used the next time the associated DLL or executable is loaded into memory. If ISAPI caching is enabled, you must stop and then restart the Web site to enforce the changes.

Removing Application Mappings

To remove application mappings, follow these steps:

1. Access the Application Configuration property sheet for the application, select the desired mapping, and then click Remove.

2. When prompted to confirm the action, click Yes, then click OK twice to return to the IIS snap-in.

3. The new settings are used the next time the associated DLL or executable is loaded into memory. If ISAPI caching is enabled, you must stop and then restart the Web site to enforce the changes.

Managing Session State

Session state plays a significant role in IIS performance and resource usage. When session state is enabled, IIS creates a session for each user who accesses an ASP application. Session information is used to track the user within the application and to pass user information from one page to another. For example, your company might want to track individual user preferences within an application, and you can use sessions to do this.

The way sessions work is fairly straightforward. The first time a user requests an ASP page with a specified application, IIS generates one of the following:

- A Session object containing all values set for the user session, including an identifier for the code page used to display the dynamic content, a location identifier, a session ID, and a time-out value.

- A Session.Contents collection, which contains all the items that the application has set in the session (except objects created in the application's Global.asa file).

- A Session.StaticObjects collection, which contains the static objects defined in the application's Global.asa file.

The Session object and its associated properties are stored in memory on the server. The user's session ID is passed to the user's browser as a cookie. As long as the browser accepts cookies, the session ID is passed back to the server on subsequent requests. This is true even if the user requests a page in a different application. The same ID is used in order to reduce the number of cookies sent to the browser. Keep in mind that if the browser doesn't accept cookies, the session ID can't be maintained and IIS can't track the user session using this technique. In this case you could track the session state on the server.

Session state is enabled by default for all IIS applications. By default, sessions time out in 20 minutes. This means that if a user doesn't request or refresh a page within 20 minutes, the session ends and IIS removes the related Session object from memory. You can change the default time-out value using the Session Timeout property on the Options tab of the Application Configuration property sheet.

 Real World Worker process recycling can affect session management. If a worker process is recycled or otherwise cleared out of memory, the session state could be lost. If this happens, you won't be able to recover the session data.

As you might imagine, tracking sessions can use valuable system resources. You can reduce resource usage by reducing the time-out interval or disabling session tracking altogether. Reducing the time-out interval allows sessions to expire more quickly than usual. Disabling session tracking tells IIS that sessions shouldn't be automatically created. You can still start sessions manually within the application. Simply place the <%@ENABLESESSIONSTATE = True%> directive in individual ASP pages.

Each application configured on your server has its own session state settings. You manage the session state for an application by completing the following steps:

1. In the IIS snap-in, right-click the site, directory, or virtual directory that's used as the starting point for the application and then select Properties.

2. Select the Home Directory, Directory, or Virtual Directory tab as appropriate and then click Configuration.

3. In the Options tab, enable automatic session creation by selecting Enable Session State. Clear this check box to disable automatic session creation.

4. If sessions are enabled, type a session time-out value in the Session Timeout field. For a high-usage application in which you expect users to move quickly from page to page, you might want to set a fairly low time-out value, such as 15 minutes. On the other hand, if it's critical that the user's session is maintained to complete a transaction, you might want to set a long time-out value, such as 60 minutes.

5. Click OK twice.

Real World These days, most large-scale, commercial Web sites are managed using multiple servers. In this situation you typically have a load balancer that distributes requests for the site Uniform Resource Locator (URL) to whichever server is available. To use ASP session management on a load-balanced site, you must ensure that all requests from a particular user are directed to the same Web server. The technique you use depends on your load balancer.

Controlling Application Buffering

Buffering is another option that affects server performance and resource usage. When buffering is enabled, IIS completely processes pages before sending content to the client browser. When buffering is disabled, IIS returns output to the client browser as the page is processed. The advantage to buffering is that it allows you to respond dynamically to events that occur while processing the page. You can take one of the following actions:

• Abort sending a page or transfer the user to a different page

• Clear the buffer and send different content to the user

• Change HTTP header information from anywhere in your ASP script

A disadvantage of buffering is that users have to wait for the entire script to be processed before content is delivered to their browser. If a script is long or complex, the user might have to wait for a long time before seeing the page. To counter potential delays associated with buffering, developers often insert Flush commands at key positions within the script. If your development team does this, they should be aware that this causes additional connection requests between the client and server, which might also cause performance problems.

As with session tracking, buffering is enabled by default for all applications. You manage buffering by completing the following steps:

1. In the IIS snap-in, right-click the site, directory, or virtual directory that's used as the starting point for the application and then select Properties.

2. Select the Home Directory, Directory, or Virtual Directory tab as appropriate and then click Configuration.

3. In the Options tab, enable buffering by selecting Enable Buffering. Clear this check box to disable buffering.

Tip If you disable buffering for an application, you can still turn on buffering for individual ASP pages. To do this, use the Response.Buffer = True statement.

4. Click OK twice to return to the IIS snap-in.

Setting Parent Paths, Default ASP Language, and ASP Script Time-Out

Additional options that you can set for applications pertain to parent paths, default ASP language, and ASP script time-out. Enable Parent Paths allows ASP pages to use relative paths to access the current directory's parent directory. For example, a script could reference ../Build.htm, where ".." is a reference to the current directory's parent directory. Parent paths are enabled by default.

Default ASP Language sets the default scripting language for ASP pages. Two scripting engines are installed with a standard IIS installation. These scripting engines are for VBScript and JScript. You can reference these scripting engines using the values VBScript and JScript, respectively. The default scripting language in a standard IIS installation is VBScript, but you can change the default value at any time. Scripts can override the default language using the <%@LANGUAGE%> directive.

ASP Script Timeout sets the length of time that IIS allows a script to run. If a script doesn't complete within the time-out interval, IIS stops the script and writes an error to the application event log. The default time-out value is 90 seconds, but you can set a new default value at any time. In an ASP page, you can override the default value using the Server.ScriptTimeout method.

To set these application options, follow these steps:

1. In the IIS snap-in, right-click the site, directory, or virtual directory that's used as the starting point for the application and then select Properties.

2. Select the Home Directory, Directory, or Virtual Directory tab as appropriate and then click Configuration. Select the Options tab.

3. Select Enable Parent Paths to allow scripts to use relative paths to reference the parent directory. Clear this check box to disable parent paths.

4. The default scripting language is VBScript. To change the default scripting language, type the scripting language name in the Default ASP Language field.

5. The default ASP script time-out is 90 seconds. To change the default time-out value, type a new time-out interval in the ASP Script Timeout field.

6. Click OK twice to return to the IIS snap-in.

Enabling and Disabling Application Debugging

One of the best ways to troubleshoot an IIS application is to enable debugging. Debugging is handled through server-side and client-side configuration options. Server-side debugging allows IIS to throw errors while processing ASP pages and to display a prompt that allows you to start the Microsoft Script Debugger. You can then use the debugger to examine your ASP pages. Client-side debugging involves sending debugging information to the client browser. You can then use this information to help determine what's wrong with IIS and the related ASP page.

You can enable server-side and client-side debugging by completing the following steps:

1. In the IIS snap-in, right-click the site, directory, or virtual directory that's used as the starting point for the application and then select Properties.

2. Select the Home Directory, Directory, or Virtual Directory tab as appropriate and then click Configuration. Select the Debugging tab.

3. To turn on server-side debugging, select Enable ASP Server-Side Script Debugging. To turn off server-side debugging, clear this option.

Caution Server-side debugging of ASP applications is designed for development and staging servers and not necessarily for production servers. If you enable server-side debugging on a production server, you might notice a severe decrease in performance for the affected application. The reason for this is that server-side debugging causes ASP to run in single-threaded mode.

4. To turn on client-side debugging, select Enable ASP Client-Side Script Debugging. To turn off client-side debugging, clear this option.

Configuring Application Error Messages

By default, applications are configured to send to clients detailed error messages that specify the file name, error message, and line number in which an error occurred. This information is great for troubleshooting problems in the code but not necessarily good for users to see when they encounter a problem. For this reason, you might want to create a text message to send instead. The text message can provide readers with an easy-to-understand text message that directs them to a location where they can get help.

You can configure application error messages by completing the following steps:

1. In the IIS snap-in, right-click the site, directory, or virtual directory that's used as the starting point for the application and then select Properties.

2. Select the Home Directory, Directory, or Virtual Directory tab as appropriate and then click Configuration. Select the Debugging tab.

3. To use detailed error messages, select Send Detailed ASP Error Messages To Client. Otherwise, select Send The Following Text Error Message To Client and type a text message that's to be displayed if an error occurs.

Unloading IIS 5 Isolated Applications

In IIS 5 mode, isolated applications are stored in a separate memory space and use a separate Dllhost.exe process. If you want to force IIS to remove the application from memory, you can do this by unloading the application. Now the next time a user accesses the application, IIS will reload the application into memory and start a new Dllhost.exe process.

You can unload an isolated application by completing the following steps:

1. In the IIS snap-in, right-click the site, directory, or virtual directory that's used as the starting point for the application and then select Properties.

2. Select the Home Directory, Directory, or Virtual Directory tab as appropriate.

3. Unload the application by clicking Unload and then click OK.

Deleting IIS Applications

If you find that you no longer need an application, you should remove it to free up the resources that it's using. To delete an application, follow these steps:

1. In the IIS snap-in, right-click the site, directory, or virtual directory that's used as the starting point for the application and then select Properties.

2. Select the Home Directory, Directory, or Virtual Directory tab as appropriate.

3. Delete the application by clicking Remove and then click OK.

Managing Custom ISAPI Filters

ISAPI filters are IIS applications that are used to filter requests for specific types of events, such as Read or Write. When a filter encounters an event for which it's been configured, it responds to the event by performing a set of tasks. You can apply ISAPI filters globally or locally. Global filters affect all Web sites. Local filters affect only the currently selected Web site.

Viewing and Configuring Global Filters

Global filters affect all IIS Web sites and are loaded into memory when the World Wide Web Publishing Service is started. Anytime you add new global filters or modify existing global filters, you must stop and then restart the World Wide Web Publishing Service.

To display and configure global filters, follow these steps:

1. In the IIS snap-in, double-click the computer node for the IIS server you want to work with. Right-click Web Sites and then select Properties.

2. In the ISAPI Filters tab, you should see a list of the currently defined global filters. Global filters are active for all Web sites on the server and are executed according to priority in the order listed.

3. The summary list for filters shows the following information:

- **Status**   The load status of the filters. Filters that have been successfully loaded show a green up arrow. Filters that aren't loaded show a red down arrow.

- **Filter Name**   The descriptive name for the filter. This name is set when you install the filter.

- **Priority**   The priority of the filter as set in the source code. Filters with higher priority are executed before filters with lower priority.

Note   You can obtain a detailed status for a filter by clicking it. The only additional information provided is the file path to the filter executable.

4. Use the following options to configure global filters:

- **Add**   Adds a filter. To add a new global filter, click Add. Type a filter name and then type the file path to the executable for the filter. If you don't know the file path, click Browse and then use the Open dialog box to find the filter.

- **Remove**   Removes a global filter. To remove a filter, select it and then click Remove.

- **Edit**   Edits a global filter. The only filter property that you can edit is the executable file path. To edit a filter, select it and then click Edit. Use the Add/Edit Filter Properties dialog box provided to change the executable file path and then click OK.

5. When several filters are configured to respond to the same events, they're executed sequentially. Filters with higher priority are executed before filters with lower priority. Filters with the same priority are executed at the global level and then at the site level. To change the execution order of a filter within a priority, use the Move Up and Move Down buttons.

6. If you've added or changed a global filter, you should stop and then restart the World Wide Web Publishing Service. Doing this causes IIS to load the new filters into memory.

Viewing and Configuring Local Filters

Local filters affect a single IIS Web site and can be dynamically loaded into memory when they're added or modified, as long as the World Wide Web Publishing Service and the Web site are running. Because of this, you don't need to stop and then restart the World Wide Web Publishing Service when you make changes to local filters.

To display and configure local filters, follow these steps:

1. In the IIS snap-in, right-click the Web site you want to manage and then choose Properties.
2. Select the ISAPI Filters tab. You should now see a list of the currently defined local filters. Local filters are active for the currently selected Web site only.

 Note You won't see any global filters inherited from the Web server's master properties. You will see only the filters installed for the currently selected Web site, even though both sets of filters are run. Although several global filters are configured by default, no local filters will exist unless an administrator has added them.

3. The summary list for filters shows the following information:
   - **Status** The load status of the filters. Filters that have been successfully loaded show a green up arrow. Filters that aren't loaded show a red down arrow.
   - **Filter Name** The descriptive name for the filter. This name is set when you install the filter.
   - **Priority** The priority of the filter as set in the source code. Filters with higher priority are executed before filters with lower priority.

Note You can obtain a detailed status for a filter by clicking it. The only additional information provided is the file path to the filter executable.

4. Use the following options to configure local filters:
   - **Add** Adds a filter. To add a new local filter, click Add. Type a filter name and then type the file path to the executable for the filter. If you don't know the file path, click Browse and then use the Open dialog box to find the filter.
   - **Remove** Removes a local filter. To remove a filter, select it and then click Remove.
   - **Edit** Edits a local filter. The only filter property that you can edit is the executable file path. To edit a filter, select it and then click Edit. Use the Add/Edit Filter Properties dialog box provided to change the executable file path and then click OK.
5. When several filters are configured to respond to the same events, they're executed sequentially. Filters with higher priority are executed before filters with lower priority. Filters with the same priority are executed at the global level and then at the site level. To change the execution order of a filter within a priority, use the Move Up and Move Down buttons.

Chapter 6

Managing ASP.NET, Application Pools, and Worker Processes

Chapter 5, "Running IIS Applications," discussed the basics of working with IIS applications. That chapter's focus was broad and discussed issues related to both the Internet Information Services (IIS) 5 isolation mode and the IIS 6.0 worker process isolation mode. In this chapter we zero in on advanced application configuration issues that are specific to applications running in IIS 6 worker process isolation mode. You'll learn techniques for:

- Managing ASP.NET configurations
- Creating application pools
- Configuring multiple worker processes for applications
- Recycling worker processes manually and automatically
- Optimizing application performance

As you might expect, the discussion in this chapter applies only when IIS is running in IIS 6 worker process isolation mode and you must be logged on as an administrator or run commands as an administrator to perform the tasks this chapter discusses.

Managing ASP.NET

Every Web administrator should become intimately familiar with ASP.NET. You should know how to configure ASP.NET and how to manage ASP.NET applications. ASP.NET configurations and applications are fairly complex. You'll need to work closely with your organization's engineering department during planning, staging, and deployment.

Installing ASP.NET

To use applications that incorporate the Microsoft Windows .NET Framework, you must install ASP.NET on your IIS servers. ASP.NET is the central Windows component that allows an IIS server to run ASP.NET applications. Like the .NET

Framework, ASP.NET technology is advancing rapidly. Several implementations of ASP.NET are already available, and many more will be developed in the coming months and years.

Unlike many application implementations, where you have to remove previous application or component versions before installing new applications or components, you don't have to remove previous versions of ASP.NET. The reason is that the .NET Framework supports side-by-side execution of applications and components running different versions of ASP.NET. Side-by-side execution is made possible because applications and the components they use run within isolated process boundaries. Each worker process runs its own instance of the ASP.NET components that it needs and is isolated from other processes.

You can check to see if ASP.NET is installed on a server by using the IIS snap-in. Follow these steps:

1. Select the Web Service Extensions node in the IIS snap-in.

2. If ASP.NET is installed, you'll see a Web Service Extension entry for each version of ASP.NET installed on the server.

To install the version of ASP.NET that ships with Windows Server 2003, you use the Windows Component Wizard by completing the following steps:

1. Click Add Or Remove Programs in Control Panel and then click Add/Remove Windows Components. This starts the Windows Component Wizard.

2. Select Application Server and then click Details. In the Application Server dialog box, shown in Figure 6-1, check the ASP.NET check box and any other application server components you want to install.

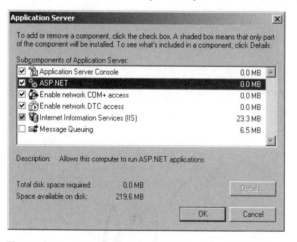

Figure 6-1. *ASP.NET isn't installed by default when you install an Application Server. You must choose ASP.NET as one of the installation components.*

Note Make sure you don't accidentally clear the Application Server check box when selecting it, which is easy to do.

3. Click OK.

4. Click Next and then, when prompted, click Finish.

Installing ASP.NET results in several Windows components and resources being installed as well. These include:

- **ASP.NET Performance Counters** Each version of ASP.NET installed on a server has a different set of performance counter objects that are associated with it. These performance counters are installed when the ASP.NET version is installed.

- **ASP.NET State Service** ASP.NET uses this service to manage session states. All compatible versions of ASP.NET installed on a server use the same state service, which is provided by the most recent version of ASP.NET installed on the computer.

- **ASP.NET SQL State Server** ASP.NET uses the SQL State Server in conjunction with the ASP.NET State Service. All compatible versions of ASP.NET installed on a server use the same state server, which is provided and managed by the most recent version of ASP.NET installed.

- **ASPNET Local User Account** On stand-alone and member servers, a local user account called ASPNET is created when you install ASP.NET. Worker processes use this account on the local machine when running in IIS 5 isolation mode. If the server is part of a domain, worker processes are configured to use the Network Service account.

Running Side-by-Side ASP.NET Configurations

You can install multiple versions of ASP.NET on an IIS server. Typically, you do this by running the .NET Framework setup program (Dotnetfx.exe) for the version you want to install. Installing a newer version of the .NET Framework could reconfigure ASP.NET applications installed on the IIS server to use the version you're installing. Specifically, this happens when the version you're installing is a new version that represents a minor revision (as determined by the version number). For example, if ASP.NET applications are currently configured to use ASP.NET version 1.1.4322 and you're installing a newer version, ASP.NET applications would be configured to use components in the new version automatically. Here, 4322 represents the build number and 1.1 are the major and minor version numbers, respectively.

After you install a new version of the .NET Framework, you'll need to configure IIS so that the new version of ASP.NET it contains can be used. You do this by completing the following steps:

1. Access the Web Service Extensions node in the IIS snap-in.

2. In the right pane, click the Web Service Extension entry for the ASP.NET version you installed and then click Allow.

Each version of the .NET Framework installed on a server has different components and tools. The base directory for the .NET Framework is %System-Root%\Microsoft.NET\Framework. Below the base directory, you'll find separate subdirectories for each version of the .NET Framework you've installed.

One of the tools in the version subdirectory is the ASP.NET IIS Registration tool. This tool controls the mapping of ASP.NET applications to a specific ASP.NET version. If you want to install an ASP.NET version so that it can be used on the server, you can use this tool to do it. Complete the following steps:

1. Display the Run dialog box by clicking Start and then choosing Run.

2. Type **cmd** in the Open field and then click OK.

3. In the command console, type **cd %SystemRoot%\Microsoft.NET\ Framework**.

4. Type **dir** to obtain a directory listing. Note the available version subdirectories and then change to the directory containing the ASP.NET version you want to use.

5. List the installed versions of ASP.NET and view how those versions are configured by typing **aspnet_regiis –lv** and then typing **aspnet_regiis –lk**.

6. If you want a single ASP.NET application to use this ASP.NET version, type **aspnet_regiis –sn** *MetabasePathLocation,* where *MetabasePathLocation* is the metabase path to the application you want to use this version of ASP.NET. See Chapter 15, "IIS Optimization and the Metabase," for details on working with the IIS metabase.

7. If you want all ASP.NET applications to use this ASP.NET version (provided that it's a newer version and represents a compatible build as determined by the version and build number), type **aspnet_regiis –i**.

8. If you want to register this ASP.NET version on the server but don't want to reconfigure applications to use it, type **aspnet_regiis –ir**.

 Tip It's important to note that each version of ASP.NET installed on a server has a separate set of performance counter objects. Because of this, if you want to monitor a particular ASP.NET application's performance, you'll need to configure monitoring of the performance counter objects specific to the version of ASP.NET used by the application.

Defining ASP.NET Directory Structures and Applications

Every ASP.NET application has an application root directory. This root directory is created in the IIS snap-in as a virtual directory that defines the application alias and the physical directory in which application components are stored. In the root directory, you'll store files needed by the application. You'll need a Bin subdirectory for the application as well, which is used to store assemblies (compiled binary files) and other dynamic-link libraries (DLLs) used by the application.

To create the directory structures for an ASP.NET application, follow these steps:

1. In the IIS snap-in, expand the Web Sites node. Right-click the Web site on which you want to define the ASP.NET application, choose New, and then click Virtual Directory. This starts the Virtual Directory Creation Wizard. Click Next.

2. In the Alias field, type the name of the application as shown in Figure 6-2. The best application names are short but descriptive. Click Next.

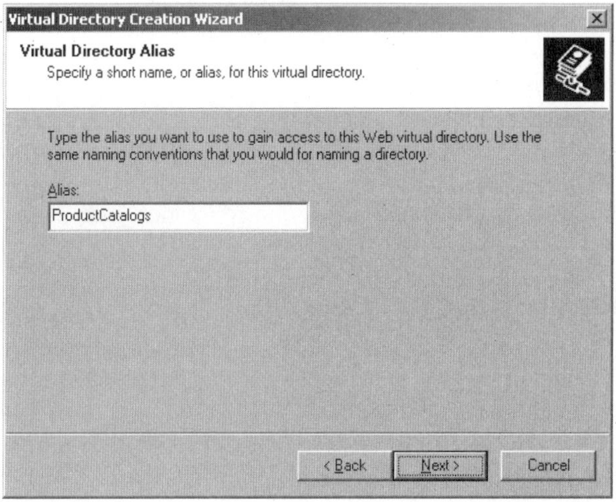

Figure 6-2. *The virtual directory alias sets the name of the application.*

3. The next page lets you set the path to the physical directory where the application content is stored. Type the directory path or click Browse to search for a directory. The directory must be created before you can select it. If necessary, click Browse and then click Make New Folder to create the directory before you select it. However, don't forget about checking and setting permissions at the operating system level as discussed in Chapter 7, "Managing Web Server Security."

4. Click Next, and then set access permissions for the applications. Normally, you'll want to set Read and Run Script permissions only. The standard permissions are these:

- **Read**   Allows users to read documents, such as Hypertext Markup Language (HTML) files.

- **Run Scripts**   Allows users to run scripts, such as Active Server Pages (ASP) files or Perl scripts.

- **Execute**   Allows users to execute programs, such as Internet Server Application Programming Interface (ISAPI) applications or executable files.

- **Write** Allows users to upload files to the site, such as with Microsoft FrontPage.

- **Browse** Allows users to view a list of files if they enter the name of a valid directory that doesn't have a default document.

5. Click Next and then click Finish. The virtual directory for the application is created.

6. Using Windows Explorer, create a Bin subdirectory under the main application directory. This directory is used as the local assembly cache. For more information on the assembly cache, see the section of this chapter entitled "Working with the Assembly Cache."

7. Configure the application to use a specific application pool and then optimize the application pool configuration as discussed later in this chapter.

8. Deploy the application by copying the application files into the appropriate directories. For more information on deploying applications, see the section of this chapter entitled "Deploying ASP.NET Applications."

Working with the Assembly Cache

ASP.NET applications can make use of many types of components. Some components, like .asmx and .aspx files, are compiled at runtime by ASP.NET when they're first requested, and then the compiled code is stored in the file cache where it can be reused without recompiling. Other components, like assemblies, must be precompiled into DLL binaries and placed in the appropriate assembly cache before they can be used.

Binary components that are specific to an application are stored in the local assembly cache. You don't need to register components in the local assembly cache. To use local assemblies, you must create a Bin directory under the main application directory and then copy the necessary binaries and assemblies into this subdirectory. You can copy files using Windows Explorer or using a command-line copy tool such as Xcopy.

Binary components that are shared between applications are called *global assemblies*. To use global assemblies, you must register them in the global assembly cache. For production servers, you configure the installation using Microsoft Windows Installer (MSI) 2. For testing and development purposes, you can use the Global Assembly Cache Tool (Gacutil.exe) to perform this task. You can find this tool in the subdirectory for the ASP.NET version you're working with, %SystemRoot%\Microsoft.NET\Framework*VersionNumber*.

To use the Global Assembly Cache Tool to install a global assembly, follow these steps:

1. Display the Run dialog box by clicking Start and then choosing Run.

2. Type **cmd** in the Open field and then click OK.

3. In the command console, type **cd %SystemRoot%\Microsoft.NET\ Framework**.

4. Type **dir** to obtain a directory listing. Note the available version subdirectories and then change to the directory containing the ASP.NET version you want to use.

5. Type **gacutil –i** *AssemblyFilePath* where *AssemblyFilePath* is the complete file path of the assembly to install in the global assembly cache.

Deploying ASP.NET Applications

Now that you've configured the application directory structure, you're ready to deploy your ASP.NET applications. You deploy applications by copying the necessary ASP.NET files, such as .asmx or .aspx files, to the application directory. Application binaries and assemblies (DLLs) are copied to the Bin subdirectory for the application.

Anytime you need to update or change the files in the deployment directory, you simply copy the new versions of the ASP.NET files and binaries to the appropriate directory. When you do this, ASP.NET automatically detects that files have been updated. In response, ASP.NET compiles a new version of the application and loads it into memory as necessary to handle new requests. Any current requests are handled without interruption by the previously created application instance. When that application instance is no longer needed, it's removed from memory.

ASP.NET handles changes to the Web.config file in the same way. If you modify the Web.config file or application pool properties while IIS is running, ASP.NET compiles a new version of the application and loads it into memory as necessary to handle new requests. Any current requests are handled without interruption by the previously created application instance. When that application instance is no longer needed, it's removed from memory.

If you need to install components in the global assembly cache, you'll need to follow the procedures discussed in the previous section.

Uninstalling ASP.NET Versions

Sometimes you'll no longer want an older version of ASP.NET to run on a server. In this case you can uninstall the ASP.NET version that's no longer needed. When you uninstall an older version of ASP.NET, ASP.NET applications that used the version are reconfigured so that they use the highest remaining version of ASP.NET that's compatible with the version you're uninstalling.

Remember, the version number determines compatibility. If no other compatible versions are installed, applications that used the version of ASP.NET you're uninstalling are left in an unconfigured state, which might cause the entire contents of ASP.NET pages to be served directly to clients, thereby exposing the code those pages contain.

If you want to uninstall a version of ASP.NET, follow these steps:

1. Display the Run dialog box by clicking Start and then choosing Run.

2. Type **cmd** in the Open field and then click OK.

3. In the command console, type **cd %SystemRoot%\Microsoft.NET\ Framework**.

4. Type **dir** to obtain a directory listing. Note the available version subdirectories and then change to the directory containing the ASP.NET version you want to use.

5. List the installed versions of ASP.NET and view how those versions are configured by typing **aspnet_regiis –lv** and then typing **aspnet_regiis –lk**.

6. To uninstall the ASP.NET version whose components are in the current subdirectory, type **aspnet_regiis –u**. This uninstalls the ASP.NET version and the performance counter objects used by the ASP.NET version.

 Note If you want to install all ASP.NET versions installed on a server, type **aspnet_regiis –ua**.

When you uninstall ASP.NET, the following Windows components and resources might also be uninstalled:

- **ASP.NET Performance Counters** Performance counters for the ASP.NET version are uninstalled.

- **ASP.NET State Service** If the ASP.NET version you're uninstalling is the most recent version of ASP.NET installed on the computer, the ASP.NET State Service of the ASP.NET version with the next highest version number is used. If this is the last ASP.NET version on the computer, the ASP.NET State Service is uninstalled.

- **ASP.NET SQL State Server** If the ASP.NET version you're uninstalling is the most recent version of ASP.NET installed on the computer, the ASP.NET SQL State Server of the ASP.NET version with the next highest version number is used. If this is the last ASP.NET version on the computer, the ASP.NET SQL State Server is uninstalled.

- **ASPNET Local User Account** If you're uninstalling the last ASP.NET version on a stand-alone or member server, the ASPNET local user account is deleted.

Working with Application Pools

Application pools set boundaries for applications and define the configuration settings that applications they contain use. Every application pool has a set of one or more worker processes assigned to it. These worker processes define the memory space that applications use. By assigning an application to a particular application pool, you're specifying that the application:

- **Can run in the same context as other applications in the application pool** All applications in a particular application pool use the same worker process or processes, and these worker processes define the isolation boundaries. These applications must use the same version of ASP.NET. If applications in the same application pool use different versions of ASP.NET, errors will occur and the worker processes might not run.

- **Should use the application pool configuration settings** Configuration settings are applied to all applications assigned to a particular application pool. These settings control recycling of worker processes, failure detection and recovery, CPU monitoring, and much more. Application pool settings should be optimized to work with all applications they contain.

The sections that follow provide techniques for creating, configuring, and optimizing application pools.

Creating Application Pools

Application pools specify the isolation boundaries for Web applications. You can use application pools to optimize the performance, recovery, and monitoring of Web applications. An application's scope can range from an entire Web site to a single virtual directory. This means you can define default applications for Web sites that your IIS server hosts and you can define Web applications with very specific scopes.

To create an application pool, follow these steps:

1. In the IIS snap-in, right-click Application Pools, choose New, and then click Application Pool. This displays the Add New Application Pool dialog box shown in Figure 6-3.

```
Add New Application Pool                               [X]

   Application pool ID:    [ AppPool #2                    ]

  ┌ Application pool settings ─────────────────────────────┐
  │   ○ Use default settings for new application pool      │
  │   ● Use existing application pool as template          │
  │       Application pool name:  [ AppPool #1      ] [▼]   │
  └────────────────────────────────────────────────────────┘

          [    OK    ]  [  Cancel  ]  [   Help   ]
```

Figure 6-3. *Use the Add New Application Pool dialog box to set the name of the application pool and determine how the default settings are obtained.*

2. In the Application Pool ID field, type the name of the application pool. The name should be short but descriptive.

Tip You might want to number the application pools to identify them uniquely. For example, you might create AppPool #1, AppPool #2, and so on. Or you might want to identify the purpose of the application pool in the name. For example, you might have CustRegPool, ProdCatPool, and TechNetPool.

3. You can now select Use Default Settings For New Application Pool or Use Existing Application Pool As Template. If you previously created an application pool and you want to apply those same settings to this pool, choose the latter option and then use the Application Pool Name drop-down list to choose the application pool to use.

4. Click OK. Right-click the node for the application pool you just created and then select Properties. Use the Properties dialog box to view or change the application pool configuration.

Assigning Applications to Application Pools

Applications assigned to the same pool share the same configuration settings. These settings control recycling of worker processes used by applications in the pool, worker process failure detection and recovery, the identity under which the worker processes run, and more. You should assign applications to the same pool only when they have similar requirements. If an application has unique requirements, you might want to assign it to a separate application pool that's used only by that application.

To assign an application to an application pool, follow these steps:

1. In the IIS snap-in, expand the Web Sites node, right-click the application that you want to assign to an application pool, and then click Properties.

2. In the Home Directory, Virtual Directory, or Directory tab, verify that the Application Name field is set. If it isn't, click Create, and then type the application name.

3. You use the Application Pool drop-down list to set the application pool for the application. Select the name of the application pool you want to use and then click OK.

 Caution Applications assigned to the same application pool can't use different versions of ASP.NET. If you assign applications that use different ASP.NET versions to the same pool, the worker process might not run at all.

Configuring Application Pool Identities

The application pool identity determines the account under which the application pool's worker processes run. In most cases this identity is the Network Service account, which has limited permissions and privileges. If a particular application needs additional permissions or privileges, it's a good idea to create a separate application pool for that application and then configure the application pool identity to use an account that has those permissions. In most cases you should use one of the other predefined accounts, such as Local Service or Local System, but you can also use the IWAM account or any other account that you configure.

To configure the application pool identity, follow these steps:

1. In the IIS snap-in, expand Application Pools, right-click the application pool that you want to configure and then select Properties.
2. Select the Identity tab as shown in Figure 6-4.

```
┌─────────────────────────────────────────────────────────┐
│ AppPool #2 Properties                             ? X    │
├─────────────────────────────────────────────────────────┤
│  ┌Recycling┐┌Performance┐┌Health┐┌Identity┐              │
│                                                           │
│  ┌─Application pool identity──────────────────────────┐  │
│  │   Select a security account for this application pool:│ │
│  │                                                      │  │
│  │   ◉ Predefined    [Network Service          ▼]      │  │
│  │                                                      │  │
│  │   ○ Configurable                                     │  │
│  │       User name:   [IWAM_CORPSERVER01    ]  [Browse] │  │
│  │                                                      │  │
│  │       Password:    [••••••••••••      ]             │  │
│  │                                                      │  │
│  └──────────────────────────────────────────────────────┘ │
│                                                           │
│              [  OK  ] [ Cancel ] [ Apply ] [ Help ]       │
└─────────────────────────────────────────────────────────┘
```

Figure 6-4. *Use the options of the Identity tab to set the application pool identity to a predefined or previously configured account.*

3. If you want to use the built-in Network Service, Local Service, or Local System accounts, select Predefined and then select the appropriate account using the drop-down list provided. Click OK and skip the remaining steps.
4. If you want to specify a user account, select Configurable. By default, the account information is filled for the IWAM account. If you don't want to use this account, click Browse and then use the Select User dialog box to choose the account that you want to use.

Security Alert   If you decide to configure an account other than the IWAM account, keep in mind that the account must be a member of the IIS_WPG group and should have been assigned only the permissions and privileges necessary for the application to run properly. If the account is assigned additional permissions and privileges, malicious users might be able to compromise the system. For detailed information on working with the Network Service, Local Service, Local System, and IWAM accounts, see the section entitled "IIS User and Group Essentials" in Chapter 7.

5. If you specified an account other than the IWAM account, type the password for this account.

6. Click OK.

Note If IIS is configured to use Kerberos authentication, the application pool identity account must be a recognized Service Principal Name (SPN). If it isn't, Kerberos authentication will fail. To resolve this problem, you must use the Set SPN tool (Setspn.exe) to register the identity account as an arbitrary SPN. Set SPN is installed with the Windows Server 2003 Support Tools, as discussed in the section entitled "Installing Administration Tools" in Chapter 1, "Overview of Microsoft Web Services."

Starting, Stopping, and Recycling Worker Processes Manually

Sometimes you might want to restart or recycle the worker processes that an application pool is using. You might want to do this if you suspect an application is leaking memory or is otherwise affecting server performance or if users are experiencing undetermined or intermittent problems.

Starting and Stopping Worker Processes Manually

When you stop worker processes for an application pool, the related IIS 6 processes (W3wp.exe) are terminated and, as a result, all resources used by the worker processes are freed. This also means, however, that any requests currently being processed will fail and that new requests for the applications aren't processed until you start the application pool again, at which time Http.sys looks for requests in the application pool queue and then starts new worker processes as necessary to handle any pending requests.

The WWW service can stop an application pool as well. Typically, this occurs when rapid-fail protection is triggered, meaning that there were a certain number of worker process failures in a specified time period. In the standard configuration, five worker process failures within a five-minute interval trigger rapid-fail protection. Application pools can also be stopped when they're incorrectly configured to use a nonexistent identity or if different applications use different versions of ASP.NET.

To stop and then start an application pool, follow these steps:

1. In the IIS snap-in, expand Application Pools. Right-click the application pool that you want to stop and then select Stop.

2. Worker processes used by applications in the application pool are terminated. To start request processing for applications in the pool, right-click the application pool and then select Start.

Tip Clients trying to access an application in a stopped application pool might see an HTTP Error 503: Service Unavailable message. If users tell you they're seeing this message and you haven't stopped the application pool, definitely check to see if the application pool is started. If it isn't, start it and then check the error logs to determine what happened while closely monitoring for additional failures.

Recycling Worker Processes Manually

An alternative to abruptly terminating worker processes used by an application pool is to mark them for recycling. Worker processes that are actively processing requests continue to run while IIS starts new worker processes to replace them. Once the new worker processes are started, Http.sys directs incoming requests to the new worker processes and the old worker processes are able to continue handling requests until they shut down. With this approach, you minimize any service interruptions while ensuring that any resources used by old worker processes are eventually freed.

With recycling, the startup and shutdown processes can be limited by the Startup Time Limit and Shutdown Time Limit values set for the application pool. If IIS can't start new worker processes within the time limit set, a service interruption would occur because IIS would be unable to direct requests to the new processes. If IIS stops old worker processes when the shutdown time limit is reached and those processes are still handling requests, a service interruption would occur because the requests wouldn't be processed further.

To recycle the worker processes used by an application pool, follow these steps:

1. In the IIS snap-in, expand Application Pools.
2. Right-click the application pool that you want to recycle and then click Recycle.

Configuring Worker Process Startup and Shutdown Time Limits

Whenever IIS starts or shuts·down worker processes, it attempts to do so within prescribed time limits. The goal is to ensure timely startup of worker processes so that Http.sys can direct incoming requests to new worker processes and shut down old worker processes after they complete the processing of existing requests.

Graceful startup and shutdown of worker processes, however, is dependent on the amount of time allowed for startup and shutdown. If these values are set too low, service might be interrupted: A new worker process might not get started in time to accept incoming requests, or an old worker process might be terminated before it can finish processing requests. If these values are set too high, system resources might be tied up waiting for a transition that isn't possible: An existing worker process might be nonresponsive, or the server might be unable to allocate additional resources to start new worker processes while the old processes are still running.

Real World Listen carefully to user complaints about failed requests, time-outs, and other errors. Frequent complaints can be an indicator that you need to take a close look at the worker process recycling configuration as discussed in the section of this chapter entitled "Configuring Worker Process Recycling." If you believe you've optimized worker process recycling and users are still experiencing problems, take a look at the startup and shutdown time limits.

Ideally, you'll select a balanced startup and shutdown time that reflects the server's load and the importance of the applications in the application pool. By default, the startup and shutdown time limits are both set to 90 seconds. Here are some rules of thumb for setting startup and shutdown time limits:

- For application pools with applications that have long-running processes, such as those that require extensive computations or extended database lookups, you might want to reduce the startup time limit and extend the shutdown time limit, particularly if the server consistently experiences a moderate or heavy load.

- For application pools where it's more important to ensure that the service is responsive than to ensure that all requests go through, you might want to reduce both the startup and shutdown time limits, particularly if applications have known problems, such as memory leaks or frequent hangs.

To configure worker process startup and shutdown time limits, complete the following steps:

1. In the IIS snap-in, expand Application Pools, right-click the application pool that you want to configure, and then select Properties.

2. On the Health tab, use the Startup Time Limit and Shutdown Time Limit fields to set the maximum time allowed for worker process startup and shutdown respectively (in seconds).

3. Click OK.

Configuring Multiple Worker Processes for Application Pools

Multiple worker processes running in their own context can share responsibility for handling requests for an application pool. This configuration is also referred to as a *Web garden*. When you define a Web garden, each new request is assigned to a worker process according to a round-robin scheme. Round-robin is a load balancing technique used to spread the workload among the worker processes that are available.

Note It's important to note that worker processes aren't started automatically and don't use resources until they're needed. Rather, they're started as necessary to meet the demand based on incoming requests. For example, if you configure a maximum of five worker processes for an application pool, there may be at any given time from zero to five worker processes running in support of applications placed in that application pool.

If a single application is placed in an application pool serviced by multiple worker processes, any and all worker processes available will handle requests queued for the application. This is a multiple worker process–single application configuration, and it's best used when you want to improve the application's request handling performance and reduce any possible contention for resources with other applications. In this case the application might have heavy usage during peak periods and moderate-to-heavy usage during other times, or individuals using the application might have specific performance expectations that must be met if possible.

If multiple applications are placed in an application pool serviced by multiple worker processes, any and all worker processes available handle requests queued for any applicable application. This is a multiple worker process–multiple application configuration, and it's best used when you want to improve request handling performance and reduce resource contention for multiple applications but don't want to dedicate resources to any single application. In this case the various applications in the application pool might have different peak usage periods or might have varying resource needs.

To configure multiple worker processes for an application pool, follow these steps:

1. In the IIS snap-in, expand Application Pools, right-click the application pool that you want to configure, and then select Properties.
2. On the Performance tab, use the Maximum Number Of Worker Processes field in the Web Garden frame to specify the number of worker processes that the application pool should use.
3. Click OK.

Real World When you assign multiple worker processes to a busy application pool, keep in mind that each worker process uses server resources when it's started and might affect the performance of applications in other application pools. Adding worker processes won't resolve latency issues due to network communications or bandwidth, and it can reduce the time it takes to process requests only if those requests were queued and waiting and not being actively processed. A poorly engineered application will still respond poorly, and, at some point, you'd need to look at optimizing the application code for efficiency and timeliness.

Configuring Worker Process Recycling

Manual recycling of worker processes might work when you're troubleshooting, but on a day-to-day basis you probably don't have time to monitor worker process resource usage and responsiveness. To have IIS handle worker process recycling for you, you'll want to configure some type of automatic worker process recycling. Automatic worker process recycling can be configured to occur:

- **After a specific time period** Recycles worker processes based on the amount of time they've been running. Best used when applications have known problems running for extended periods of time.

- **When a certain number of requests are processed** Recycles worker processes based on the number of requests processed. Best used when applications fail based on usage.

- **At specific scheduled times during the day** Recycles worker processes based on a defined schedule. Best used when applications have known problems running for extended periods of time and you don't want processes to be recycled during a peak usage period. Here, you'd schedule recycling when you expect application usage to be at its lows for the day.

- **When memory usage grows to a specific point** Recycles worker processes when they use a certain amount of virtual (paged) or physical (nonpaged) memory. Best used when applications have known or suspected memory leaks.

- **When requested by the application** Recycles worker processes based on requests from applications. ISAPI extension applications can be coded to declare themselves unhealthy using the server support function HSE_REQ_REPORT_UNHEALTHY.

The sections that follow discuss techniques for configuring automatic worker process recycling. When you configure recycling, keep in mind that active worker processes continue to run while IIS starts new worker processes to replace them. Once the new worker processes are started, Http.sys directs incoming requests to the new worker processes and the old worker processes are able to continue handling requests until they shut down. The startup and shutdown processes can be limited by the Startup Time Limit and Shutdown Time Limit values set for the application pool. If these values are set inappropriately, new worker processes might not start and old worker processes might shut down before they've finished processing current requests.

Recycling Automatically by Time and Number of Requests

When applications have known problems running for extended periods of time and handling requests in peak loads, you probably want to configure automatic recycling by time, by number of requests, or both. To configure automatic recycling by time and number of requests, follow these steps:

1. In the IIS snap-in, expand Application Pools, right-click the application pool that you want to configure, and then select Properties. The Recycling tab should be selected by default, as shown in Figure 6-5.

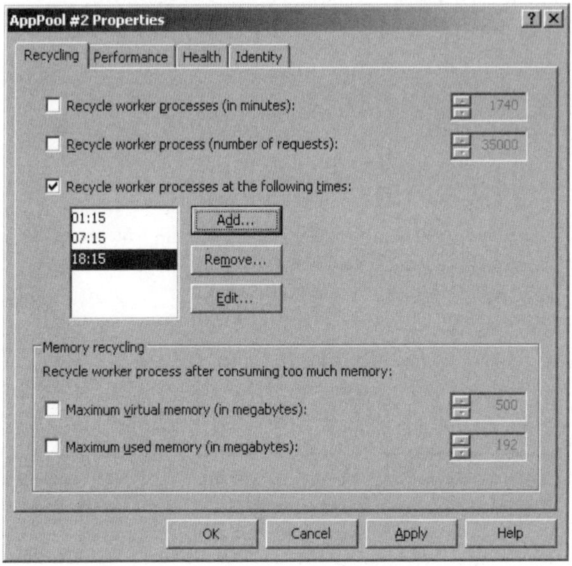

Figure 6-5. *Worker processes can be recycled automatically based on time, number of requests, and memory usage.*

2. To recycle worker processes after a specified period of time, select Recycle Worker Processes (In Minutes) and then type the number of minutes that you want to elapse before worker processes are recycled.

Tip   In most cases it's prudent to schedule worker process recycling to take place at specific off-peak usage times rather than to set hard limits based on runtime or number of requests handled. If you schedule recycling, you control when recycling occurs and can be reasonably sure that it won't occur when the application usage is high.

3. To recycle a worker process after processing a specified number of requests, select Recycle Worker Processes (Number Of Requests) and then type the number of requests that you want to be processed before the worker process is recycled.

4. To recycle worker processes according to a specific schedule, select Recycle Worker Processes At The Following Times. You now have the following options:

   • **Add a scheduled recycle time**   Click Add. Use the Select Time dialog box to set the recycle time on a 24-hour clock. Select the hours or minutes and then use the up and down arrows to set the time. Click OK.

- **Edit a scheduled recycle time**   Click the recycle time you want to change and then click Edit. Change the recycle time using the Select Time dialog box and then click OK.

- **Remove a scheduled recycle time**   Click the recycle time you want to delete and then click Remove.

5. Click OK to apply the settings.

Recycling Automatically by Memory Usage

When applications have known or suspected memory leaks, you probably want to configure automatic recycling based on virtual or physical memory usage. To configure automatic recycling of worker processes based on memory usage, follow these steps:

1. In the IIS snap-in, expand Application Pools, right-click the application pool that you want to configure, and then select Properties. The Recycling tab should be selected by default, as shown previously in Figure 6-5.

2. Virtual memory usage refers to the amount of paged memory written to disk that the worker process uses. To limit virtual memory usage and automatically recycle a worker process when this limit is reached, select Maximum Virtual Memory (In Megabytes) and then type the virtual memory limit in the field provided.

 Tip   In most cases you'll want to establish the baseline virtual and physical memory usage for an application before configuring memory recycling. If you don't do this, you might find that worker processes are being recycled at the most inopportune times, such as when the server is experiencing peak usage loads. A good rule of thumb is to allow physical memory usage of at least 1.5 times the baseline usage you see and to allow virtual memory usage of at least 2 times the physical memory usage. For example, if your baseline memory usage monitoring shows that the application typically uses 128 MB of physical memory and 96 MB of virtual memory, you might allow memory usage up to at least 192 MB for physical memory and 256 MB for virtual memory.

3. Physical memory usage refers to the amount of RAM that the worker process uses. To limit physical memory usage and automatically recycle a worker process when this limit is reached, select Maximum Used Memory (In Megabytes) and then type the memory limit in the field provided.

4. Click OK to apply the settings.

Maintaining Application Health and Performance

Maintaining the health and performance of Web applications is an important part of your job as a Web administrator. Fortunately, IIS has many built-in functions to make this task easier, including:

- CPU monitoring and automated shutdown of runaway worker processes
- Worker process failure detection and recovery
- Request queue limiting to prevent server flooding
- Idle worker process shutdown to recover resources

Each of these tasks is discussed in the sections that follow.

Configuring CPU Monitoring

Typically, when a process consistently uses a high percentage of CPU time, there's a problem with the process. The process might have failed or might be running rampant on the system. You can configure IIS to monitor CPU usage and perform either of the following CPU performance monitoring options:

- **Take No Action** IIS logs the CPU maximum usage event in the System event log but takes no corrective action.

- **Shutdown** IIS logs the event and requests that the application pool's worker processes be recycled, based on the Shutdown Time Limit, set in the Health tab.

To configure IIS to monitor the CPU usage of worker processes, follow these steps:

1. In the IIS snap-in, expand Application Pools, right-click the application pool that you want to configure, and then select Properties.
2. Select the Performance tab as shown in Figure 6-6 on the following page.
3. To allow CPU monitoring, select the Enable CPU Monitoring check box.
4. Use the Maximum CPU Use (Percentage) field to set the percentage of CPU usage that triggers event logging, worker process recycling, or both.

Tip Typically, you'll want to set a value to at least 90 percent. However, to ensure that worker processes are recycled only when they're blocking other processes, you should set the value to 100 percent.

5. Use the Refresh CPU Usage Numbers (In Minutes) field to specify how often IIS checks the CPU usage.

Caution In most cases you won't want to check the CPU usage more frequently than every five minutes. If you monitor the CPU usage more frequently, you might waste resources that could be better used by other processes.

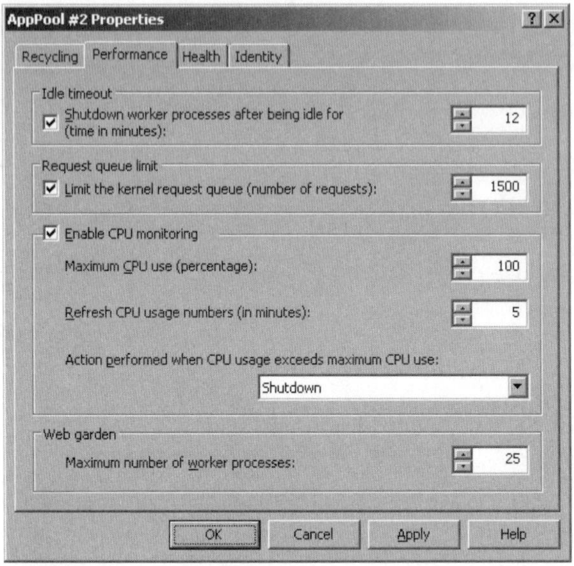

Figure 6-6. *Configure CPU monitoring to ensure that runaway processes are reported or terminated.*

6. If you want to log the CPU usage event but not have IIS attempt to shut down worker processes, set the Action Performed... drop-down list to No Action.

7. If you want to log the CPU usage event and have IIS attempt to shut down the worker processes used by the application pool, set the Action Performed... drop-down list to Shutdown.

8. Click OK.

Configuring Failure Detection and Recovery

You can configure application pools to monitor the health of their worker processes. This monitoring includes processes that detect worker process failure and then take action to recover or prevent further problems on the server.

Central to health monitoring is process pinging. With process pinging, IIS periodically checks to see if worker processes are responsive. This means that the WWW Service (Svchost.exe) sends a ping request at a specified interval to each worker process (W3wp.exe). If a worker process fails to respond to the ping request, either because it doesn't have additional threads available for processing incoming requests or because it's hung up, the WWW service flags the worker process as unhealthy. If the worker process is in an idle but unresponsive state, the WWW service terminates it immediately and a replacement worker process is created. Otherwise, the worker process is marked for recycling as discussed previously in this chapter.

You can also configure application pools for rapid-fail protection. When rapid-fail protection is enabled, the WWW service stops an application pool if there are a certain number of worker process failures in a specified time period. In the standard configuration, five worker process failures within a five-minute interval trigger rapid-fail protection.

To configure health monitoring, complete the following steps:

1. In the IIS snap-in, expand Application Pools, right-click the application pool that you want to configure, and then select Properties.

2. Select the Health tab as shown in Figure 6-7.

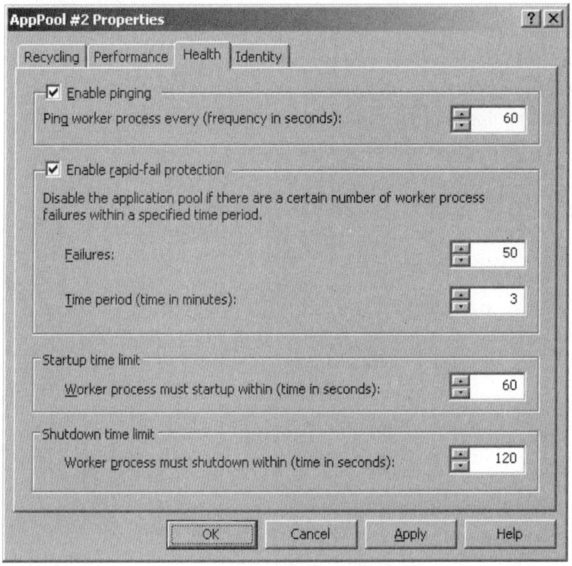

Figure 6-7. *Pinging and rapid-fail protection are important monitoring techniques for detecting and recovering from problems.*

3. To enable process pinging, select the Enable Pinging check box and then use the field provided to set the ping interval in seconds. Here are some guidelines:

   • For low priority applications or applications that are used infrequently, you might want to set an interval of several minutes. This ensures that the responsiveness of applications is checked only as often as necessary.

- On a busy server or a server with many configured applications, you might want to set a longer interval than usual. This will reduce resource usage due to ping requests.

- For high-priority applications where it's critical that applications run and be responsive, you might want to set an interval of one minute (60 seconds) or less. This ensures that the responsiveness of applications is checked frequently.

4. To prevent idle processes from being shut down after a specified period of time, on the Performance tab, clear the Shutdown Worker Processes After Being Idle For check box.

5. Click OK.

Note Keep in mind that these monitoring techniques aren't perfect, but they're helpful. They won't detect all types of failures. For instance, they won't detect problems with the application code, such as conditions that cause the application to return an internal error, and they won't detect a nonblocking error state, such as when the worker process can allocate new threads but is unable to process current threads.

Shutting Down Idle Worker Processes

Although worker processes start on demand based on incoming requests and thus resources are allocated only when necessary, worker processes don't free up the resources they use until they're shut down. In a standard configuration, worker processes are shut down after they've been idle for 20 minutes. This ensures that any physical or virtual memory used by the worker process is made available to other processes running on the server, which is especially important if the server is busy.

Tip Shutting down idle worker processes is a good idea in most instances, and if system resources are at a premium you might even want idle processes shut down sooner than 20 minutes. For example, on a moderately busy server with many configured sites and applications where there are intermittent resource issues, reducing the idle time-out could resolve the problems with resource availability.

Caution Shutting down idle worker processes can have unintended consequences. For example, on a dedicated server with ample memory and resources, shutting down idle worker processes clears cached components out of memory. These components must be reloaded into memory when the worker process starts and requires them, which might make the application seem unresponsive or sluggish.

To configure the idle process shutdown time, follow these steps:

1. In the IIS snap-in, expand Application Pools; right-click the application pool that you want to configure, and then select Properties.
2. Select the Performance tab as shown in Figure 6-8.

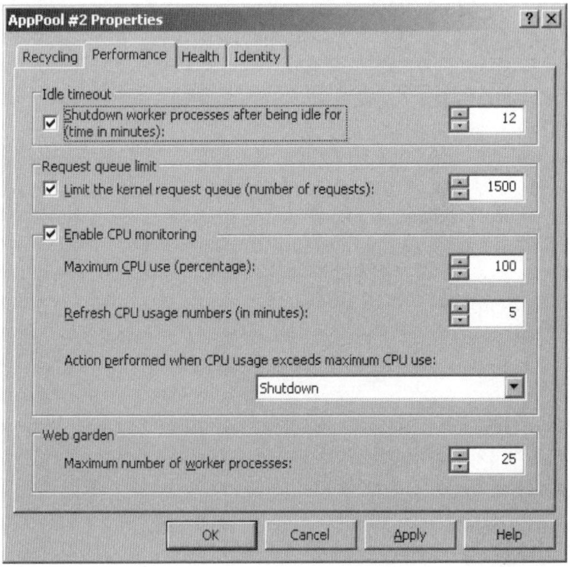

Figure 6-8. *Set the idle time-out to meet your application environment's needs.*

3. To allow idle processes to be shut down after a specified period of time, select the Shutdown Worker Processes After Being Idle For check box and then use the field provided to set the shutdown time in minutes.
4. To prevent idle processes from being shut down after a specified period of time, clear the Shutdown Worker Processes After Being Idle For check box.
5. Click OK.

Limiting Request Queues

When hundreds or thousands of new requests pour into an application pool's request queue, the IIS server can become overloaded and overwhelmed. To prevent this from occurring, you can limit the length of the application pool request queue. Once a queue limit is set, IIS checks the queue size each time before adding a new request to the queue. If the queue limit has been reached, IIS rejects the request and sends the client an HTTP Error 503: Service Unavailable message.

Real World The standard limit for the default application pool is 1000 requests. On a moderately sized server with few applications configured, this might be a good value. However, on a server with multiple CPUs and lots of RAM, this value might be too low. On a server with limited resources or many applications configured, this value might be too high. Here, you might want to use a formula of Memory Size in Megabytes × Number of CPUs × 10 / Number of Configured Applications to determine what the size of the average request queue should be.

This is meant to be a guideline to give you a starting point for consideration and not an absolute rule. For example, on a server with two CPUs, 512 MB of RAM, and eight configured applications, the size of the average request queue limit would be around 1280 requests. You might have some applications configured with request queue limits of 1000 and others with request queue limits of 1500. However, if the same server had only one configured application, you probably wouldn't want to configure a request queue limit of 10,000.

To configure the request queue limit, follow these steps:

1. In the IIS snap-in, expand Application Pools, right-click the application pool that you want to configure, and then select Properties.
2. Select the Performance tab as shown previously in Figure 6-8.
3. To specify and enforce a request queue limit, select the Limit The Kernel Request Queue check box and then use the field provided to specify the request limit.
4. Click OK.

Note Requests that are already queued remain queued even if you change the queue limit to a value that's less than the current queue length. The only consequence here would be that new requests wouldn't be added to the queue until the current queue length is less than the queue limit.

Chapter 7

Managing Web Server Security

In this chapter you'll learn how to manage Web server security. Web servers have different security considerations from those of standard Microsoft Windows servers. On a Web server you have two levels of security:

- **Windows security** At the operating system level, you create user and group accounts, configure access permissions for files and directories, and set policies.

- **IIS security** At the level of Internet Information Services (IIS), you set content permissions, authentication controls, and operator privileges.

Windows security and IIS security can be completely integrated. The integrated security model allows you to use authentication based on user and group membership as well as standard Internet-based authentication. It also allows you to use a layered permission model to determine access rights and permissions for content. Before users can access files and directories, you must ensure that the appropriate users and groups have access at the operating system level. Then you must set IIS security permissions that grant permissions for content that IIS controls.

You'll use the security discussion in this chapter as a stepping-stone to later discussions that cover security for other IIS resources, including File Transfer Protocol (FTP), Simple Mail Transfer Protocol (SMTP), and Network News Transfer Protocol (NNTP). Later discussions focus on what's different rather than rehashing what's already been discussed in this chapter.

Managing Windows Security

Before setting IIS security permissions, you use operating system security settings to do the following tasks:

- Create and manage accounts for users and groups
- Configure access permissions for files and folders
- Set group policies for users and groups

Each of these topics is discussed in the sections that follow.

Working with User and Group Accounts

Microsoft Windows Server 2003 provides user accounts and group accounts. User accounts determine permissions and privileges for individuals. Group accounts determine permissions and privileges for multiple users.

IIS User and Group Essentials

You can set user and group accounts at the local computer level or at the domain level. Local accounts are specific to an individual computer and aren't valid on other machines or in a domain unless you specifically grant permissions. Domain accounts, on the other hand, are valid throughout a domain, which makes resources in the domain available to the account. Typically, you'll use specific accounts for specific purposes:

- Use local accounts when your IIS servers aren't part of a domain or you want to limit access to a specific computer.

- Use domain accounts when the servers are part of a Windows domain and you want users to be able to access resources throughout that domain.

User accounts that are important on IIS servers include:

- **ASPNET**   A local user account used with ASP.NET. This account is used to run the ASP.NET worker process (aspnet_wp.exe) when the server is operating in IIS 5 isolation mode. The account grants the user the right to log on as a service or batch job but denies the right to log on locally or through Terminal Services.

- **Local System**   By default, all IIS and Indexing Service users log on using the local system account. This account has many access rights and privileges. The account grants the user the right to log on locally, as a service, or as a batch job. If you configure worker processes to use this account, those processes have full access to the server system.

- **Local Service**   A limited-privilege account that grants access to the local system only. The account grants the user the right to log on as a batch job. Configure worker processes to use this account only when the processes don't need to access other servers.

- **Network Service**   When the server is running in IIS 6.0 worker process mode, Web applications use this account by default. This account provides fewer permissions and privileges than the Local System account but more than the Local Service account. Specifically, processes running under this account can log on as a service and can also access other servers using the current account credentials.

- **IUSR_*ComputerName***   Internet guest account used by anonymous users to access Internet sites. The account grants the user the right to log on locally or as a batch job. If this account is disabled or locked out, anonymous users won't be able to access Internet services. If this IIS server is in a domain, this account is a member of the Domain Users and Guests groups.

- **IWAM_*ComputerName*** Web application account used with Web applications. The account grants the user the right to log on as a batch job. If this account is disabled or locked out and the server is running in IIS 5 isolation mode, out-of-process applications won't be able to start. With IIS 6 worker process mode, this account is used only when configured for a specific application pool or pools. If this IIS server is in a domain, this account is a member of the Domain Users and IIS_WPG groups.

The IIS_WPG group is used with the Web application account (IWAM_*ComputerName*). This group is created at the local level and at the domain level (if applicable). At the local level, the members of this group are IWAM_*ComputerName*, Local Service, Network Service, and System.

Table 7-1 details key user rights assigned to IIS user and group accounts by default. You can make changes to these accounts if necessary. For added security, you can configure IIS to use different accounts from the standard accounts provided. You can also create additional accounts.

Table 7-1. Important User Rights Assigned by Default to IIS User and Group Accounts

Default User Right	ASPNET	Local Service	Network Service	IUSR	IWAM	IIS_WPG
Access this computer from the network	X	X	X	X	X	X
Adjust memory quotas for a process		X	X		X	
Allow log on locally				X		
Bypass traverse checking		X	X	X	X	
Generate security audits		X	X			
Impersonate a client after authentication	X					X
Log on as a batch job	X	X		X	X	X
Log on as a service	X		X			
Replace a process-level token		X	X		X	

Managing the IIS and Indexing Service Logon Accounts

The IIS and Indexing Service use the local system account to log on to the server. Using the local system account allows the services to run system processes and perform system-level tasks. You really shouldn't change this configuration unless you have very specific needs or want to have strict control over the IIS logon account's privileges and rights. If you decide not to use this account, you can reconfigure the logon account for IIS and Indexing Service by completing the following steps:

1. Start the Computer Management console. Click Start, then Administrative Tools, and finally Computer Management.

2. In the Computer Management console, connect to the computer whose services you want to manage.

3. Expand the Services And Applications node by clicking the plus sign (+) next to it and then select Services.

4. Right-click the service you want to configure and then choose Properties.

5. Select the Log On tab, as shown in Figure 7-1.

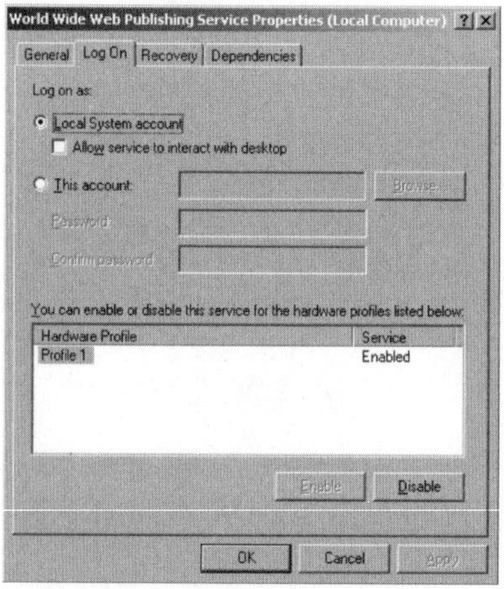

Figure 7-1. *Use the Log On tab to configure the service logon account.*

6. Select Local System Account if the service should log on using the system account (the default for most services).

7. Select This Account if the service should log on using a specific user account. Be sure to type an account name and password in the fields provided. Use the Browse button to search for a user account if necessary.

8. Click OK.

Note If you don't use the local system account, you'll need to assign privileges and logon rights to the account you use. For more information on these and other account permissions, see Chapter 8, "Understanding User and Group Accounts," in the *Microsoft Windows Server 2003 Administrator's Pocket Consultant* (Microsoft Press, 2003).

Managing the Internet Guest Account

You manage the Internet Guest account at the IIS security level and at the Windows security level. At the IIS security level, you specify the user account to use for anonymous access. Normally, you manage anonymous access at the site level, and all files and directories within the site inherit the settings you use. You can change this behavior for individual files and directories as necessary.

To change the configuration of the anonymous user account for all Web sites and directories on a Web server, complete the following steps:

1. In the IIS snap-in, right-click the Web Sites node and then select Properties. This displays a Properties dialog box.

2. Select the Directory Security tab and then click Edit in the Authentication And Access Control frame.

Note When Anonymous Access is enabled, users don't have to log on using a user name and password. IIS automatically logs the user on using the anonymous account information provided for the resource. If the Enable Anonymous Access check box isn't selected, the resource is configured for named account access only. You can enable anonymous access by selecting this check box. However, you should do this only if you're sure the resource doesn't need to be protected.

3. The Username field specifies the account used for anonymous access to the resource. If you desire, type the account name you want to use instead of the existing account or click Browse to display the Select User dialog box.

4. Leave the password blank. You don't need to enter a specific password when anonymous access is enabled.

5. Click OK twice to save your changes.

To change the configuration of the anonymous user account at the site, directory, or file level, complete the following steps:

1. In the IIS snap-in, right-click the Web site, directory, or file you want to work with, and then choose Properties.

2. Follow steps 2 to 5 in the previous listing.

At the Windows security level you perform all other account management tasks, including:

- Enabling or disabling accounts
- Unlocking the account after it has been locked out
- Changing group membership

Managing the Web Application Account

You manage the Web application account at the Windows security and IIS security levels. At the Windows security level you perform all other account management tasks for the Web application account. These tasks include the following:

- Enabling or disabling the account
- Unlocking the account after it has been locked out
- Changing group membership

> **More Info** For details on working with user and group accounts, see Chapter 8, "Understanding User and Group Accounts," Chapter 9, "Creating User and Group Accounts," and Chapter 10, "Managing Existing User and Group Accounts," in the *Microsoft Windows Server 2003 Administrator's Pocket Consultant*.

At the IIS security level, you use the IIS snap-in to specify the account used by applications. Applications can all use the same account or you can assign different accounts as necessary to meet individual requirements. The management technique you use depends on the processing mode of IIS.

Updating the Web Application Account in IIS 6 Worker Process Mode
Once you've started the IIS snap-in, you can manage the account for pooled applications by completing the following steps:

1. Right-click Application Pools to manage the application account globally. Or right-click the specific application pool you want to work with.

2. On the shortcut menu, select Properties and then, in the Properties dialog box, select the Identity tab.

3. As shown in Figure 7-2, you can now use a predefined account or an account you've created as the application account.

4. The drop-down list for predefined accounts has three options: Network Service, Local Service, and Local System. To use one of these accounts, select Predefined and then make the appropriate selection.

5. If you want to use a different account, choose Configurable. By default, the IWAM account is selected. If you want to use this account, you don't need to do anything further. If you want to use a different account, type the account name you want to use instead of the existing account and enter the account password. If you don't know the name of the account, click Browse to display the Select User dialog box. Afterward, you'll need to enter the account password.

6. Click OK.

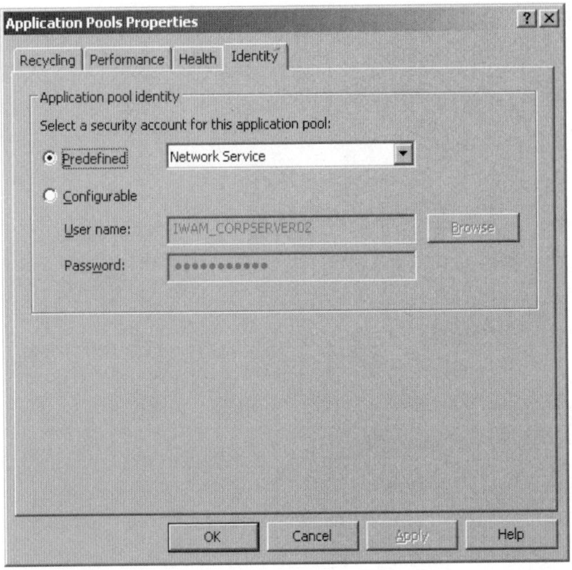

Figure 7-2. *Set the Web application account identity as Predefined or Configurable.*

Updating the Web Application Account in IIS 5 Isolation Mode

Once you've started the Component Services snap-in from the Administrative Tools menu, you can manage the account for pooled applications by completing the following steps:

1. Expand the Component Services node by clicking the plus sign (+) next to it. You should now see the Computers node.

2. If you're connecting to a remote computer, right-click Computers, choose New, and then select Computer. Type the name of the computer you want to manage and then click OK. If you don't know the computer name, click Browse, and then use the Select Computer dialog box to select a computer.

3. Expand the node for the computer and then expand the COM+ Applications node.

4. Right-click IIS Out-Of-Process Pooled Applications, select Properties, and then select the Identity tab.

5. As shown in Figure 7-3 on the following page, you can now use a system account or an account you've created as the application account.

6. The options for system accounts include: Interactive User (not recommended for security reasons), Local Service, Network Service, and Local System. To use one of these accounts, choose System Account and then make the appropriate selection.

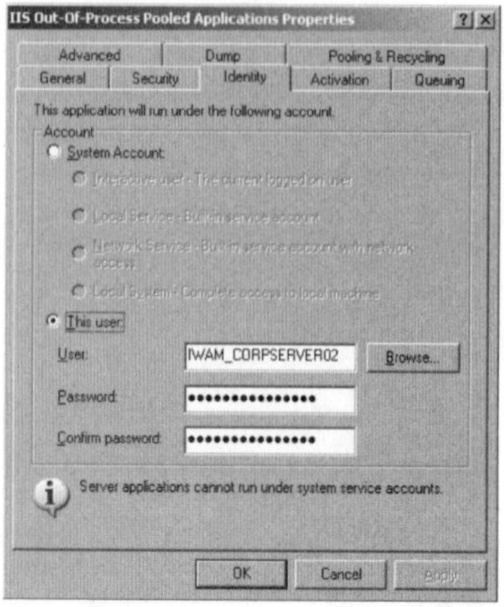

Figure 7-3. *For IIS 5 isolation mode, set the Web application account identity in the Component Services snap-in.*

7. If you want to use a different account, choose This User. By default, the IWAM account is selected. If you want to use this account, you don't need to do anything further. If you want to use a different account, type the account name you want to use instead of the existing account and enter the account password. If you don't know the name of the account, click Browse to display the Select User dialog box. Afterward, you'll need to enter the account password.

8. Click OK.

Working with File and Folder Permissions

Every folder and file used by IIS can have different access permissions. You set these access permissions at the Windows security level. The sections that follow provide an overview of permissions. You'll learn the basics, including how to view and set permissions.

File and Folder Permission Essentials

The basic permissions you can assign to files and folders are summarized in Table 7-2. The basic permissions are created by combining special permissions, such as traverse folder and execute file, into a single easily managed permission. If you want granular control over file or folder access, you can use advanced permissions to assign special permissions individually. For more information on special permissions, see Chapter 14, "Data Sharing, Security, and Auditing," in the *Microsoft Windows Server 2003 Administrator's Pocket Consultant.*

Table 7-2.   File and Folder Permissions Used by Windows Server 2003

Permission	Meaning for Folders	Meaning for Files
Read	Permits viewing and listing files and subfolders	Permits viewing or accessing the file's contents
Write	Permits adding files and subfolders	Permits writing to a file
Read & Execute	Permits viewing and listing files and subfolders as well as executing files; inherited by files and folders	Permits viewing and accessing the file's contents as well as executing the file
List Folder Contents	Permits viewing and listing files and subfolders as well as executing files; inherited by folders only	N/A
Modify	Permits reading and writing of files and subfolders; allows deletion of the folder	Permits reading and writing of the file; allows deletion of the file
Full Control	Permits reading, writing, changing, and deleting files and subfolders	Permits reading, writing, changing, and deleting the file

Whenever you work with file and folder permissions, you should keep the following in mind:

- Read is the only permission needed to run scripts. Execute permission applies only to executables.

- Read access is required to access a shortcut and its target.

- Giving a user permission to write to a file but not to delete it doesn't prevent the user from deleting the file's contents. A user can still delete the contents.

- If a user has full control over a folder, the user can delete files in the folder regardless of the permission on the files.

IIS uses the following users and groups to configure file and folder access:

- **Administrators**   Allows administrators to access IIS resources.

- **Creator Owner**   Allows the account that created a resource to access the resource.

- **System**   Allows the local system to access the resource.

- **Users**   Allows named accounts to access the resource (including the Internet Guest and Web Application accounts, which are user accounts).

- **Internet Guest Account**   Allows you to set specific permission for IUSR or the other accounts you've configured as Internet guests. To prevent malicious users from gaining access to files and modifying them, you can deny this account Write permission on important directories.

When you grant Read permission to these users and groups, anyone who has access to your Internet or intranet Web site will be able to access the files and folders. If you want to restrict access to certain files and folders, you should set specific user and group permissions and then use authenticated access rather than anonymous access. With authenticated access, IIS authenticates the user before granting access and then uses the Windows permissions to determine what files and folders the user can access.

As you evaluate the permissions you might want to use for files and folders used by IIS, refer to Table 7-3. This table provides general guidelines for assigning permissions based on content type.

Table 7-3. General Guidelines for Permissions Based on Content Type

File Type	File Extension	Permission
CGI scripts and executables	.exe, .dll, .cmd	Users (Execute) Administrators (Full Control) System (Full Control)
Dynamic content	.asp, .aspx, .vbs, .js, .pl	Users (Read Only) Administrators (Full Control) System (Full Control)
Include files	.inc, .shtm, .shtml, .stm	Users (Read Only, Deny Write) Administrators (Full Control) System (Full Control)
Static content	.txt, .rtf, .gif, .jpg, .jpeg, .htm, .html, .doc, .ppt, .xls	Users (Read Only, Deny Write) Administrators (Full Control) System (Full Control)

Instead of setting permissions on individual files, you should organize content by type in subdirectories. For example, if your Web site used static, script, and dynamic content, you could create subdirectories called WebStatic, WebScripts, and WebDynamic. You would then store static, script, and dynamic content in these directories and assign permissions on a per directory basis. Don't forget to consider whether it's prudent to specifically deny Write permission.

Viewing File and Folder Permissions

You view security permissions for files and folders by completing the following steps:

1. In Windows Explorer, right-click the file or folder you want to work with.

2. From the shortcut menu, select Properties, and then, in the Properties dialog box, select the Security tab.

3. In the Group Or User Names list box, select the user, contact, computer, or group whose permissions you want to view. If check boxes in the Permissions For list are dimmed, it means the permissions are inherited from a parent object.

Setting File and Folder Permissions

You can set permissions for files and folders by completing the following steps:

1. In Windows Explorer, right-click the file or folder you want to work with.

2. From the shortcut menu, select Properties, and then, in the Properties dialog box, select the Security tab, shown in Figure 7-4.

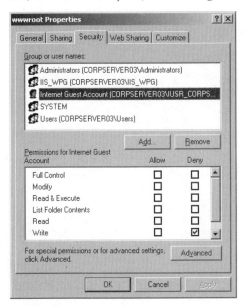

Figure 7-4. *Use the Security tab to configure basic permissions for the file or folder.*

3. Users or groups that already have access to the file or folder are listed in the Group Or User Names list box. You can change permissions for these users and groups by doing the following:
   - Select the user or group you want to change.
   - Use the Permissions For list box to grant or deny access permissions.

Note Inherited permissions are dimmed. If you want to override an inherited permission, select the opposite permission. For example, if a user is granted a permission you don't want them to have due to inheritance, you could override the inheritance by explicitly denying the permission in the Permissions For list box.

4. Click Add to set access permissions for additional users, contacts, computers, or groups. This displays the Select Users, Computers, Or Groups dialog box. You can select computer accounts and configure their permissions only if you are part of a domain.

5. Use the Select Users, Computers, Or Groups dialog box to select the users, computers, or groups for which you want to set access permissions. Click OK.

6. In the Group Or User Names list box, select the user, computer, or group you want to configure, and then use the fields in the Permissions For list box to allow or deny permissions. Repeat for other users, computers, or groups.

7. Click OK when you're finished.

Working with Group Policies

Group policies are another aspect of Windows security that you need to understand. You'll use group policies to automate key security administration tasks and to manage IIS resources more effectively. Site, domain, and organizational unit group policies can be configured only for computer, group, and user accounts that are part of a domain.

Group Policy Essentials

Group policies provide central control over privileges, permissions, and capabilities of users and computers. You can think of a policy as a set of rules that you can apply to multiple computers and to multiple users. Because computers can be a part of larger organizational groups, you can apply multiple policies. The order in which policies are applied is extremely important in determining which rules are enforced and which rules are not.

When multiple policies are in place, the policies are applied in the following order:

1. Windows NT 4 policies from Ntconfig.pol files

2. Local group policies that affect the local computer only

3. Site group policies that affect all computers that are part of the same site, which can include multiple domains

4. Domain polices that affect all computers in a specific domain

5. Organizational unit policies that affect all computers in an organizational unit

6. Child organizational unit policies that affect all computers in a subcomponent of an organizational unit

As successive policies are applied, the rules in those policies override the rules set in the previous policy. For example, domain policy settings have precedence over the local group policy settings. Exceptions allow you to block, override, and disable policy settings; a discussion of exceptions is outside the scope of this book.

Policy settings are divided into two broad categories: those that affect computers and those that affect users. Computer policies are applied during system startup. User policies are applied during logon. You configure and manage policies for sites, domains, and organizational units with the Group Policy snap-in. To access this snap-in, follow these steps:

1. For sites, start the Active Directory Sites And Services console from the Administrative Tools menu.

2. For domains, start the Active Directory Users And Computers console from the Administrative Tools menu.

3. In the console root, right-click the site, domain, or organizational unit in which you want to create or manage a group policy. Then, from the shortcut menu, select Properties. This opens a Properties dialog box.

4. In the Properties dialog box, select the Group Policy tab. As Figure 7-5 shows, existing policies are listed in the Group Policy Object Links list.

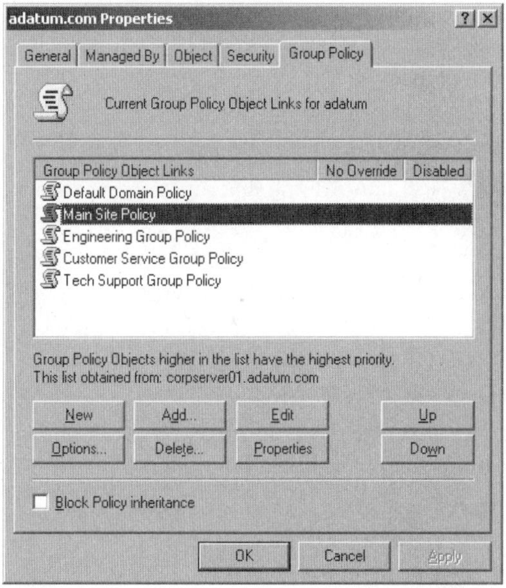

Figure 7-5. *Use the Group Policy tab of the Properties dialog box to create and edit policies.*

5. You can now create a new policy, edit an existing policy, or change the priority of a policy as follows:

   - To create a new policy, click New. You can now configure the policy.

   - To edit an existing policy, select the policy and then click Edit. You can now edit the policy.

   - To change the priority of a policy, use the Up or Down button to change its position in the Group Policy Object Links list.

You manage local group policies for an individual computer by completing the following steps:

1. Open the Run dialog box by clicking Start and then clicking Run.
2. Type **MMC** in the Open field and then click OK. This opens the Microsoft Management Console (MMC).
3. In the MMC, click File, and then click Add/Remove Snap-In. This opens the Add/Remove Snap-In dialog box.
4. In the Standalone tab, click Add.
5. In the Add Standalone Snap-In dialog box, click Group Policy Object Editor and then click Add. This opens the Select Group Policy Object dialog box.
6. Click Finish to edit the local policy on your computer or Browse to find the local policy on another computer.
7. Click Close, and then click OK.
8. You can now manage the local policy on the selected computer.

Group policies for passwords, account lockout, and auditing are essential to your Web server's security. Guidelines for password policies are as follows:

- Set a minimum password age for all accounts. I recommend 2-3 days.
- Set a maximum password age for all accounts. I recommend 30 days.
- Set a minimum password length. I suggest the minimum be set at eight characters to start.
- Enable secure passwords by enforcing password complexity requirements.
- Enforce password history. Use a value of 5 or more.

Guidelines for account lockout polices include the following:

- Set an account lockout threshold. In most cases accounts should be locked after five bad attempts.
- Set account lockout duration. In most cases you'll want to lock out accounts indefinitely.
- Reset the lockout threshold after 30 to 60 minutes.

Guidelines for auditing include the following:

- Audit system event success and failure
- Audit logon event success and failure
- Audit failed object access attempts
- Audit successful and failed policy changes
- Audit successful and failed account management
- Audit successful and failed account logon

Techniques for managing these policies are examined in the sections that follow. For more detailed information on policy management, see Chapter 4, "Automating Administrative Tasks, Policies, and Procedures," in *Microsoft Windows Server 2003 Administrator's Pocket Consultant.*

Setting Account Policies for IIS Servers

You can set account policies by completing the following steps:

1. Access the group policy container you want to work with as described in the section of this chapter entitled "Working with Group Policies." Expand the Computer Configuration node, then Windows Settings, then Security Settings, and finally Account Policies.

2. As shown in Figure 7-6, you can now manage account policies. For domains, sites, and organizational units, you'll have Password Policy, Account Lockout Policy, and Kerberos Policy nodes. For local computers, you'll have Password Policy and Account Lockout Policy nodes only.

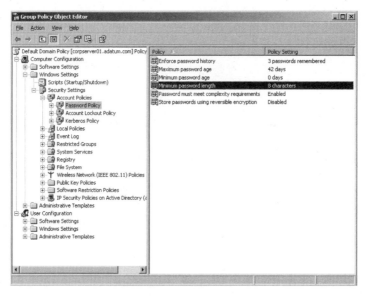

Figure 7-6. *Set policies for passwords and general account use.*

3. To configure a policy, double-click its entry or right-click it and select Properties. This opens a Properties dialog box for the policy.

4. For a local policy, the Properties dialog box is similar to the one shown in Figure 7-7 on the following page. The policy for the computer is displayed. Use the fields provided to configure the local policy. Skip the remaining steps; they apply to global group policies.

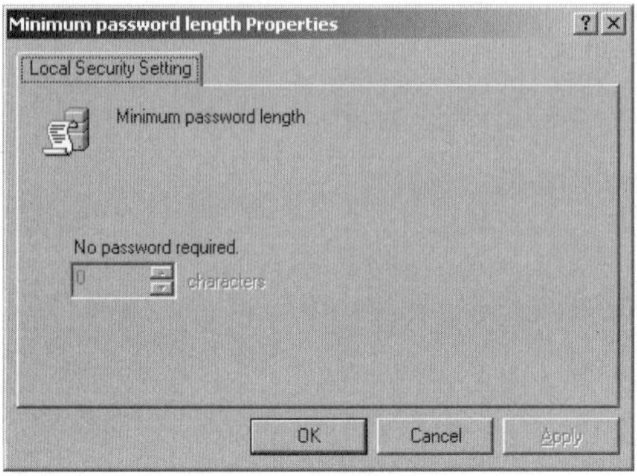

Figure 7-7. *With local policies, you'll see the current policy setting.*

5. For a site, domain, or organizational unit, the Properties dialog box is similar to the one shown in Figure 7-8.

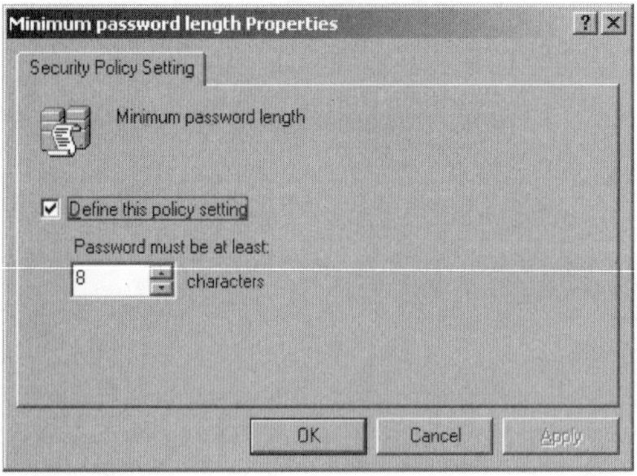

Figure 7-8. *Define and configure global group policies using the Properties dialog box.*

6. All policies are either defined or not defined—that is, they're either configured for use or not configured for use. A policy that isn't defined in the current container could be inherited from another container.

7. Select or clear the Define This Policy Setting check box to determine whether a policy is defined.

8. Policies can have additional fields for configuring the policy. Often, these fields have the following option buttons:

   - **Enabled** Turns on the policy restriction
   - **Disabled** Turns off the policy restriction

Setting Auditing Policies

Auditing is the best way to track what's happening on your IIS server. You can use auditing to collect information related to resource usage, such as file access, system logon, and system configuration changes. Whenever an action occurs that you've configured for auditing, the action is written to the system's security log, where it's stored for your review. You access the security log from Event Viewer.

You can set auditing policies by completing the following steps:

1. Access the group policy container you want to work with as described in the section of this chapter entitled "Working With Group Policies." Expand the Computer Configuration node, Windows Settings, Security Settings, and Local Policies. Then select Audit Policy.

2. You can now have access to the following auditing options:

   - **Audit Account Logon Events**   Tracks events related to user logon and logoff.

   - **Audit Account Management**   Tracks account management. Events are generated anytime user, computer, or group accounts are created, modified, or deleted.

   - **Audit Directory Service Access**   Tracks access to the Active Directory service. Events are generated whenever users or computers access the directory.

   - **Audit Logon Events**   Tracks events related to user logon, logoff, and remote connections to network systems.

   - **Audit Object Access**   Tracks system resource usage for files, directories, shares, printers, and Active Directory objects.

   - **Audit Policy Change**   Tracks changes to user rights, auditing, and trust relationships.

   - **Audit Privilege Use**   Tracks the use of user rights and privileges, such as the right to back up files and directories, but doesn't track system logon or logoff.

   - **Audit Process Tracking**   Tracks system processes and the resources they use.

   - **Audit System Events**   Tracks system startup, shutdown, and restart, as well as actions that affect system security or the security log.

3. To configure an auditing policy, double-click its entry or right-click it and select Properties. This opens a Properties dialog box for the policy.

4. Select Define These Policy Settings, and then select the Success check box, the Failure check box, or both. Success logs successful events, such as successful logon attempts. Failure logs failed events, such as failed logon attempts.

5. Click OK when you're finished.

Managing IIS Security

After setting operating system security, use IIS security to:

- Set the Web server and execute permissions for content
- Configure Web Distributed Authoring and Versioning (WebDAV)
- Configure authentication methods
- Control access by IP address or Internet domain name

Each of these topics is discussed in the sections that follow. It's important to note that IIS 6 doesn't use the concept of Web site operators.

Setting Web Server Permissions

Sites, directories, and files have permissions in IIS in addition to the Windows security settings. These permissions are set the same for all users. This means you can't set different permissions for different users at the Web content level. You can, however, create secure areas of your Web site and then use Windows file and folder permissions to provide the necessary additional controls.

Understanding Web Server Permissions

The permissions you assign to Web content are applied in combination with the authentication methods and access restrictions currently being enforced for the resource. This means that user requests must meet the requirements for Web content permissions, authentication, and access before they're executed. Keep in mind that all directories and files within the site inherit permissions set at the site level and that you can override site-level permissions by setting permissions on individual directories and files.

Web server permissions also set the permissible actions for Web Distributed Authoring and Versioning (WebDAV). WebDAV publishing allows remote users to publish, lock, and manage resources on a Web server through a Hypertext Transfer Protocol (HTTP) connection. Windows 2000, Microsoft Office 2000, and Internet Explorer 5 or later are all WebDAV-enabled. If you have WebDAV-enabled applications, use Web server permissions to determine permitted actions for these applications and their users. You'll find more detailed information on WebDAV in the "Configuring Distributed Authoring and Versioning" section of this chapter.

You can set Web server permissions in two ways:

- **Globally** You configure global permissions using the Web Sites Properties dialog box. When you set Web server permissions globally, you must also specify how these properties are inherited. When a site or directory has settings that conflict with permission changes you've made, you're given the opportunity to override the site or directory permissions with the global permissions. If you override permissions, the global permissions are applied to the site or directory and its contents. If you don't override permissions, the original settings for the site or directory are maintained.

- **Locally** You configure local permissions at the site, directory, or file level. As with global permissions, local permissions for sites and directories can be inherited. Because of this, when you make permission changes that conflict with existing permissions on a subdirectory, you're given the opportunity to override the site or directory permissions with the local permissions. If you override permissions, the local permissions are applied to the site or directory and its contents. If you don't override permissions, the original settings for the site or directory are maintained.

IIS manages inheritance of permissions changes at the node level. Because of this, the top-level directory for a site and the individual directories within a site are seen as separate nodes. If you apply changes to a site node, the permissions are applied to the site's root folder and to files in this folder. Changes aren't applied to subdirectories within the site unless you specify that they should be.

Setting Web Server Permissions Globally

To manage Web server permissions globally, complete the following steps:

1. In the IIS snap-in, right-click the Web Sites node and then select Properties. This displays a Properties dialog box.

2. As shown in Figure 7-9 on the following page, select the Home Directory tab, and then use the following fields to set the Web server permissions that you want sites and directories on this computer to inherit:

   - **Script Source Access** Allows users to access source code, including scripts in Active Server Pages (ASP). This option is available only when Read permission is also selected. If Write permission is also selected, users will be able to write to the source file.

Note Be careful when granting Script Source Access on production servers that are on the Internet. With this permission, anyone will be able to read the contents of your scripts, and this might open your servers to mischievous users. Because of this, you should enable this feature only in a directory that requires users to authenticate themselves before being granted access.

   - **Read** Allows users to view the resource. For a directory, this grants the user access to the directory. For a file, this means the user can read the file and display it.

   - **Write** Allows users to change the resource. For a directory, this allows the user to create or publish files. For a file, this allows the user to change the content.

Note You should grant Write permission to only a limited number of resources. If possible, you should create separate subdirectories that contain only writeable files, or you should write-enable individual files rather than entire directories. To execute application files, you must assign Read permission to all files used by the application or to the site or directory used to store these files. If the application posts content to a file on the site, you must also assign Write permission (but you should limit this to a specific file or directory).

- **Directory Browsing** Allows users to view a list of files and sub-directories within the designated directory.

- **Log Visits** Used with server logging to log requests related for resource files.

- **Index This Resource** Allows the Indexing Service to index the resource. Indexing allows users to perform keyword searches for information contained in the resource.

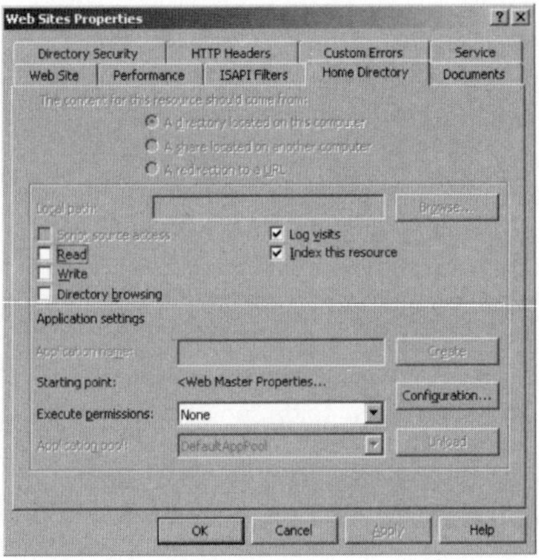

Figure 7-9. *Manage Web server permissions globally using the Home Directory tab on the Web Sites Properties dialog box.*

3. If the selected resource is part of an IIS application, you might also want to set the level of program execution that's allowed for the application. To do this, use the Execute Permissions selection list to choose one of the following options:

- **None** Only static files, such as .html or .gif files, can be accessed.

- **Scripts Only** Only scripts, such as ASP scripts, can be run.

- **Scripts And Executables** All file types can be accessed and executed.

4. Click Apply. Before applying permission changes, IIS checks the existing permissions in use for all Web sites and directories within Web sites. Each time a site or directory node uses a different value for a permission, an Inheritance Overrides dialog box is displayed. Use this dialog box to select the site and directory nodes, which should use the new permission value, and then click OK.

Setting Web Server Permissions Locally

To set content permissions for a site, directory, or file, complete the following steps:

1. In the IIS snap-in, right-click the site, directory, or file that you want to work with and then select Properties.

2. Select the Home Directory, Directory, or Virtual Directory tab as appropriate. This displays the dialog box shown in Figure 7-10 on the following page. Then use the following fields to set the permissions for the selected resource:

   • **Script Source Access**   Allows users to access source code, including scripts in Active Server Pages (ASP). This option is available only when Read permission is also selected. If Write permission is also selected, users will be able to write to the source file.

Note   Be careful when granting Script Source Access on production servers that are on the Internet. With this permission, anyone will be able to read the contents of your scripts, and this might open your servers to mischievous users. Because of this, you should enable this feature only in a directory that requires users to authenticate themselves before being granted access.

   • **Read**   Allows users to view the resource. For a directory, this grants the user access to the directory. For a file, this means the user can read the file and display it.

   • **Write**   Allows users to change the resource. For a directory, this allows the user to create or publish files. For a file, this allows the user to change the content.

Note   You should grant Write permission to only a limited number of resources. If possible, you should create separate subdirectories that contain only writeable files, or you should write-enable individual files rather than entire directories. To execute application files, you must assign Read permission to all files used by the application or to the site or directory used to store these files. If the application posts content to a file on the site, you must also assign Write permission (but you should limit this to a specific file or directory).

   • **Directory Browsing**   Allows users to view a list of files and subdirectories within the designated directory.

- **Log Visits** Used with server logging to log requests related for resource files.

- **Index This Resource** Allows the Indexing Service to index the resource. Indexing allows users to perform keyword searches for information contained in the resource.

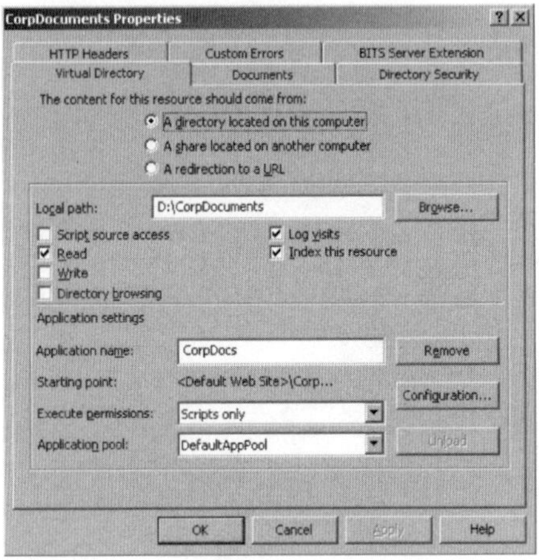

Figure 7-10. *Manage permissions for individual sites, virtual directories, and files using the Properties dialog box for that site, virtual directory, or file.*

3. If the selected resource is part of an IIS application, you might also want to set the level of program execution that's allowed for the application. To do this, use the Execute Permissions selection list to choose one of the following options:

   - **None** Only static files, such as .html or .gif files, can be accessed.

   - **Scripts Only** Only scripts, such as ASP scripts, can be run.

   - **Scripts And Executables** All file types can be accessed and executed.

4. Click Apply. Before applying permission changes, IIS checks the existing permissions in use for all sites and directories within the site you are working with. Each time a site or directory node uses a different value for a permission, an Inheritance Overrides dialog box is displayed. Use this dialog box to select the site and directory nodes, which should use the new permission value, and then click OK.

Configuring Distributed Authoring and Versioning

WebDAV is an extension to the HTTP 1.1 protocol that allows remote users to manage Web server resources. Using WebDAV, clients can:

- Perform standard file operations, such as cut, copy, and paste

- Create and edit files and their properties at the operating system level

- Create and edit directories and their properties at the operating system level
- Lock and unlock resources to allow only one person to modify a resource while allowing multiple users to read the resource
- Search the contents and properties of files in a directory

Because WebDAV is integrated into IIS, all Web site directories on your IIS server are accessible for distributed authoring and versioning. This makes it easy to access and publish documents to your IIS server.

Permitting Distributed Authoring and Versioning

You control the permitted actions for WebDAV application using the standard Web server permissions. The Web server permissions that are directly applicable to WebDAV are:

- **Script Source Access** Allows WebDAV clients to download source files for scripts.

- **Read** Allows WebDAV clients to view and run files and subdirectories within the WebDAV directory.

- **Write** Allows WebDAV clients to create files or directories and to write to existing files.

- **Directory Browsing** Allows WebDAV clients to view the contents of directories.

- **Index This Resource** If your Web server is running the Indexing Service, WebDAV clients can search the directory using special search utilities.

To publish to a directory and see a list of files in that directory, users need Read, Write, and Browse access permissions. If users need to update script files, you must also grant Script Source Access permission. To protect your Web content, you should grant these permissions only in directories that require users to authenticate themselves. For example, you could create a directory called For-Publishing, configure permissions on this directory so that anonymous access isn't allowed, and then configure the necessary authoring and publishing permissions (Read, Write, and Browse).

When you allow script source access, you need to ensure that your source code and executables are protected. Any extension designated in the application mappings for the site is considered a script source file. Files with extensions that aren't mapped are treated as static .html or text files. Files with the .dll or .exe extension are also treated as static files, unless the Scripts And Executables permission is set, which means they could be overwritten even if Script Source Access isn't enabled. When the Scripts And Executables permission is set, .dll and .exe files aren't treated as static files—they're treated as executable files, and they can only be overwritten when Script Source Access is enabled.

Accessing and Publishing Documents with WebDAV

Windows 2000 or later and Office 2000 and later products are all WebDAV-enabled, and you can connect to Web directories on IIS servers quite easily. In Windows Explorer, select My Network Places and then click the Web directory you want to work with. If the directory isn't shown, you can connect to it by completing the following steps:

1. In Windows Explorer, select My Network Places and then double-click Add Network Place in the right pane. This starts the Add Network Place Wizard. Click Next.

2. After the wizard gathers the necessary information, ensure Choose Another Network Location is selected and then Click Next again.

3. In the Add Network Place Wizard, type a Universal Naming Convention (UNC) path of the WebDAV directory to which you want to connect, such as \\Corpserver01\CorpWWW, or a Uniform Resource Locater (URL) path, such as *http://www.adatum.com/CorpWWW* or *ftp://ftp.adatum.com/CorpFTP*

4. Click Next, type a descriptive name for the directory, and then click Next again.

5. Click Finish. Windows automatically accesses the directory.

Once you've created a network place for the WebDAV directory, you can easily publish documents to it from Office 2000 or later. Simply create a document in any Office application and then follow these steps:

1. Select Save As from the File menu and then, in the left column of the Save As dialog box, click My Network Places.

2. Select the shortcut for the WebDAV directory you want to use or type the UNC path, and then click OK.

You can also connect to WebDAV directories through Internet Explorer 5 on Windows 95 or later operating systems. Simply complete the following steps:

1. Start Internet Explorer 5 or later, and then display the Open dialog box by selecting Open from the File menu.

2. In the Open combo box, type the UNC path for the WebDAV directory to which you want to connect.

3. Select the Open As Web Folder check box and then click OK.

Setting Authentication Modes

Authentication modes control access to IIS resources. You can use authentication to allow anonymous access to public resources, to create secure areas within a Web site, and to create controlled access Web sites. When authentication is enabled, IIS uses the account credentials supplied by a user to determine whether or not the user has access to a resource and to determine which permissions the user has been granted.

Understanding Authentication

Five authentication modes are available. These modes are:

- **Anonymous Authentication**   With anonymous authentication, IIS automatically logs users on with an anonymous or guest account. This allows users to access resources without being prompted for user name and password information.

- **Basic Authentication**   With basic authentication, users are prompted for logon information. When it's entered, this information is transmitted unencrypted (clear text) across the network. If you've configured secure communications on the server as described in the "Working with SSL" section of Chapter 8, "Managing Microsoft Certificate Services and SSL," you can require clients to use Secure Sockets Layer (SSL). When you use SSL with basic authentication, the logon information is encrypted before transmission.

- **Integrated Windows Authentication**   With integrated Windows authentication, IIS uses standard Windows security to validate the user's identity. Instead of prompting for a user name and password, clients relay the logon credentials that users supply when they log on to Windows. These credentials are fully encrypted without the need for SSL, and they include the user name and password needed to log on to the network. Only Internet Explorer browsers support this feature.

- **Digest Authentication**   With digest authentication, user credentials are transmitted securely between clients and servers. Digest authentication is a feature of HTTP 1.1 and uses a technique that can't be easily intercepted and decrypted. This feature is available only when IIS is configured on a Windows Server 2003 server, and part of a Windows 2000 Server, or later, Active Directory domain. The client is required to use a domain account, and the request made by Internet Explorer 5.0 or later.

- **.NET Passport authentication**   With .NET Passport authentication, the user credentials aren't checked directly. Instead, the server checks for a Passport Authentication ticket as one of the cookie files on the user's computer. If the ticket exists and has valid credentials, the server authenticates the client. If the ticket doesn't exist or the credentials aren't valid, the user is redirected to the Passport Logon Service. Once the user logs on to the Passport service, the user is directed back to the original URL.

By default, both anonymous authentication and Integrated Windows Authentication are enabled for IIS resources. Because of this, the default authentication process looks like this:

1. IIS attempts to access the resource using the Internet Guest account. If this has the appropriate access permissions, the user is allowed to access the resource.

2. If validation of the credentials fails or the account is disabled or locked, IIS attempts to use the user's current account credentials. If the credentials can be validated and the user has the appropriate access permissions, the user is allowed to access the resource.

3. If validation fails or the user doesn't have appropriate access permissions, the user is denied access to the resource.

As with Web server permissions, you can apply authentication on a global or local basis. You configure global authentication modes using the master Web Sites Properties. You set local authentication modes using site, directory, or file properties. Anytime you make changes that conflict with existing settings, IIS displays a dialog box that allows you to specify which resources inherit the new settings.

Before you start working with authentication modes, you should keep the following in mind:

- When you combine anonymous access with authenticated access, users have full access to resources that are accessible to the Internet Guest account. If this account doesn't have access to a resource, IIS attempts to authenticate the user using the authentication techniques you've specified. If these authentication methods fail, the user is denied access to the resource.

- When you disable anonymous access, you're telling IIS that all user requests must be authenticated using the authentication modes you've specified. Once the user is authenticated, IIS uses the user's account credentials to determine access rights.

- When you combine basic authentication with integrated or digest authentication, Internet Explorer attempts to use integrated Windows authentication or digest authentication before using basic authentication. This means users who can be authenticated using their current account credentials won't be prompted for a user name and password.

In addition, before you can use digest authentication, you must enable reversible password encryption for each account that will connect to the server using this authentication technique. IIS and the user's Web browser use reversible encryption to manage secure transmission and unencryption of user information. To enable reversible encryption, follow these steps:

1. Start Active Directory Users And Computers. Click Start, choose Administrative Tools, and then Active Directory Users And Computers.

2. Double-click the user name that you want to use with digest authentication.

3. On the Account tab, under Account Options, select Store Password Using Reversible Encryption.

4. Click OK.

5. Repeat steps 1 to 4 for each account that you want to use with digest authentication.

Enabling and Disabling Authentication

You can enable or disable anonymous access to resources at the server, site, directory, or file level. If you enable anonymous access, users can access resources without having to authenticate themselves (provided the Windows permissions on the resource allow this). If you disable anonymous access, users must authenticate themselves before accessing resources. Authentication can occur automatically or manually depending on the browser used and the account credentials the user previously entered.

You can enable or disable authentication at the server level by completing the following steps:

1. In the IIS snap-in, right-click the Web Sites node and then select Properties. This displays a Properties dialog box.

2. Select the Directory Security tab and then click Edit in the Authentication And Access Control frame. This displays the Authentication Methods dialog box shown in Figure 7-11.

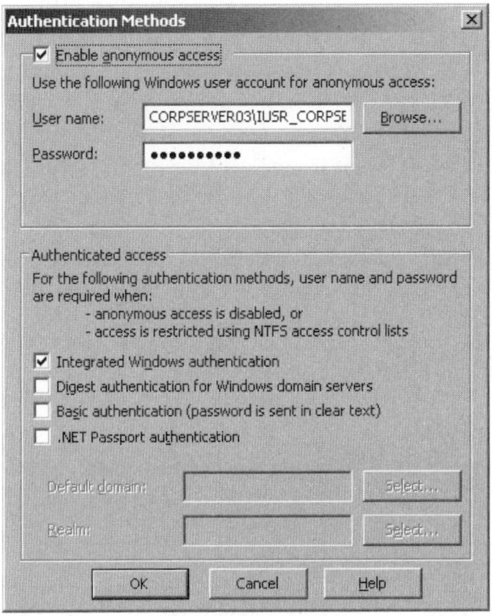

Figure 7-11. *Use the Authentication Methods dialog box to enable or disable authentication methods to meet your organization's needs. With basic authentication, it's often helpful to set a default domain as well.*

3. To enable anonymous access, select the Enable Anonymous Access check box. To disable anonymous access, clear this check box.

4. Configure the authentication methods you want to use. Keep the following in mind:

   - Disabling basic authentication might prevent some clients from accessing resources remotely. Clients can log on only when you enable an authentication method that they support.

- A default domain isn't set automatically. If you enable basic or .NET Passport authentication, you can choose to set a default domain that should be used when no domain information is supplied during the logon process. Setting the default domain is useful when you want to ensure that clients authenticate properly.

- With basic and digest authentication, you can optionally define the realm or realms that can be accessed. Essentially, a realm is a level within the metabase hierarchy. The default realm name is the computer name, which provides access to all levels within the metabase hierarchy. You could limit this by defining specific realms, such as W3SVC (for the Web Sites root) or W3SVC/1/root (for the root of the first Web instance).

- If you enable .NET Passport authentication, all other authentication settings are ignored. As a result, the server will only authenticate using this technique for the specified resource.

5. Click OK. Before applying changes, IIS checks the existing authentication methods in use for all Web sites and directories within Web sites. If a site or directory node uses a different value, an Inheritance Overrides dialog box is displayed. Use this dialog box to select the site and directory nodes that should use the new setting, and then click OK.

You can enable or disable authentication at the site, directory, or file level by completing these steps:

1. In the IIS snap-in, right-click the site, directory, or file that you want to work with and then select Properties. This displays a Properties dialog box.

2. Select the Directory Security tab and then click Edit in the Authentication And Access Control frame. This displays the Authentication Methods dialog box shown previously in Figure 7-11.

3. Follows steps 3-5 as listed in the previous procedure.

Configuring IP Address and Domain Name Restrictions

By default, IIS resources are accessible to all IP addresses, computers, and domains, which presents a security risk that might allow your server to be misused. To control use of resources, you might want to grant or deny access by IP address, network ID, or domain. As with other Web server settings, you can apply restrictions through the master Web Sites properties or through the properties for individual sites, directories, and files.

- Granting access allows a computer to make requests for resources but doesn't necessarily allow users to work with resources. If you require authentication, users still need to authenticate themselves.

- Denying access to resources prevents a computer from accessing those resources. Therefore, users of the computer can't access the resources—even if they could have authenticated themselves with a user name and password.

You can establish or remove restrictions globally through the Web Sites node by completing the following steps:

1. In the IIS snap-in, right-click the Web Sites node and then select Properties. This displays a Properties dialog box.

2. Select the Directory Security tab and then click Edit in the IP Address And Domain Name Restrictions frame This displays the IP Address And Domain Name Restrictions dialog box shown in Figure 7-12.

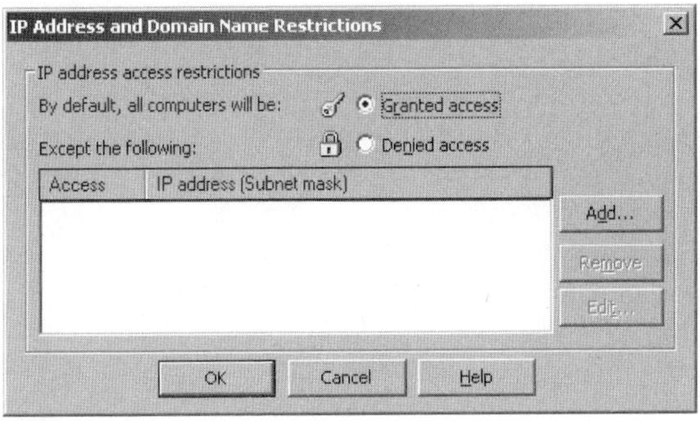

Figure 7-12. *You can grant or deny access by IP address, network ID, and domain.*

3. Select Granted Access to grant access to all computers and deny access to specific computers, groups of computers, or domains.

4. Select Denied Access to deny access to all computers and grant access to specific computers, groups of computers, or domains.

5. Create the Access list. Click Add and then, in the Access dialog box, specify Single Computer, Group Of Computers, or Domain Name. The settings you can specify for each option are as follows:

   - For a single computer, type the IP address for the computer, such as 192.168.5.50.

   - For groups of computers, type the subnet address, such as 192.168.0.0, and the subnet mask, such as 255.255.0.0.

   - For a domain name, type the fully qualified domain name (FQDN), such as *eng.microsoft.com*.

Note When you grant or deny by domain, IIS must perform a reverse Domain Name System (DNS) lookup on each connection to determine whether the connection comes from the domain. These reverse look-ups can severely increase response times for the first query each user sends to your site.

6. If you want to remove an entry from the Access list, select the related entry in the Access list and then click Remove.

7. Click Apply.

You can establish or remove restrictions at the site, directory, or file level by completing these steps:

1. In the IIS snap-in, right-click the site, directory, or file that you want to work with and choose Properties. This displays a Properties dialog box.

2. Select the Directory Security tab and then click Edit in the IP Address And Domain Name Restrictions frame. This displays the IP Address And Domain Name Restrictions dialog box shown previously in Figure 7-12.

3. Select Granted Access to grant access to all computers and deny access to specific computers, groups of computers, or domains.

4. Select Denied Access to deny access to all computers and grant access to specific computers, groups of computers, or domains.

5. Create the Access list. Click Add and then, in the Access dialog box, specify Single Computer, Group Of Computers, or Domain Name. The settings you can specify for each option are as follows:

   - For a single computer, type the IP address for the computer, such as 192.168.5.50.

   - For groups of computers, type the subnet address, such as 192.168.0.0, and the subnet mask, such as 255.255.0.0.

   - For a domain name, type the FQDN, such as *eng.microsoft.com*.

6. If you want to remove an entry from the Access list, select it and then click Remove.

7. Click Apply.

More Tips for Enhancing Web Server Security

Your Web server is only as secure as you make it. To improve your server's security, read the additional tips provided here and apply the ones that make sense for your server environment.

Using Firewalls

Maintaining your Web server's security is an ongoing task that requires continual vigilance. To shield your Web servers from attacks, you need a firewall, such as the Microsoft Internet Security and Acceleration (ISA) Server or a hardware-based firewall solution. When you install a firewall, close all ports that you aren't using and open only ports that are needed.

The ports you'll want to open depend on the types of IIS resources you're using. FTP uses ports 20 and 21. SMTP uses port 25 and might require port 53 for DNS resolution. HTTP uses ports 80 and 443. NNTP uses ports 119 and 563.

Renaming the Administrator Account

The Administrator account is a known account that has extensive privileges on your Web server. Malicious users often target this account in an attempt to take control of the server. You can deter malicious users by changing the name of this account. Simply select a new name for the account and then rename it using either Active Directory Users and Computers or the Computer Management console, depending on your environment. You might want to tell other administrators in your company the new name for the administrator account.

Disabling the Default Web Site

In IIS 6, the default Web site normally doesn't have the open security issues that were in previous versions and caused most administrators to delete the default site and create a new one. Here, the default site is installed with good security precautions in mind. As a result, you probably don't need to delete the default Web site as you would with previous IIS installations.

If you want, however, you can still disable the default site. To do this, follow these steps:

1. In the IIS snap-in, right-click the default Web site, and then select Stop.
2. Exit the IIS snap-in to save this configuration state.
3. From now on, the default Web site should be stopped when you or other administrators access the IIS snap-in.

Note You can also delete the default Web site to prevent its use in the future.

Disabling Remote Administration from the Web

As you know from previous discussions, Web sites can be managed remotely through a browser. Administrators connect to IIS through the Administration Web site. If you want to tightly control access to your server, you should disable remote administration from the Web and allow access to the server only through the IIS snap-in.

To disable remote administration from the Web, you should do the following:

1. In the IIS snap-in, right-click the Administration Web site and then select Stop.
2. Exit the IIS snap-in to save this configuration state.
3. From now on, the Administration site should be stopped when you or other administrators access the IIS snap-in.

Disabling Directory Browsing

Directory browsing allows users to see the contents of directories. Most users don't need to see directory contents, so you should disable directory browsing globally. To do this, clear this Web server permission in the Web Sites Properties dialog box.

Creating Legal Notices

Every user who logs on to the Web server locally or through a telnet session should see a legal notice that tells the user that this is a private computer system and its use is restricted to authorized personnel only. Legal notices have a caption and message text. You set the caption using the Registry key:

HKEY_LOCAL_MACHINE

```
\Software
\Microsoft
\Windows
\CurrentVersion
\Policies
\System
\LegalNoticeCaption
```

You set the message text using the Registry key:

HKEY_LOCAL_MACHINE

```
\Software
\Microsoft
\Windows
\CurrentVersion
\Policies
\System
\LegalNoticeText
```

You can modify both keys using the Registry Editor, a Windows script, or configured local or domain policies. You might want to use text, as in the following example:

```
This is a private system. Use of this system is restricted to
authorized personnel only. Violators will be prosecuted!
```

Applying Service Packs, Hot Fixes, and Templates

Microsoft regularly provides service packs and hot fixes for the Windows operating system. To maintain the server's security, you should apply the service packs and hot fixes to production servers as soon as you've had a chance to review and test these updates on similarly configured test servers.

Microsoft also publishes security templates that you can apply to your Web servers. Security templates are available in all Windows Server 2003 installations.

You can preview existing templates and create your own templates using the Security Templates snap-in. You apply a template and analyze its security constraints using the Security Configuration And Analysis snap-in. You can access these snap-ins by completing the following steps:

1. Open the Run dialog box by clicking Start and then clicking Run.
2. Type **MMC** in the Open field and then click OK. This opens the Microsoft Management Console (MMC).
3. In MMC, click File and then click Add/Remove Snap-In. This opens the Add/Remove Snap-In dialog box.
4. On the Standalone tab, click Add.
5. In the Add Standalone Snap-In dialog box, click Security Templates and then click Add.
6. Click Security Configuration And Analysis and then click Add.
7. Close the Add Standalone Snap-In dialog box by clicking Close and then click OK.

The security templates that you'll want to use are securews and hisecws. Securews is a template for Web servers that need strong security. Hisecws is a template for Web servers that need very strong security. As shown in Figure 7-13, these templates configure security for the following:

- Password, account lockout, and Kerberos policies
- Auditing, user rights assignment, and security options policies
- Event logs, system services, and file system permissions
- Registry keys for the local machine and the current user

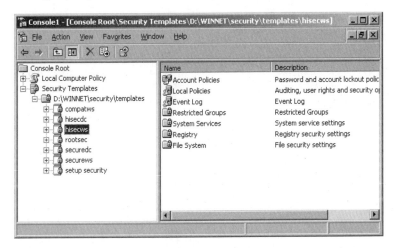

Figure 7-13. *Use the Security Templates snap-in to access existing security templates and to create new ones.*

After you select the template that you want to use, you should go through each setting that the template will apply and evaluate how the setting will affect your environment. If a setting doesn't make sense, you should modify or delete it as appropriate. When you're ready to configure and analyze the settings, complete the following steps:

1. Access the Security Configuration And Analysis snap-in in an MMC.

2. Right-click the Security Configuration And Analysis node and then select Open Database. This displays the Open Database dialog box.

3. Type a new database name in the File Name field and then click Open.

4. The Import Template dialog box is displayed. Select the security template that you want to use and then click Open.

5. Right-click the Security Configuration And Analysis node and then choose Analyze Computer Now. When prompted to set the error log path, click OK. The default path should work just fine.

6. Wait for the snap-in to complete the analysis of the template. Afterward, review the findings and update the template as necessary. You can view the error log by right-clicking the Security Configuration And Analysis node and choosing View Log File.

7. When you're ready to apply the template, right-click the Security Configuration And Analysis node and choose Configure Computer Now. When prompted to set the error log path, click OK. The default path should be just fine.

8. View the configuration error log by right-clicking the Security Configuration And Analysis node and choosing View Log File. Note any problems and act as necessary.

Checking for Malicious Input in Forms and Query Strings

The text that users type into forms might contain values designed to cause problems on your system. If you pass this input directly to a script or ASP page, you might allow a malicious user to gain access to the system and cause problems. To prevent this, you should check all input before passing it to a script or ASP page.

One way to ensure that input contains only text and numbers is to remove characters that aren't alphanumeric. You can do this with the following Microsoft Visual Basic Scripting Edition (VBScript) example:

```
'Start a regular expression
Set reg = New RegExp

'Check for characters that aren't 0-9a-zA-Z or '_'
reg.Pattern = "\W+"

'Remove invalid characters from input string
goodString = reg.Replace(inputString, "")
```

If you want users to be able to enter punctuation but don't want to permit possible malicious input, you should check for and remove the pipe character (|). The pipe character is used to string commands together, which could allow a user to execute a command on your server. The following command removes the pipe character and all text that follows it from an input string:

```
'Start a regular expression
Set reg = New RegExp

'Check for the pipe character
reg.Pattern = "^(.+)\|(.+)"

'Remove pipe character and any text after it
goodString = reg.Replace(inputString, "$1")
```

Many other techniques for checking user input before using it are available. See the Microsoft TechNet at *http://www.microsoft.com/technet/* for more information.

Removing Unused Application Mappings

Application mappings are used to specify the Internet Server Application Programming Interface (ISAPI) extensions and CGI programs that are available to applications. IIS is preconfigured to support many common ISAPI applications, including ASP, Internet Database Connector, and Index Server. If your Web site doesn't use some of these ISAPI applications, you can enhance security by prohibiting all related extensions of a specific type or by removing individual application mappings that are not needed.

To prohibit a specific type of application extension from being used, select the extension type in the Web Service Extensions node of the IIS snap-in and then click Prohibit.

To remove individual application mappings globally for all Web sites on a server, follow these steps:

1. In the IIS snap-in, right-click the Web Sites node and then select Properties. This displays a Properties dialog box.

2. Select the Home Directory tab and then click Configuration in the Application Settings frame. This displays the Application Configuration dialog box.

3. In the Mappings tab, under Application Extensions, select the application mappings that you want to remove and then click Remove. When prompted to confirm the action, click Yes.

4. Click Apply.

Chapter 8

Managing Microsoft Certificate Services and SSL

The focus of the previous chapter was on Web server security. This chapter shows how you can extend Web server security using Microsoft Certificate Services and Secure Sockets Layer (SSL). Certificate Services and SSL provide an extra layer of security to your Web server.

You use Certificate Services and SSL to protect sensitive information, such as passwords, credit card numbers, or payment information. Certificate Services and SSL protect sensitive information by encrypting the data sent between client browsers and your server. *Encryption* is the process of encoding information using a mathematical algorithm that makes it difficult for anyone other than the intended recipient to view the original information.

Internet Information Services (IIS) transfers encrypted data to a client browser using the SSL protocol. With SSL, servers and clients can use certificates to provide proof of identity prior to establishing a secure connection. Once a connection is established, clients and servers use the secure SSL channel to transfer information. This information is encrypted using a technique that the clients and servers can interpret to extract the original information.

Understanding SSL

IIS supports SSL protocol version 3. SSL 3 enables encrypted data transfers between client browsers and Web servers. The sections that follow provide an overview on how SSL works and how it's used.

Using SSL Encryption

As stated previously, encryption is the process of encoding information using a mathematical algorithm that makes it difficult for anyone other than the intended recipient to view the original information. The encryption algorithm uses a mathematical value, called a *key*, to scramble the data so that it can be recovered only by using the key.

Many techniques are available for encrypting information so that it can be exchanged. Some encryption techniques use a combination of public and private keys—one key can be shared and the other key can't. Some encryption techniques use shared secret keys that are transferred between authenticated systems. SSL uses a technique called *public key encryption*, which combines private, public, and shared secret (session) keys.

In public key encryption there are three keys:

- A public key available to any application that requests it
- A private key known only to its owner
- A session key created using public and private key data

IIS uses the public key encryption component in SSL to establish sessions between clients and servers. You should use SSL whenever you want to provide additional protection for data that's transferred between clients and servers. Some specific instances in which you might want to use Certificate Services and SSL are the following:

- When you remotely manage the Web server using the Administration Web site or operator administration pages
- When your Web site has secure areas that contain sensitive company documents
- When your Web site has pages that collect sensitive personal or financial information from visitors
- When your Web site processes orders for goods or services and you collect credit or other personal information from customers

With SSL, users connect to Web pages using a secure Uniform Resource Locator (URL) that begins with *https://*. The *https* designator tells the browser to try to establish a secure connection with IIS. SSL connections for Web pages are made on port 443 by default, but you can change the port designator as necessary. As you set out to work with SSL, keep in mind that you can't use host headers with SSL. With SSL, Hypertext Transfer Protocol (HTTP) requests are encrypted, and the host header name within the encrypted request can't be used to determine the correct site to which a request must be routed.

After the client browser contacts the server using a secure URL, the server sends the browser its public key and server certificate. Next, the client and server negotiate the level of encryption to use for secure communications. The server always attempts to use the highest level of encryption it supports. Once the encryption level is established, the client browser creates a session key and uses the server's public key to encrypt this information for transmission. Anyone intercepting the message at this point wouldn't be able to read the session key—only the server's private key can decrypt the message.

The IIS server decrypts the message sent by the client using its private key. The SSL session between the client and the server is now established. The session key can be used to encrypt and decrypt data transmitted between the client and server.

To recap, secure SSL sessions are established using the following technique:

1. The user's Web browser contacts the server using a secure URL.
2. The IIS server sends the browser its public key and server certificate.
3. The client and server negotiate the level of encryption to use for the secure communications.
4. The client browser encrypts a session key with the server's public key and sends the encrypted data back to the server.
5. The IIS Server decrypts the message sent by the client using its private key, and the session is established.
6. Both the client and the server use the session key to encrypt and decrypt transmitted data.

Using SSL Certificates

Not reflected in the previous discussion is the way in which SSL uses certificates. You can think of a certificate as an identity card that contains information needed to establish the identity of an application or user over a network. Certificates enable Web servers and users to authenticate one another before establishing a connection. Certificates also contain keys that need to establish SSL sessions between clients and servers.

In most cases certificates used by IIS, Web browsers, and Certificate Services conform to the X.509 standard. For this reason, they're often referred to as X.509 certificates. Different versions of the X.509 standard have been issued (see *RFC 3280* for more information on this standard). These versions have been extended from time to time as well. Two types of X.509 certificates are used:

- Client certificates, which contain identifying information about a client
- Server certificates, which contain identifying information about a server

Certificate authorities issue both types of certificates. A *certificate authority (CA)* is a trusted agency responsible for confirming the identity of users, organizations, and their servers and then issuing certificates that confirm these identities. Before issuing a client certificate, CAs require that you provide information that identifies you, your organization, and the client application you're using. Before issuing a server certificate, CAs require that you provide information that identifies your organization and the server you're using.

This chapter focuses on server certificates. When you're choosing CAs to create your server certificates, you have several options. If you use Certificate Services, your organization can act as its own CA. When you act as your own CA, you enable SSL on your Web server using the following process:

1. Install Certificate Services on a server in the domain and then generate the root CA certificate.
2. Generate a certificate request file for each Web site on your server that has a unique name, and then use the certificate request files to create server certificates for your Web sites.

3. Install the certificates and then enable SSL on each applicable Web site.

4. Client browsers won't recognize and trust your root CA certificate. To get browsers to trust the root CA, the user must install the certificate in the browser's authorities store.

5. Initiate SSL connections by using URLs that begin with *https://*.

You can also use third-party CAs—and there's an advantage to doing so. The third-party authority can vouch for your identity, and dozens of vendors are already configured as trusted CAs in Web browsers. In Microsoft Internet Explorer 5 or later, you can obtain a list of trusted authorities by completing the following steps:

1. From the Tools menu, select Internet Options. This displays the Internet Options dialog box.

2. Select the Content tab and then click Certificates. This displays the Certificates dialog box.

3. Select the Trusted Root Certification Authorities tab. You should now see a list of trusted root CAs.

When you use a trusted third-party authority, you enable SSL on your Web server using a different process from when you act as your own root CA. This process is as follows:

1. Generate a certificate request file for each Web site on your server that has a unique name.

2. Submit the certificate request files to a trusted third-party authority, such as Entrust, Equifax, Valicert, or Verisign. The CA will process the requests and send you certificates.

3. Install the certificates and then enable SSL on each applicable Web site.

4. Client browsers initiate SSL sessions using a secure URL beginning with *https://*.

Regardless of whether you act as your own CA or use a trusted CA, you must still manage the server certificates, and you use Certificate Services to do this. Server certificates can expire or be revoked, if necessary. For example, if your organization is an Internet service provider (ISP) that issues its own certificates, you might want your customers' server certificates to expire annually. This forces customers to update their certificate information at least once a year to ensure that it's current. You also might want to revoke a certificate when a customer cancels service.

Understanding SSL Encryption Strength

An SSL session's encryption strength is directly proportional to the number of bits in the session key. This means that session keys with a greater number of bits are considerably more difficult to crack and, thus, are more secure.

The two most commonly used encryption levels for SSL sessions are 40-bit and 128-bit. Encryption at the 40-bit level is adequate for most needs, including e-commerce. Encryption at the 128-bit level provides added protection for sensitive personal and financial information. Most versions of Microsoft Windows Server 2003 shipped in the United States are configured with 128-bit encryption. Export versions of Windows Server 2003 have 40-bit encryption. To upgrade a server from 40-bit encryption to 128-bit encryption, you must install the 128-bit upgrade patch, which is available from Microsoft.

Don't confuse the encryption level for SSL sessions (the strength of the session key expressed as bits) with the encryption level for SSL certificates (the strength of the certificate's public and private keys expressed as bits). Most encryption keys (public and private) have a bit length of 512 or 1024. Domestic U.S. and export versions of most applications and operating systems support encryption keys with a bit length of 512. However, encryption keys with a bit length of 1024 or greater aren't supported in the export versions of most applications and operating systems.

When a user attempts to establish an SSL session with your Web server, the user's browser and the server use the bit length of their encryption keys to determine the strongest level of encryption possible. If the encryption keys use 512 bits, the level of encryption is set to 40 bits. If the encryption keys use 1024 bits, the level of encryption is set to 128 bits. Other key bit lengths and encryption levels are available.

Working with Microsoft Certificate Services

Microsoft Certificate Services allows you to issue and revoke digital certificates. You can use these certificates to enable SSL sessions and to authenticate the identity of your intranet, extranet, or Internet Web site.

Understanding Certificate Services

Certificate Services is a Windows service that runs on a designated certificate server. Certificate servers can be configured as one of four types of CAs:

- **Enterprise root CA** The certificate server at the root of the hierarchy for a Windows domain. It's the most trusted CA in the enterprise and must be a member of the Active Directory service and have access to it.

- **Enterprise subordinate CA** A certificate server that will be a member of an existing CA hierarchy. It can issue certificates but must obtain its own CA certificate from the enterprise root CA.

- **Stand-alone root CA** The certificate server at the root of a non-enterprise hierarchy. It's the most trusted CA in its hierarchy and doesn't need access to Active Directory.

- **Stand-alone subordinate CA**   A certificate server that will be a member of an existing non-enterprise hierarchy. It can issue certificates but must obtain its own CA certificate from the stand-alone root CA in its hierarchy.

Certificate servers don't have to be dedicated to Certificate Services and can be the same servers you use for Web publishing. However, it's a good idea to designate specific servers in your domain that will act as certificate servers and to use these servers only for that purpose.

Security Alert   To safeguard the root CA from malicious users, you should create multiple levels in the CA hierarchy. For example, in an enterprise, you'd set up an enterprise root CA and then set up one or more enterprise subordinate CAs. You'd then issue certificates to users and computers only through the subordinate CAs. This safeguard should help ensure that the root CA's private key can't be easily compromised.

Once you install Certificate Services on a computer, you're limited in what you can and can't do with the computer. Specifically, you can't do the following:

- You can't rename a computer running Certificate Services.

- You can't change the domain membership of a computer running Certificate Services.

You manage Certificate Services using a Microsoft Management Console (MMC) snap-in called the Certification Authority snap-in and a Web-based Active Server Pages (ASP) application that can be accessed in a standard Web browser. In the snap-in, you have full control over Certificate Services. The Web-based application, on the other hand, is primarily used to retrieve Certificate Revocation Lists (CRLs), to request certificates, and to check on pending certificates. You can access the Web-based application from the following URL: *http://hostname/certsrv*.

Figure 8-1 shows the Certification Authority snap-in's main window. As you can see, five containers are under the root authority. These containers are used as follows:

- **Revoked Certificates**   Contains all certificates that have been issued and then revoked.

- **Issued Certificates**   Contains all certificates that have been approved and issued by the Certificate Services administrator.

- **Pending Requests**   Contains all pending certificate requests for this CA. If you're an administrator on the certificate server, you can approve requests by right-clicking them and selecting Issue. The default configuration is to process requests automatically, which means that no administrator involvement is required.

- **Failed Requests** Contains any declined certificate requests for this CA. If you're an administrator on the certificate server, you can deny requests by right-clicking them and selecting Deny.

Note The label for the root node of the snap-in is set to the name of the CA. In the example, the CA name is Corporate Root CA.

- **Certificate Templates** Contains a set of certificate templates that are configured for different intended purposes. These templates provide basic rules for the various types of certificates. Additional certificate templates can be installed by right-clicking Certificate Templates, selecting New, and then clicking Certificate Template To Issue. (Certificate Templates are available only with enterprise root and subordinate CAs.)

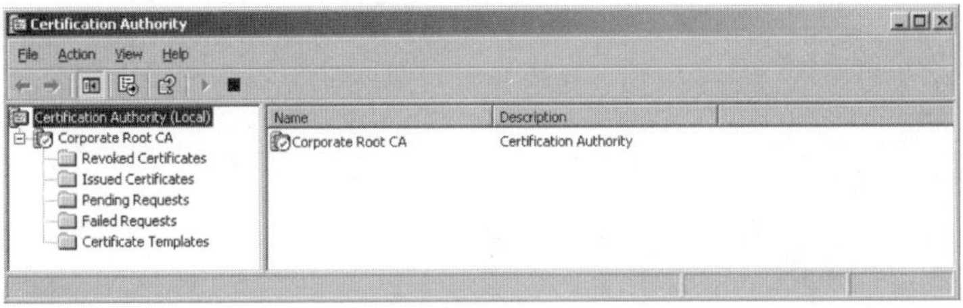

Figure 8-1. *Use the Certification Authority snap-in to manage Certificate Services.*

Installing Certificate Services

If the server isn't running IIS and you want to be able to retrieve CRLs to request certificates or to check on pending certificates through a browser, you must install IIS prior to installing Certificate Services. To install Certificate Services, complete the following steps:

1. Log on to the certificate server using an account with Administrator privileges or, if you're creating an enterprise CA, Enterprise Administrator privileges.

2. Click Start, choose Control Panel, and then Add Or Remove Programs. This displays the Add Or Remove Programs dialog box.

3. Start the Windows Components Wizard by clicking Add/Remove Windows Components.

4. Select the Certificate Services check box. When prompted to confirm the action, click Yes and then click Next.

5. As shown in Figure 8-2 on the following page, select the CA type. The options are as follows:

    - **Enterprise Root CA** Establishes the root CA in an Active Directory domain. This option is available only if your server participates in a domain.

- **Enterprise Subordinate CA** Establishes a subordinate CA that will be a member of an existing hierarchy. This option also requires connectivity to Active Directory.

- **Stand-Alone Root CA** Establishes a stand-alone root CA that doesn't require connectivity to Active Directory.

- **Stand-Alone Subordinate CA** Establishes a subordinate CA that will be a member of an existing hierarchy. The server doesn't require connectivity to Active Directory.

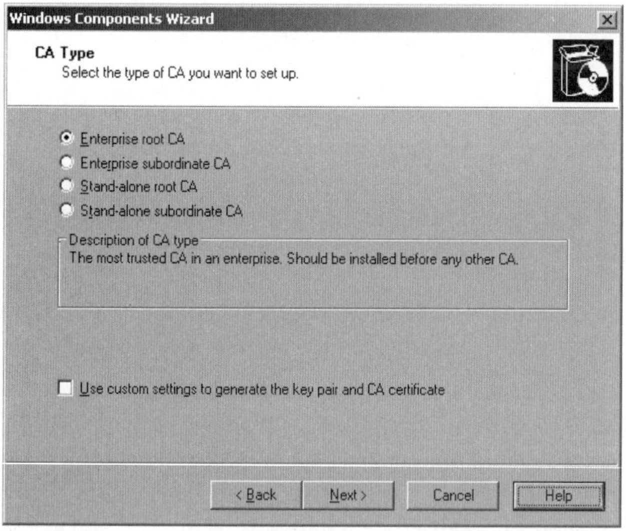

Figure 8-2. *Choose the type of CA that you want to install.*

Note Select the Use Custom Settings... check box if you want to choose the cryptographic service provider (CSP) and hashing algorithms used to generate keys. In most cases, however, the default values are acceptable.

6. As shown in Figure 8-3, enter the common name for the CA, such as Corporate Root CA, and set the CA certificate's expiration date. Most CA certificates are valid for at least five years. Click Next.

7. Specify the storage location for the configuration database and log. By default, the certificate database and log are stored in the \%SystemRoot%\ System32\CertLog folder. Click Next.

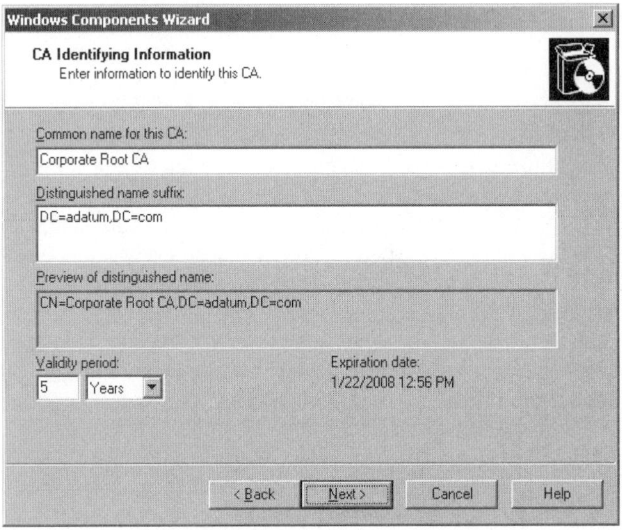

Figure 8-3. *Identify the CA and set an expiration date for the root CA certificate.*

Tip   If hundreds or thousands of users use your CA, you might want the database and log files to be stored on separate drives. By placing these files on separate drives, you can improve the CA's performance and responsiveness. In all cases the database and log files should be on NTFS volumes. This ensures that the security permissions can be set to restrict access to these files by user account.

8. If IIS is running on the certificate server, Windows will need to shut down the related services before continuing. Click Yes when prompted to do this. The Windows Components Wizard begins installing and configuring Certificate Services.

9. Click Finish to complete the process. If you installed Certificate Services on a computer running IIS, you can configure these services for Web access (see the following section of this chapter).

Accessing Certificate Services in a Browser

When you install Certificate Services on a computer running IIS, the default (or primary) Web site is updated so that you can perform key certificate tasks through a Web browser. These tasks include:

- Retrieving CRLs
- Requesting certificates
- Checking on pending certificates

The structures that make Web-based requests possible are files configured for use in three virtual directories:

- **CertSrv**   Contains files necessary for Web-based access to Certificate Services and is located in \%SystemRoot%\System32\CertSrv by default. This directory is set up as a pooled application called CertSrv.

- **CertControl**   Contains files necessary for controlling Certificate Services and is located in \%SystemRoot%\System32\CertSrv\CertControl by default.

- **CertEnroll**   Contains files necessary for controlling Certificate Services and is located in \%SystemRoot%\System32\CertSrv\CertEnroll by default.

> **Tip**   If these directories aren't available for some reason, you can create virtual directories that map aliases to their physical locations. In a command prompt, type **certutil –vroot**. The command-line utility Certutil creates the necessary virtual directories for you and maps them to their default locations.

Once you've configured Web-based access to Certificate Services, you can access these services by typing **http://*hostname*/certsrv/,** where *hostname* is the Domain Name System (DNS) or NetBIOS name of the host server, such as *ca.microsoft.com* or CASrvr. Figure 8-4 shows the main page for Certificate Services.

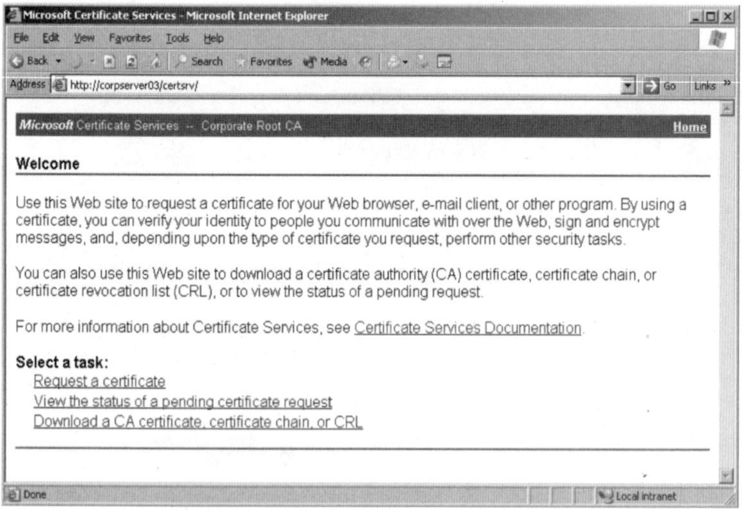

Figure 8-4. *Use the Web-based interface to retrieve CA certificates or revocation lists, to request certificates, or to check on pending certificates.*

Starting and Stopping Certificate Services

Microsoft Certificate Services runs as a Windows service on the certificate server. You can stop and start this service on a local system by completing the following steps:

1. Start the Certification Authority snap-in by clicking Certification Authority in Administrative Tools.
2. Right-click the root node for the CA, and then select All Tasks.
3. Select Stop Service to stop Certificate Services.
4. Select Start Service to start Certificate Services.

You can stop and start services on a remote system by completing the following steps:

1. Start the Certification Authority snap-in by clicking Certification Authority in Administrative Tools, then right-click the Certification Authority node.
2. To display the Certification Authority dialog box, from the shortcut menu, select Retarget Certification Authority.
3. As shown in Figure 8-5, select Another Computer, type the name of the computer to which you want to connect and then click Finish. You can also type the server's Internet Protocol (IP) address or fully qualified domain name (FQDN), or click Browse to search for the computer.

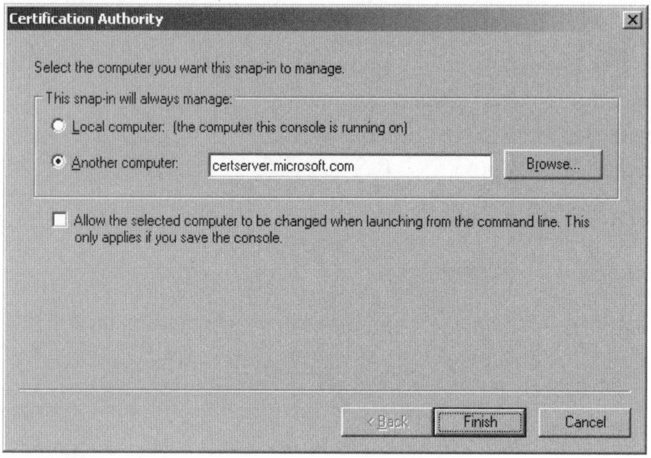

Figure 8-5. *You can connect to both local and remote CAs.*

4. In the Certification Authority snap-in, right-click the root node for the CA and then select All Tasks.
5. Select Stop Service to stop Certificate Services.
6. Select Start Service to start Certificate Services.

Backing Up and Restoring the CA

If your organization publishes its own CA, you should back up the CA information routinely. Backing up the CA information ensures that you can recover critical CA data, including:

- CA private key and certificate
- CA configuration information
- CA log and pending request queue

You can perform two types of backups:

- **Standard**   Creates a full copy of certificate database, logs, and pending request queues.
- **Incremental**   Creates a partial copy of certificate database, logs, and pending request queues. This copy contains only the changes since the last standard backup.

In a very large CA implementation, you can perform incremental backups of the database, logs, and queues by selecting Perform Incremental Backups. To use incremental backups, you must do the following:

1. First perform a standard backup.
2. Perform successive incremental backups at later dates.

When you use incremental backups, you must also restore incrementally. To do this, complete the following steps:

1. Stop Certificate Services.
2. Restore the last standard backup.
3. Restore each incremental backup in order.
4. Start Certificate Services.

Creating CA Backups

To back up the CA information on your certificate server, complete the following steps:

1. Create a folder that Certificate Services can use to store the backup information. This directory must be empty, and you should create it on the local machine where Certificate Services is installed.
2. Start the Certification Authority snap-in, right-click the root node for the CA, choose All Tasks, and then select Back Up CA. This starts the Certification Authority Backup Wizard.

Note   Certificate Services must be running when you back up the CA. If the service isn't running, you'll see a prompt asking you if you want to start the service. Click OK.

3. Click Next and then select the items you want to back up, as shown in Figure 8-6. The options are:

   • Private Key And CA Certificate
   • Certificate Database And Certificate Database Log

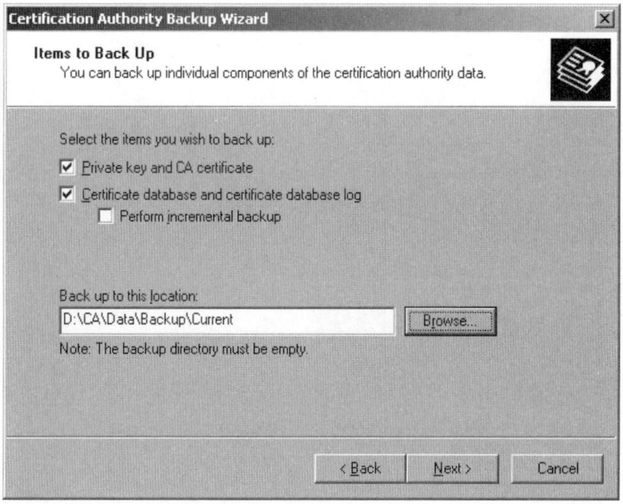

Figure 8-6. *Specify the certification items that you want to back up.*

4. If this is an incremental backup, select Perform Incremental Backup. Incremental backups can be performed only when backing up the certificate database and log.

5. Type the file path to the backup folder in the Back Up To This Location field or click Browse to search for this folder. If you specify a folder that doesn't exist, you'll be given the option of creating it.

6. Click OK or Next. Type and then confirm a password that will be used to protect the private key and CA certificate files.

7. Click Next and then click Finish. The wizard creates a backup of the selected data.

Recovering CA Information

If you ever need to recover the CA information, you can do this by completing the following steps:

1. The Certificate Services can't be running when you restore the CA. In the Certification Authority snap-in, right-click the root node for the CA, choose All Tasks, and then select Stop Service.

2. Right-click the root node a second time, choose All Tasks, and then select Restore CA. This starts the Certification Authority Restore Wizard.

3. Click Next and then select the items you want to restore, as shown in Figure 8-7. The options are:
   - Private Key And CA Certificate
   - Certificate Database And Certificate Database Log

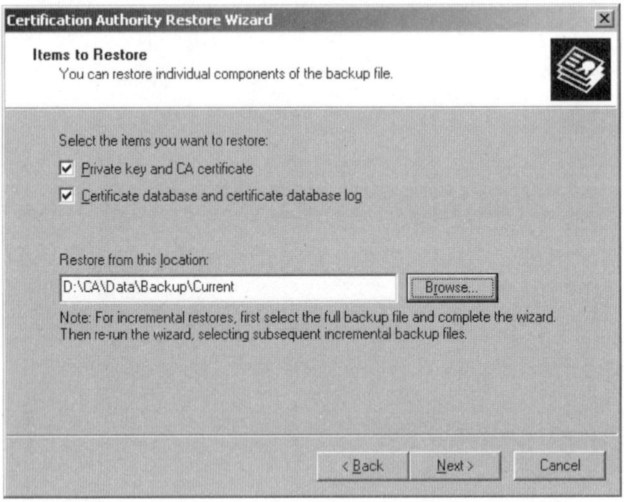

Figure 8-7. *Specify the certification items that you want to restore from a backup.*

4. Type the file path to the backup folder in the Restore From This Location field or click Browse to search for this folder. You should always restore the last complete backup before restoring any incremental backups.

5. Click Next. Type the password used to protect the CA files and then click Next again.

6. Click Finish. The wizard restores the selected data and starts the Certificate Services service.

Configuring Certificate Request Processing

Unlike previous versions of Certificate Services, the version shipping with IIS 6 is configured for autoenrollment by default. This means authorized users can request a certificate, and the CA automatically processes the certificate request so that the user can immediately install the certificate.

If you want to view or change the default request processing policy, follow these steps:

1. Start the Certification Authority snap-in by clicking Certification Authority in Administrative Tools.

2. Right-click the CA node and then select Properties. This displays the Properties dialog box.

3. Select the Policy Module tab and then click Properties.

4. If you want to process requests manually, select Set The Certificate Request Status To Pending. The Administrator Must Explicitly Issue The Certificate.

5. If you want the CA to automatically process requests, select Follow The Settings In The Certificate Template, If Applicable. Otherwise, Automatically Issue The Certificate.

6. Click OK twice.

Approving and Declining Pending Certificate Requests

If you've configured the CA so that certificates must be manually processed, you'll find that pending certificate requests are displayed in the Certification Authority snap-in's Pending Requests container.

You can approve pending requests by completing the following steps:

1. Start the Certification Authority snap-in by clicking Certification Authority in Administrative Tools.

2. Select the Pending Requests container. You will see a list of pending requests, if any.

3. Right-click the request that you want to approve, choose All Tasks, and then select Issue.

4. Certificate Services generates a certificate based on the request and places this certificate in the Issued Certificates container.

5. Certificates are valid for one year. After this period they must be renewed.

You can decline pending certificate requests by doing the following:

1. Start the Certification Authority snap-in by clicking Certification Authority in Administrative Tools.

2. Select the Pending Requests container. You should see a list of pending requests.

3. Right-click the request that you want to decline, choose All Tasks, and then select Deny.

4. When prompted to confirm the action, select Yes.

Caution   Denied requests are moved to the Failed Requests container and can't be restored. The user must resubmit a new request.

Generating Certificates Manually in the Certification Authority Snap-In

Once you've issued a certificate, you can manually create the certificate file that you need to install. To do this, complete the following steps:

1. Start the Certification Authority snap-in, by clicking Certification Authority in Administrative Tools.
2. Select the Issued Certificates container. You should see a list of certificates issued by this root CA, if any.
3. Right-click the certificate that you want to generate and select Open. This displays the Certificate dialog box.
4. Select the Details tab and then select Copy To File. This starts the Certificate Export Wizard. Click Next.
5. Select the Base-64 Encoded X.509 (.CER) export file format and then click Next.
6. Specify the name of the file you want to export. Be sure to use .cer as the file extension. Click Browse if you want to use the Save As dialog box to set the file location and name.
7. Click Next and then click Finish. Click OK after the Certificate Export Wizard confirms that the certificate was successfully exported. You can now install the certificate file as described in the section of this chapter entitled "Processing Pending Requests and Installing Site Certificates."

Revoking Certificates

Server certificates are valid for one year and can be revoked if necessary. Typically, you revoke a certificate when there's a change in the site's status or when the customer for whom you issued the certificate cancels the service subscription. To revoke a certificate, complete the following steps:

1. Start the Certification Authority snap-in by clicking Certification Authority in Administrative Tools.
2. Select the Issued Certificates container. You should see a list of issued certificates.
3. Right-click the certificate that you want to revoke, choose All Tasks, and then select Revoke Certificate. The Certificate Revocation dialog box is displayed.
4. As shown in Figure 8-8, use the Reason Code drop-down list to specify a reason for the revocation and then click Yes.

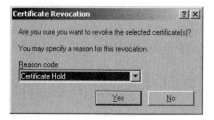

Figure 8-8. *In the Certificate Revocation dialog box, specify the reason you're revoking the certificate.*

5. The CA marks the certificate as revoked and moves it to the Revoked Certificates container.

By default, CAs publish CRLs weekly and CRL changes daily. You can change this setting through the Revoked Certificates Properties dialog box by performing the following steps:

1. Start the Certification Authority snap-in by clicking Certification Authority in Administrative Tools.

2. Right-click the Revoked Certificates container, then select Properties and use the CRL Publication Interval fields to set a new interval for publishing the CRL and CRL changes, as shown in Figure 8-9.

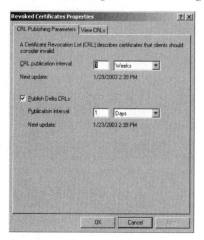

Figure 8-9. *Set the schedule for publishing the CRL. By default, the publication interval is a week.*

3. Click OK.

Reviewing and Renewing the Root CA Certificate

The root CA certificate is valid for the period that was specified when the certificate was created. To view the expiration date or to review the certificate properties, complete the following steps:

1. Start the Certification Authority snap-in by clicking Certification Authority in Administrative Tools.

2. Right-click the root node for the CA and then select Properties. This displays the Root CA Properties dialog box.

3. Click View Certificate in the General tab.

4. As shown in Figure 8-10, use the Certificate dialog box to review the root CA certificate's properties, including the valid from and to dates.

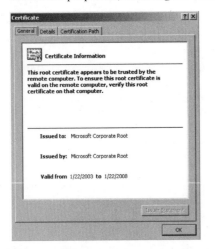

Figure 8-10. *The Certificate dialog box shows the root CA certificate's properties.*

The root CA certificate is usually valid for five years. If you're approaching the end of the five-year period, you should renew the certificate. You should also renew the root CA certificate if one of the following situations exists:

• The signing key is compromised.

• A program requires a new signing key to be used with a new certificate.

• The current CRL is too big and you want to move some of the information to a new CRL.

To renew the root CA certificate, complete the following steps:

1. Log on locally to the CA server.

2. Right-click the root node for the CA again, choose All Tasks, and then select Renew CA Certificate.

Figure 8-11. *When you renew the root CA certificate, you can generate new public and private keys. Do this if the key has been compromised or a new key is required.*

3. If prompted to stop Certificate Services, click Yes. Certificate Services can't be running when you renew the CA. The Renew CA Certificate dialog box shown in Figure 8-11 is displayed.

4. In the Renew CA Certificate dialog box, select Yes if you want to generate a new public and private key pair. Otherwise, select No.

5. Click OK. Certificate Services is restarted automatically and a new certificate is issued.

Creating and Installing Certificates

You have two options for creating and installing certificates. You can use your own Certificate Services to generate your certificates or you can use a trusted third-party authority. When you use Certificate Services, you manage the certificate creation, expiration, and revocation process. When you create certificates through trusted third-party authorities, you let the trusted authority manage the certificate creation, expiration, and revocation process. Either way, the basic tasks you need to perform to create and install a certificate are as follows:

1. Create a certificate request.

2. Submit the request to the authority of your choice or to your own root authority.

3. When you receive the response from the authority, process the pending request and install the certificate.

4. Ensure that SSL is enabled and that secure communications are configured properly.

Creating Certificate Requests

Each Web site hosted on your Web server needs a separate certificate if you want SSL to work properly. The first step in the certificate creation process is to generate a certificate request. You can generate a certificate request by completing the following steps:

1. In the IIS snap-in, right-click the site for which you want to generate the certificate and then select Properties.

2. From the Directory Security tab, select Server Certificate. This starts the Web Server Certificate Wizard. Click Next.

Note If you or someone else has already generated a certificate request for the site, you'll see the Pending Certificate Request dialog box shown in Figure 8-16 later in the chapter. You must either process the request or delete the request to continue. For more information, see the sections of this chapter entitled "Processing Pending Requests and Installing Site Certificates" and "Approving and Declining Pending Certificate Requests."

3. As shown in Figure 8-12, select Create A New Certificate and then click Next.

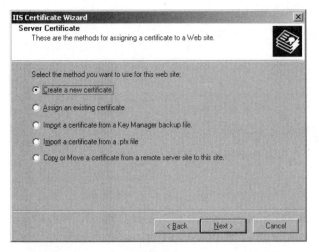

Figure 8-12. *To create a certificate, select Create A New Certificate.*

4. Select Prepare The Request Now, But Send It Later to prepare a request and submit it manually to an authority, and then click Next.

5. As shown in Figure 8-13, you must assign the certificate a name and select a bit length. The name should be descriptive and easy to refer to. The bit length sets the encryption strength of your public and private keys. In most cases you should choose the maximum bit length you're allowed to use.

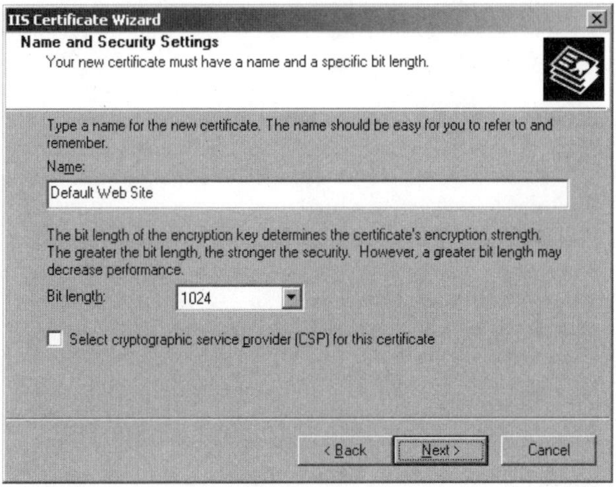

Figure 8-13. *Specify a descriptive name and bit length for the certificate.*

Caution A high level of encryption might slow down a CPU-intensive application when it's running over SSL. If you use SSL with ASP applications extensively and your Web server demonstrates high CPU utilization, you might want to experiment with different levels of encryption and determine where the acceptable levels of performance are achieved.

6. Click Next. You have now created a public and private key pair. These keys are stored locally on the Web server. The final steps are used to create a certificate-signing request (CSR). The information in the request identifies the key's owner and is displayed on your certificate.

Note The CSR is used only to request the certificate. Certain characters must be excluded from your CSR fields, or your certificate might not work. Don't use any of the following characters:
! @ # $ % ^ * ( ) ~ ? > < & / \

7. Enter your organization information in the fields provided as follows:

- **Organization** Sets your company's legal name, such as Microsoft Corporation
- **Organizational Unit** Sets the division in your company responsible for the certificate, such as Technology Department

 Note Third-party authorities will use the organization name, the site's common name, and the geographical information you supply to validate your request for a certificate. If you don't enter this information correctly, you won't be issued a certificate.

8. Click Next and enter your Web site's common name. When the certificate will be used on an intranet (or internal network), the common name may be one word, and it can also be the server's NetBIOS name, such as CorpIntranet. When the certificate will be used on the Internet, the common name must be a valid DNS name, such as *www.microsoft.com.* Click Next.

9. As shown in Figure 8-14, enter the geographic information for your company in the fields provided and then click Next:

- **Country/Region** Select the country or region for your company.
- **State/Province** Type the full name of the state or province in which your company is located.
- **City/Locality** Type the city or locality in which your company is located.

IIS Certificate Wizard

Geographical Information
The certification authority requires the following geographical information.

Country/Region:
US (United States)

State/province:
Washington

City/locality:
Redmond

State/province and City/locality must be complete, official names and may not contain abbreviations.

< Back   Next >   Cancel

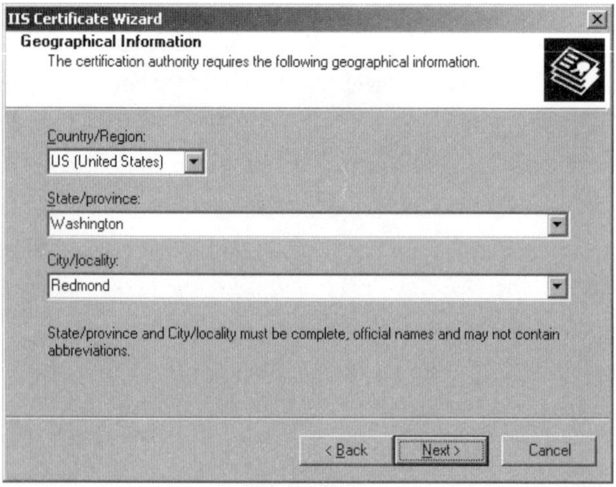

Figure 8-14. *Type complete entries for geographic information.*

 Caution Don't use abbreviations when entering geographic data. Some authorities won't accept abbreviated geographic information, and you'll have to resubmit your request.

10. You need to specify the file name and path for the certificate request file. By default, the file name and path are set to %SystemDrive%\Certreq.txt. Type a new path, or click Browse to select a path and file name using the Save As dialog box.

11. Click Next twice and then click Finish to complete the request generation process.

Real World The common name is typically composed of *Host + Domain Name*, such as *www.microsoft.com* or *products.microsoft.com*. Certificates are specific to the common name that they have been issued to at the Host level. The common name must be the same as the Web address you'll be accessing when connecting to a secure site. For example, a certificate for the domain *microsoft.com* will receive a warning if accessing a site named *www.microsoft.com* or *services.microsoft.com*, as *www.microsoft.com* and *services.microsoft.com* are different from *microsoft.com*. You'd need to create a certificate for the correct common name.

Submitting Certificate Requests to Third-Party Authorities

After you create a CSR, you can submit it to a third-party authority, such as Entrust, Equifax, Valicert, or Verisign. The CSR is stored as American Standard Code of Information Interchange (ASCII) text in the file you specified in step 10 in the section entitled "Creating Certificate Requests." It contains your site's public key and your identification information. When you open this file, you'll find the encrypted contents of the request, such as:

```
--BEGIN NEW CERTIFICATE REQUEST--

MIXCCDCCAnECAQAwczERMA8GA1UEAxMIZW5nc3ZyMDExEzARBgNVBAsTClRlY2hu

b2xvZ3kxEzARBgNVBAoTCkRvbWFpbi5Db20xEjAQBgNVBAcTCVZhbmNvdXZlcjET

MBEGA3UECBMKV2FzaGluZ3RvbjELMAkGA1UEBhMCVVMwgZ8wDQYJKoZIhvcNAQEB

BQADgY0AMIGJAoGBALElbrvIZNRB+gvkdcf9b7tNns24hB2Jgp5BhKi4NXc/twR7

C+GuDnyTqRs+C2AnNHgb9oQkpivqQNKh2+N18bKU3PEZUzXH0pxxjhaiT8aMFJhi

3bFvD+gTCQrw5BWoV9/Ff5Ud3EF5TRQ2WJZ+JluQQewo/mXv5ZnbHsM+aLy3AgMB

AAGgggFTMBoGCisGAQQBgjcNAgMxDBYKNS4wLjIxOTUuMjA1BgorBgEEAYI3AgEO

MScwJTAOBgNVHQ8BAf8EBAMCBPAwEwYDVR01BAwwCgYIKwYWWQUHAwEwEwgf0GCisG

AQQBgjcNAgIxge4wgesCAQEeWgBNAGkAYwByAG8AcwBvAGYAdAAgAFIAUwBBACAA

UwBDAGgAYQBuAG4AZQBsACAAQwByAHkAcAB0AG8AZwByAGEAcABoAGkAYwAgAFAA

cgBvAHYAaQBkAGUAcgOBiQBfE24DPqBwFplR15/xZDY8Cugoxbyymtwq/tAPZ6dz

Pr9Zy3MNnkKQbKcsbLR/4t9/tWJIMmrFhZonrx12qBfICoiKUXreSK89OILrLEto

1frm/dycoXHhStSsZdm25vszv827FKKk5bRW/vIIeBqfKnEPJHOnoiG6UScvgA8Q
```

```
fgAAAAAVVAAAMA0GCSqGSIb3DQEBBQUAA4GBAFZc6K4S04BMUnR/8Ow3J/MS3TYi
HAvFuxnjGOCefTq8Sakzvq+uazU03waBqHxZ1f32qGr/karoD+fq8dX27nmh0zpp
RzlDXrxR35mMC/yP/fpLmLb51sxOt1379PdS4trvWUFkfY93/CkUi+nrQt/uZHY3
N0SThxf73VkfbsE3
--END NEW CERTIFICATE REQUEST--
```

Most CAs have you submit the certificate request as part of a formal site registration process. In this registration process you'll be asked to submit the request file in an e-mail or through an online form. When using e-mail, you simply attach the request file to the e-mail and send it. When using an online form, you can copy the entire text of the request—including the BEGIN and END statements—to the clipboard and paste this into the online form. You can use Microsoft Notepad to do this. Or you might be able to browse for the file to insert and let the server paste the data into the form for you.

After the CA reviews your certificate request, the CA either approves or declines your request. If the CA approves the request, you'll receive an e-mail with the signed certificate attached or a notice to visit a location where you can retrieve the signed certificate. The certificate is an ASCII text file that you can view in Notepad, and it can only be decrypted with the private key you generated previously. As before, the contents of the file are encrypted and include BEGIN and END statements, as in this example:

```
--BEGIN CERTIFICATE--
MXXCWjCCAgQCED1pyIenknxBt43eUZ7JF9YwDQYJKoZIhvcNAQEEBQAwgakxFjAU
BgNERAoTDVZ1cm1TaWduLCBJbmMxRzBFBgNVBAsTPnd3dy52ZXJppc2lnbi5jb20v
cmVwb3NpdG9yeS9UZXN0Q1BTIE1uY29ycC4gQnkgUmVmLiBMaWFiLiBMVEQuMUYw
RAYDVQQLEz1G45IgVmVyaVNpZ24gYXV0aG9yaXp1ZCB0ZXN0aW5nIG9ubHkuIeev
IGFzc3VyYW5jZXMgKEM345MxOTk3MB4XDTAwMTEwNzAwMDAwMFoXDTAwMTEyMTIz
NTk1OVowczELMAkGA1UEBhMCVVMxEzARBgNVBAgTC1dhc2hpbmd0b24xEjAQBgNV
BAcUCVZhbmNvdXZ1cjETMBEGA1UEChQKRG9tYWluLkNvbTETMBEGA1UECxQKVGVj
aG5vbG9neTERMA8GA1UEAxQIZW5nc3ZyQWEwgZ8wDQYJKoZIhvcNAQEBBQADgY0A
MIGJAoGBALE1brvIZNRB+gvkdcf9b7tNns24hB2Jgp5BhKi4NXc/twR7C+GuDnyT
qRs+C2AnNHgb9oQkpivqQNKh2+N18bKU3PEZUzXH0prtyhaiT8aMFJhi3bFvD+gT
CQrw5BWoV9/Ff5Ud3EF5TRQ2WJZ+J1uQQewo/mXnTZnbHsM+aLy3AgMBAAEwDQYJ
KoZIhvcNAQEEBQADQQCQIrhq5UmsPYzwzKVHIiLDDnkYunbhUpSNaBfUSYdvlAU1
Ic/37OrdN/E1ZmOut0MbCWIXKr0Jk5q8F6T1bqwe
--END CERTIFICATE--
```

Save the certificate file to a location that you can access when using the IIS snap-in. You should use .cer as the file extension. Then process and install the certificate as described in the "Processing Pending Requests and Installing Site Certificates" section of this chapter.

Submitting Certificate Requests to Certificate Services

After you create a CSR, you can submit it to Certificate Services using the Web-based interface. To do this, complete the following steps:

1. The CSR is stored as ASCII text in the file you specified in step 10 in the section entitled "Creating Certificate Requests." Open this file in Notepad and copy the entire text of the request, including the BEGIN and END statements, to the clipboard (press Ctrl+A and then press Ctrl+C).

2. You're now ready to submit the request to Certificate Services. Start your Web browser and type in the Certificate Services URL, such as *http:// ca.microsoft.com/certsrv/*. You should see the main page for Certificate Services, as shown in Figure 8-15.

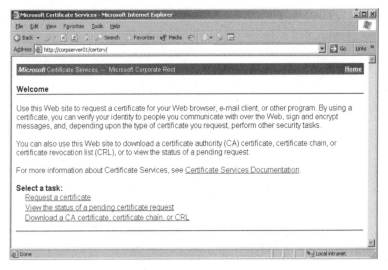

Figure 8-15. *When you access the Certificate Services URL, you should see the main page for the Web-based interface. If you don't, you might not have configured Web access correctly.*

3. Select Request A Certificate.

4. On the Request A Certificate page, select Advanced Certificate Request.

5. Select Submit A Certificate Request Using A Base-64-Encoded.... Request. This option tells Certificate Services that you're going to submit a request that's Base64-encoded.

6. Paste the request into the Saved Request field (press Ctrl+V).

7. Click Submit.

8. If you've completed this process correctly, the final page shows you that your request has been received and is pending approval by the CA. If there's a problem with the request, you'll see an error page telling you to contact your administrator for further assistance. On the error page you can click Details to get more information on the error. You might need to recreate the certificate request or go back to ensure that you haven't accidentally inserted additional spacing or characters in the request submission.

9. If you're also the CA, you can use the Certification Authority snap-in to handle the request. See the "Approving and Declining Pending Certificate Requests" section of this chapter.

Once the request has been approved, use the Web-based interface to retrieve the signed certificate. To do this, complete the following steps:

1. Start your Web browser and type in the Certificate Services URL, such as *http://ca.microsoft.com/certsrv/*.

2. Click View The Status Of A Pending Certificate Request.

3. You should see a list of pending requests. Requests are listed with a description and a date/time stamp. Click the request for the site you want to work with.

 Note If you can't access the certificate file online, you can have the certificate administrator generate the certificate manually. See the section of this chapter entitled "Generating Certificates Manually in the Certification Authority Snap-In."

4. If a certificate has been issued for the request, you should see a page stating that the certificate you requested was issued to you. On this page, select Base 64 Encoded and then click Download Certificate.

5. You should see a File Download dialog box. Select Save.

6. Use the Save As dialog box to select a save location for the certificate file, click Save, then Close. You should use .cer as the file extension. Then process and install the certificate as described in the following section of this chapter.

 Tip I recommend placing all certificate files and requests in a common folder on the Web server's local file system. You should safeguard this folder so that only administrators have access.

Processing Pending Requests and Installing Site Certificates

Once you receive the certificate back from the authority, you can install it by completing the following steps:

1. In the IIS snap-in, right-click the site for which you want to process the certificate and then select Properties.

2. From the Directory Security tab, select Server Certificate. This starts the Web Server Certificate Wizard. Click Next.

3. As shown in Figure 8-16, select Process The Pending Request And Install The Certificate and then click Next.

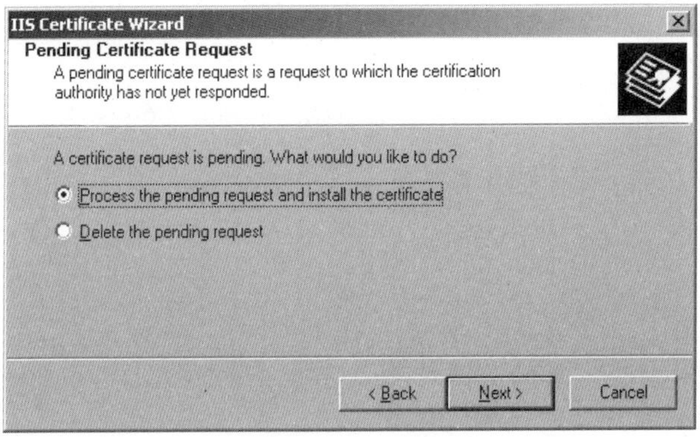

Figure 8-16. *Process the pending request and install the certificate file.*

4. Type the path and file name to the certificate file returned by the authority, or click Browse to search for the file. Click Next to continue.

5. Select the SSL port the Web site should use. The default SSL port is 443. Click Next.

6. The next page provides summary information on the certificate. If this is the correct certificate, click Next and then click Finish to complete the installation process. Otherwise, click Back to choose a different certificate file and then repeat steps 3 to 5.

7. Click OK. Check the SSL configuration and manage the certificate as described in the sections of this chapter entitled "Working with SSL" and "Managing Site Certificates in the Internet Information Services Snap-In."

Deleting Pending Certificate Requests

If you made a mistake in a certificate request that has already been generated, the only way to fix it is to delete the request and then create a new one. You delete pending certificate requests by completing the following steps:

1. In the IIS snap-in, right-click the site for which you want to generate the certificate and then select Properties.

2. From the Directory Security tab, select Server Certificate. This starts the Web Server Certificate Wizard. Click Next.

3. Select Delete The Pending Request and then click Next.

4. Click Next and then click Finish. This deletes the request association in IIS but doesn't remove the actual request file. This file contains your site's public key and should be deleted. Click OK.

Working with SSL

Installing a site certificate automatically enables SSL so that it can be used, but you might need to change the default settings. You'll need to configure and troubleshoot SSL as necessary.

Configuring SSL Ports

Once you install a certificate on a Web site, you can change the SSL port for the site. The SSL port is used for secure communications with client browsers. To view or change the SSL port, follow these steps:

1. In the IIS snap-in, right-click the site you want to work with and then select Properties.

2. The SSL Port field in the Web Site tab shows the currently configured SSL port (if any).

3. As shown in Figure 8-17, change the SSL port by typing a new value in the SSL Port field. Multiple sites can use the same SSL port, provided that the sites are configured to use different IP addresses.

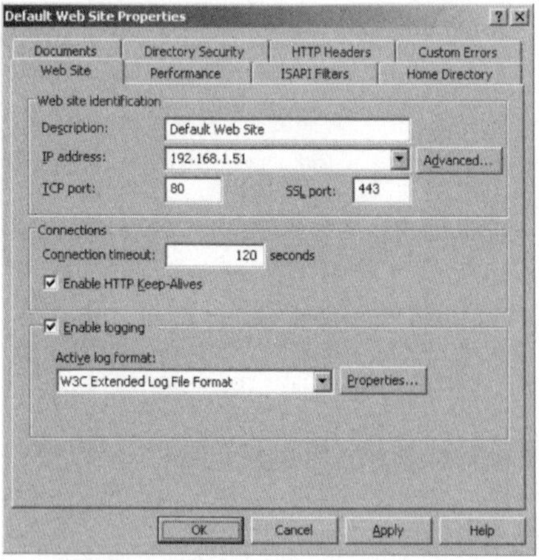

Figure 8-17. *Specify a port value for SSL.*

4. Click OK.

A site can also have multiple SSL identities (meaning the site can answer on different SSL ports). The SSL port configured in the Web Site tab is the one the site responds to by default. All other SSL ports must be specified in the browser request. For example, if you configure SSL for ports 443, 444, and 445, a request for *https://yoursite/* is handled by port 443 automatically, but you must specify the other ports to use them, such as *https://yoursite:445/*.

To configure multiple SSL identities for a site, complete these steps:

1. In the IIS snap-in, right-click the Web site you want to manage, and then select Properties.

2. In the Web Site tab of the Properties dialog box, click Advanced. The Advanced Web Site Identification dialog box is displayed.

3. As shown in Figure 8-18, use the Multiple SSL Identities For This Web Site frame to manage SSL port settings as follows:

   - **Add**   Adds a new SSL identity. Click Add, select the IP address you want to use, and then type an SSL port value. Click OK when you're finished.

   - **Remove**   Allows you to remove the currently selected entry from the SSL Identities list box.

   - **Edit**   Allows you to edit the currently selected entry in the SSL Identities list box.

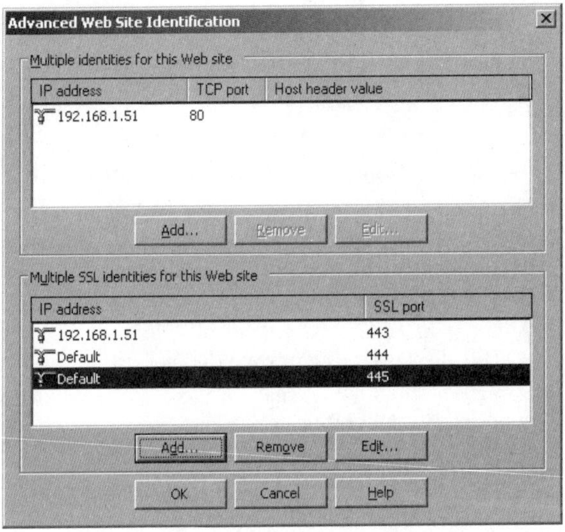

Figure 8-18. *Web sites can have multiple SSL identities. The port that is set in the Web Site tab is the primary identity; the others are alternatives that must be specified in a URL request.*

4. Click OK and then click OK again to save your settings. Click OK a final time to close the Properties dialog box.

Adding the CA Certificate to the Client Browser's Root Store

Most root CA certificates issued by third-party CAs are configured as trusted CAs in Web browsers. However, if you're acting as your own CA, client browsers won't recognize and trust your root CA certificate. To get browsers to trust the root CA certificate, the user must install the certificate in the browser's authorities store.

To install the root CA certificate, users need to complete the following steps:

1. Connect to your site using a secure URL that begins with *https://*.

2. As shown in Figure 8-19, the user's browser displays a security alert stating that there's a problem with the site's security certificate.

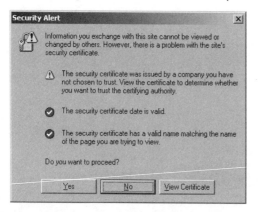

Figure 8-19. *A security alert warns that the browser doesn't trust your root CA.*

3. The alert is displayed because the user hasn't chosen to trust your root CA. At this point, the user can elect to proceed by clicking Yes, to cancel the request by clicking No, or to view the root CA certificate by clicking View Certificate.

4. Click View Certificate. This displays the Certificate dialog box.

5. The General tab information should state that the CA Root certificate isn't trusted. To enable trust, click Install Certificate.

6. This starts the Certificate Import Wizard. Click Next.

7. Choose Automatically Select The Certificate Store Based On The Type Of Certificate, as shown in Figure 8-20, and then click Next.

8. Click Finish. The default options allow the browser to select the certificate store based on the type of certificate.

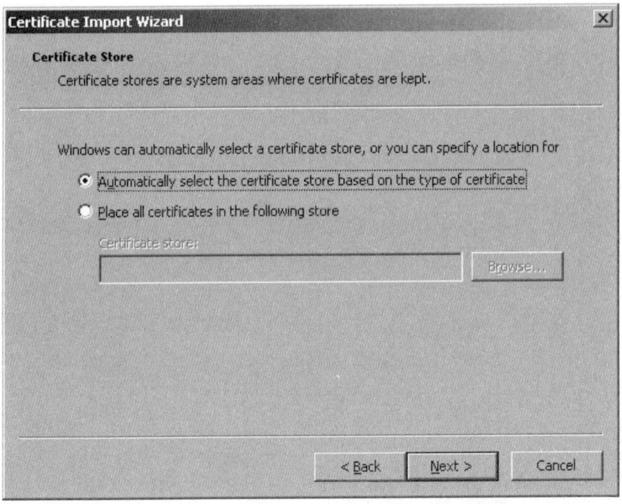

Figure 8-20. *In the Certificate Import Wizard, select Automatically Select The Certificate Store Based On The Type Of Certificate.*

9. Click OK in response to the successful import message that appears, and then click OK to close the Certificate dialog box. The user shouldn't see the security alert again.

Confirming that SSL Is Correctly Enabled

Secure connections can be established only when the browser connects to the server using a secure URL beginning with *https://*. Browsers display a warning if any embedded content (such as images) on a secure Web page are retrieved using an insecure (*http://*) connection. This warning tells users that some of the content on the page is insecure and asks them if they want to continue.

Once you've enabled SSL on your server, you should confirm that SSL is working and that the encryption level is set properly. To confirm that SSL is working in Internet Explorer, complete these steps:

1. Access your Web site using a secure URL beginning with *https://*. A padlock displayed in the bar at the bottom of the Internet Explorer window indicates that an SSL session has been established. If the padlock isn't displayed, the SSL session wasn't established.

2. Right-click anywhere on the Web page and then select Properties. This displays a Properties dialog box, which provides summary information on the Web page.

3. Click Certificates and then select the Details tab. Scroll down to display details concerning the certificate and the level of encryption used.

To confirm that SSL is working in Netscape Navigator 7, complete the following steps:

1. Access your Web site using a secure URL beginning with *https://*. The padlock in the lower right corner of the Navigator window should be closed instead of open. This indicates that an SSL session has been established. If the padlock is open, the SSL session wasn't established.

2. Click the padlock icon. This displays the Security tab of the Page Info dialog box, which also indicates the level of encryption currently being used.

Resolving SSL Problems

If SSL isn't working, ensure that you've installed the server certificate on the correct Web site and that you've enabled SSL on the site. These steps should resolve a server-based SSL problem.

If the encryption level isn't what you expected, you should check to make sure the browser supports the encryption level you're using. If a browser supports 128-bit encryption and the encryption level in use according to the browser's Properties dialog box is 40-bit, the problem is the server certificate. The server certificate must be upgraded to 128-bit encryption.

In Internet Explorer, check encryption support by completing the following steps:

1. From the Help menu, select About Internet Explorer.

2. The Cipher Strength field shows the level of encryption supported. You must have 128-bit support to establish a 128-bit session.

3. Click OK.

4. From the Tools menu, select Internet Options. From the Internet Options dialog box, select the Advanced tab.

5. Scroll down through the Advanced options until you see the Security heading. Ensure that Use SSL 2.0 and Use SSL 3.0 are selected.

6. Click OK.

In Netscape Navigator 7, check encryption support by completing these steps:

1. Click the Edit menu and then select Preferences. This displays the Preferences dialog box.

2. On the left, select the Privacy & Security category, and then select SSL. In the SSL frame, there are three check boxes, all selected by default: Enable SSL Version 2, Enable SSL Version 3, and Enable TLS. Make sure that at least both versions of SSL are selected.

3. Click OK to save your settings.

Managing Site Certificates in the IIS Snap-In

Once you've installed a certificate on a Web site, you can use the IIS snap-in to manage it. Key management tasks are discussed in this section.

Viewing and Modifying Issued Certificates

Certificates contain the identity and geographic information specified in the original certificate request. They also have a number of properties set by the CA. These properties describe the certificate, set its authorized uses, and define the site for which the certificate is valid. If needed, you can modify the certificate to do the following:

- Update the friendly name assigned when the certificate was created
- Specify a detailed description of the certificate
- Enable or disable purposes for which the certificate can be used

You can view or modify a site's certificate by completing the following steps:

1. In the IIS snap-in, right-click the Web site you want to manage and then select Properties.
2. In the Directory Security tab, click View Certificate. This displays the Certificate dialog box, shown in Figure 8-21.

Figure 8-21. *The Certificate dialog box provides summary information on the site certificate, and you can use it to modify properties and export the certificate to a file.*

3. To view properties set when the certificate was issued, select the Details tab. Fields in the Details tab include:

- **Version**   The X.509 version used in creating the certificate
- **Serial Number**   The unique serial number for the certificate
- **Signature Algorithm**   The encryption algorithm used to create the certificate's signature
- **Issuer**   The issuer of the certificate
- **Valid From**   The date from which the certificate is valid
- **Valid To**   The date after which the certificate expires
- **Subject**   Used to set the subject of the certificate, which typically includes the identification and geographic information
- **Public Key**   The certificate's encrypted public key
- **Thumbprint Algorithm**   The encryption algorithm used to create the certificate's thumbprint
- **Thumbprint**   The encrypted thumbprint of the signature
- **Friendly Name**   The descriptive name assigned to the certificate

4. To view or edit a list of purposes for which the certificate can be used, in the Details tab, click Edit Properties. You can then use the Certificate Properties dialog box, shown in Figure 8-22, to view or edit the certificate purposes.

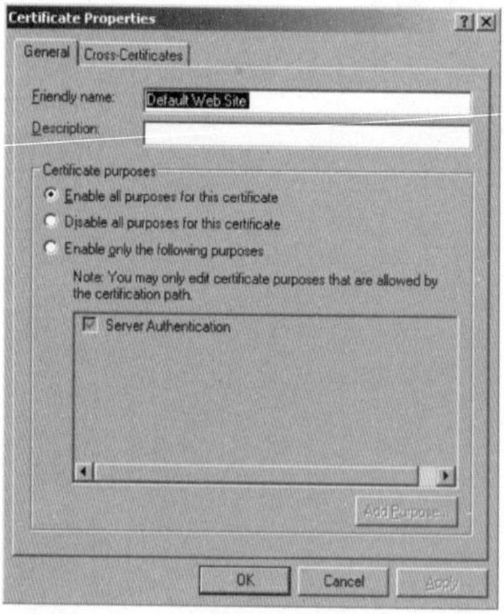

Figure 8-22. *You can modify certificate purposes to meet your organization's needs.*

Renewing, Removing, and Replacing Certificates

Normally, certificates are valid for one year from the date they were issued. This means certificates must be renewed annually. You can also remove or replace certificates as necessary. To renew, remove, or replace a certificate, follow these steps:

1. In the IIS snap-in, right-click the Web site you want to manage and then select Properties.

2. Select the Directory Security tab and then click Server Certificate on the Secure Communications frame. This starts the Web Server Certificate Wizard. Click Next.

3. As shown in Figure 8-23, you can now elect to renew, remove, or replace the current certificate. Make your selection and then continue through the remaining wizard pages.

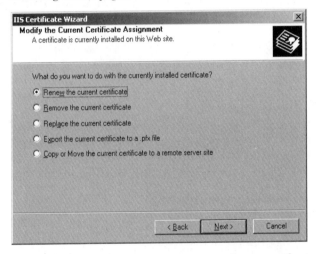

Figure 8-23. *You can renew, remove, or replace a certificate at any time using the Web Server Certificate Wizard.*

Exporting Site Certificates

You can export site certificates to a file, if necessary. To do this, complete the following steps:

1. In the IIS snap-in, right-click the Web site you want to manage and then select Properties.

2. In the Directory Security tab, click View Certificate. This displays the Certificate dialog box, shown previously in Figure 8-21.

3. Select the Details tab and then select Copy To File. This starts the Certificate Export Wizard. Click Next.

4. You can export the certificate file with or without the associated private key. If you want to export the private key, select Yes. Otherwise, select No. Click Next.

5. The next page lets you choose the export file format. The default format should be adequate, so note the format that will be used and then click Next.

6. If you elected to export the private key, you must now set a password for the certificate file. After you type and then confirm the password in the fields provided, click Next.

7. Specify the name of the file you want to export. Click Browse if you want to use the Save As dialog box to set the file location and name.

8. Click Next and then click Finish. Click OK to confirm a successful export. Click OK twice more to return to the IIS snap-in.

Ignoring, Accepting, and Requiring Client Certificates

Client certificates allow users to authenticate themselves through their Web browser. You might want to use client certificates if you have a secure external Web site, such as an extranet. If a Web site accepts or requires client certificates, you can configure client certificate mappings that permit access control to resources based on client certificates. A client certificate mapping can be mapped to a specific Windows account using a one-to-one mapping, or it can be mapped based on rules you specify.

By default, IIS doesn't accept or require client certificates. You can change this behavior. Keep in mind that accepting client certificates isn't the same as requiring client certificates. When a site requires client certificates, the site is secured for access using SSL only and can't be accessed using standard HTTP. When a site accepts client certificates rather than requires them, the site can use either HTTP or Hypertext Transfer Protocol Secure (HTTPS) for communications.

To configure client certificate usage, follow these steps:

1. In the IIS snap-in, right-click the Web site you want to manage and then select Properties.

2. Select the Directory Security tab and then click Edit on the Secure Communications frame. This displays the Secure Communications dialog box, shown in Figure 8-24.

3. If you want to require SSL (and preclude the use of insecure communications), select Require Secure Channel (SSL). Optionally, you can also select Require 128-Bit Encryption if your server has a 128-bit encryption installed and enabled.

4. In the Client Certificates frame, select the Ignore, Accept, or Require Client Certificates option as necessary.

Note   You can only require client certificates when secure SSL communications are required as well. Because of this, you must check Require
Secure Channel (SSL) when you want to require client certificates.

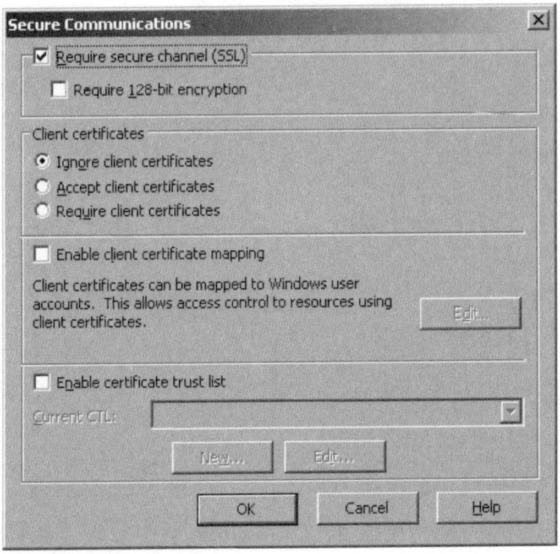

Figure 8-24. *Sites can ignore, accept, or require client certificates.*

5. If you want to map client certificates to Windows user accounts, select
   Enable Client Certificate Mapping and then click Edit. Then use the Account
   Mappings dialog box to configure certificate mappings.

6. If you want to accept client certificates only from specific CAs, select Enable
   Certificate Trust List and then click New. This starts the Certificate Trust List
   Wizard, which you can use to specify the root CA certificates that are trusted.
   Client certificates from trusted root CAs will be accepted. Client certificates
   from other root CAs won't be accepted.

7. Click OK twice.

Requiring SSL for All Communications

In some cases you'll want to create sites that can only be accessed using secure
communications. You can do this by requiring SSL and prohibiting the use of
insecure communications. To require SSL for communications with a Web site,
follow these steps:

1. In the IIS snap-in, right-click the Web site you want to manage and then
   select Properties.

2. Select the Directory Security tab and then click Edit on the Secure Communications frame. This displays the Secure Communications dialog box, shown
   previously in Figure 8-24.

3. Select Require Secure Channel (SSL) if you want to require SSL and preclude the use of insecure communications.

4. Optionally, select Require 128-Bit Encryption if your server has a 128-bit encryption installed and enabled.

5. Click OK twice.

Part III
Essential Services Administration

This part of the book focuses on the administration of essential services. By essential services, we mean those services you'll deploy time and again on your Web servers. Chapter 9 covers techniques for managing File Transfer Protocol (FTP). You'll find information on configuring FTP servers, controlling access to directories, managing user sessions, and maintaining FTP server security. Chapter 10 discusses key issues related to working with Simple Mail Transfer Protocol (SMTP) and Post Office Protocol 3 (POP3) e-mail services. With POP3 e-mail services, you can receive incoming mail on your Web server. Chapter 11 continues this discussion with a look at advanced configuration issues. Chapter 12 examines indexing services. You'll learn to configure the Indexing Service, to create and manage catalogs, to optimize performance, and to test the indexing installation.

Chapter 9
Managing FTP Servers

File Transfer Protocol (FTP) is used to transfer files from one host to another. Managing FTP sites and servers is similar to managing World Wide Web sites and servers. You configure FTP sites for use on the Internet and on corporate intranets. Internet FTP sites typically use fully qualified domain names (FQDNs) and public Internet Protocol (IP) addresses. Intranet FTP sites typically use private IP addresses and computer names that resolve locally.

As with Web sites, FTP site properties identify a site, set its configuration values, and determine where and how documents are accessed. You can set FTP site properties at several levels:

- As global defaults
- As site defaults
- As directory defaults

You set global defaults through the master properties using the FTP Sites Properties dialog box, and they apply to all new FTP sites created on the server. You set individual defaults through the *Sitename* Site Properties dialog box, and they apply only to the selected FTP site. You set directory defaults through the *Directoryname* Properties dialog box, and they apply only to the selected directory.

Understanding FTP

The following sections examine how FTP is used. You'll learn how FTP file transfers work, how FTP servers are accessed, and how FTP sessions are established.

FTP Essentials

FTP is a client/server protocol used for transferring files. Using FTP, you can log on to an FTP server, browse a directory structure to locate a file, and download the file. FTP also enables you to upload files to an FTP server. The difference between a file upload and a file download is important. When you upload a file, you transfer a file from a client to a server. When you download a file, you transfer a file from a server to a client.

With the increasing popularity of Hypertext Transfer Protocol (HTTP), the use of FTP is decreasing. Although it's true that HTTP has taken over some of the functions of FTP, FTP continues to have a place when you need a dedicated resource for transferring files that's easy to use and to maintain. Like HTTP, FTP uses Transmission Control Protocol (TCP) as its transport protocol. Unlike HTTP, FTP is session-oriented. This means that FTP connections are persistent. When you connect to an FTP server, the connection remains open after you transfer files.

The maintenance of persistent connections requires system resources. A server with too many open connections quickly gets bogged down. Consequently, many FTP servers are configured to limit the number of open connections and to time out connections after a certain period of time. By default, Internet Information Services (IIS) FTP servers limit the number of connections to 100,000 and use a connection time-out of 120 seconds.

Because FTP is a client/server protocol, the successful transfer of files depends on several factors. A computer acting as a server must run FTP server software, such as IIS. A computer acting as a client must run FTP client software, such as Microsoft Internet Explorer or the command-line FTP utility built into Microsoft Windows Server 2003.

File transfers can be either American Standard Code of Information Interchange (ASCII) or binary. You can use ASCII file transfers when you're working with text documents and want to preserve the end-of-line designators. You must use binary file transfers when you're working with executables. You can use binary file transfers with other file types as well.

Controlling FTP Server Access

Most FTP clients and servers are configured to allow anonymous file transfers. In an anonymous file transfer, the server allows users to connect to the server and transfer files anonymously. As the name implies, anonymous file transfers are designed to allow anyone to connect to the server and transfer files. When you use Internet Explorer or another FTP client, anonymous transfers can be started automatically in most cases. For example, you could connect to the Microsoft FTP server by typing this Uniform Resource Locator (URL) into your browser's Address field: **ftp://ftp.microsoft.com/public/**.

In this example, *ftp://* designates the protocol as FTP, *ftp.microsoft.com* identifies the server to which you want to connect, and *public* is the name of a directory on the server. Behind the scenes, the FTP client fills in the necessary user name and password information. With an anonymous FTP connection, this means setting the user name to *anonymous* and the password to your e-mail address or an empty string. If the client is unable to fill in the necessary information automatically, you'll be prompted for a user name and password. Enter **anonymous** as the user name and set the password to your e-mail address.

You can also configure FTP servers for restricted access. When you restrict access to a server, only authenticated users can gain access to the server. When users try to connect to the server, they're prompted to authenticate themselves by typing a user name and password. The user name and password must be for an account that exists on the local computer or in the domain the computer is a member of. User name and password information can also be specified in the URL used to access the server. To do this, use this URL format: *ftp://user-name:password@hostname:port/path_to_resource.*

Here, *ftp://* designates the protocol as FTP, *username* sets the account name, and *password* sets the account password. In this example, the user name is set to wrstanek and the password is set to mydingo123: *ftp://wrstanek:mydingo123@ftp.microsoft.com/public/.*

Security Alert   Don't allow FTP passwords to become a back door into your server. FTP passwords encoded in URLs are passed to the server as plain text. The URL containing the password might also be saved in the history cache of the user's browser. Anyone monitoring the network and anyone with access to the user's computer might be able to gain unauthorized access to the FTP server. Help to safeguard the server and data by changing passwords periodically and by setting NTFS file system (NTFS) permissions that restrict user access to files and folders on the server. The FTP user isolation feature could also be useful to prevent security issues. See the section in this chapter entitled "FTP User Isolation for Busy Upload Sites" for more information.

Being granted access to a server, either anonymously or through authentication, doesn't mean a user can upload or download files. The specific actions available to the user depend on the security settings. As discussed in Chapter 7, "Enhancing Web Server Security," security settings are set at two levels: Windows and IIS. Windows security settings are configured through user and group accounts, file and folder permissions, and group policy. IIS security settings are set through FTP server permissions, authentication, and Transmission Control Protocol/Internet Protocol (TCP/IP) access restrictions.

Working with FTP Sessions

Once a user is granted access to a server, either anonymously or through authentication, a TCP connection is established, and this connection remains open until the user session is terminated or the server issues a time-out. The FTP client and the server establish this connection using a three-way handshake. This handshake involves two dedicated TCP ports on the FTP server and two dynamically assigned TCP ports on the client that are mapped to the dedicated server ports.

TCP/IP connections are also established using a three-way handshake. TCP/IP connections are established at the Network Layer (Layer 3) of the Open Systems Interconnection (OSI) model. FTP connections are established at the Application Layer (Layer 7).

The two ports used by FTP servers are ports 20 and 21, by default. Port 20 is used for sending and receiving FTP data and is open only when data is being transferred. Port 21 is used for sending and receiving FTP control information.

Port 21 listens for clients that are trying to establish a connection. Once an FTP session is established with a client, the connection on port 21 remains open for the entire session.

 Tip If clients connecting through a firewall or proxy can connect to an FTP server but can't retrieve data, it's likely that the control port, port 21, was opened for FTP access, but not the data port. To resolve this, have your network administrator check the firewall or proxy settings, ensuring that clients are granted access on both the FTP control port and the FTP data port.

The two ports used by FTP clients are dynamically assigned and range from 1024 to 5000. When an FTP session is started, the client opens a control port that connects to port 21 on the server. This connection is used to manage the FTP session. The client doesn't automatically connect to the data port on the server. This port connection is established only when data needs to be transferred between the client and server. When data needs to be transferred, the client opens a new data port and then connects to the server's data port (port 20 by default). Once the file transfer is complete, the client releases the data port. The next time data needs to be transferred, the client opens a new data port, which typically isn't the same as the last port number used for data transfers.

More Info The dynamically assigned port numbers are outside the ranges that are normally reserved for other TCP and User Datagram Protocol (UDP) services. Thus, because ports 0 to 1023 (well-known ports) are reserved for other TCP and UDP services, FTP uses ports ranging from 1024 to 5000 (limited by a Windows Registry setting with a theoretical limit of 65,535). You can find a complete list of current TCP and UDP ports used for well-known services in \%System-Root%\System32\Drivers\Etc\Services.

Now that you know how FTP servers and clients use ports, let's look at how FTP sessions are established and then used in actual data transfers. The process of establishing and using an FTP session can be summarized as follows:

1. The FTP server listens for client requests on a dedicated control port. By default, the control port is 21.

2. When a user makes a request for resources on the FTP server, the client dynamically assigns a control port and then maps this control port to the server's control port. For example, the client might assign port 1025 and map this to server port 21.

3. Once a connection has been established with the server, the client and server can communicate over the control port.

4. Before the client initiates a data transfer, the client must dynamically assign a data port and map this to the server's data port, port 20. Each time a file is

transferred, a new data port is opened by the client and then released. For example, port 1057 might be used for the first data transfer, port 1058 for the next data transfer, and so on.

5. The FTP session remains open until the session is terminated or the connection times out. The user or the server can terminate the session.

A useful tool for monitoring FTP sessions on clients and servers is Netstat. Netstat is a command-line utility that displays the status of network connections. When you call Netstat, you should specify that you want to see connections that TCP is using and that you want to redisplay the statistics at a specific interval. In this example you tell Netstat to display connection statistics every 15 seconds:

```
netstat -p tcp 15
```

You can run Netstat on a client to monitor FTP activity. When the client establishes an FTP connection to the server, you'll see output similar to the following:

```
Active Connections

  Proto Local Address Foreign Address State
  TCP engsvr01:ftp engsvr01:1043 ESTABLISHED
  TCP engsvr01:1043 engsvr01:ftp ESTABLISHED
```

Here, the FTP connection is established on port 1043 and this port is mapped to the FTP control port. Whenever the client retrieves data from the server, a data port is mapped as well. After the data has been transferred, the data port enters the TIME_WAIT state. The port remains in the TIME_WAIT state until it times out and is closed. The control port continues to reflect the ESTABLISHED state as long as the connection is open. These port states are reflected in the following statements:

```
Active Connections

  Proto Local Address Foreign Address State
  TCP engsvr01:ftp-data engsvr01:1045 TIME_WAIT
  TCP engsvr01:ftp engsvr01:1043 ESTABLISHED
  TCP engsvr01:1043 engsvr01:ftp ESTABLISHED
```

When the client closes the connection to the FTP server, the only TCP entry that remains is the client-to-server control port mapping. As shown in this example, the client-to-server control port mapping enters the TIME_WAIT state and remains in this state until the session times out:

```
Active Connections

  Proto Local Address Foreign Address State
  TCP engsvr01:1043 engsvr01:ftp TIME_WAIT
```

Note Keep in mind that clients can establish multiple connections to a server. If this is the case for the client you're monitoring, you'll see multiple control and data ports in various states. To see the complete list of available Netstat command line options, type **netstat -?.**

FTP Site Naming and Identification

Each FTP site deployed in your organization has a unique identity that it uses to receive and respond to requests. The identity includes the following:

- A computer or Domain Name System (DNS) name
- A port number
- An IP address

The way these identifiers are combined to identify an FTP site depends on whether the host server is on a private or public network. On a private network, a computer called CorpFTP could have an IP address of 10.0.10.25. If so, you could access the FTP site on the server in one of these ways:

- Using the Universal Naming Convention (UNC) path name: \\CorpFTP or \\10.0.10.25
- Using a URL: *ftp://CorpFTP/* or *ftp://10.0.10.25/*
- Using a URL and port number: *ftp://CorpFTP:21/* or *ftp://10.0.10.25:21/*

On a public network, a computer called MoonShot could be registered to use the DNS name *ftp.microsoft.com* and the IP address 207.46.230.210. If so, you could access the FTP site on the server in one of these ways:

- Using a URL: *ftp://ftp.microsoft.com/* or *ftp://207.46.230.210/*
- Using a URL and port number: *ftp://ftp.microsoft.com:21/* or *http://207.46.230.210:21/*

Using different combinations of IP addresses and port numbers, you can host multiple sites on a single computer. Hosting multiple sites on a single server has definite advantages. For example, rather than installing three different FTP servers, you could host ftp.*microsoft.com*, *ftp.msn.com*, and *ftp.adatum.com* on the same FTP server.

FTP User Isolation for Busy Upload Sites

In some environments where FTP is used extensively for uploading files, you might want more control over where and how users can upload files. Instead of allowing users to upload files to a common directory, such as Upload, you might want users to have separate home directories where they can safely upload files without fear of overwriting each others' files and without being able to see files uploaded by other users. In this case you'd install the FTP site in FTP user isolation.

 Note Keep in mind that you can't change the user isolation mode after the FTP site is installed.

IIS 6.0 supports two isolation modes for FTP users:

- **Standard** Isolates users by local and domain user account names. Here, users log on to the server root directory using their Windows account. When the logon is authenticated, they're mapped transparently to their isolated user directory.

- **Active Directory–integrated** Authenticates user credentials using Active Directory service. Here, users log on to the server root directory and their Windows credentials are authenticated in Active Directory. If authenticated, the user's FTPRoot and FTPDir environment variables are used to determine which isolated user directory is used.

Note The FTPRoot and FTPDir environment variables are important in determining how the isolated user directories are mapped. FTPRoot sets the base directory of the server file share to use, such as \\ZETA\FTP. FTPDir sets the actual home directory to use, such as WRSTANEK. Together, these two variables specify the full UNC path to the user's isolated directory, such as \\ZETA\FTP\WRSTANEK. These variables can be set through individual user environment variable settings or through the Active Directory User object. Note that by setting FTPDir to %UserName%, the home directory value is set automatically on a user-by-user basis. Also, keep in mind that only User objects in Windows Server 2003 environments have the FTPRoot and FTPDir attributes included by default.

When user isolation is used, users see only the FTP root directory and don't know they're in a separate directory. With Active Directory–integrated mode, users are mapped through an arbitrary root directory to the directory specified by concatenating the values of FTPRoot and FTPDir. These values must be set for users to log on to the FTP site.

With the standard mode, you'll need to create a directory structure for all users who will access the server. Two directories are at the base of this directory structure:

- **LocalUser** A top-level directory for all local user accounts configured on the server. If you enable user isolation and also want to permit anonymous access, you'll need to create a directory named LocalUser and then create a directory named Public below it. Anonymous users will be transparently mapped to the LocalUser\Public directory.

- **Domain** A top-level directory for all domain users who access the server, where *Domain* is the pre–Windows 2000 domain name. For example, if the domain name is *Adatum.com*, you would create a directory called ADATUM under the FTP root directory.

After you create the LocalUser and *Domain* directories, you'll need to create subdirectories for each user that will access the FTP site. Following this, if you were the administrator of Adatum.com and wanted to take advantage of the standard FTP user isolation feature and also allow anonymous access to the FTP server, your directory structure might look like this:

LocalUser

   \Public

Adatum

   \JohnE

   \MikeJ

   \TomW

   \WilliamS

Here, the LocalUser\Public virtual directory enables anonymous access on the user-isolated FTP server and four users have been configured for isolated access to the server: JohnE, MikeJ, TomW, and WilliamS.

When working with FTP user isolation modes, it's important to note that you can't change the mode after you've created an FTP site. So if you create a site in one mode and later discover you should have used another mode, you'll need to create a new site to use this mode.

FTP Site Operators

In previous versions of IIS, you could designate FTP site operators for each FTP site on your server. FTP site operators were a special group of users who had limited administrative privileges. IIS 6 eliminates the notion of both FTP and Web site operators. FTP and Web site operator accounts were rarely used and presented more of a security risk than was desired. Don't worry; you can designate administrators with limited privileges in IIS 6 and Windows Server 2003. To do this, you delegate authority to a user who needs specific permissions or privileges.

Managing Global FTP Service Properties

You use the global FTP service properties to set default property values for new FTP sites created on a server. Existing FTP sites on a server inherit changes you make to the master service properties. The only changes that are applied optionally are permission changes. If you set new access permissions, a prompt is displayed asking you to specify the sites and directories that should inherit the new access permissions.

To change the global FTP service properties for a server, follow these steps:

1. In the IIS snap-in, double-click the icon for the computer you want to work with. If the computer isn't shown, connect to it as discussed in the "Connecting to Other Servers" section of Chapter 2, "Core IIS Administration," and then perform these tasks.

2. Right-click FTP Sites and then select Properties.

3. Use the tabs and fields of the FTP Sites Properties dialog box to configure the default property values for new FTP sites. When you're finished making changes, click OK.

Creating FTP Sites

When you install FTP Service for IIS, a default FTP site is created. Typically, the default FTP site is installed in %SystemDrive%\Inetpub\Ftproot. By adding subdirectories to this location, you can create the FTP site's directory structure. By adding files to this directory or to subdirectories, you provide content for users to download. Users can access the FTP site using the FTP server name or by typing an appropriate URL in their browsers.

The default FTP site isn't configured for isolated user directories. If you want to use this feature of IIS 6, you should create a new FTP site, specifying the type of user isolation you want to use. If you want the FTP site to use a new IP address, you must configure the IP address before installing the site. For details, refer to Chapter 16, "Managing TCP/IP Networking," in the *Microsoft Windows Server 2003 Administrator's Pocket Consultant* (Microsoft Press, 2003).

Creating Non-Isolated FTP Sites

You can create FTP sites that don't use isolation by completing the following steps:

1. In the IIS snap-in, access the node for the computer you want to work with, right-click FTP Sites, choose New from the shortcut menu, and then select FTP Site. If the computer isn't shown, connect to it as discussed in the "Connecting to Other Servers" section of Chapter 2 and then perform this task.

2. The FTP Site Creation Wizard starts. Click Next. In the Description field, type a descriptive name for the FTP site, such as Corporate FTP Server. Click Next.

3. As shown in Figure 9-1, use the IP Address drop-down list to select an available IP address. Select (All Unassigned) to allow FTP to respond on all unassigned IP addresses that are configured on the server. Multiple FTP sites can use the same IP address if the sites are configured to use different port numbers.

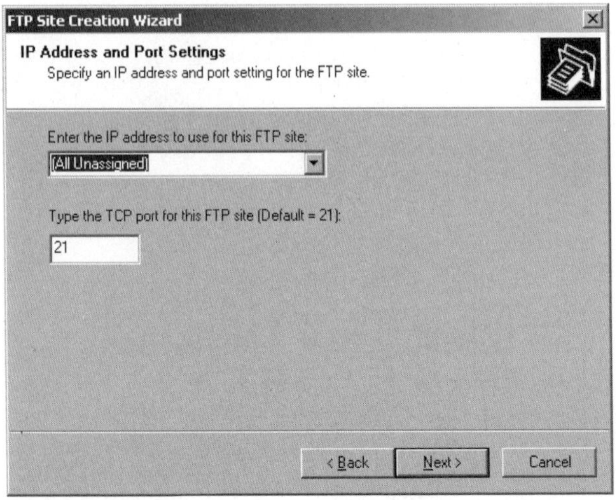

FTP Site Creation Wizard ⊠

IP Address and Port Settings
Specify an IP address and port setting for the FTP site.

Enter the IP address to use for this FTP site:

[All Unassigned] ▼

Type the TCP port for this FTP site (Default = 21):

21

< <u>B</u>ack   <u>N</u>ext >   Cancel

Figure 9-1. *Set the IP address and port values for the new FTP site.*

 Note FTP has no equivalent of HTTP host headers. This means you can't use host header names with FTP sites.

4. The TCP port for the FTP site is assigned automatically as port 21. If necessary, type a new port number in the TCP Port field. Multiple sites can use the same port if the sites are configured to use different IP addresses. Click Next.

5. The following options are available:

- **Do Not Isolate Users** With this setting, users log on to the server and aren't mapped transparently to separate isolated user directories. Depending on directory settings, users might be able to view and access the directories of other users. Users writing files to the same directory could also accidentally overwrite another user's files.

- **Isolate Users** This mode isolates users by local and domain user account names. Here, users log on to the server root directory using their Windows account. When the logon is authenticated, they're mapped transparently to their isolated user directory and won't be able to overwrite other users' files.

- **Isolate Users Using Active Directory** With this setting, IIS authenticates user credentials using Active Directory. If authenticated, users are mapped transparently to their isolated user directory based on the values of FTPRoot and FTPDir and won't be able to overwrite other users' files.

As shown in Figure 9-2, select Do Not Isolate Users and then click Next.

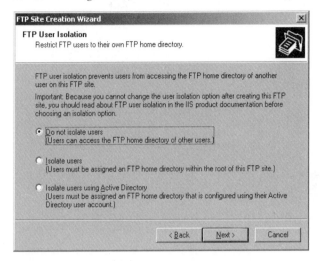

Figure 9-2. *Set user isolation mode for the FTP site.*

Caution You can't change the user isolation mode after an FTP site has been created. Because of this, you should carefully determine the mode you need to use and then develop an implementation plan to support this mode.

6. The FTP Site Home Directory page lets you set the home directory for the FTP site. Click Browse to search for a folder. This folder must be created before you can select it. If necessary, click Browse and then Make New Folder in the Browse For Folder dialog box. Click Next.

7. You can set access permissions for the FTP site. Normally, you'll want to set Read permissions only. The standard permissions are the following:

   * **Read** Allows users to download documents, which means that their clients can transfer documents from the server

   * **Write** Allows users to upload documents, which means that their clients can transfer documents to the server

8. Click Next and then click Finish. The FTP site is created automatically. The new FTP site may or may not be started. You should update the site's properties before you make it accessible to users.

Creating Isolated FTP Sites Without Active Directory

You can create isolated FTP sites that don't use Active Directory by completing the following steps:

1. In the IIS snap-in, access the node for the computer you want to work with, right-click FTP Sites, choose New from the shortcut menu, and then select FTP Site. If the computer isn't shown, connect to it as discussed in the "Connecting to Other Servers" section of Chapter 2 and then perform this task.

2. The FTP Site Creation Wizard is started. Click Next. In the Description field, type a descriptive name for the FTP site, such as Corporate FTP Server. Click Next.

3. As shown previously in Figure 9-1, use the IP Address drop-down list to select an available IP address. Select (All Unassigned) to allow FTP to respond on all unassigned IP addresses that are configured on the server. Multiple FTP sites can use the same IP address if the sites are configured to use different port numbers.

4. The TCP port for the FTP site is assigned automatically as port 21. If necessary, type a new port number in the TCP Port field. Multiple sites can use the same port if the sites are configured to use different IP addresses. Click Next.

5. Select Isolate Users and then click Next.

6. The FTP Site Home Directory page lets you set the home directory for the FTP site. Click Browse to search for a folder. This folder must be created before you can select it. If necessary, click Browse and then Make New Folder in the Browse For Folder dialog box. Click Next.

7. You can set access permissions for the FTP site. Normally, you'll want to set Read permissions only. The standard permissions are the following:

   • **Read** Allows users to download documents, which means that their clients can transfer documents from the server

   • **Write** Allows users to upload documents, which means that their clients can transfer documents to the server

8. Click Next and then click Finish. The FTP site is created automatically. The new FTP site may or may not be started. You should update the site's properties before you make it accessible to users.

9. If anonymous access to the FTP site is allowed, create a directory called LocalUser under the root directory and then create a subdirectory of LocalUser called Public.

10. If users access the FTP site using local user accounts, create a directory called LocalUser under the root directory and then create subdirectories for each user account that will be used. These directories should be named the same as the user account (%UserName%).

11. If users access the FTP site using domain user accounts, create directories for the domain under the root directory and then create subdirectories under the domain directories for each user. These directories should be named the same as the user account (%UserName%).

Creating Isolated FTP Sites with Active Directory

You can create isolated FTP sites that use Active Directory by completing the following steps:

1. In the IIS snap-in, access the node for the computer you want to work with, right-click FTP Sites, choose New from the shortcut menu, and then select FTP Site. If the computer isn't shown, connect to it as discussed in the "Connecting to Other Servers" section of Chapter 2 and then perform this task.

2. The FTP Site Creation Wizard is started. Click Next. In the Description field, type a descriptive name for the FTP site, such as Corporate FTP Server. Click Next.

3. As shown previously in Figure 9-1, use the IP Address drop-down list to select an available IP address. Select (All Unassigned) to allow FTP to respond on all unassigned IP addresses that are configured on the server. Multiple FTP sites can use the same IP address if the sites are configured to use different port numbers.

4. The TCP port for the FTP site is assigned automatically as port 21. If necessary, type a new port number in the TCP Port field. Multiple sites can use the same port if the sites are configured to use different IP addresses. Click Next.

5. Select Isolate Users Using Active Directory and then click Next.

6. Type the user name of an account with administrator privileges that can be used to access the Active Directory domain, so that users can be authenticated, such as ADATUM\Administrator. To search for an account to use, click Browse.

7. Enter the password for the specified account.

8. Enter the default domain to be used, such as adatum.com, or click Browse to use the Browse For Domain dialog box to search for a domain to use.

9. Click Next. When prompted, confirm the password for the previously specified account.

10. Set access permissions for the FTP site. Normally, you'll want to set Read permissions only, but since you can't change this option later, be sure to plan accordingly. The standard permissions are the following:

    • **Read** Allows users to download documents, which means that their clients can transfer documents from the server

    • **Write** Allows users to upload documents, which means that their clients can transfer documents to the server

11. Click Next and then click Finish. The FTP site is created automatically.

Tip Note that you didn't have to specify a root directory for the FTP site. Sites isolated using Active Directory don't have an actual home directory. Instead, users map directly to their isolated directories using an arbitrary (not actual) root directory. Because of this, the site's Properties dialog box doesn't have a Home Directory tab and any options on this tab can't be set.

Managing FTP Sites

The sections that follow examine key tasks for managing FTP sites. You configure most FTP site properties through the IIS snap-in.

Configuring an FTP Site's Home Directory

Each FTP site on a server has a home directory. The home directory is the base directory for all document transfers. The home directory is mapped to your site's domain name or to the server name. FTP clients connect to the server and access this directory by default.

With FTP sites configured to use Active Directory, the home directory is arbitrarily assigned at logon and users are mapped directly to their isolated directory. With other types of FTP sites, the home directory is a physical location on the server's hard disk drive. You can view or change this home directory by completing the following steps:

1. In the IIS snap-in, access the node for the computer you want to work with and then double-click FTP Sites.

2. Right-click the FTP site you want to manage and then select Properties.

3. Select the Home Directory tab, as shown in Figure 9-3.

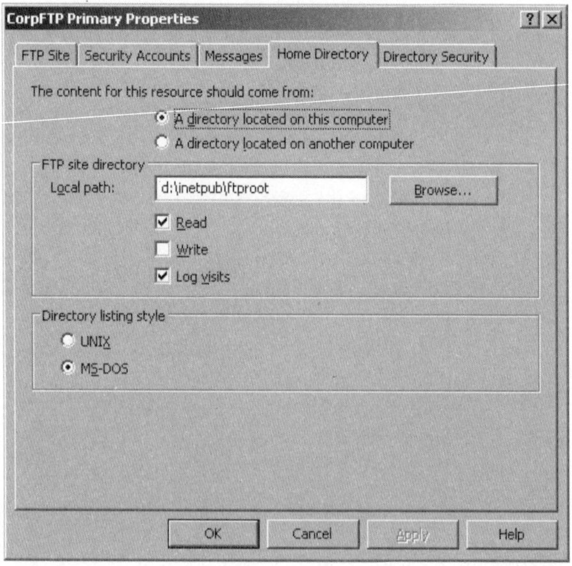

Figure 9-3. *You can change a site's home directory at any time.*

4. If the directory you want to use is on the local computer, select A Directory Located On This Computer and then type the directory path in the Local Path field, such as **C:\Inetpub\FTProot**. To browse for the folder, click Browse.

5. If the directory you want to use is on another computer and is accessible as a shared folder, select A Directory Located On Another Computer and then type the UNC path to the share in the Network Share field. The path should be in the form *ServerName**SharedFolder*\, such as \\Gandolf\CorpFTP\.

Tip By default, the user's credentials are validated prior to accessing the shared folder. If you don't want users to be prompted or otherwise use their authenticated credentials, click Connect As. This displays the Network Directory Security Credentials dialog box. Clear the Always Use the Authenticated User's Credentials ... check box, and then enter the user name and password that should be used to connect to the shared folder, such as ADATUM\IUSR_CORPSEVER01.

6. Click OK twice.

Configuring Ports and IP Addresses Used by FTP Sites

Each FTP site has a unique identity. The identity consists of a TCP port and an IP address. The default TCP port is 21. The default IP address setting is to use any available IP address.

To change the identity of an FTP site, complete the following steps:

1. If you want the FTP site to use a new IP address, you must configure the IP address before updating the site. For details, refer to Chapter 16, "Managing TCP/IP Networking," in *Microsoft Windows Server 2003 Administrator's Pocket Consultant*.

2. In the IIS snap-in, access the node for the computer you want to work with. If the computer isn't shown, connect to it as discussed in the "Connecting To Other Servers" section of Chapter 2 and then perform this task.

3. Right-click the FTP site you want to manage and then select Properties. The dialog box shown in Figure 9-4 is displayed.

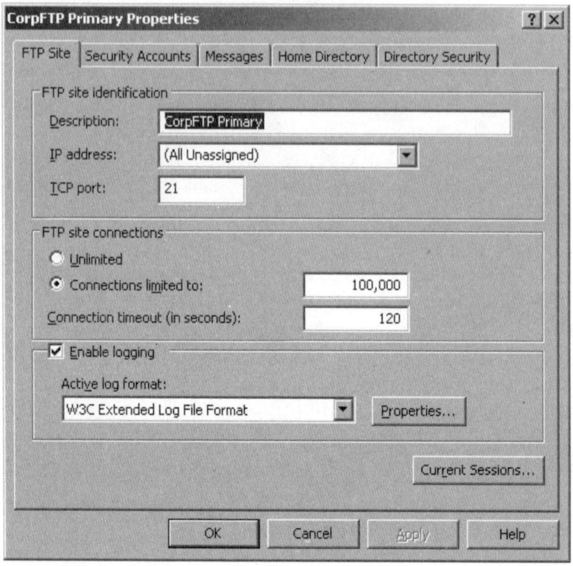

Figure 9-4. *You modify a site's identity through the FTP Site tab in the Properties dialog box.*

4. The Description field shows the descriptive name for the FTP site. The descriptive name is displayed in the IIS snap-in and isn't used for other purposes. You can change the current value by typing a new name in the Description field.

5. The IP Address drop-down list shows the current IP address for the FTP site. If you want to change the current setting, use the drop-down list to select an available IP address, or select (All Unassigned) to allow FTP to respond on all unassigned IP addresses. Multiple FTP sites can use the same IP address if the sites are configured to use different port numbers.

6. The TCP port for the FTP site is assigned automatically to port 21. If necessary, type a new port number in the TCP Port field. Multiple FTP sites can use the same TCP port if the sites are configured to use different IP addresses.

7. Click OK.

Restricting Incoming Connections and Setting Time-Out Values

You use connection limits and time-out values to control the number of simultaneous FTP sessions that are allowed. Normally, FTP sites are limited to 100,000 connections and have a time-out of 120 seconds. If you have a server with limited resources, you might want to reduce the number of allowable connections. Keep in mind that once the limit is reached, no other clients are permitted to access the server. The clients must wait until the connection load on the server decreases and connections become available.

The connection time-out value determines when idle user sessions are disconnected. With the default FTP site, sessions time out after they've been idle for 120 seconds (2 minutes). This is a good time-out for most FTP uses. If you find that users are complaining about getting disconnected from idle sessions, you might want to increase the time-out value.

You can modify connection limits and time-outs by completing the following steps:

1. Start the IIS snap-in and then, in the left pane (Console Root), click the plus sign (+) next to the computer you want to work with. Next, double-click FTP sites, right-click the FTP site you want to manage, and then choose Properties.

2. On the FTP Site tab, the FTP Site Connections frame has two option buttons: Unlimited and Connections Limited To. The Unlimited option removes connection limits, which isn't a good idea for FTP servers. The Connections Limited To option restricts the number of connections to a specific value. If you select the Connections Limited To option, you must also specify the maximum number of connections that are permitted at any one time.

3. The Connection Timeout field controls the connection time-out. Type a new value to change the current time-out.

4. Click OK.

Tip Each connection to an FTP server uses system resources. To reduce the load on the server, you should set a specific connection limit. The default option is Connections Limited To, which allows 100,000 simultaneous connections. On an average-sized server, this is a good value. If a server has limited resources or is used for other purposes, such as publishing your Web site, you might want to reduce this value. If a server is dedicated to FTP or is an enterprise class server, you might want to increase this value.

Creating Physical Directories for FTP Sites

FTP sites can be used for file uploads and downloads. Typically, directories used for uploading data are configured separately from directories used for retrieving data. Separate directory structures provide a clear separation between files that your organization has made available and files that users have uploaded. Here's a typical directory tree for an FTP site:

- **%SystemDrive%\Inetpub\FTProot**   Base directory for the site
- **%SystemDrive%\Inetpub\FTProot\Public**   Base directory for downloads
- **%SystemDrive%\Inetpub\FTProot\Upload**   Base directory for uploads

Once you establish the base directory structure, you can add directories to the tree. For example, a software company might have the following subdirectories under %SystemDrive%\Inetpub\FTProot\Public\:

- **Documentation**   Directory for product documentation
- **Patches**   Directory for patches to software
- **Service_Packs**   Directory for service packs

 Tip   To help visitors understand your site's directory structure, you should create a Welcome message that provides both an overview of how the site is meant to be used and a directory map. A directory map is a text file that describes in detail the available directories and what they're used for. Save the directory map as a .txt file in the base directory for the site.

You might want to configure separate FTP sites for uploads and downloads. On the upload site, you configure write-only access for upload directories. On the download site, you configure read-only access for download directories. In this way, visitors can only perform one very specific task at the site, and you have an easier job as an administrator.

You create physical directories for FTP sites using Windows Explorer. You can create subdirectories within the home directory by completing the following steps:

1. Start Windows Explorer. Click Start and choose All Programs, Accessories, and then Windows Explorer.

2. In the Folders pane, select the home directory for the FTP site.

3. In the Contents pane, right-click a blank area and then, from the shortcut menu, select New and then Folder. A new folder is added to the Contents pane. The folder name defaults to New Folder and is selected for editing.

4. Edit the name of the folder and press Enter. The best folder names are short but descriptive, such as Documentation, Service_Packs, or Patches.

5. The new folder inherits the home directory's default file permissions and the FTP site's default IIS permissions.

 Note   The IIS snap-in doesn't automatically display new folders. You might need to click Refresh on the toolbar (or press F5) to display the folder.

Creating Virtual Directories for FTP Sites

To create virtual directories, you first need to create a physical directory. You can create a physical directory using Windows Explorer or create one using the Virtual Directory Creation Wizard. You can configure virtual directories on FTP sites to allow file uploads, file downloads, or both. The way you control file transfers is simple. You set these configurations:

- Read access on directories that should allow downloads
- Write access on directories that should allow uploads
- Read and write access on directories that should allow uploads and downloads

Don't forget, however, that permissions at the file and folder level also control user permissions. With an anonymous connection, the Internet Guest account must have the appropriate directory permissions. With an authenticated connection, the user or a group in which the user is a member must have the appropriate directory permissions.

You can create a virtual directory by completing the following steps:

1. Start the IIS snap-in and then, in the left pane (Console Root), click the plus sign (+) next to the computer you want to work with.

2. Double-click FTP sites and then right-click the FTP site on which you want to create the virtual directory. From the shortcut menu, choose New and then Virtual Directory. This starts the Virtual Directory Creation Wizard. Click Next.

3. In the Alias field, type the name you want to use to access the virtual directory. As with directory names, the best alias names are short but descriptive.

4. The next page lets you set the path to the physical directory where your content is stored. Type the directory path or click Browse to search for a directory. The directory must be created before you can select it. If necessary, click Make New Folder in the Browse For Folder dialog box to create the directory before you select it.

5. Set access permissions for the virtual directory. Read permission allows users to download files. Write permission allows users to upload files.

6. Click Next and then click Finish. The virtual directory is created.

Redirecting Requests to a Network Share

When the FTP site is configured to use the non-isolated or standard isolated modes, you can redirect a site's file requests to locations on a network share. This option is useful if you have network attached storage or a dedicated server for file transfers.

To redirect requests to a network share, complete the following steps:

1. In the IIS snap-in, right-click the FTP site you want to work with and then select Properties.

2. Select the Home Directory tab and then select A Directory Located On Another Computer.

3. Type the UNC path to the network share in the Network Share field. The path should be in the form *ServerName**SharedFolder*\, such as \\Gandolf\CorpFTP\. By default, the user's credentials are validated prior to accessing the shared folder. If you don't want users to be prompted or otherwise use their authenticated credentials, click Connect As and then specify the credentials to use.

4. Click OK twice. Now all requests for files on the FTP site are mapped to files on the specified network share.

Setting the Directory Listing Style

When an FTP client accesses an FTP site, it automatically retrieves a directory listing from the server. If the FTP site is configured to use the non-isolated or standard isolated modes, you can configure the style of directory listing in one of two ways:

- **MS-DOS style**   Provides MS-DOS-style file names, dates, and directory listings
- **UNIX style**   Provides UNIX-style file names, dates, and directory listings

MS-DOS style listings are the preferred format, as they're friendlier and easier to navigate. UNIX style listings are compatible with older browsers that might not understand the MS-DOS format. You set directory listing style at the site level. To do this, complete the following steps:

1. In the IIS snap-in, right-click the FTP site you want to work with and then select Properties.

2. Select the Home Directory tab and then, under Directory Listing Style, select either UNIX or MS-DOS.

3. Click OK.

Setting Banner, Welcome, Exit, and Maximum Connections Messages

IIS FTP sites can display four different types of messages: Banner, Welcome, Exit, and Maximum Connections. These messages are called information messages and are set at the site level. Each FTP site configured on your server can have a different set of information messages. Generally, these messages aren't displayed in Internet Explorer or other graphical FTP client tools. Most command-line FTP clients will, however, display these messages.

Each information message has a different use:

- **Banner messages**   Banner messages are displayed when users first connect to the FTP server. They can contain information about the site's purpose, rules for using the site, locations of mirror sites, administrator contact, and more. The best Banner messages are informative and contain 8 to 10 lines of text. To offset the message, you can start and end the message with a line of banner text, such as a line of asterisks.

- **Welcome messages**   Welcome messages are displayed when users first log on the FTP server. If their client automatically logs on when accessing the site, the Welcome message generally is the first message they see. Like a Banner message, a Welcome message can contain information about the site's purpose, rules for using the site, locations of mirror sites, administrator contact, and more.

- **Exit messages** Exit messages display final text to users when they leave your site. Exit messages are displayed when clients log off using the FTP command QUIT in an active session. Exit messages aren't displayed when clients terminate an FTP session through a different technique, such as clicking Close in a browser window. Exit messages can be only one line long and should be short and to the point.

- **Maximum Connections messages** Maximum Connections messages display when the server's connection threshold has been reached. These messages can be only one line long and should be short and to the point. Keep in mind that you can change the number of simultaneous connections allowed. To do this, follow the procedure discussed in the "Restricting Incoming Connections and Setting Time-Out Values" section of this chapter.

You can configure information messages by completing the following steps:

1. In the IIS snap-in, right-click the FTP site you want to work with and then select Properties.

2. Select the Messages tab.

3. In the Banner field, type your Banner message. Because you'll usually want to have the same text in your Welcome message, you should copy this text into the Welcome field. Otherwise, type a separate Welcome message.

Note Each line of text should end with a return (carriage return and line feed). If you don't end each line of text, Internet Explorer's FTP client might not display your message properly.

4. In the Exit field, type your Exit message.

5. In the Maximum Connections field, type your Maximum Connections message.

6. Click OK.

Managing FTP User Sessions

Each connection to an FTP site uses resources on the FTP server. To help you monitor resource usage, IIS allows you to view statistics on sessions. Each FTP site has separate session statistics.

Viewing FTP User Sessions

You can view session information for an FTP site by completing the following steps:

1. In the IIS snap-in, right-click the FTP site you want to work with and then select Properties.

2. Click Current Sessions in the FTP Site tab. This displays the FTP User Sessions dialog box shown in Figure 9-5. This dialog box displays the following information:

- **Connected Users** The account name of authenticated users or the password value entered by anonymous users.

 Tip Keep in mind that anonymous users are asked to enter their e-mail addresses as the password value. You can distinguish between authenticated and anonymous users by the icon that's displayed. Icons for anonymous users have a red question mark. Icons for authenticated users have a standard user image.

- **From** The IP address or DNS name of the computer from which the user is connecting.

- **Time** The total elapsed time since the session started. The format is HH:MM:SS.

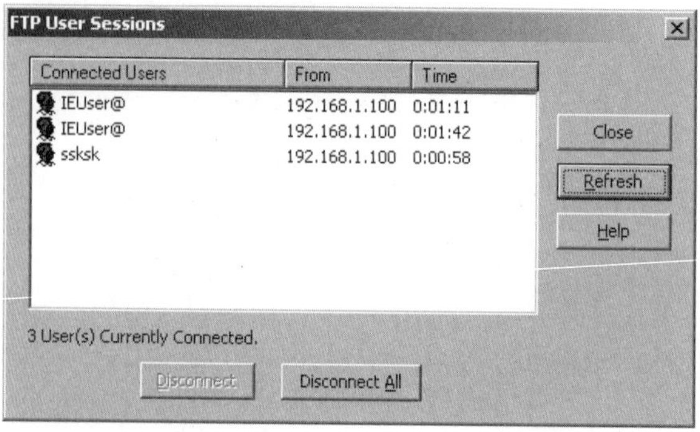

FTP User Sessions			⊠
Connected Users	From	Time	
🧑 IEUser@	192.168.1.100	0:01:11	
🧑 IEUser@	192.168.1.100	0:01:42	Close
🧑 ssksk	192.168.1.100	0:00:58	Refresh
			Help
3 User(s) Currently Connected.			
	Disconnect	Disconnect All	

Figure 9-5. *Current FTP user sessions are displayed by user name, IP address, and connection duration.*

3. Click Refresh to renew the session statistics or click Close when you're finished monitoring user sessions.

Viewing the Total Number of Connected Users

In the lower-left corner of the FTP User Sessions dialog box, IIS displays the total number of users who are connected to an FTP site. You can access this dialog box and view the total number of connected users by completing the following steps:

1. In the IIS snap-in, right-click the FTP site you want to work with and then select Properties.

2. Click Current Sessions in the FTP Site tab. This displays the FTP User Sessions dialog box.

3. The total number of connected users is displayed in the lower-left corner of the dialog box. Click Refresh to get an updated count.

Terminating FTP User Sessions

You can terminate individual user sessions or all user sessions that are active on an FTP site. Typically, you want to do this when the session lasts too long or there are problems with resources on the server. If the user is uploading or downloading a file when you terminate the session, the file transfer terminates immediately, and the user gets a message stating that the remote host has closed the connection.

To disconnect an individual session, follow these steps:

1. In the IIS snap-in, right-click the FTP site you want to work with and then select Properties.

2. In the FTP Site tab, click Current Sessions.

3. Select the session you want to terminate and then click Disconnect.

4. When prompted to confirm the action, click Yes.

5. Click Close and then click OK to return to the IIS snap-in.

To disconnect all user sessions on an FTP site, follow these steps:

1. In the IIS snap-in, right-click the FTP site you want to work with and then select Properties.

2. Click Current Sessions in the FTP Site tab.

3. Click Disconnect All and then, when prompted to confirm the action, click Yes.

4. Click Close and then click OK to return to the IIS snap-in.

Managing FTP Server Security

You handle FTP server security much like Web server security. You manage security at two levels: Windows and IIS. At the operating system level, you create user accounts, configure access permissions for files and directories, and set policies. At the IIS level, you set content permissions, authentication controls, and user privileges.

Note Most FTP server security tasks are identical to those for Web server security. This section focuses only on what's different. For a complete discussion of IIS security, see Chapter 7.

Managing Anonymous Connections

You manage anonymous access to FTP sites using a named account that has the appropriate permissions for the directories and files you make available for uploading and downloading files. By default, the anonymous access account is the Internet guest account (IUSR_*ComputerName*) discussed in Chapter 7.

When anonymous access is enabled, users don't have to log on using a user name and password. IIS automatically logs the user on using the anonymous account information provided for the resource. If anonymous access isn't allowed, the site is configured for named account access only. Unlike Web sites, you can manage anonymous access only at the global or site level. You can't manage anonymous access at the directory or file level.

Setting Anonymous Access Globally

When the FTP site is configured to use the non-isolated or standard isolated modes, you can manage anonymous access for all FTP sites on a server by completing the following steps:

1. After accessing the computer node you want to work with in the IIS snap-in, right-click FTP Sites and then select Properties. This displays the FTP Sites Properties dialog box.

2. Select the Security Accounts tab in the Properties dialog box, as shown in Figure 9-6.

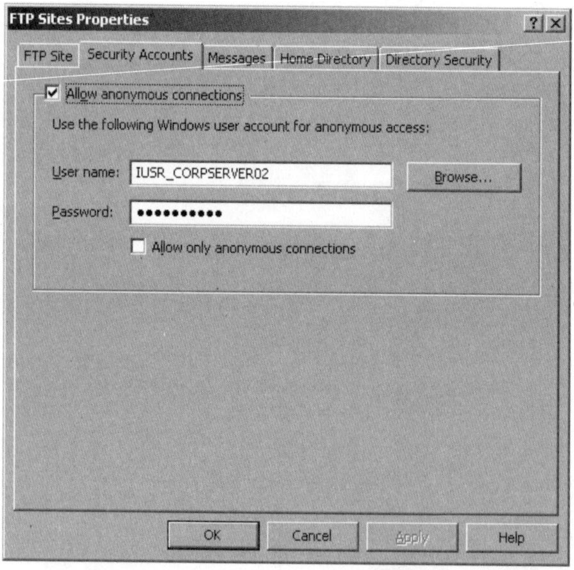

Figure 9-6. *Use the Security Accounts tab to configure anonymous access.*

3. To enable anonymous access, select Allow Anonymous Connections and complete the remaining steps in this procedure.

4. To disable anonymous access, clear Allow Anonymous Connections and skip the remaining steps in this procedure. With anonymous connections disabled, only authenticated users can access the server. You must configure local or domain accounts that can be used to access the sites on this server.

5. The User Name field specifies the account used for anonymous access to the resource. If you desire, type the account name you want to use instead of the existing account, or click Browse to display the Select User dialog box. As necessary, enter the password for the account in the Password field.

6. Allow Only Anonymous Connections prevents users from logging on to the server with user names and passwords. Select this option if you want only the anonymous user account to be available. If you want to allow users to log on to the server with named accounts, clear this option.

7. Click OK, and then, if you browsed for a user account, click OK again to save your settings. All FTP sites on the server inherit the changes automatically.

Setting Anonymous Access Locally

You can manage anonymous access for a specific FTP site by completing these steps:

1. In the IIS snap-in, right-click the FTP site you want to work with and then select Properties.

2. Select the Security Accounts tab.

3. To enable anonymous access, select Allow Anonymous Connections and complete the remaining steps in this procedure.

4. To disable anonymous access, clear Allow Anonymous Connections and skip the remaining steps in this procedure. With anonymous connections disabled, only authenticated users can access the site. You must configure local or domain accounts that can be used to access the site.

5. The User Name field specifies the account used for anonymous access to the resource. If you desire, type the account name you want to use instead of the existing account or click Browse to display the Select User dialog box. As necessary, enter the password for the account in the Password field.

6. Allow Only Anonymous Connections prevents users from logging on to the site with user names and passwords. Select this option if you want only the anonymous user account to be available. If you want to allow users to log on to the site with named accounts, clear this option.

7. Click OK.

Configuring Windows Permissions on FTP Servers

Every folder and file used by IIS can have different access permissions. You set these access permissions at the Windows security level. Anytime you work with file and folder permissions on an FTP server, you should keep the following in mind:

- Only administrators should have full control over folders and files. If users have full control, they'll be able to create, rename, and delete resources.

- Authenticated users should be assigned specific permissions based on the types of tasks they need to perform. Users who can download files should have Read permission on the appropriate folders and files. Users who can upload files should have Write permission on the appropriate folders (and Read permission if you want them to view folder contents).

- The Users group should have limited permissions. Set Read permission on folders and files used with downloads. Set Write permission on folders used with uploads (and Read permission if you want users to view folder contents).

- If the server is part of an Active Directory domain, the Internet Guest account is a member of the Domain Users group. Otherwise, the Internet Guest account is a member of the Guests group. This ensures that anonymous users can access the FTP site's directories. To prevent anonymous users from gaining permissions they shouldn't have, you can specifically deny permissions, such as Write. You could also deny advanced permissions, such as Delete and Delete Subfolders And Files.

 Tip If you modify the properties of the base directory for the Default FTP Site, you'll need to clear the Allow Inheritable Permissions From Parent check box before you can set specific permissions on the directory. You can access this check box by clicking Advanced in the Security tab.

Configuring FTP Server Permissions

FTP sites and directories have permissions in IIS in addition to the Windows security settings. These permissions are set the same for all users. This means you can't set different permissions for different users at the IIS level. You can, however, create specific areas of your FTP site that are designed for these specific functions:

- Download only
- Upload only
- Download and upload

You can set FTP permissions globally through the master properties or locally at the site or directory level. When you set FTP permissions in the master properties, you must also specify how these properties are inherited. If a site or directory has settings that conflict with permission changes you've made, you're given the opportunity to override the site or directory permissions with the global permissions.

Similarly, if you make site-level permission changes that conflict with existing permissions on a subdirectory, you're given the opportunity to override the site or directory permissions with the local permissions. In both cases the changes are applied when you choose to override the existing permissions.

Setting FTP Permissions Globally

To set FTP permissions globally, complete the following steps:

1. After accessing the computer node you want to work with in the IIS snap-in, right-click FTP Sites and then select Properties. This displays the FTP Site Properties dialog box.

2. As shown in Figure 9-7, select the Home Directory tab and then use the fields in the FTP Site Directory frame to set the permissions that you want sites and directories on this computer to inherit. The available options are the following:

   - **Read** Allows users to read or download files stored in the directory
   - **Write** Allows users to upload files to the directory
   - **Log Visits** Used with server logging to log requests related for resource files

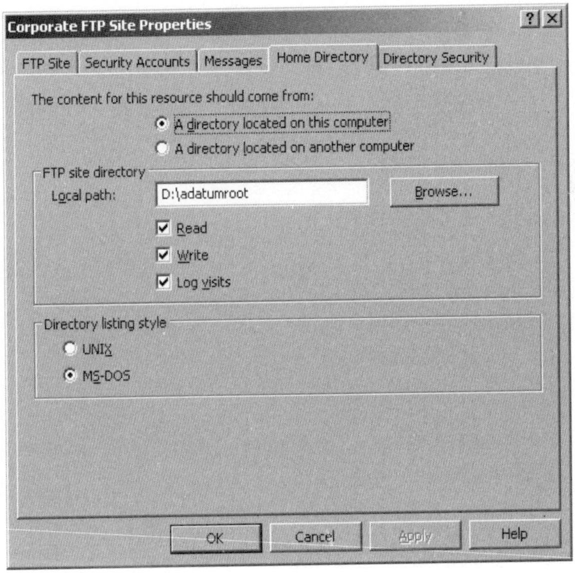

Figure 9-7. *Use the FTP Sites Properties dialog box to configure FTP permissions.*

3. Click Apply. Before applying permission changes, IIS checks the existing permissions in use for all FTP sites and directories within FTP sites. If a site or directory node uses a different value for a permission, the Inheritance

Overrides dialog box is displayed. Use this dialog box to select the site and directory nodes, which should use the new permission value, and then click OK.

Setting FTP Permissions Locally

To set FTP permissions for a site or directory, complete the following steps:

1. In the IIS snap-in, right-click the site or directory.
2. Select the Home Directory, Directory, or Virtual Directory tab as appropriate. This displays the dialog box shown in Figure 9-8. Then use the following fields to set the permissions for the selected resource:
   - **Read**   Allows users to read or download files stored in the directory
   - **Write**   Allows users to upload files to the directory
   - **Log Visits**   Used with server logging to log requests related for resource files

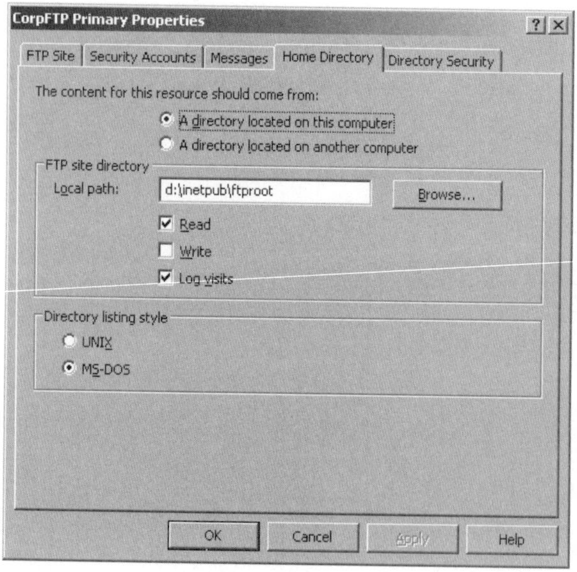

Figure 9-8. *Use the site's Properties dialog box to configure FTP permissions.*

3. Click Apply. Before applying FTP permission changes, IIS checks the existing permissions in use for all subdirectories. If a subdirectory uses a different value for a permission, the Inheritance Overrides dialog box is displayed. Use this dialog box to select the site and directory nodes, which should use the new permission value, and then click OK.

Configuring IP Address and Domain Name Restrictions

By default, FTP resources are accessible to all IP addresses, computers, and domains, which presents a security risk that might allow your server to be misused. To control use of resources, you might want to grant or deny access by IP address, network identification, or domain. As with other FTP server settings, you can apply restrictions through the master FTP server properties or through the properties for individual sites, directories, and files.

- Granting access allows a computer to make requests for resources but doesn't necessarily allow users to work with resources. If you require authentication, users still need to authenticate themselves.

- Denying access to resources prevents a computer from accessing those resources. Consequently, users of the computer can't access the resources—even if they could have authenticated themselves with a username and password.

You can establish or remove restrictions globally through the master FTP Site Properties dialog box by completing the following steps:

1. After accessing the computer node you want to work with in the IIS snap-in, right-click FTP Sites and then select Properties. This displays the FTP Sites Properties dialog box.

2. Select the Directory Security tab, as shown in Figure 9-9.

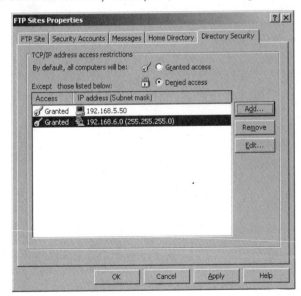

Figure 9-9. *You can grant or deny access by IP address, network identification, and domain.*

3. Click Granted Access to grant access to specific computers and deny access to all others.

4. Click Denied Access to deny access to specific computers and grant access to all others.

5. Create the Access list. Click Add, and then, in the Grant Access Or Deny Access dialog box, specify Single Computer or Group Of Computers as follows:

   • For a Single Computer, type the IP address for the computer, such as **192.168.5.50**.

   • For Groups Of Computers, type the Network ID, such as **192.168.6.0**, and the Subnet Mask, such as **255.255.255.0**.

6. If you want to remove an entry from the Access list, select the related entry and then click Remove.

7. Click Apply. Before applying changes, IIS checks the existing restrictions for all FTP sites and directories within FTP sites. If a site or directory node uses a different value, the Inheritance Overrides dialog box is displayed. Use this dialog box to select the site and directory nodes that should use the new setting and then click OK.

You can establish or remove restrictions at the site or directory level by completing these steps:

1. In the IIS snap-in, right-click the site or directory that you want to work with. This displays a Properties dialog box.

2. Select the Directory Security tab.

3. Click Granted Access to grant access to specific computers and deny access to all others.

4. Click Denied Access to deny access to specific computers and grant access to all others.

5. Create the Access list. Click Add and then, in the Grant Access Or Deny Access dialog box, specify Single Computer or Group Of Computers as follows:

   • For a Single Computer, type the IP address for the computer, such as **192.168.5.50**.

   • For Groups Of Computers, type the Network ID, such as **192.168.6.0**, and the Subnet Mask, such as **255.255.255.0**.

6. If you want to remove an entry from the Access list, select the related entry and then click Remove.

7. Click Apply. Before applying changes, IIS checks the existing restrictions for all child nodes of the selected resource (if any). If a child node uses a different value, the Inheritance Overrides dialog box is displayed. Use this dialog box to select the site and directory nodes that should use the new setting and then click OK.

Chapter 10

Configuring and Maintaining E-Mail Services

E-mail services are an important part of most Internet, intranet, and extranet server operations. Often, you'll find that applications installed on a server generate e-mails that need to be delivered or users connected to a server need to be able to send or receive e-mail. Microsoft Windows Server 2003 ships with several components that make this possible, including Simple Mail Transfer Protocol (SMTP) and Post Office Protocol 3 (POP3).

SMTP is used to transfer and route e-mail messages. SMTP is available for installation as a component of Internet Information Services (IIS). Most organizations use the SMTP features in IIS to send e-mail rather than to allow World Wide Web servers to receive e-mail—and this is the purpose for which the SMTP service was designed. If you want to receive e-mail and store it on the server so that users and applications can retrieve it, you need to install POP3.

SMTP and POP3 are two of the three components that make up a typical e-mail system. The other component is a POP3 e-mail client that actually sends or receives e-mail using these protocols. Managing SMTP and POP3 is very different from any administration process you must perform in your normal duties as a Web administrator. Instead of managing content or file transfers, you're managing the way in which e-mail messages are handled and delivered. Before diving in to core administration tasks, let's look at fundamentals. A discussion of fundamentals will help build the essential background for successful e-mail services administration.

Using Mail Services

You manage the configuration of SMTP through virtual servers. These virtual servers are used to handle mail submission and transport services for one or more e-mail domains and each SMTP virtual server. When you install the SMTP service as part of an IIS installation, a default SMTP virtual server is created.

The default virtual server is preconfigured so that locally generated messages can be handled and delivered. The configuration restricts the sending of messages that are generated by remote users, which include the Internet Guest account and any other named user on the Web server. The configuration also restricts relaying of e-mail through the SMTP virtual server. With these settings you can use the default virtual server in most environments without having to make further adjustments. That said, there are many times when you'll want to optimize configuration settings to meet your environment's needs.

You manage the configuration of POP3 using e-mail domains. Each POP3 server has a specific configuration that's inherited by the e-mail domains configured on the server. You install the POP3 service separate from the IIS installation. To do this, you install the E-Mail Services Windows component. Because the POP3 installation is dependent on IIS and SMTP, these components are also installed if they aren't already installed on the server.

The SMTP and POP3 services are designed to provide basic messaging services for one or more domains and you can configure them in different ways. To understand how e-mail services are used and managed, you need to understand the following concepts:

- How e-mail domains are used
- How the mail root is used
- How SMTP messages are processed

Understanding E-Mail Domain Usage

The SMTP and POP3 services use the e-mail address provided in a message's To, Cc, Bcc, and From fields to determine how the message should be handled. To, Cc, and Bcc fields are used to determine where the message should be delivered. The From field determines from where the message originated.

E-mail addresses, such as *williams@tech.microsoft.com*, have three components:

- An e-mail account, such as *williams*
- An at symbol (@), which separates the account name from the domain name
- An e-mail domain, such as *tech.microsoft.com*

The key component that determines how the server handles messages is the e-mail or service domain. Service domains can be either local or remote. A local service domain is a Domain Name System (DNS) domain that's serviced locally by the server. A remote service domain is a DNS domain that's serviced by another server or mail gateway.

Any message with a local domain name in a message's To, Cc, or Bcc fields is delivered locally. With SMTP you can designate a local domain as the default domain or an alias domain. The default domain serves as the default for all messages transferred into or out of the domain. Messages addressed to the default domain are stored in the virtual server's Drop directory and, if POP3 is configured, delivered to the appropriate mailbox, if it's available. Outgoing messages that don't have a domain set in the From field of the e-mail address use the default domain as their domain of origin. An SMTP virtual server can have only one default domain.

Any other local domains that you create on an SMTP virtual server are specified as *alias domains.* Alias domains allow you to create secondary domains that point to the default domain and use its settings. When working with alias domains, keep in mind that any message sent to an alias domain is stamped with the default domain name. This means that the alias domain uses the same configuration settings and the same Drop directory as the default domain. For example, an SMTP virtual server could specify *tech.microsoft.com* as the default domain and *dev.microsoft.com* as an alias domain. Any messages that specify either of these domains are handled locally by the SMTP virtual server on which they're configured and are stamped with the default domain name.

Any message with a nonlocal domain in a message's To, Cc, or Bcc fields is queued for delivery to a remote server. If you have unique delivery require-ments for a specific remote domain, you can add a remote domain to the SMTP server and configure settings that allow you to handle its messages appropri-ately. For example, you could configure a remote domain with separate out-bound security that requires message encryption. Or you could forward messages destined for a remote domain through a specific mail server desig-nated as a smart host.

To receive e-mail, the server must be registered as the mail exchange for the domain in DNS. For example, if you wanted to receive mail for *dev.microsoft.com*, you'd need to have your Internet service provider (ISP) create a Mail Exchange (MX) record in DNS. This record would designate the server as an authorized mail exchange for the *dev.microsoft.com* domain.

When you create an MX record, you must specify a preference number for the mail server. This value denotes the mail server's priority within the domain. The server with the lowest priority is the first to receive mail. If mail delivery to this server fails, the mail server with the next lowest priority is tried.

For example, you could configure netmail01 and netmail02 as mail servers for your organization's data center. If netmail01 had a priority of 10 and netmail02 had a priority of 15, mail would first be routed to the netmail01 server. If deliv-ery to that server failed, the mail would be routed to netmail02.

Generally speaking, you can't route mail to multiple servers—only one server will receive the mail, and because of this, you'll want to plan out the imple-mentation very carefully. In most cases you wouldn't want mail for your com-pany's primary domain to be routed to your Internet, intranet, or extranet servers. For example, if *microsoft.com* is your primary domain and you already have a mail exchange server configured for the company, you wouldn't want POP3 e-mail services for your Web servers to interfere with mail delivery to the *microsoft.com* domain. Here, you might configure a new e-mail domain, such as *dev.microsoft.com*, and use this domain for your Internet, intranet, or extra-net servers.

Understanding the Mail Root

During the installation of mail services, a default SMTP virtual server is installed. Both SMTP and POP3 use this default virtual server, and you can't delete it.

The default virtual server uses the Inetpub\Mailroot folder to manage message submission and delivery. You can install additional SMTP virtual servers. When you do this, each virtual server has a separate mail root that's located in the directory you specify during creation. The only mail root shared by POP3 servers, however, is Inetpub\Mailroot or the directory you specify when configuring the POP3 mail server.

Each mail root has seven subfolders associated with it. These folders are used as follows:

- **Badmail** Used to store messages that are undeliverable and can't be returned to the sender. Each badmail message has an error message associated with it that you can use to help diagnose the problem. You should periodically monitor the Badmail folder to ensure that messages are flowing through the system as expected.

- **Drop** Drop box for all incoming messages addressed to recipients located on the server, such as the virtual server's postmaster. If an incoming message is addressed to a local recipient, the SMTP service moves the message from the Queue folder to this folder. This folder becomes the final destination unless POP3 is configured. When POP3 is configured, the message is passed from the Queue folder to the appropriate mailbox store, bypassing the Drop folder.

- **Mailbox** Used to store mailboxes. For the Inetpub\Mailroot folder, this is where you'd look to find mailboxes for users who have POP3 e-mail domains. Each domain configured has a separate folder and within this folder are subfolders for any mailboxes you've created for the domain. With Mailbox folders, individual e-mail messages are stored as flat files.

- **Pickup** Used as a pickup point for messages that are to be delivered by the SMTP service. The SMTP service monitors this mailbox continuously for new messages. Any message placed in this folder is picked up by the SMTP service and transferred to the Queue folder for further processing and delivery.

- **Queue** Holds messages that are ready for processing and delivery. Messages are transferred to the Queue folder from the Pickup folder when they're received by SMTP. Messages that the SMTP service is unable to deliver due to bad connections or busy destination servers are stored in the Queue folder as well. These messages remain in the Queue folder until they can be delivered or until they're deemed undeliverable and transferred to the Badmail folder.

- **Route** Used to store temporary data needed to route messages along specific paths. Typically used when you configure a route domain for an SMTP virtual server.

- **SortTemp** Serves as a temporary sorting area for messages. Temporary files are created in this directory and are cleared out after messages are sorted and queued for delivery.

When you configure e-mail services for use on a server, you should periodically monitor the Badmail and Queue folders. The Badmail folder provides the best indicator that you might have a problem with e-mail transfer. Messages in this folder couldn't be delivered to the intended recipients, and they couldn't be returned to the sender. If the number of messages in this folder is growing, your mail server might have a problem accessing the network or delivering mail. Likewise, if the number of queued messages is growing and messages aren't clearing out of the Queue folder, your mail server might have a problem connecting to the network or delivering mail.

Understanding Mail Processing

The SMTP service is very systematic in the way it processes mail messages. Mail messages can originate from two sources:

- **Pickup folder**   Message files placed in the Pickup folder by an application, such as an Active Server Page, or by a user, such as an administrator
- **SMTP**   Message files received using the SMTP network protocol

When a message is copied to the Pickup folder or comes in through the SMTP network protocol, it's placed in the Queue folder for processing and delivery. What happens to a message next depends on the type of recipient. Mail recipients fall into two categories:

- **Local recipients**   A local recipient is a recipient with an e-mail domain serviced locally by the SMTP server. Locally serviced domains are the default domain and any alias domains configured on the server. Mail messages for local recipients are handled locally.

- **Remote recipients**   A remote recipient is a recipient with an e-mail domain serviced remotely by the SMTP server. Mail messages for remote recipients can be relayed directly, routed through DNS, or forwarded to a designated mail gateway.

Note   The e-mail domain is the portion of the e-mail address to the right of the at symbol (@). For example, the e-mail domain for the *williams@tech.microsoft.com* address is *tech.microsoft.com*. E-mail addresses and domain names are always processed by the server from right to left.

If a message is for local recipients and POP3 isn't configured, the message is moved from the Queue folder to the Drop folder designated for the default domain. After the message is placed in the Drop folder, the SMTP service is done processing the message. By default, the Drop folder is located at Inetpub\Mailroot\Drop. However, the Drop folder's location is configurable and you can change it using the Properties dialog box for the default domain.

If a message is for local recipients and POP3 is configured, the message is moved from the Queue folder to the appropriate mailbox store. The Drop folder isn't used in this case.

If a message is for remote recipients, the recipients for the message are sorted by domain so the SMTP service can deliver the messages to these recipients as a group and thereby attempt to deliver multiple messages in a single mail session. After sorting, the message is queued for delivery.

Messages in the queue are handled in first in, first out (FIFO) order, which means that the first message into the queue is the first message that SMTP attempts to deliver. When a message is at the front of the queue, the SMTP service attempts to connect to the destination mail server. If the SMTP service is able to establish a connection, the recipients are verified, the message is sent, and it's up to the destination server to confirm receipt. If the destination server fails to respond or isn't ready to receive the message, the message remains in the queue and the SMTP service attempts to deliver the message according to the retry intervals you've specified. Processing will continue on lower-ranked messages while the SMTP service waits to retry delivery.

Messages that can't be delivered within a specific expiration period are marked as non-deliverable, and the SMTP service generates a non-delivery report. The non-delivery report provides an error message that explains why delivery failed, along with the original message. The SMTP service then attempts to deliver this report to the sender of the original message.

The message delivery process for the non-delivery report is the same as it is for any other message. The SMTP service places the message in the Queue folder and processes the message according to whether the sender is a local or remote recipient. However, if the non-delivery report can't be delivered to the sender of the original message, the non-delivery report is moved to the Badmail folder and the SMTP service is finished processing the message.

Starting, Stopping, and Pausing E-Mail Services

As an administrator, you'll often have to start, stop, or pause e-mail services. You can manage e-mail services directly through the Computer Management console or the Services utility. The services you want to work with are:

- Microsoft POP3 Service, to control POP3 e-mail services for e-mail storage and receipt
- Simple Mail Transfer Protocol (SMTP), to control e-mail transfer and routing

When you control e-mail services at this level, you're controlling all virtual servers and e-mail domains that use the service. For example, if a system manages e-mail for two domains and you stop the Microsoft POP3 Service, both domains are stopped and e-mail can't be received or retrieved. An alternative to stopping a service is to pause it. Pausing a service prevents new client connections but doesn't disconnect current connections.

In addition to being able to start, stop, or pause all POP3 or SMTP servers by stopping the related services, you can manage individual resources through the Microsoft Management Console (MMC). You manage SMTP through the IIS snap-in. You can start, stop, or pause an SMTP virtual server by completing the following steps:

1. Start the IIS snap-in.

2. In the left pane, select the icon for the computer you want to work with. If the computer isn't shown, connect to it as discussed in the "Connecting To Other Servers" section of Chapter 2, "Core IIS Administration."

3. Right-click the SMTP virtual server you want to manage. You can now perform any of the following actions:

   - Select Start to start the SMTP virtual server.

   - Select Stop to stop the SMTP virtual server.

   - Select Pause to pause the SMTP virtual server. After you pause an SMTP virtual server, click Pause again when you want to resume normal operations.

You manage POP3 through the POP3 Service snap-in. You can start, stop, or pause the POP3 e-mail domains running on a system by completing the following steps:

1. Select POP3 Service by clicking Start and selecting All Programs and then Administrative Tools.

2. In the left pane, right-click the icon for the computer you want to work with. If the computer isn't shown, right-click POP3 Service and select Connect. From the shortcut menu, choose All Tasks. You can now perform any of the following actions:

   - Select Start to start the POP3 e-mail service. If the POP3 e-mail service is already started, this option will be listed as Restart. If the POP3 e-mail service is stopped, Start will be the only option listed.

   - Select Stop to stop the POP3 e-mail service.

   - Select Pause to pause the POP3 e-mail service. After you pause the POP3 e-mail service, click Resume when you want to resume normal operations.

Core SMTP Administration

Core SMTP administration has to do with creating SMTP virtual servers, managing a server's port and Internet Protocol (IP) address configuration, checking server health, and monitoring user sessions. These tasks are examined in the sections that follow.

Creating SMTP Virtual Servers

When you install the SMTP service, a default SMTP virtual server is created. The default SMTP virtual server handles message delivery for the default domain and any other domains you've configured. In most cases you won't need to create an additional SMTP virtual server. However, if you're hosting multiple domains and you want to have more than one default domain, you might want to create additional SMTP virtual servers to service these domains. You might also want to create additional virtual servers when you need to set separate messaging restrictions on each domain that you host.

You can create additional SMTP virtual servers by completing the following steps:

1. If you're installing the SMTP virtual server on a new server, ensure that the SMTP service has been installed on the server.

2. If you want the virtual server to use a new IP address, you must configure the IP address before installing the site. For details, refer to Chapter 16, "Managing TCP/IP Networking," in *Microsoft Windows Server 2003 Administrator's Pocket Consultant* (Microsoft Press, 2003).

3. In the IIS snap-in, right-click the icon for the computer you want to work with, choose New, and then select SMTP Virtual Server. If the computer isn't shown, connect to it as discussed in the "Connecting to Other Servers" section of Chapter 2, and then perform this task.

4. The New SMTP Virtual Server Wizard is started, as shown in Figure 10-1. In the Name field, type a descriptive name for the Web site, such as TechNet SMTP Server, and then click Next.

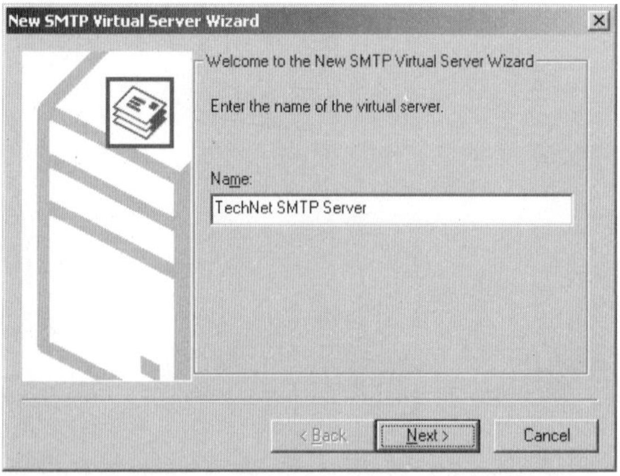

Figure 10-1. *Use the New SMTP Virtual Server Wizard to create additional virtual servers.*

5. Use the IP Address drop-down list to select an available IP address. Choose (All Unassigned) to allow SMTP to respond on all unassigned IP addresses that are configured on the server. The Transmission Control Protocol (TCP) port is assigned automatically to port 25. Click Next to continue.

Note   The IP address and TCP port combination must be unique on every virtual server. Multiple virtual servers can use the same port, provided that the servers are configured to use different IP addresses.

6. The next page lets you set the home directory for the virtual server. Type the path to the directory, such as **C:\SMTPRoot\SMTPMain**. If the directory doesn't exist, it is created automatically. If you already created the necessary directory and don't remember the path, click Browse to search for the directory. When you have finished setting the directory, click Next to continue.

Tip   The folder you select becomes the mail root for the new SMTP virtual server. For SMTP to function properly, the Local Service and Network Service accounts are configured as Operators. This configuration gives SMTP the privileges and permissions necessary to process e-mail messages.

7. You must specify the default domain for the virtual server. The default domain is a DNS domain that's serviced locally by the SMTP server. Typically, the default domain is the domain name specified in the DNS tab of the TCP/IP Properties dialog box for the server.

8. Click Finish to create the virtual server. If the default startup setting for the SMTP service is set to Automatic, the new SMTP virtual server should start automatically as well. However, if you select an IP address and TCP port combination that's already in use, the virtual server won't start automatically and you'll need to change the IP address or TCP port before you can start the virtual server.

Configuring Ports and IP Addresses Used by SMTP Servers

Each SMTP virtual server has a unique identity. The identity includes TCP port and IP address settings. The default TCP port is 25. The default IP address setting is to use any available IP address. To change the identity of an SMTP virtual server, complete the following steps:

1. If you want the SMTP virtual server to use a new IP address, you must configure the IP address before updating the site. For details, refer to Chapter 16, "Managing TCP/IP Networking," in *Microsoft Windows Server 2003 Administrator's Pocket Consultant*.

2. Start the IIS snap-in and then, in the left pane (Console Root), click the plus sign (+) next to the computer you want to work with. If the computer isn't shown, connect to it as discussed in the "Connecting to Other Servers" section of Chapter 2.

3. Right-click the SMTP virtual server you want to manage and then choose Properties. The dialog box shown in Figure 10-2 is displayed.

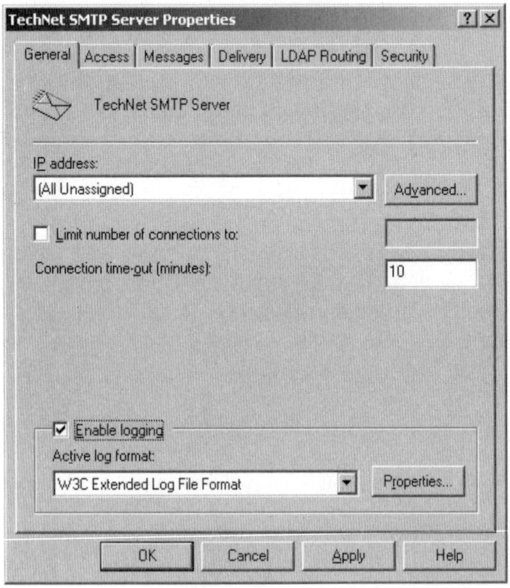

Figure 10-2. *You modify a site's identity through the General tab in the SMTP Virtual Server Properties dialog box.*

4. The IP Address drop-down list shows the current IP address for the SMTP virtual server. If you want to change the current setting, use the drop-down list to select an available IP address or choose (All Unassigned) to allow SMTP to respond on all unassigned IP addresses. Multiple SMTP virtual servers can use the same IP address, provided that the servers are configured to use different port numbers.

5. The TCP port for the SMTP virtual server is assigned automatically to port 25. If you want to change the default value, display the Advanced dialog box by clicking Advanced. Next, select the IP address entry that you want to change and then click Edit. Type a new port number in the TCP Port field and click OK. Then click OK again to save your settings. Multiple SMTP virtual servers can use the same TCP port, provided that the sites are configured to use different IP addresses.

6. Click OK to close the SMTP Virtual Server Properties dialog box.

Configuring Multiple Identities for SMTP Virtual Servers

An SMTP virtual server is capable of handling incoming messages on multiple IP addresses and ports. In some instances you might want a single SMTP virtual server to have multiple identities. For example, you could configure the server to receive mail on multiple TCP ports.

To assign multiple identities to an SMTP virtual server, complete the following steps:

1. In the IIS snap-in, right-click the SMTP virtual server you want to manage, and then choose Properties.

2. In the General tab, click Advanced and then use the Advanced dialog box shown in Figure 10-3 to configure new IP address and TCP port settings. The key buttons in this dialog box are the following:

   • **Add**   Adds a new identity. Click Add, select the IP address you want to use, and then type a TCP port. Click OK when you're finished.

   • **Edit**   Allows you to edit the currently selected entry in the Address list box.

   • **Remove**   Allows you to remove the currently selected entry from the Address list box.

3. Click OK and then click OK again to save your settings.

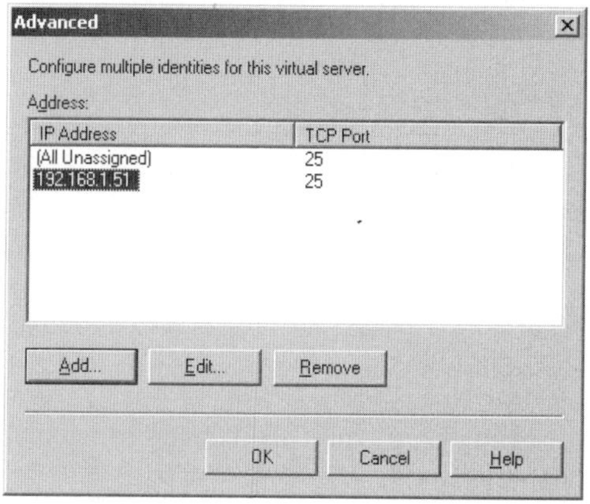

Figure 10-3. *SMTP virtual servers can respond on multiple IP addresses and ports. Configure additional identities using the Advanced dialog box.*

Monitoring SMTP Virtual Server Health

When you configure SMTP for use on a server, you should periodically monitor the folders under the Mailroot folder. These folders provide the best indicator of the SMTP installation's health. The key folders you'll want to monitor are the following:

- **Badmail** Messages in this folder couldn't be delivered to the intended recipients, and they couldn't be returned to the sender. If the number of messages in this folder is growing, your mail server might have a problem accessing the network or delivering mail. Try pinging the external network or the problem servers.

- **Drop** Messages in this folder have been processed by SMTP and are addressed to locally serviced domains. You might find messages addressed to *postmaster@yourwebserver.com* here. Read the messages and forward them as necessary to individuals in your organization.

- **Queue** Messages in this folder have been sorted and are queued for delivery to remote domains. If the number of queued messages is growing and messages aren't clearing out of this folder, your server might have a problem connecting to the network or delivering mail. Try pinging the external network or the problem servers.

- **Pickup** Messages should pass through this folder quickly. If messages remain in this folder, they might be unreadable or there might be a problem with the SMTP service. You might, for example, have set permissions on the folder that don't allow the SMTP service to read its contents. Check the folder permissions and the status of the SMTP service.

Note Each SMTP virtual server has a separate Mailroot folder. The location of the Mailroot folder was set when the SMTP virtual server was installed. Note also that you can configure alternate Badmail folders in the Messages tab in the Properties dialog box for the virtual server.

Managing User Sessions

A user session is started each time a user connects to a virtual server. The session lasts for the duration of the user's connection. Each virtual server tracks user sessions separately. By viewing the current sessions, you can monitor server load and determine which users are logged on to a server as well as how long users have been connected. If an unauthorized user is accessing a virtual server, you can terminate the user session, which immediately disconnects the user. If you want to disconnect all users who are accessing a particular virtual server, you can do this as well.

To view or end user sessions, complete the following steps:

1. Start the IIS snap-in and then double-click the entry for the virtual server you want to work with.

2. You should now see a node called Current Sessions. When you select this node in the left pane, current sessions are displayed in the right pane.

3. To disconnect a single user, right-click a user entry in the right pane and then select Terminate.

4. To disconnect all users, right-click in the right pane and then select Terminate All.

Configuring SMTP Service Domains

SMTP virtual servers are configured to support specific service domains. The only types of service domains you can create are alias and remote domains. The default domain is set automatically when you install the virtual server. If necessary, you can set an alias domain as the default.

Viewing Configured Service Domains

Before you create additional service domains on an SMTP virtual server, you should check the domains that are already being serviced by the SMTP virtual servers installed on the Web server. Each virtual server has separate service domains. You can view the configured service domains by completing the following steps:

1. Start the IIS snap-in and then double-click the entry for the virtual server you want to work with.

2. You should now see a node called Domains. When you select this node in the left pane, configured service domains are displayed in the right pane, as shown in Figure 10-4. The domain entries depict two characteristics:

   - **Domain Name**   The DNS name of the service domain, such as *microsoft.com*

   - **Type**   The type of the service domain such as Local (Default), Local (Alias), or Remote

Figure 10-4. *SMTP virtual servers can have local alias, local default, and remote service domains.*

Note Any domains you've designated for use with POP3 are listed as domains serviced by the default SMTP Virtual Server. The domain type is set to Local (Custom).

3. To view the properties of a service domain, right-click the domain entry and then select Properties from the shortcut menu.

Working with Local Domains

Local service domains are domains that are serviced locally by SMTP. Two types of local domains are available: default and alias. The default domain serves as the default for incoming and outgoing messages. Alias domains allow you to create secondary domains that point to the default domain and use its settings. Messages addressed to the default domain and any associated alias domains are stored in the virtual server's Drop directory. Outgoing messages use the default domain as their domain of origin.

With local domains you have several administration options. You can:

- Create alias domains
- Set the default domain
- Configure Drop directory location and quota settings

Creating Alias Domains

Alias domains allow you to create secondary domains that point to the default domain. Alias domains use the same configuration settings and the same Drop directory as the default domain.

You can create an alias domain by completing the following steps:

1. Start the IIS snap-in and then double-click the entry for the virtual server you want to work with.

2. Right-click Domains, choose New, and then select Domain. This starts the New SMTP Domain Wizard.

3. Select Alias as the domain type and then click Next.

4. Type the DNS domain name of the alias in the Name field.

 Note You can't use wildcard characters in domain names. For example, you can use *tech.microsoft.com*, but not **.microsoft.com*.

5. Click Finish to create the alias domain.

Setting the Default Domain

The default domain serves as the default for all messages transferred into or out of the domain. Messages addressed to the default domain are stored in the virtual server's Drop directory. Outgoing messages that don't have a domain set in the From field of the e-mail address use the default domain as their domain of origin. An SMTP virtual server can have only one default domain.

For the default SMTP virtual server (the one created automatically when you install the SMTP Service), the default domain name is set automatically based on the full computer name as set in the Computer Name tab of the System Properties dialog box. For example, if the system name is corpserver01 and the domain is *adatum.com*, the full computer name is corpserver01.adatum.com and the default SMTP virtual server sets this name as the default domain service. If you change the computer name or domain association in the System Properties dialog box, the default domain used is updated the next time you start the SMTP service.

If you need to set a new default service domain for other SMTP virtual servers, you do this by renaming the default domain. Follow these steps:

1. Start the IIS snap-in and then double-click the entry for the virtual server you want to work with.

2. Select the Domains node in the left pane. You should see a list of service domains configured on the server.

3. Right-click the default domain and then select Rename from the short-cut menu.

4. Type the domain name you want to use as the default and then press Enter.

Changing the Drop Directory Settings for the Default Domain

The Drop directory is the final destination for all incoming messages addressed to local domains. This means that messages addressed to the local domain and any alias domains are transferred from the Queue to the Drop directory. By default, the Drop directory is located at Inetpub\Mailroot\Drop. You can change the Drop directory settings by completing the following steps:

1. Start the IIS snap-in and then double-click the entry for the virtual server you want to work with.

2. Select the Domains node in the left pane. You should see a list of service domains configured on the server.

3. Right-click the default domain and then select Properties. The Properties dialog box shown in Figure 10-5 on the following page is displayed.

4. Type the new location of the Drop directory in the field provided or click Browse to search for a folder. The folder you want to use must be created before you can select it, and it must be on a local drive. If necessary, use Windows Explorer to create the directory before you browse for a folder.

5. You can enforce a quota policy for the Drop directory by selecting Enable Drop Directory Quota. Otherwise, clear this option.

Tip   Quotas are useful to restrict the total size of the messages stored in the Drop directory. Quotas are enforced according to the quota policies configured for the directory owner. For more information about working with quotas, see the section entitled "Using, Configuring, and Managing Disk Quotas" in Chapter 14, "Data Sharing, Security, and Auditing" of the *Microsoft Windows Server 2003 Administrator's Companion* (Microsoft Press, 2003).

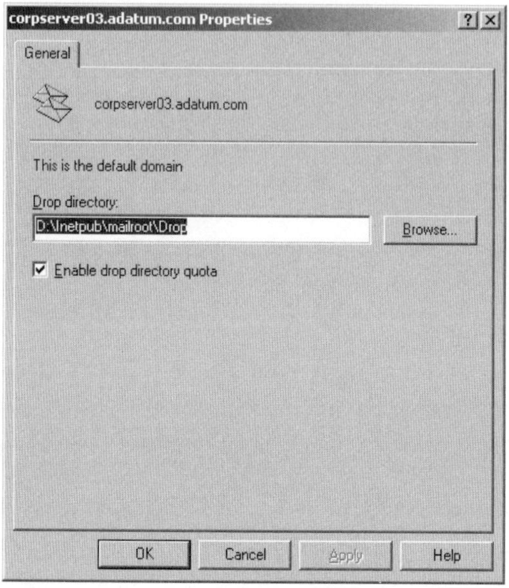

Figure 10-5. *The Drop directory is used by the default domain and all alias domains configured on the virtual server. You can change the directory location and quota configuration at any time.*

6. Click OK.

Working with Remote Domains

Any message with a nonlocal destination address is queued for delivery to a remote server. By default, the SMTP Service forwards messages directly to the destination SMTP servers as listed in DNS. If you have unique delivery requirements for a specific remote server, you can add a remote domain to the SMTP virtual server and configure the necessary delivery requirements.

Once you create a remote domain, you have different configuration options. The key options are the following:

- To set relay restrictions
- To configure support for Extension to SMTP (ESMTP) or standard SMTP
- To set outbound access and authentication security
- To queue messages for remote triggered delivery
- To configure route domains with smart hosts

Creating Remote Domains

Remote domains allow you to set delivery paths and routing for other SMTP servers and mail gateways. You typically configure remote domains for domains to which you commonly send messages. For each remote domain, you can set specific delivery options and require authentication before delivering mail to the domain.

You can create a remote domain by completing the following steps:

1. Start the IIS snap-in and then double-click the entry for the virtual server you want to work with.

2. Right-click Domains, choose New, and then select Domain. This starts the New SMTP Domain Wizard.

3. Select Remote as the domain type and then click Next.

4. Specify the domain's address space. Typically, this is the DNS domain name of the remote domain.

Tip   You can also use a wildcard character in the name so that all-inclusive domains use the same settings. Use an asterisk (*) as the first character, followed by a period (.), and then type the remaining portion of the domain name, such as *.com for all .com domains or *.microsoft.com for all domains ending with microsoft.com.

5. Click Finish to create the remote domain. Select Domains in the left pane of the IIS snap-in. Right-click the remote domain entry in the right pane and then select Properties. You should now set properties for routing and securing message delivery to the remote domain. Click OK when your changes are completed.

Setting and Removing Relay Restrictions for Remote Domains

Mail relaying allows external users to use your mail system to relay messages bound for another organization. By default, the SMTP service is configured to prevent mail relaying, and you typically should maintain this setting to prevent the systems from being used to distribute spam. In this way, external users are unable to relay mail through your SMTP virtual server. Sometimes, however, you'll want users to be able to relay mail to designated mail gateways. The way you do this is to create a remote domain that specifies the target service domain and then authorizes mail relaying to this service domain.

You can set or remove relay restrictions by completing the following steps:

1. Start the IIS snap-in and then double-click the entry for the virtual server you want to work with.

2. Select the Domains node in the left pane. You should see a list of service domains configured on the server.

3. Right-click the remote domain to which you want to relay mail and then select Properties. The Properties dialog box shown in Figure 10-6 on the following page is displayed.

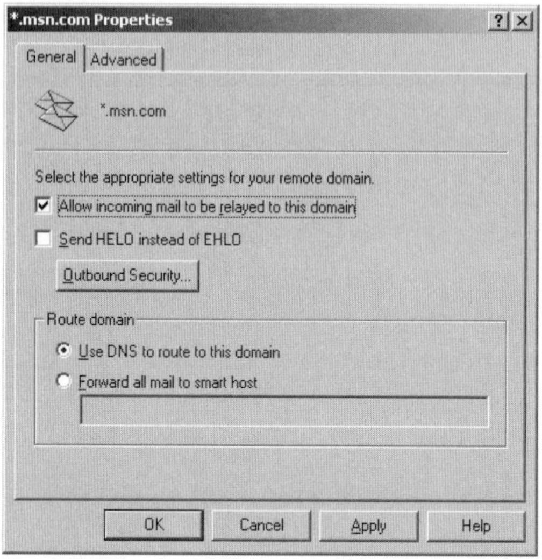

Figure 10-6. *You can configure remote domains to allow or prevent mail relaying. Mail relaying is prevented by default.*

4. To allow mail relaying to the remote domain, select Allow Incoming Mail To Be Relayed To This Domain.

5. To prevent mail relaying to the remote domain, clear Allow Incoming Mail To Be Relayed To This Domain.

6. Click OK.

Switching SMTP Modes Used with Remote Domains

The SMTP service supports standard SMTP and ESMTP. Although ESMTP is more efficient and secure than SMTP, you might want to configure a specific remote domain to use SMTP instead. The most likely scenario in which you'd do this is when the e-mail system in the remote domain doesn't support ESMTP and you're receiving error messages when initiating the ESMTP session (see RFC 1651 for more information on ESMTP).

By default, SMTP virtual servers always try to initiate ESMTP sessions using the EHLO session command, but you can change this to the more widely compatible SMTP HELO command. The SMTP service initiates SMTP sessions with other mail servers by issuing a HELO start command. The SMTP service initiates ESMTP sessions with other mail servers by issuing an EHLO start command.

You can change SMTP modes by completing the following steps:

1. Start the IIS snap-in and then double-click the entry for the virtual server you want to work with.

2. Select the Domains node in the left pane. You should see a list of service domains configured on the server.

3. Right-click the remote domain you want to work with and then select Properties. The Properties dialog box shown previously in Figure 10-6 is displayed.

4. The Send HELO Instead Of EHLO check box controls the use of SMTP or ESMTP. To use SMTP, select this option. To use ESMTP (which is the default), clear this option.

5. Click OK.

Queuing Messages for Remote Triggered Delivery

The SMTP service can hold mail for mail clients or gateways that periodically connect to a virtual server and download mail. In this case the client initiates delivery of the mail by issuing an Authenticated Turn (ATRN) command. The ATRN command tells the SMTP service to start sending messages to the remote domain. When you configure remote triggered delivery, you must specify the domain accounts in the enterprise that are authorized to use this feature. You do this by adding the domain accounts to an authorization list.

You can enable remote triggered delivery for named accounts in a remote domain by completing the following steps:

1. Start the IIS snap-in and then double-click the entry for the virtual server you want to work with.

2. Select the Domains node in the left pane. You should see a list of service domains configured on the server.

3. Right-click the remote domain you want to work with and then select Properties.

4. Select the Advanced tab, as shown in Figure 10-7.

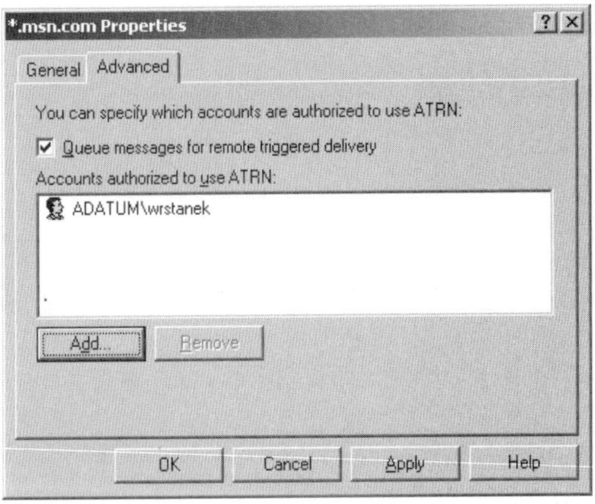

Figure 10-7. *You can queue messages addressed to specific users in a remote domain; then the user's mail client can trigger delivery of those messages.*

5. To enable remote triggered delivery, select Queue Messages For Remote Triggered Delivery.

6. To specify an authorized account, click Add. This displays the Select Users Or Groups dialog box, which you can use to select users or groups that are in the same Active Directory domain forest or tree.

7. To remove an authorized account, select the account in the Accounts Authorized To Use ATRN list box and then click Remove.

8. Click OK.

Configuring Authentication for Remote Domains

By default, the SMTP service doesn't authenticate connections to remote domains. This means that the connectors anonymously access remote domains to send messages. You can configure an SMTP virtual server to pass authentication credentials to remote domains, however. The key reasons to do this are when a specific level of authentication is required to access a remote domain and when you're sending messages to a specific address in the remote domain that requires authentication.

You can use several types of authentication:

- **Basic** Standard authentication with wide compatibility. With basic authentication, the user name and password specified are passed as clear text to the remote domain.

- **Integrated Windows authentication** Secure authentication for Windows-compatible domains. With this authentication level, the user name and password specified are passed securely to the remote domain using Windows security.

- **Transport Layer Security (TLS) encryption** Encrypted authentication for servers with smart cards or X.509 certificates. This type of authentication is combined with basic or Windows authentication.

To configure outbound security for a remote domain, follow these steps:

1. Start the IIS snap-in and then double-click the entry for the virtual server you want to work with.

2. Select the Domains node in the left pane. You should see a list of service domains configured on the server.

3. Right-click the remote domain you want to work with and then select Properties.

4. Click Outbound Security in the General tab to display the dialog box shown in Figure 10-8.

5. To set standard authentication for maximum compatibility, select Basic Authentication.

6. To set secure authentication for Windows-compatible domains, select Integrated Windows Authentication.

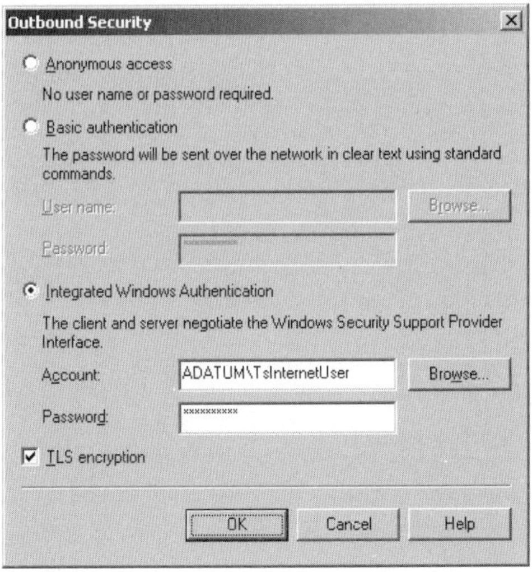

Outbound Security ☒

○ Anonymous access
No user name or password required.

○ Basic authentication
The password will be sent over the network in clear text using standard commands.

    User name: [   ] [Browse...]

    Password: [**********]

● Integrated Windows Authentication
The client and server negotiate the Windows Security Support Provider Interface.

    Account: [ADATUM\TsInternetUser] [Browse...]

    Password: [xxxxxxxxxx]

☑ TLS encryption

[OK] [Cancel] [Help]

Figure 10-8. *Select the outbound security options and add TLS encryption if it's supported by the remote domain.*

7. Each authentication mode has associated user account and password fields. Use these fields to set the authentication credentials. If the remote domain is in the same Active Directory domain forest or tree, click Browse to find an account in the remote domain using the Select User dialog box, and then type the account password.

8. If you want to encrypt message traffic and the destination servers in the remote domain support smart cards or X.509 certificates, select the TLS Encryption check box.

9. Click OK.

Tip When you select TLS encryption, the destination servers in the remote domain must support smart cards or X.509 certificates. If the servers don't, all messages sent to the remote domain are returned with a non-delivery report.

Configuring Smart Hosts for Remote Domains

You can route all outgoing messages for a remote domain through a smart host instead of sending them directly to the destination domain. This allows you to route messages for the remote domain to a specific server. The goal is to route messages over a connection that might be more direct or less costly than the standard route.

You can add or remove a smart host for a remote domain by completing the following steps:

1. Start the IIS snap-in and then double-click the entry for the virtual server you want to work with.

2. Select the Domains node in the left pane. You should see a list of service domains configured on the server.

3. Right-click the remote domain you want to work with and then select Properties.

4. To add a smart host, in the General tab of the Properties dialog box, select Forward All Mail To Smart Host, and then type the IP address or the DNS name of the smart host in the field provided.

 Tip If you use an IP address to identify a smart host, enclose the IP address in brackets [] to prevent the SMTP service from attempting to perform a DNS lookup on the address. Note also that smart host settings for remote domains override smart host settings configured for the SMTP virtual server itself.

5. To remove a smart host, select Use DNS To Route To This Domain.

6. Click OK.

Renaming and Deleting SMTP Service Domains

The service domain name determines how e-mail messages are serviced and routed. If the domain name is incorrect, e-mail can't be handled properly. For example, if you created a service domain called *tec.microsoft.com* that should have been *tech.microsoft.com*, e-mail for *tech.microsoft.com* won't be handled properly. Don't worry, there's an easy way to fix this. Simply follow these steps to rename the service domain:

1. Start the IIS snap-in and then double-click the entry for the virtual server you want to work with.

2. Select the Domains node in the left pane. You should see a list of service domains configured on the server.

3. Right-click the default domain and then select Rename from the shortcut menu.

4. Type the domain name you want to use as the default and then press Enter.

If you no longer need a service domain, you can delete it. Keep in mind, however, that you can't delete the default domain.

You delete a service domain by completing the following steps:

1. Start the IIS snap-in and then double-click the entry for the virtual server you want to work with.

2. Select the Domains node in the left pane. You should see a list of service domains configured on the server.

3. Right-click the remote domain you want to delete and then select Delete from the shortcut menu. When prompted to confirm the action, click Yes.

Core POP3 Administration

POP3 Service is installed when you add the E-Mail Services Windows component to a system. Click Add Or Remove Programs in Control Panel and then click Add/Remove Windows Components. This starts the Windows Component Wizard. Select E-Mail Services, click Next, and then, when prompted, click Finish. The POP3 e-mail service is installed, as well as any additional components that are required, including SMTP and IIS.

Unlike SMTP, which you manage through the IIS snap-in, you manage POP3 Service through a separate console snap-in. You can access this snap-in, called POP3 Service, from the Administrative Tools menu, or you can add it to any updateable MMC.

When you install E-Mail Services, POP3 Service is installed but no e-mail domains are configured for e-mail receipt and storage. After you've planned the necessary modifications to DNS and coordinated with your ISP, you can specify the e-mail domains you want to service. You do this by creating the domains on the server. However, before you do this, you should configure the server properties.

Configuring POP3 E-Mail Client and Server Authentication

When you install the POP3 Service, no default domains are created. You can create and manage e-mail domains as discussed in the section of this chapter entitled "Working with POP3 Domains." However, before you do this, you should configure the e-mail server authentication method.

You can't modify the authentication method once you define the e-mail domains that the server will handle. The only way to change the authentication method is by following these steps:

1. Delete all existing e-mail domains for the POP3 Service.

2. Change to the desired authentication method.

3. Recreate the e-mail domains for the POP3 Service and the mailboxes you want to use.

Three authentication methods are available. The best one for you depends on your network's configuration and how you plan to use e-mail services. The authentication methods are summarized in Table 10-1.

Table 10-1. Authentication Methods for POP3 Servers

Authentication Method	Description	When to Use
Local Windows Accounts	Integrates the POP3 Service with the local system's Security Accounts Manager (SAM). This has several benefits: when you're creating mailboxes for users, you can automatically create their user account as well; users can utilize the same account name and password to be authenticated on the system and for POP3; and you can more easily manage accounts. A limitation of this method is that you can't use the same user name across domains. For example, if *dev.microsoft.com* and *tech. microsoft.com* are configured, you can't have a user account for *wrstanek@dev.microsoft.com* and a user account for *wrstanek@tech. microsoft.com*.	If you're not using Active Directory but want to associate user accounts with mailboxes that you create, use this authentication technique. You'll then be able to manage accounts associated with mailboxes through the Local Users And Groups node in Computer Management. (This option is available only when the system isn't part of Active Directory.)
Active Directory Integrated	Integrates the POP3 Service with an Active Directory domain. This mode has the same benefits as the Local Windows Accounts authentication method. Here, you integrate the POP3 Service into your existing Active Directory domain to gain the benefits mentioned previously. As long as the domains are available through Active Directory and are in the same forest, you can use the same user name across domains. For example, if the system services *dev.microsoft.com* and *tech. microsoft.com*, you can have a user account for *wrstanek@dev. microsoft.com* and a user account for *wrstanek@tech.microsoft.com*.	If the server is a member of an Active Directory domain or a domain controller, use this authentication technique. You'll then be able to manage accounts associated with mailboxes through Active Directory Users And Computers. (This option is available only when the system is part of Active Directory.)

Table 10-1.   Authentication Methods for POP3 Servers

Authentication Method	Description	When to Use
Encrypted Password File	Instead of managing mailboxes through user accounts, you use encrypted password files to set passwords for mailboxes. This file is stored in the user's mailbox directory and read during the authentication process. In some cases this might allow you to support a larger number of mailboxes while reducing management overhead, since there are no user accounts. However, the only way to change mailbox passwords is to use the Winpop utility, located in %SystemRoot%\System32.	If you're not using Active Directory and don't want to associate user accounts with mailboxes, use this authentication technique. You'll then use the Winpop utility to reset mailbox passwords.

By default, POP3 is configured to pass the user name and password information as clear text when users attempt to connect to the server. With Local Windows Account authentication and Active Directory Integrated authentication, you can also require Secure Password Authentication (SPA) for all client connections. You can't require SPA for the Encrypted Password File method, but secure authentication is supported.

To set the server authentication method, follow these steps:

1. In the POP3 Service snap-in, right-click the icon for the computer you want to work with and then select Properties. This displays the *Server* Properties dialog box shown in Figure 10-9.

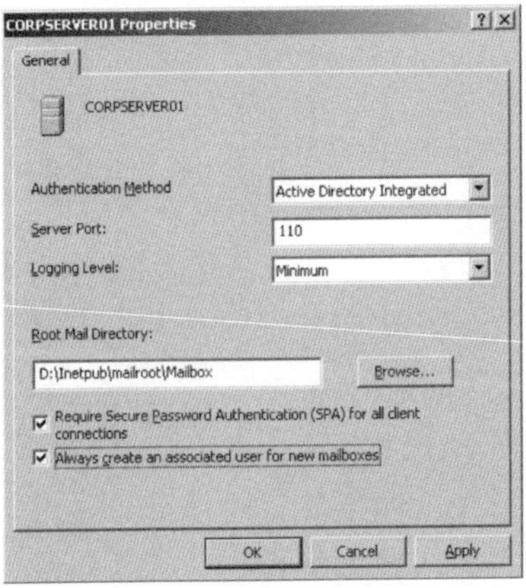

Figure 10-9. *Use the Properties dialog box to configure properties for all POP3 domains on a server.*

2. Use the Authentication Method drop-down list to set the authentication method for the server and all e-mail domains it services. Remember, you can't modify the method once you define e-mail domains.

3. If you chose Local Windows Account or Active Directory Integrated authentication, you can also require Secure Password Authentication for all client connections. Select Require Secure Password Authentication (SPA) For All Client Connections. Click OK.

4. If prompted, click Yes to restart the POP3 Service. Otherwise, right-click the icon for the computer you're working with, select All Tasks from the shortcut menu, and then click Restart. You should restart the POP3 service in order for these changes to take effect.

Configuring POP3 Port Settings

By default, POP3 responds on TCP port 110. If you want the server to use a different port for all e-mail domains serviced, you can configure this through the server properties dialog box. Follow these steps:

1. In the POP3 Service snap-in, right-click the icon for the computer you want to work with and then select Properties.

2. Type the new port number in the Server Port field.

3. Click OK. Next, right-click the icon for the computer you're working with, select All Tasks from the shortcut menu, and then click Restart. You should restart the POP3 service in order for this change to take effect.

Configuring the POP3 Root Mail Directory

The Root Mail Directory field sets the physical location used to store mailboxes. Each e-mail domain configured has a separate folder, and within this folder are subfolders for any mailboxes you've created for the domain. Individual e-mail messages are stored as flat files within the mailbox folders.

By default, the Root Mail directory is set to Intepub\mailroot\Mailbox. You can change this to any local or remote folder you want if desired. To do this, follow these steps:

1. In the POP3 Service snap-in, right-click the icon for the computer you want to work with and then select Properties.

2. In the Root Mail Directory field, type the directory path to the folder in which you want to store mail. If you don't know the full path for the folder, click Browse and then use the Browse For Folder dialog box to find the folder you want to use. It's recommended that you use a directory on an NTFS partition.

3. Click OK to set the new Root Mail directory. If the folder is available and can be used, you'll see a message stating that the new mail root is set but any existing domains won't have mail stored properly.

With NTFS, the permissions on the folder are reset so that only local administrators and services accounts have access to the Root Mail directory. If you examine the permissions, you'll see that Administrators, System, and Network Service are all given full control and any previously assigned access for individual users or groups is removed.

Note   If the folder can't be found, you'll see a warning telling you this. To resolve the problem, you'll need to ensure that the folder is created or shared as necessary, and then repeat this procedure.

4. Using Windows Explorer, copy any existing domain directories (and all their subdirectories) to the new Root Mail directory. This ensures that mail for any previously defined domains or user mailboxes can be stored properly.

5. Click OK. If prompted, click Yes to restart the POP3 Service. Otherwise, right-click the icon for the computer you're working with, select All Tasks from the shortcut menu, and then click Restart. You should restart the POP3 service in order for these changes to take effect.

Working with POP3 Domains

After you configure basic server properties, including the authentication method, you can create and manage e-mail domains. The tasks for creating and managing e-mail domains are examined in the sections that follow.

Viewing Domain Information

Anytime you want to view the currently configured domains, simply select the computer node in the POP3 Service snap-in. If e-mail domains are configured on the server, as shown in Figure 10-10 on the following page, you'll see the following statistics for each domain:

- **Name**   The name of the e-mail domain.
- **Mailboxes**   The number of mailboxes in the e-mail domain.
- **Domain Size**   The total disk space used by all mailboxes in the e-mail domain.
- **Messages**   The total number of messages stored in all mailboxes in the domain.
- **State**   The state of the domain. A locked state means that clients can't connect to the server to access e-mail in this domain. However, e-mail can still be delivered and routed.

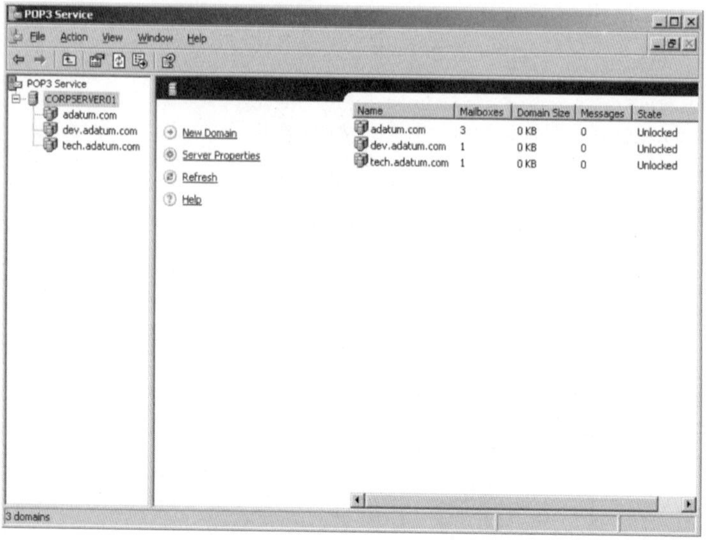

Figure 10-10. *Domain statistics provide a quick overview of mailboxes, messages, and state of the mailboxes for each domain.*

Creating Domains

The POP3 Service handles top-level domains, such as *adatum.com*, and second-level domains, such as *dev.adatum.com* or *tech.adatum.com*. DNS determines how mail is routed on the Internet and you'll need to contact your ISP if you want mail for specific domains to be routed to your POP3 server.

Once DNS is configured properly, you'll need to ensure that the TCP ports for POP3 and SMTP are open to the server. This ensures that the e-mail system will function properly. By default, SMTP is on TCP port 25 and POP3 is on TCP port 110. If your network has a firewall or proxy server, you'll need to configure these ports so that inbound and outbound connections can be made.

When you install E-Mail Services, POP3 Service is installed but no e-mail domains are configured for e-mail receipt and storage. After you've planned the necessary modifications to DNS and coordinated with your ISP, you can specify the e-mail domains you want to service. You do this by creating the domains on the server. However, before you do this, you should configure the server properties.

Once you've done the necessary planning and configuration, creating the e-mail domain is easy. Follow these steps:

1. In the POP3 Service snap-in, right-click the icon for the computer you want to work with, choose New, and then select Domain. This displays the Add Domain dialog box.

2. In the Domain Name field, type the name of the e-mail domain you want the server to handle. Be sure to use the DNS domain name format, such as *adatum.com*, rather than *adatum*.

3. Click OK to create the domain. A folder is created in the Mailroot directory for the domain. If you examine the permissions for this directory, you'll see that they're the same as those assigned to the mail root itself. Administrators, System, and Network Service are all given full control.

Locking and Unlocking Domains

You can restrict access to an e-mail domain temporarily by locking the domain. When the domain is locked, POP3 clients can't connect to the server to access e-mail in the domain. However, e-mail can still be delivered and routed. You can lock and unlock domains as follows:

- To lock a domain, right-click the domain name in the POP3 Service snap-in and then select Lock from the shortcut menu.

- To unlock a domain, right-click the domain name in the POP3 Service snap-in and then select Unlock from the shortcut menu.

Deleting Domains

When you no longer want to support an e-mail domain on a server, you can delete the e-mail domain from the POP3 server. Deleting an e-mail domain permanently removes the domain directory and the complete contents of the associated mail store. As a result, all user mailboxes are deleted, as well as any messages they might contain.

To delete a domain, follow these steps:

1. In the POP3 Service snap-in, select the icon for the computer you want to work with.

2. Right-click the domain you want to remove and then select Delete.

3. When prompted, click Yes to confirm the action. If you're unsure that this is the desired action, click No.

Deleting an e-mail domain doesn't stop mail from being routed to the server, nor does it delete the user accounts that might have been created with the mailboxes. To stop mail from being routed to the server, you'll need to contact your ISP. They'll need to modify the DNS mail exchange (MX) record to point to a new server or delete the record. To close access to the server, you'll need to lock or remove user accounts as necessary.

Real World DNS changes can takes several days or weeks to take effect, depending on the DNS configuration. Because of this, you should contact your ISP several weeks before you plan to make DNS changes. Your ISP can then modify the DNS configuration so that upcoming changes can be more rapidly disseminated.

Working with Mailboxes

Mailboxes are used to store incoming e-mail for users. Each mailbox is created as a separate folder in the mail store. The name of this folder is P3_*accountName*.mbx, where *accountName* is the actual name of the mailbox, the user account, or both, associated with the mailbox. When users connect to the server using a POP3 client, such as Microsoft Outlook Express, the mailbox name is the name they must provide to retrieve their e-mail.

With Active Directory Integrated or Local Windows Account authentication, a user account can be associated with the mailbox. This user account has the same name as the mailbox. You can't create two mailboxes with the same name in a domain. But with Active Directory Integrated and Encrypted Password File authentication, you can use the same user name across domains in the same forest. For example, if *dev.microsoft.com* and *tech.microsoft.com* are configured, you could have a mailbox for *wrstanek* in both domains. The complete e-mail address of these mailboxes would be *wrstanek@dev.microsoft.com* and *wrstanek@tech.microsoft.com*, respectively.

In the mailbox directory, individual mail messages are stored as separate files. Mail files are named in the form P3*messageNumber*.eml, where *messageNumber* is a unique identifier for the message.

Checking Mailbox Size, Messages, and State

Any time you want to check the size, number of messages, or state of mailboxes in a domain, simply select the domain in the POP3 Service snap-in. You'll then see the following statistics for each mailbox:

- **Mailbox Name** The name of the mailbox. If an account was associated with the mailbox, the user account has the same name.
- **Size Of Mailbox** The total disk space used by messages in the mailbox.
- **Messages** The total number of messages stored in the mailboxes.
- **State** The state of the mailbox. A locked state means that mailbox can't be connected to. However, e-mail can still be delivered and routed to the mailbox.

Creating Mailboxes

When you use Active Directory Integrated or Local Windows Account authentication, you should always create an associated user account with new mailboxes. In this way you can manage the user account to control access and privileges on the server. You can also use the standard techniques for locking accounts and changing passwords to control access to the mailbox. To help ensure that user accounts are created when these authentication methods are used, follow these steps:

1. In the POP3 Service snap-in, right-click the icon for the computer you want to work with and then select Properties.

2. In the server properties dialog box, select Always Create An Associated User For New Mailboxes.

3. Click OK. Now user accounts will be created with mailboxes by default.

Another thing to consider before creating mailboxes is the naming scheme you want to use. When you're using Local Windows Accounts authentication, mailbox names can be up to 20 characters. Mailbox names can be up to 64 characters when you're using Encrypted Password File or Active Directory Integrated authentication. The minimum length for a mailbox name is one character. You should follow the same naming conventions as those for domain accounts—even if you don't plan on creating user accounts for mailboxes. Having a defined naming structure for mailboxes makes it easier to manage the POP3 server.

The naming schemes I recommend for mailboxes are the same as the ones I recommend for user accounts. Guidelines for naming schemes you might want to use include:

- **User's first name and last initial**   You take the user's first name and combine it with the first letter of the last name to create the logon name. For William Stanek, you'd use *williams* or *bills*. Because it's very likely that several people will have the same first name and last initial, this naming scheme might not be practical for large organizations.

- **User's first initial and last name**   You take the user's first initial and combine it with the last name to create the logon name. For William Stanek, you'd use *wstanek*. Because it's very likely that several people will have the same first initial and last name, this naming scheme might not be practical for large organizations, either.

- **User's first initial, middle initial, and last name**   You combine the user's first initial, middle initial, and last name to create the logon name. For William R. Stanek, you'd use *wrstanek*.

- **User's first initial, middle initial, and first five characters of the last name**   You combine the user's first initial, middle initial, and the first five characters of the last name to create the logon name. For William R. Stanek, you'd use *wrstane*. Because it's less likely several people will have the same first initial, middle initial, and last name fragment, this naming scheme works well with medium and large organizations. You'll also have a more uniform naming structure, and if by chance there are several logons that match, you can have a *wrstane, wrstane2, wrstane3*, and so on.

- **User's first name and last name**   You combine the user's first and last name. To separate the names, you could use the underscore character (_) or hyphen (-). For William Stanek, you could use *william_stanek* or *william-stanek*. Because it's very likely that several people will have the same first and last name, this naming scheme might not be practical for large organizations.

When you're ready to create mailboxes, follow these steps:

1. In the POP3 Service snap-in, select the e-mail domain you want to work with. A complete list of mailboxes in this domain is displayed.

2. If the mailbox you want to create doesn't already exist in the domain, click Add Mailbox. This displays the Add Mailbox dialog box shown in Figure 10-11.

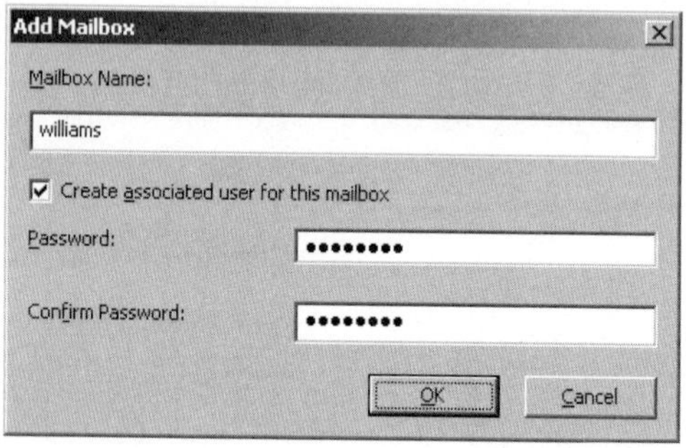

Figure 10-11. *Use the Add Mailbox dialog box to create mailboxes for the e-mail domain. Mailboxes should follow the same naming and strict password requirements as any other type of account.*

3. In the Mailbox Name field, type a name for the mailbox. When you're using Local Windows Accounts authentication, mailbox names can be up to 20 characters. Mailbox names can be up to 64 characters when you're using Encrypted Password File or Active Directory Integrated authentication. The minimum length for a mailbox name is one character, and it can't be the same as any other mailbox already created in the domain.

Note With Local Windows Account authentication, the mailbox name must be unique across all domains. For example, if *dev.microsoft.com* and *tech.microsoft.com* are configured, you can't have a mailbox for *wrstanek* in both domains.

Tip The e-mail address for the mailbox is the mailbox name + @ + the e-mail domain name. For example, if the mailbox name is *tomg* and the e-mail domain name is *adatum.com*, the e-mail address for sending messages to this mailbox is *tomg@adatum.com*.

4. With Active Directory Integrated or Local Windows Account authentication, you'll want to create a user account with the mailbox, so Create Associated User For This Mailbox should be selected.

5. Type and confirm the password for the mailbox. With Active Directory Integrated or Local Windows Account authentication, the password is set for the user account, which means that authentication of the password is against the user account. With Encrypted Password File authentication, the password is set in an encrypted file and the only way to change or reset this password is to use the Winpop utility.

6. Click OK to create the mailbox. A folder is created in the e-mail domain directory for the mailbox. If you examine the permissions for this directory, you'll see that they're the same as those assigned to the mail root itself. Administrators, System, and Network Service are all given full control. Any user account associated with this directory doesn't need direct access. The POP3 Service itself manages the files in this directory.

Locking and Unlocking Mailboxes

You can temporarily restrict access to a mailbox by locking it. When the mailbox is locked, POP3 clients can't connect to the mailbox. However, e-mail messages can still be delivered to the mailbox. You can lock and unlock mailboxes as follows:

- To lock a mailbox, right-click the mailbox in the POP3 Service snap-in and then select Lock from the shortcut menu.

- To unlock a mailbox, right-click the mailbox in the POP3 Service snap-in and then select Unlock from the shortcut menu.

Resetting or Changing Mailbox Passwords

With Active Directory Integrated or Local Windows Account authentication, user accounts should have been associated with the mailbox. The user account password is the mailbox password, and in this case you can use Active Directory Users And Computers snap-in or the Local Users And Groups node on the Computer Management console, respectively, to manage mailbox passwords.

If you're using Encrypted Password File authentication, you use the Winpop utility to change the mailbox password. Follow these steps:

1. Click Start and then select Run. In the Run dialog box, type **cmd** and then click OK. This starts a command prompt.

2. Type **cd %SystemRoot%\system32\pop3server** and then type **winpop changepwd** *mailboxName@domainName newPassword*, where *mailboxName@domainName* specifies the e-mail address for the mailbox and *newPassword* is the password you want to use.

Deleting Mailboxes

When a mailbox is no longer needed, you can delete it from the POP3 server. Deleting a mailbox permanently removes the mailbox and all the messages it contains.

To delete a mailbox, follow these steps:

1. In the POP3 Service snap-in, select the domain you want to work with.

2. Right-click the mailbox you want to remove and then select Delete.

3. A prompt is displayed asking you to confirm the action. If a user account was associated with the mailbox, you also have the opportunity to delete that account. If desired, select Also Delete The User Account Associated With This Mailbox.

4. Click Yes.

Chapter 11

Advanced E-Mail Service Configuration Options

As you've seen in the previous chapter, there's a lot to configuring and managing e-mail services for Internet, intranet, and extranet sites. Working with Simple Mail Transfer Protocol (SMTP) and Post Office Protocol 3 (POP3) isn't as straightforward as working with Web or File Transfer Protocol (FTP) services—there's a lot going on behind the scenes and a lot of configuration options to consider. With all the options available, don't overlook the importance of securing connections and properly managing message delivery. Not only do these advanced configuration options ensure that the e-mail services work properly, but they also help safeguard the system.

Securing Incoming Connections

You can control incoming connections to SMTP virtual servers in several ways. You can do the following:

- Grant or deny access using Internet Protocol (IP) addresses or Internet domain names
- Require secure incoming connections
- Require authentication for incoming connections
- Restrict concurrent connections and set connection time-out values

Each of these tasks is discussed in the sections that follow.

Note With SMTP, you can configure both incoming and outbound connection restrictions. To learn how to configure outbound connections, see the "Controlling Outgoing Connections" section of this chapter.

Securing Access by IP Address, Subnet, or Domain

By default, virtual servers are accessible to all IP addresses, which presents a security risk that might allow your messaging system to be misused. To control use of a virtual server, you might want to grant or deny access by IP address, subnet, or domain.

- Granting access allows a computer to access the virtual server but doesn't necessarily allow users to submit or retrieve messages. Users still need to authenticate themselves if you require authentication.

- Denying access prevents a computer from accessing the virtual server. As a result, users of the computer can't submit messages to, or retrieve messages from, the virtual server—even if they could have authenticated themselves with a user name and password.

To grant or deny access to a virtual server by IP address, subnet, or domain, follow these steps:

1. In the Internet Information Services (IIS) snap-in, right-click the SMTP virtual server you want to manage and then choose Properties.

2. Click Connection in the Access tab. As shown in Figure 11-1, the Computers list shows the computers that currently have connection controls.

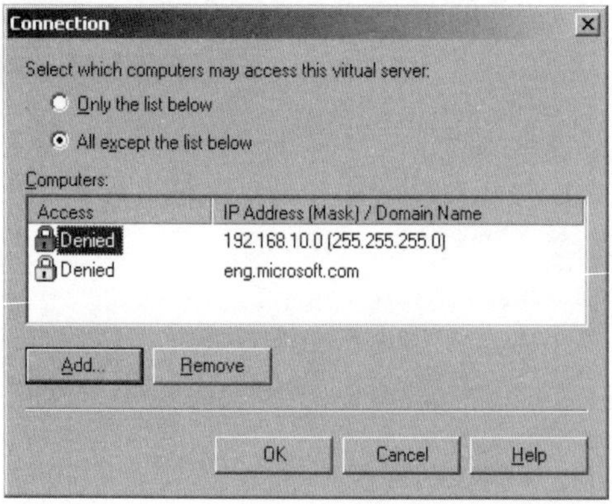

Figure 11-1. *You can control connections by IP address, subnet, or domain.*

3. To grant access to specific computers and deny access to all others, click Only The List Below.

4. To deny access to specific computers and grant all others access, click All Except The List Below.

5. Create the Access list. Click Add and then, in the Computer dialog box, specify Single Computer, Group Of Computers, or Domain. When you have specified the computer or group, click OK.

   - With a single computer, enter the IP address for the computer, such as 192.168.5.50.

   - With a group of computers, enter the subnet address, such as 192.168.10.0, and the subnet mask, such as 255.255.255.0.

   - With a domain name, enter the fully qualified domain name (FQDN), such as *eng.domain.com*.

Caution   When you grant or deny by domain, the SMTP service must perform a reverse Domain Name System (DNS) lookup on each connection to determine if the connection comes from the domain. These reverse lookups can severely affect the performance of the SMTP service, and this performance impact increases as the number of concurrent users and connections increases.

6. If you want to remove an entry from the Access list, select the related entry in the Computers list and then click Remove.

7. Click OK.

Controlling Secure Communications for Incoming Connections

By default, mail clients pass connection information and message data through an insecure connection. If corporate security is a high priority, however, your information security team might require that mail clients connect over secure communication channels. You configure secure communications by completing the following steps:

1. Create a certificate request for the SMTP virtual server for which you want to use secure communications. Each server that will be exchanging messages with other secure SMTP virtual servers must have a certificate.

2. Submit the certificate request to a certificate authority (CA). The CA then issues you a certificate (usually for a fee).

3. Install the certificate on the SMTP virtual server. Repeat steps 1 to 3 for each SMTP virtual server that needs to communicate over a secure channel.

4. Configure the server to require secure communications on a per virtual server basis.

You can create, install, and enable a certificate for use on a virtual server by completing the following steps:

1. In the IIS snap-in, right-click the SMTP virtual server on which you want to secure communications and then select Properties.

2. In the Access tab, click Certificate. This starts the Web Server Certificate Wizard. Use the wizard to create a new certificate.

3. Send the certificate request to your CA. When you receive the certificate back from the CA, access the Web Server Certificate Wizard from the virtual server's Properties dialog box again. Now you'll be able to process the pending request and install the certificate.

4. When you're finished installing the certificate, don't close the Properties dialog box. Instead, click Communicate in the Access tab.

5. In the Security dialog box, click Require Secure Channel, and then, if you've also configured 128-bit security, select Require 128-Bit Encryption.

6. Click OK and then click OK again to save your settings.

Controlling Authentication for Incoming Connections

The SMTP service supports the following authentication modes:

- **Anonymous access** With anonymous access, users are able to connect to the server and submit messages for delivery anonymously. Most Web servers have SMTP virtual servers configured for anonymous connections. This allows applications and external users to submit mail for delivery to the domain without needing to be authenticated. The way you prevent users from abusing the system is to set restrictions that allow only authorized users to relay mail on the server.

- **Basic authentication** With basic authentication, users are prompted for logon information before they're allowed to connect to the SMTP virtual server. When the logon information is entered, the information is transmitted unencrypted across the network. If you've configured secure communications on the server as described in the section of this chapter entitled "Controlling Secure Communications for Incoming Connections," you can require that clients use Secure Sockets Layer (SSL). When you use SSL with basic authentication, the logon information is encrypted before transmission.

- **Integrated Windows authentication** With integrated Windows authentication, the SMTP service uses standard Windows security to validate the user's identity. Instead of prompting for a user name and password, clients relay the logon credentials users supply when they log on to Windows. These credentials are fully encrypted without the need for SSL and include the user name and password needed to log on to the network.

All three authentication methods are available for SMTP virtual servers. As necessary, you can enable or disable support for these authentication methods by performing the following steps:

1. In the IIS snap-in, right-click the SMTP virtual server that you want to work with and then select Properties.

2. On the Access tab, click Authentication. This displays the dialog box shown in Figure 11-2.

3. You can now choose the acceptable authentication methods. Keep in mind that if you disable anonymous access, clients must authenticate themselves before they can submit messages for delivery and you might need to reconfigure Web-based applications on your server so that they use authentication.

4. If you enable basic authentication, you can set a default domain that should be used when no domain information is supplied during the logon process. Setting the default domain is useful when you want to ensure that clients authenticate properly.

Figure 11-2. *You can enable or disable authentication methods to meet your organization's needs. With basic authentication it's often helpful to set a default domain as well.*

5. With basic authentication, you can also require Transport Layer Security (TLS) encryption. With TLS encryption, clients must have smart cards or certificates installed to establish a secure connection to the server.

6. Click OK and then click OK again to save your settings.

Restricting Incoming Connections and Setting Time-Out Values

You can control incoming connections to SMTP virtual servers in two key ways. You can set a limit on the number of simultaneous connections, and you can set a connection time-out value.

Normally, SMTP virtual servers accept an unlimited number of connections, and this is an optimal setting in most environments. However, when you're trying to prevent a virtual server from becoming overloaded, you might want to limit the number of simultaneous connections. Once the limit is reached, no other clients are permitted to access the server. The clients must wait until the connection load on the server decreases.

The connection time-out value determines when idle connections are disconnected. Normally, connections time out after they've been idle for 10 minutes. In most situations, a 10-minute time-out is ideal. Still, there are times when you'll want to increase the time-out value, and this primarily relates to clients that get disconnected when transferring large messages. If you discover that clients get disconnected during large message transfers, the time-out value is one area to examine.

You can modify connection limits and time-outs by completing the following steps:

1. In the IIS snap-in, right-click the SMTP virtual server that you want to work with and then select Properties. This displays the Properties dialog box shown in Figure 11-3.

```
┌────────────────────────────────────────────────────────────┐
│ Default SMTP Virtual Server Properties              ? │ X │  │
├────────────────────────────────────────────────────────────┤
│  General │ Access │ Messages │ Delivery │ LDAP Routing │ Security │ │
│                                                            │
│     ◇▷  Default SMTP Virtual Server                        │
│  ──────────────────────────────────────────────────────   │
│   IP address:                                              │
│  ┌──────────────────────────────────────┐  ┌───────────┐ │
│  │(All Unassigned)                    ▼ │  │ Advanced...│ │
│  └──────────────────────────────────────┘  └───────────┘ │
│                                                            │
│   ☑ Limit number of connections to:        ┌──────────┐  │
│                                            │100       │  │
│   Connection time-out (minutes):           └──────────┘  │
│                                            ┌──────────┐  │
│                                            │10        │  │
│                                            └──────────┘  │
│                                                            │
│                                                            │
│  ┌─ ☑ Enable logging ────────────────────────────────┐   │
│  │  Active log format:                                │   │
│  │ ┌────────────────────────────────┐  ┌───────────┐ │   │
│  │ │W3C Extended Log File Format  ▼ │  │Properties..│ │   │
│  │ └────────────────────────────────┘  └───────────┘ │   │
│  └────────────────────────────────────────────────────┘   │
│  ──────────────────────────────────────────────────────   │
│      ┌──────┐   ┌───────┐   ┌──────┐   ┌──────┐           │
│      │  OK  │   │Cancel │   │ Apply│   │ Help │           │
│      └──────┘   └───────┘   └──────┘   └──────┘           │
└────────────────────────────────────────────────────────────┘
```

Figure 11-3. *Connection limits and time-outs can help reduce server load. They can also help to resolve connection problems.*

2. To set a connection limit, select Limit Number Of Connections To and then type the limit value. To remove connection limits, clear Limit Number Of Connections To.

3. The Connection Time-Out field controls the connection time-out. Type the new time-out value in minutes. In most cases you'll want to use a time-out value between 10 and 30 minutes.

4. Click OK to save your settings.

Securing Outgoing Connections

As with incoming connections, you can control outgoing connections to external SMTP virtual servers in several ways. You can do the following:

- Require authentication for outgoing connections
- Restrict concurrent connections and set connection time-out values
- Configure message limits

- Handle non-delivery, bad mail, and unresolved recipients
- Set relay restrictions for message delivery

Each of these tasks is discussed in the following sections.

Configuring Outbound Security

By default, SMTP virtual servers deliver messages to other servers without authenticating themselves. This mode of authentication is referred to as *anonymous*. You can also configure SMTP virtual servers to use basic authentication or integrated Windows authentication. However, you'll rarely use an authentication method other than anonymous with SMTP virtual servers.

One time when you'll use basic authentication or integrated Windows authentication with outgoing connections is if the SMTP virtual server must deliver all e-mail to a specific server or e-mail address in another domain. In other words, the server delivers mail to only one destination and doesn't deliver mail to other destinations. If you need to configure authentication for e-mail delivered to a particular server and need to deliver mail to other servers, you should configure a remote service domain to send mail to that specific server and use anonymous authentication for all other mail.

To view or change the outbound security settings for an SMTP virtual server, complete the following steps:

1. In the IIS snap-in, right-click the SMTP virtual server that you want to work with and then select Properties.

2. In the Delivery tab, click Outbound Security. To use standard delivery for outgoing messages, select Anonymous Access.

3. To set basic authentication for outgoing messages, select Basic Authentication and then, in the User Name and Password fields, type the user name and password that are required to connect to the remote server.

4. To set Windows authentication for outgoing messages, select Integrated Windows Authentication and then, under Account and Password, type the Windows account name and password that are required to connect to the remote server.

5. When you require authentication, you can also require encryption. To do this, select TLS Encryption.

Note   When you select TLS encryption, the destination servers must support smart cards or X.509 certificates. If the servers don't, all messages sent to noncompliant servers are returned with a non-delivery report.

6. Click OK and then click OK again to save your settings.

Controlling Outgoing Connections

With SMTP virtual servers, you have much more control over outgoing connections than you do over incoming connections. You can limit the number of simultaneous connections and the number of connections per domain. These limits set the maximum number of simultaneous outbound connections. By default, the total number of connections is limited to 1000, and the total number of connections per domain is limited to 100. To improve performance, you should optimize these values based on the capacity of your Web server.

You can set a connection time-out that determines when idle connections are disconnected. Normally, outbound connections time out after they've been idle for 10 minutes. Sometimes you'll want to increase the time-out value, and this primarily relates to times when you're experiencing connectivity problems and messages aren't getting delivered.

You can also map outbound SMTP connections to a Transmission Control Protocol (TCP) port other than port 25. If you're connecting through a firewall or proxy, you might want to map outgoing connections to a different port and then let the firewall or proxy deliver the mail over the standard SMTP port (port 25).

You set outgoing connection controls by completing the following steps:

1. In the IIS snap-in, right-click the SMTP virtual server that you want to work with and then select Properties.

2. On the Delivery tab, click Outbound Connections. This displays the Outbound Connections dialog box shown in Figure 11-4.

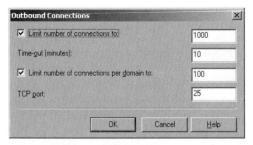

Figure 11-4. *As with incoming connections, limits and time-outs on outbound connections can help reduce server load and resolve connection problems.*

3. To remove outgoing connection limits, clear Limit Number Of Connections To. To set an outgoing connection limit, select Limit Number Of Connections To and then type the limit value.

4. The Time-Out field controls the connection time-out. Type the new time-out value in minutes. In most cases you'll want to use a time-out value between 10 minutes and 30 minutes.

5. To set an outgoing connection limit per domain, select Limit Number Of Connections Per Domain To and then type the limit value. You can remove the per domain limit by clearing Limit Number Of Connections Per Domain To.

6. To map outgoing connections to a different port, type the outbound port that the firewall or proxy expects in the TCP Port field.

7. Click OK and then click OK again to save your settings.

Configuring Outgoing Message Limits for SMTP

You can use outgoing message limits to control SMTP usage and to improve throughput for message delivery. You can set the maximum allowable message size for incoming messages. Clients attempting to send messages larger than this size get a non-delivery report that states that the message exceeds this limit. The default limit is 2048 KB (2 MB).

You can set the maximum size of all messages that can be sent in a single connection. The session limit should always be set so that it's several times larger than the message size limit. The default limit is 10,240 KB (10 MB). Clients attempting to send multiple messages in sessions whose total size exceeds this limit receive a non-delivery report stating that the maximum session size has been exceeded.

You can control the number of messages that can be sent in a single connection. When the number of messages exceeds this value, the SMTP service starts a new connection and transfer continues until all messages are delivered. Optimizing this value for your environment can improve server performance, especially if users typically send large numbers of messages to the same external domains. The default is 20. So, if you had 50 messages queued for delivery to the same destination server, the SMTP service would open three connections and use these connections to deliver the mail. Because message delivery would take less time if you optimize the number of connections, you can considerably enhance the SMTP service's performance.

You can also control the number of recipients for a single message. When the number of recipients exceeds this value, the SMTP service opens a new connection and uses this connection to process the remaining recipients. The default is 100. Using the 100-recipient limit, a message queued for delivery to 300 recipients would be sent over three connections. Again, because message delivery would take less time if you optimize the number of connections, you can considerably enhance the SMTP service's performance.

You set outgoing connection controls by completing the following steps:

1. In the IIS snap-in, right-click the SMTP virtual server that you want to work with and then select Properties.
2. Select the Messages tab, as shown in Figure 11-5.

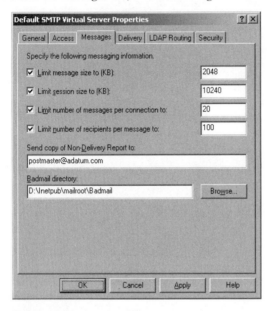

Figure 11-5. *You can use messaging limits to control SMTP usage and to improve performance.*

3. Use the message size limit to strictly control the maximum message size. To disable this limit, clear Limit Message Size To. Otherwise, select the Limit Message Size To check box and use the related field to set a message size limit.

4. Use session limits to strictly control the maximum size of all messages that can be sent in a single session. To disable this limit, clear Limit Session Size To. Otherwise, select the Limit Session Size To check box and use the related field to set a session size limit.

5. Use the messages per connection limit to force the SMTP service to open new connections when messages queued for delivery to the same destination exceed the messages per connection limit. To disable this limit, clear Limit Number Of Messages Per Connection To. Otherwise, select the Limit Number Of Messages Per Connection To check box and use the related field to set a limit.

6. Use recipient limits to force the SMTP service to open new connections when the number of messages addressed to multiple recipients exceeds the

recipients-per-connection limit. To disable this limit, clear Limit Number Of Recipients Per Message To. Otherwise, select the Limit Number Of Recipients Per Message To check box and use the related field to set a limit.

7. Click OK.

Handling Non-Delivery, Bad Mail, and Unresolved Recipients

When a message is undeliverable or a fatal error occurs during delivery, the SMTP service generates a non-delivery report that it attempts to deliver to the sender. SMTP virtual server options provide several ways to handle non-delivery.

For tracking purposes, you can send a copy of all non-delivery reports to a specific e-mail address. The e-mail address specified is also placed in the non-delivery report's Reply To field. This allows users to respond to the error message and potentially reach someone who can help resolve the problem.

If a non-delivery report can't be delivered to the sender, a copy of the original message is placed in the Badmail folder. Messages placed in the Badmail folder can't be delivered or returned. You can use the Badmail folder to track potential abuse of your messaging system. By default, the Badmail folder is located at Inetpub\Mailroot\Badmail. You can change the Badmail folder's location at any time, as long as you use a local drive.

You can configure these non-delivery options by completing the following steps:

1. In the IIS snap-in, right-click the SMTP virtual server that you want to work with and then select Properties.

2. Select the Messages tab, as shown previously in Figure 11-5.

3. In the Send Copy Of Non-Delivery Report To field, type the e-mail address of the organization's postmaster account or other account that should receive a copy of non-delivery reports.

4. In the Badmail Directory field, type the full path to the directory in which you want to store bad mail. If you don't know the full path, click Browse, and then use the Browse For Folder dialog box to find the folder you want to use.

5. Click OK.

Setting and Removing Relay Restrictions

Mail relaying can occur when users outside the organization use your mail system to send messages bound for another organization. The SMTP service normally prevents unauthorized users and computers from relaying mail through your organization—and you typically should use this setting. In this way only users and computers that are able to authenticate themselves can use your mail system to relay messages.

If necessary, you can grant or deny relaying permissions to specific computers, networks, and domains, overriding the default configuration. To do this, follow these steps:

1. In the IIS snap-in, right-click the SMTP virtual server that you want to work with and then select Properties.

2. Select the Access tab and then click Relay. You should now see the Relay Restrictions dialog box shown in Figure 11-6.

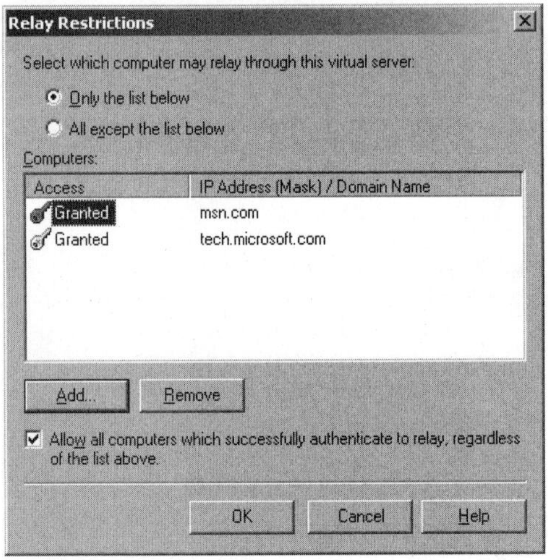

Figure 11-6. *If necessary, you can grant or deny computers, groups of computers, or domains the right to relay mail through your organization.*

3. To grant relay rights to specific computers and deny relay rights to all others, click Only The List Below.

4. To deny relaying for specific computers and grant all others the right to relay, click All Except The List Below.

- Create the Access list. Click Add and then, in the Computer dialog box, specify Single Computer, Group Of Computers, or Domain. When you have specified the computer or group, click OK.

- With a single computer, enter the IP address for the computer, such as 192.168.5.50.

- With a group of computers, enter the subnet address, such as 192.168.5.0, and the subnet mask, such as 255.255.255.0.

- With a domain name, enter the FQDN, such as *eng.domain.com.*

Caution   When you grant or deny relaying by domain, the SMTP service must perform a reverse DNS lookup on each connection to determine if the connection comes from the domain. These reverse lookups can severely affect the performance of the SMTP service, and this performance impact increases as the number of concurrent users and connections increases.

5. If you want to remove an entry from the Access list, select the entry in the Computers list and then click Remove.

6. By default, any computer that can authenticate itself is permitted to relay messages through the SMTP virtual server. To change this behavior and strictly control relaying using the authorization list, clear the Allow All Computers Which Successfully Authenticate To Relay, Regardless Of The List Above option.

7. Click OK, and then click OK again to save your settings.

Managing Message Delivery

SMTP delivery options determine how mail is delivered once a connection has been established and the receiving computer has acknowledged that it's ready to receive the data transfer. This section shows you how to use the configuration options that determine how message delivery and transfer occur.

You can set the following options to control message delivery:

- Outbound retry intervals
- Outbound and local delay notification
- Outbound and local expiration time-out values
- Message hop count
- Domain name options
- Reverse DNS lookups
- External DNS server lists

Setting Outbound Retry Intervals, Delay Notification, and Expiration Time-Out

Once a connection has been established and the receiving computer has acknowledged that it's ready to receive the data transfer, the SMTP service attempts to deliver messages queued for delivery to the computer. If a message can't be delivered on the first attempt, the SMTP service tries to send the message again after a specified time. The SMTP service keeps trying to send the message at the intervals you've specified until the expiration time-out is reached. When the time limit is reached, the message is returned to the sender with a non-delivery report. The default expiration time-out value is two days.

After each failed attempt to deliver a message, a delay notification is generated and queued for delivery to the user who sent the message. Notification doesn't occur immediately after failure. Instead, the delay notification message is sent only after the notification delay interval, and then only if the message hasn't been delivered already. The default delay notification value is 12 hours.

The SMTP service handles delay notification and expiration time-out values differently, depending on whether the message originated within the organization or outside the organization. Messages that originate within the organization are handled using the local delay notification and expiration time-out values. Messages that originate outside the organization are handled using the outbound delay notification and expiration time-out values. By default, both the local and outbound delay notification and expiration time-outs are set to the same values.

You can view or change the retry interval, delay notification, and expiration time-out values by completing the following steps:

1. In the IIS snap-in, right-click the SMTP virtual server that you want to work with and then select Properties.

2. Select the Delivery tab as shown in Figure 11-7, and then use the following options to set the retry values:

   - **First Retry Interval**   Sets the amount of time to wait after the first delivery attempt. The default is 15 minutes.

   - **Second Retry Interval**   Sets the amount of time to wait after the second delivery attempt. The default is 30 minutes.

   - **Third Retry Interval**   Sets the amount of time to wait after the third delivery attempt. The default is 60 minutes.

   - **Subsequent Retry Interval**   Sets the amount of time to wait after the fourth and subsequent delivery attempts. The default is 240 minutes.

3. With the Delivery tab still selected, you can set the outbound delay notification and expiration time-out values using the Delay Notification and Expiration Timeout fields in the Outbound frame. These values can be set in minutes, hours, or days, and they apply to messages addressed to remote domains and other external locations.

4. Set the local delay notification and expiration time-out values using the Delay Notification and Expiration Timeout fields in the Local frame. These values can be set in minutes, hours, or days, and they apply to messages addressed to local and alias service domains.

5. Click OK.

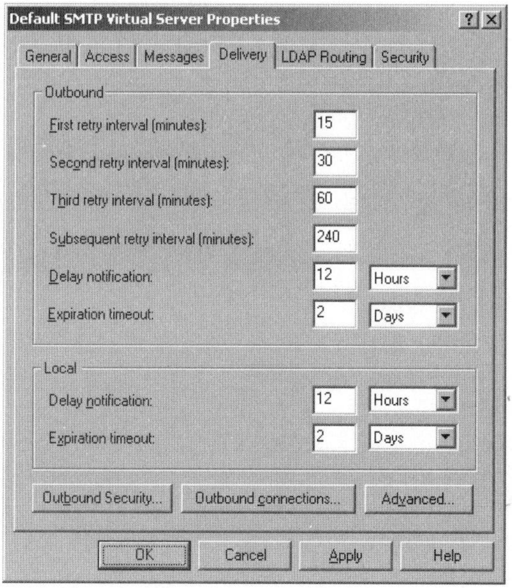

Figure 11-7.   *Use the options in the Delivery tab to control message delivery in the organization.*

Setting Message Hop Count

Messages can be routed through many different servers before reaching their final destination. The number of servers a message passes through is called the *hop count*. As an administrator, you can control the maximum allowable hop count, and you'll usually want to do this to prevent a message from being misrouted repeatedly.

The default maximum hop count is 15, which works well for most network configurations. However, if users frequently get non-delivery reports that state that the maximum hop count was reached and the message wasn't delivered, you might want to consider increasing the maximum allowable hop count. The number of Received: lines in the message header determines the total hops.

Caution   Don't automatically increase the hop count without first examining the SMTP routing on your network. Non-delivery reports due to the hop count can also indicate SMTP routing problems.

You can view or set the maximum hop count by completing the following steps:

1. In the IIS snap-in, right-click the SMTP virtual server that you want to work with and then select Properties.

2. In the Delivery tab, click Advanced. This displays the Advanced Delivery dialog box.

3. If you want to change the hop count, type a new value in the Maximum Hop Count field. Valid values are between 10 and 256.

4. Click OK and then click OK again to save your settings.

Setting Domain Name Options

Domain names play an important role in determining how mail is delivered, and you have two options for configuring domain name usage. You can set a masquerade domain, and you can set a FQDN for the SMTP virtual server.

A masquerade domain replaces the local domain name in any Mail From: lines in the message header. Mail From information is used to determine the address for sending non-delivery reports and doesn't replace the From: lines in the message body that are displayed to mail clients. The name replacement occurs only on the first hop.

The virtual server's FQDN is used in mail delivery. The server must have an FQDN, and this FQDN is associated with an e-mail domain through a DNS mail exchanger (MX) record. You have two options for specifying an FQDN:

• You can use the name specified in the Computer Name tab of the System Properties dialog box.

• You can specify a unique FQDN for the SMTP virtual server you're configuring.

The name in the Computer Name tab is used automatically. If you change the name in this tab, the new name is used the next time the computer is rebooted. No action is required to update the FQDN for the virtual server. However, if you want to override the setting in the Computer Name tab, you can do so by specifying a unique FQDN for the SMTP virtual server.

You can set the masquerade domain name or override the default FQDN by completing the following steps:

1. In the IIS snap-in, right-click the SMTP virtual server that you want to work with and then select Properties.

2. On the Delivery tab, click Advanced. This displays the Advanced Delivery dialog box shown in Figure 11-8.

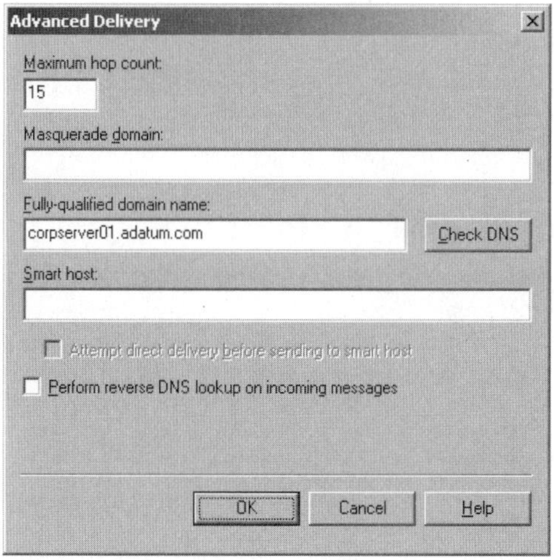

Figure 11-8. *Domain name options play an important role in determining how mail is delivered.*

3. In the Masquerade Domain field, type the domain name where you'd like non-delivery reports to be sent. This will replace the default domain name in outgoing message headers.

4. If you want to override the default FQDN, type a new value in the Fully-Qualified Domain Name field. Click Check DNS to ensure that you've entered the correct value and that DNS resolution is configured properly.

5. Click OK and then click OK again to save your settings.

Configuring Reverse DNS Lookups

With reverse lookups enabled, the SMTP service attempts to verify that the mail client's IP address matches the host and domain submitted by the client in the start session command. If the IP and DNS information match, the SMTP service passes the message through without modifying its contents. If the IP and DNS information can't be verified, the SMTP service modifies the message header so that the key word "unverified" is inserted into the message header's Received: line.

As stated previously, reverse lookups can severely affect the performance of the SMTP service, and this performance impact increases as the number of concurrent users and connections increases. Because of this, you'll want to be very cautious of enabling reverse lookups.

To enable reverse DNS lookups, complete the following steps:

1. In the IIS snap-in, right-click the SMTP virtual server that you want to work with and then select Properties.

2. In the Delivery tab, click Advanced. This displays the Advanced Delivery dialog box shown previously in Figure 11-8.

3. To enable reverse lookups, select Perform Reverse DNS Lookup On Incoming Messages. Clear this option to disable reverse lookups.

4. Click OK and then click OK again to save your settings.

Routing Outgoing Messages to Smart Hosts

You can route all outgoing messages through a smart host instead of sending them directly to the destination domain. This allows you to route messages to a specific server that can relay or deliver the messages. The goal is to route messages over a connection that might be more direct or less costly than the standard route.

You can add or remove a smart host for a remote domain by completing the following steps:

1. In the IIS snap-in, right-click the SMTP virtual server that you want to work with, and then select Properties.

2. In the Delivery tab, click Advanced. This displays the Advanced Delivery dialog box shown previously in Figure 11-8.

3. To add a smart host, type the IP address or DNS name of the smart host in the Smart Host field. If you want the SMTP service to attempt direct delivery before using the smart host, select Attempt Direct Delivery Before Sending To Smart Host.

 Tip If you use an IP address to identify a smart host, enclose the IP address in brackets [] to prevent the SMTP service from attempting to perform a DNS lookup on the address. Note also that smart host settings for remote domains override smart host settings configured for the SMTP virtual server itself.

4. To remove a smart host, delete the contents of the Smart Host field.

5. Click OK and then click OK again to save your settings.

Chapter 12

Administering the Indexing Service

You use the Indexing Service to build catalogs of documents that can be searched. When you add this capability to a World Wide Web site, it allows users to search for topics of interest using a standard Hypertext Markup Language (HTML) form. Like Internet Information Services (IIS), the Indexing Service is integrated into the Microsoft Windows operation system and can be used on intranets, extranets, and the Internet. As the Web administrator, you set up the catalogs that the Indexing Service needs, configure content indexing, and manage indexing on a day-to-day basis.

Managing the Indexing Service is very different from managing IIS. Before you can use the Indexing Service, you must perform the following tasks:

1. Install the Indexing Service using the Windows Components Wizard. Then configure the Indexing Service on the site or virtual server you want to index. Once the Indexing Service is installed on the server, it's configured to start automatically by default.

2. Create a catalog of documents to be searched. Each catalog should associate with a specific Web site, and each catalog can be associated with a Network News Transfer Protocol (NNTP) virtual server as well if you like.

3. Specify the directories and files to be indexed. You specify content indexing options using the IIS snap-in.

4. Create a search page on the Web site. This page is used to access the catalog and retrieve information that matches the user's search parameters. The search page must specify the catalog's physical location using the CiCatalog variable. Other variables are available to configure index searching as well.

Once you configure the Indexing Service for a site or virtual server, the service automatically creates and updates indexes. The service also attempts to manage its catalogs so that the data they contain is consistent and current. Data within catalogs occasionally gets out of sync, and when this happens, you might need to rebuild the catalog or force the Indexing Service to rescan directories for documents that should be indexed. These and other administration tasks are covered in this chapter.

Getting Started with the Indexing Service

The Indexing Service extracts information from designated documents and orga-
nizes the results into a catalog that can be searched quickly and easily. The
extracted information includes the content (text) within documents as well as
document properties, such as the document title and author. To understand how
the Indexing Service works, let's look at the following subjects:

- How you can use and install the Indexing Service
- How the Indexing Service builds indexes and catalogs
- How you can search and manipulate indexes

Using the Indexing Service

The Indexing Service indexes the following types of documents:

- HTML (.htm or .html)
- American Standard Code of Information Interchange (ASCII) text files (.txt)
- Microsoft Word documents (.doc)
- Microsoft Excel spreadsheets (.xls)
- Microsoft PowerPoint presentations (.ppt)
- Internet mail and news (when you index NNTP virtual servers)

Other documents for which a document filter is installed can be indexed as well.
The Indexing Service isn't installed on your Web server by default, but you can
install it using the Windows Components Wizard. To access and use this wizard,
follow these steps:

1. Log on to the computer using an account with administrator privileges.
2. Access Control Panel. Double-click Add Or Remove Programs. This displays
   the Add Or Remove Programs dialog box.
3. Start the Windows Components Wizard by clicking Add/Remove Windows
   Components.
4. In the Components list box, select Indexing Service and then click Next to
   continue. The wizard then installs the Indexing Service.
5. Click Finish when prompted.

Once you've installed the Indexing Service, you manage the service using the
Indexing Service snap-in for the Microsoft Management Console (MMC) or the
Indexing Service node in Computer Management. Regardless of the option you
choose, you can work with both local and remote servers using the same techniques. The only task that's different is connecting to remote servers.

With the Indexing Service snap-in, you set the server you want to work with
when you add the snap-in to a management console. Here are the steps for adding the Indexing Service snap-in to a management console and selecting a server
to work with:

1. Open the Run dialog box by clicking Start and then clicking Run.
2. Type **mmc** in the Open field and then click OK. This opens the MMC.
3. In MMC, click File, and then click Add/Remove Snap-In. This opens the Add/Remove Snap-In dialog box.
4. On the Standalone tab, click Add.
5. In the Add Standalone Snap-In dialog box, click Indexing Service and then click Add.
6. Select Local Computer to connect to the computer on which the console is running. Or select Another Computer and then type the name of a remote computer.
7. Click Finish. Afterward, click Close and then click OK.

With the Computer Management console, you connect to the local server automatically when you start the utility. You can connect to a different computer by right-clicking the Computer Management node, selecting Connect To Another Computer, and then following the prompts. Figure 12-1 shows the Indexing Service node in the Computer Management console.

Catalog	Location	Size (Mb)	Total Docs	Docs to Index	Deferred for Indexing	Word Lists	Saved Indexes
System	D:\System...	1	453	240	0	0	1
Web	d:\inetpub	14	2911	122	96	0	5

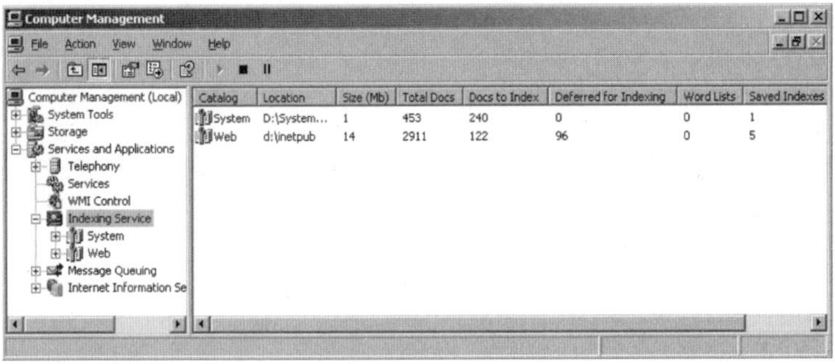

Figure 12-1. *Use the Indexing Service node in the Computer Management console to manage the Indexing Service.*

As you can see, selecting the Indexing Service node displays an overview of the currently installed catalogs, which include the default System and Web catalogs. The catalog summary provides the following information:

- **Catalog**   The descriptive name set when the catalog was created
- **Location**   The physical location of the catalog, such as D:\Catalogs\WWW\
- **Size (Mb)**   The size of the catalog in megabytes

Note   The typical catalog is 25 percent to 40 percent of the total size of the documents indexed. This means that if you index 1 GB of documents, you'll need an additional 250 MB–400 MB of storage space for the associated catalog.

- **Total Docs** The total number of documents designated for indexing in this catalog
- **Docs To Index** The total number of documents that remain to be indexed
- **Deferred For Indexing** The total number of documents that need to be indexed but can't be indexed because they're in use

 Note The Indexing Service defers indexing of documents being used and attempts to index the documents when they're no longer in use.

- **Word Lists** The number of word lists associated with the catalog and stored in system memory
- **Saved Indexes** The number of indexes within the catalog that have been saved to disk.
- **Status** The status of the indexing process

If you access the Indexing Service using Computer Management, you'll find that two default catalogs were created when you installed the service. These catalogs are the following:

- **System** The System catalog contains an index of all documents on all hard disk drives attached to the server.
- **Web** The Web catalog contains an index of the default Web site.

 Tip I recommend deleting the System catalog. This catalog typically isn't used on an IIS server, and maintaining the catalog uses system resources that could be better used elsewhere.

You can create additional catalogs at any time. When you create a catalog, you can associate the catalog with a Web site and an NNTP virtual server. The service then uses the indexing settings on the directories associated with the site or virtual server to determine which documents should be indexed. You configure indexing settings on directories as detailed in the section of this chapter entitled "Setting Web Resources to Index."

Indexing Service Essentials

The Indexing Service stores catalog information in Unicode format. This allows the service to index and query content in multiple languages. The Indexing Service performs three main functions to process document contents:

- **Indexing** Indexing is the process of extracting information from documents. The index contains contents from the main body of documents but doesn't include words on any exception word lists associated with the catalog. Indexes are compressed to save space.

- **Catalog building** Catalog building is the process of storing the index information in a named location. Catalogs contain extracted content in the form of indexes and stored properties for a set of documents.

- **Merging** Merging is the process of combining temporary indexes to create combined or master indexes. Merging indexes improves the performance of the Indexing Service and reduces the amount of RAM used to store temporary indexes in memory.

Indexing and catalog building take place automatically in the background when the Indexing Service is running. When first started, the Indexing Service takes an inventory of the directories associated with each catalog to determine which documents should be indexed. This process is referred to as *scanning*. The Indexing Service can perform two types of scans:

- Full
- Incremental

Full scans take a complete look at all documents associated with a catalog. The Indexing Service performs a full scan under the following circumstances:

- When the service is run for the first time after installation
- When a folder is added to a catalog
- As part of recovery if a serious error occurs
- When you manually choose to do so

Incremental scans look only at documents modified since the last full or incremental scan. The Indexing Service performs incremental scans under the following circumstances:

- When you start or restart the Indexing Service
- When you change a local document
- When the Indexing Service loses change notifications
- Any time you manually start an incremental scan

Note File system change notifications are important parts of the incremental scanning process. Whenever local documents are modified, the operating system generates change notifications and the Indexing Server reads them. In most cases change notifications for documents on remote systems won't reach the local Indexing Service. To account for this, the Indexing Service periodically performs incremental scans on any remote directories associated with a catalog.

After completing a scan of documents to be indexed, the Indexing Service begins to build the necessary catalogs. It does this by reading each document using a document filter. Filters are software components that interpret the structure of a particular kind of document, such as an ASCII text file, a Word document, or an HTML document. Using the appropriate filter, the Indexing Service extracts the document contents and property values, storing the property values and the path to the document in the index. Next, the Indexing Service uses the filter to determine the language in which the document is written and breaks the document body (content) into individual words. Each supported language has an exception list that provides a list of words that the Indexing Service should ignore.

You'll find exception lists in the \%SystemRoot%\System32 directory. These files are stored as ASCII text files and are named Noise.*lang*, where *lang* is a three-letter extension that indicates the language of the exception list. You can add entries to or remove entries from the exception list using a standard text editor or word processor.

The Indexing Service also stores values of selected document properties in the property cache. The property cache is a storage place for values of properties that you might want to search on or display in the list of search results. Within the property cache are two storage levels: primary and secondary. The primary storage level is for values that are frequently accessed, and, as such, these values are stored in a way that makes them quick and easy to retrieve. The secondary storage level is for additional values that are used infrequently.

After discarding words on the exception list and updating the property cache, the Indexing Service stores the remaining document content in a word list. Each document can have one or more word lists associated with it. Word lists are combined to form temporary indexes called *shadow indexes*. Shadow indexes are stored on disk in a compressed file format. Multiple shadow indexes can be, and usually are, in the catalog at any given time. The Saved Indexes entry, mentioned previously, lists the number of shadow and master indexes in a catalog. Over time, the number of shadow indexes can grow substantially. This occurs as documents are added to and modified within indexed directories.

The Indexing Service uses a process called *shadow merging* to combine word lists and temporary indexes, thereby reducing the number of temporary resources used and improving the service's overall responsiveness. Shadow merges occur during scans and as part of the normal housekeeping process implemented by the Indexing Service. The key events that trigger a shadow merge are when there are too many word lists stored in memory (1012 by default) or when the total size of all word lists exceeds a preset value (2560 KB by default).

The result of the indexing process is a master index. Each catalog has one, and only one, master index. The master index is created the first time you create a catalog and is kept up to date by periodically merging it with shadow indexes to create a new master index. This process of merging shadow indexes with the master index is called *master merging*. Once a master merge has occurred, there's only one saved index associated with a catalog—namely, the master index.

Master merges are triggered automatically based on the size of the shadow indexes, the amount of free disk space on the catalog drive, and the number of document changes in indexed directories. Automatic master merges, regardless of condition, are scheduled to occur nightly at midnight as well. If necessary, you can force a master merge. The key reason for forcing a master merge is to cause the Indexing Service to update a catalog so that all changes are reflected in search results immediately. As you might imagine, the master merge process is resource-intensive, so you normally wouldn't force a master merge during peak usage hours.

Settings that control scanning, merging, and other Indexing Service processes are found in the Registry and are stored here:

```
HKEY_LOCAL_MACHINE

\SYSTEM
\CurrentControlSet
\Control
\ContentIndex
```

Registry settings, given in decimal value, that control scanning and merging include the following:

- **MasterMergeCheckpointInterval**   Sets the interval for determining whether a master merge should be performed. The default value is 8192 seconds.

- **MasterMergeTime**   Sets the default time for when a daily master merge should be performed. The default value is 60, meaning 60 seconds after the start of a new day.

- **MaxFilesizeFiltered**   Sets the maximum size of filtered content for a particular document. By default, this is set to 256 KB.

- **MaxFreshCount**   Sets the maximum number of document updates and changes that triggers a master merge. By default, if more than 10,000 documents are changed, a master merge is triggered.

- **MaxIndexes**   Sets the maximum number of indexes that should be associated with a catalog before shadow merging is forced. By default, if more than 25 indexes are associated with a catalog, the Indexing Service will perform a shadow merge.

- **MaxShadowIndexSize**   Sets a maximum size value for shadow indexes in 128 KB increments. Used with MinDiskFreeForceMerge to force master merges when disk space is low and the size of the shadow index exceeds this value. The default is 15 (15 × 128 KB = 1920 KB).

- **MaxWordLists**   Sets the maximum number of word lists that can exist in a catalog. When this number is exceeded, a shadow merge is triggered. By default, this value is set to 20.

- **MaxWordlistSize**   Sets the maximum size of all word lists associated with a catalog. This value is set in increments of 128 KB and when exceeded, a shadow merge is triggered. By default, this value is set to 20 (20 × 128 KB = 2560 KB).

- **MinDiskFreeForceMerge** Sets a minimum free disk space value. If a drive containing catalogs has less disk space than this value and the total size used by shadow indexes exceeds MaxShadowIndexSize, the Indexing Service performs a master merge. The default is 15 MB.

- **MinSizeMergeWordlists** Sets the minimum size threshold for merging word lists with a shadow index. If the word lists' size exceeds this value, a shadow merge is triggered. The default is 256 KB.

Searching Catalogs

Searching is the process of looking through the catalog to find information. Users can search the catalog in several ways. The technique most often used with Web servers is to build a query form that can be used to search the catalog. The Indexing Service includes a query form for each catalog that can be used to test the installation. You can also create query forms using Active Server Pages (ASP) and Internet data query (IDQ) files.

With ASP, you create the query form and handle the results using a combination of server-side scripts that use ASP objects, HTML, and client-side scripts. The scripts you use can be written in any installed scripting language, and both Microsoft VBScript and Microsoft JScript are installed by default. Typically, you'll use the same page to implement the query form and display the results once the user has entered search parameters. For example, you could create a page called Query.asp that implements the query form and has an embedded script that submits the search parameters and then formats the search results.

IDQ, on the other hand, is a special language designed for submitting queries to the Indexing Service. With IDQ you create separate pages for handling each step in the query process. You use the following elements:

- An HTML page that ends with the .htm or .html extension to implement the query form

- An IDQ page that ends with the .idq extension to define the fixed query parameters for searches

- An HTML extension file that ends with the .htx extension to format the results of the query

An advantage of IDQ over ASP is that IDQ queries are much faster and more efficient in their use of Indexing Service resources. Regardless of whether you use ASP or IDQ to handle searches, you must set basic parameters that provide default values for the Indexing Service. The parameters you should set are summarized in Table 12-1.

Table 12-1.   Basic Parameters for the Indexing Service

Parameter	Description	Sample Value for IDQ
CiCatalog	Sets the file location of the catalog to be searched. If you don't set this parameter, the Indexing Service searches the Inetpub directory for a default catalog.	CiCatalog = D:\Catalogs\WWW
CiFlags	Sets the search flags for the query. The DEEP flag tells the Indexing Service to search all subdirectories within the current scope.	CiFlags = DEEP
CiMaxRecords In ResultSet	Sets the maximum number of records to return in the result set.	CiMaxRecordsInResultSet = 100
CiMaxRecords PerPage	Sets the maximum number of records to return in a single page.	CiMaxRecordsPerPage = 20
CiRestriction	Stores the search values entered by the user as passed from the query form.	CiRestriction = %CiRestriction%
CiScope	Sets the scope of the query within the catalog. If scope is set to /, the search begins at the top (or root) of the document tree.	CiScope = /Docs

Note   Most organizations have Web developers whose job is to create the Web pages needed for searching, handling, and displaying results. As the Web administrator, you assist the development team in setting parameters and publishing the Web pages when they're completed.

Core Indexing Service Administration

Now that you know how the Indexing Service works, let's look at the core techniques for managing it. In this section you'll learn how to specify the resources to index, create catalogs, tune performance, and more.

Setting Web Resources to Index

You configure Web resources for indexing using the IIS snap-in. You can apply indexing settings globally or locally. Global settings affect all IIS Web sites that inherit the settings, which means that all indexable files on all sites and in all subdirectories use this setting. To configure global indexing settings, follow these steps:

1. In the IIS snap-in, expand the node for the IIS server you want to work with. Then right-click Web Sites and select Properties.

2. In the Web Sites Properties dialog box, select the Home Directory tab.

3. Enable indexing for all Web sites on the server by selecting Index This Resource and then clicking OK. All Web sites inherit the indexing settings automatically. The changes also are propagated automatically to all directories within sites.

4. Disable indexing for all Web sites on the server by clearing Index This Resource and then clicking OK. Before applying these settings, IIS checks the existing settings in use for all Web sites. If a Web site uses a different value, an Inheritance Overrides dialog box is displayed. Use this dialog box to select the sites that should use the new setting and then click OK.

You can apply local settings to individual Web sites and directories. With sites, the root folder and all associated directories automatically inherit the site's indexing settings, which means that the indexable files within the root folder and associated directories use this setting. With directories, the selected directory and its subdirectories inherit the directory's indexing settings, which means that the indexable files within the selected directory and subdirectories use this setting.

To configure indexing settings for individual sites or directories, perform the following steps:

1. In the IIS snap-in, right-click the Web site or directory you want to manage and then select Properties.

2. Select the Home Directory, Directory, or Virtual Directory tab as appropriate.

3. Enable indexing for the currently selected resource and all its subdirectories by selecting Index This Resource and then clicking OK. The indexing settings are inherited automatically.

4. Disable indexing for the currently selected resource and all its subdirectories by clearing Index This Resource and then clicking OK. The indexing settings are inherited automatically.

Viewing and Creating Catalogs

You create and manage catalogs at the site level. Each site that you want to index should have a catalog. A site can have multiple catalogs. For example, you could create a catalog for indexes of your product directories and another catalog for indexes of your services directories.

You should store each catalog you create on a local file system in a folder separate from other catalogs. To help manage multiple catalogs, you could create a top-level directory called Catalogs and then create subdirectories within this directory for each catalog you want to create. You must create the catalog directory before you create the catalog.

You create a catalog for a site by completing the following steps:

1. Start Computer Management and then expand the Services And Applications node by clicking the plus sign (+) next to it.

Note When first accessed, the Computer Management console automatically connects to the local system. You can connect to a different
computer by right-clicking the Computer Management node, selecting
Connect To Another Computer, and then following the prompts. Keep in
mind that you can't add a catalog to a remote computer if the default
administration shares on the remote computer have been removed.

2. Right-click the Indexing Service node, choose New, and then click Catalog.
   This displays the Add Catalog dialog box shown in Figure 12-2.

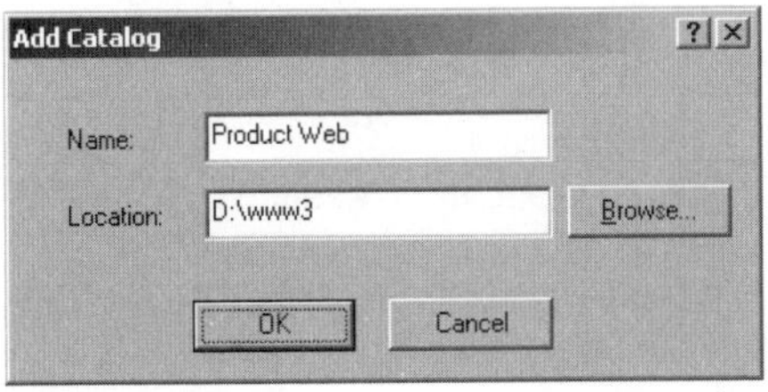

Figure 12-2. *Use the Add Catalog dialog box to create a new catalog on
the server.*

3. In the Name field, type the name of the catalog.

4. In the Location field, type the complete file path to the catalog folder, or
   click Browse and then select the folder in which you want the catalog to be
   located.

Security Alert Don't place the catalog in a Web site folder. If you do
this, the Indexing Service might not be able to maintain the catalog.
Keep in mind that as long as the catalog is on an NTFS file system
(NTFS) volume, Windows security permissions for documents are
maintained. This means that if the user doesn't have permission to
access a document, the document won't be listed in the query results.
However, if you index a shared folder from another system, documents
in the shared folder are listed in result sets regardless of access permissions, and it's only when the user tries to access the document
that access permissions are enforced.

5. Click OK.

After you create a catalog, you must stop and then restart the Indexing Service to
populate the catalog with indexes. To do so, follow these steps:

1. In the Computer Management console, right-click the Indexing Service node
   and then click Stop.

2. Right-click the Indexing Service node again and then click Start.

Viewing Indexing Status

You should monitor indexing periodically to make sure that catalogs are being maintained. One of the values you can use to keep track of the Indexing Service is the indexing status. As Table 12-2 shows, the indexing status tells you the indexing engine's current state. If users are experiencing problems retrieving search results, the Indexing Service might be paused or stopped, a merge might be in progress, or the service might be rescanning catalogs. Typically, you'll see an indexing state followed by the keyword Started. The Started keyword is a reference to the state of the Indexing Service itself. In this case, the service is active.

Table 12-2. Quick Reference for Indexing Service Status Conditions

Status	Description
Blank	Indexing Service is stopped and must be started to resume indexing.
Indexing Paused (High I/O)	Indexing is paused due to a high level of input/output (I/O) activity. You might want to close some applications to reduce the I/O activity.
Indexing Paused (Low Memory)	Indexing is paused because of low virtual memory. You might want to close some applications to make more memory available.
Indexing Paused (Power Management)	Indexing is paused to save battery power. Typically only seen on laptop systems.
Indexing Paused (User Active)	Indexing is paused to minimize interference with user activity. Users might be working with a large number of files that the indexer needs, or an administrator might be making changes to the Indexing Service configuration in Computer Management.
Master Merge (Paused)	Master merge is paused because of low resource availability. You might have a problem with the amount of memory, file space, or throughput of the system.
Merge	A merge is in progress. Merging is resource-intensive and might cause a temporary performance problem on the system.
Query Only	Indexing Service is started and is available only for querying.
Recovering	Indexing Service is recovering from an abrupt shutdown.
Scan Required	One or more documents have been added or modified within directories of this catalog. The indexer should perform a scan automatically. If it doesn't, check the Windows Event log.
Scanning	One or more directories are being scanned for newly added or modified documents.
Scanning (NTFS)	One or more NTFS volumes are being scanned for new or modified documents.

Table 12-2. **Quick Reference for Indexing Service Status Conditions**

Status	Description
Started	Indexing Service for this catalog has started.
Starting	Indexing Service is in the process of starting.
Stopped	Indexing of the catalog has been stopped.

You can view Indexing Service status conditions by completing the following steps:

1. Start the Computer Management console and then expand the Services And Applications node by clicking the plus sign (+) next to it.

2. Select the Indexing Service node in the left pane. The right pane displays the status conditions for each individual catalog. Keep in mind that each catalog can have a different status condition.

Starting, Stopping, and Pausing the Indexing Service

You can start, stop, and pause the Indexing Service like any other service. Users can perform queries and obtain results only when the Indexing Service is running. Users won't be able to obtain query results when the Indexing Service is stopped.

You can manage the Indexing Service by completing the following steps:

1. Start the Computer Management console, and then expand the Services And Applications node by clicking the plus sign (+) next to it.

2. Select the Indexing Service node in the left pane. The right pane displays the status conditions for each individual catalog.

3. Right-click the Indexing Service node in the left pane. You can now do the following:

   * Select Start to start the Indexing Service.

   * Select Stop to stop the Indexing Service.

   * Select Pause to pause the Indexing Service. After you pause indexing, click Start to resume normal operations.

Note Whenever you stop and then restart indexing, the Indexing Service performs an incremental scan of all the catalogs associated with all the sites on the server.

Setting Indexing Service Properties

The Indexing Service has several properties that you can configure to customize the way indexing works. These properties are summarized in Table 12-3 on the following page. As with most other Indexing Service properties, you can set these values globally or locally. All catalogs inherit global property settings unless you override the global settings.

Table 12-3. Configurable Properties for the Indexing Service

Property Tab	Property	Description
Generation	Index Files With Unknown Extensions	Specifies whether the Indexing Service indexes files with unregistered extensions. These files are not indexed by default. Indexing these files could slow down the indexing process if you have a large number of files with unregistered extensions.
	Generate Abstracts	Specifies whether the Indexing Service generates abstracts for files found in a search and returns them with the results. Abstracts contain key information gathered from documents that match the search parameters. Abstracts are not generated by default.
	Maximum Size	Sets the maximum number of characters in the abstracts returned with a search. The default value is 320. The range of permitted values is from 10 to 10,000. Keep in mind that this property is available only when you enable Generate Abstracts.
Tracking	Add Network Shares Alias Automatically	Specifies whether the Indexing Service automatically uses network share names as aliases for shared network drives. If you don't select this option, you must manually configure aliases for each network share you want to index, as described in the "Adding Physical Directories to a Catalog" section of this chapter.

You configure global property settings by completing the following steps:

1. Start the Computer Management console and then expand the Services And Applications node by clicking the plus sign (+) next to it.

2. Right-click the Indexing Service node and then select Properties.

3. In the Generation tab, you set properties that control the way indexing and search results are handled. Set or clear these properties as appropriate.

4. In the Tracking tab, you set properties for tracking network shares. Set or clear the related property as appropriate.

5. Click OK. If you want catalogs to inherit these values, check the properties of each catalog to ensure that Inherit Above Settings From Service is selected as appropriate in the Generation and Tracking tabs.

Individual catalogs can inherit or override the global settings. To perform these tasks, complete the following steps:

1. Start the Computer Management console. Expand the Services And Applications node by clicking the plus sign (+) next to it, and then expand the Indexing Service node.

2. You should see a list of catalogs configured on the server. Right-click the catalog you want to work with and then select Properties.

3. In the Generation tab, you set properties that control the way indexing and search results are handled. If you want the catalog to inherit the global settings, select Inherit Above Settings From Service. Otherwise, clear this check box and then change the properties as necessary.

4. In the Tracking tab, you set properties for tracking network shares. If you want the catalog to inherit the global settings, select Inherit Above Settings From Service. Otherwise, clear this check box and then change the properties as necessary.

5. Click OK.

Optimizing Indexing Service Performance

You can optimize the Indexing Service performance based on expected usage. You do this by controlling the way the Indexing Service manages the indexing and querying processes. Each process has different performance settings that you can set by using fixed or custom optimization values. For indexing, the performance options are the following:

- **Lazy**   The Indexing Service minimizes the amount of system resources reserved for indexing. In addition, the Indexing Service doesn't immediately respond to change notification requests from the operating system and consequently reduces the frequency of scanning. This is best for environments in which documents are infrequently updated or modified.

- **Moderate**   The Indexing Service reserves the normal amount of system resources for indexes and attempts to handle change notification requests in a timely manner. This is the default setting. It's best for the typical environment in which changes are made daily to documents configured for indexing.

- **Instant**   The Indexing Service reserves additional system resources for indexing and aggressively responds to change notification requests, which means higher than normal scanning for new and changed documents. As a result, document changes and additions appear quickly in catalogs. This is best for environments in which documents are changing rapidly and in which you need to reflect the changes quickly.

The available optimization settings are:

- **Low Load**   The Indexing Service reduces the amount of system resources reserved for querying. Therefore, the Indexing Service can handle only a limited number of simultaneous queries. This is best for environments in which queries are infrequent. If the number of queries increases too much, the responsiveness of the service will be poor.

- **Moderate Load**   The Indexing Service reserves the normal amount of system resources for querying and attempts to handle multiple simultaneous requests. This is the default setting. It's best for the typical environment in which users are regularly performing queries and you want to handle them appropriately.

- **High Load** The Indexing Service reserves additional system resources for querying and is able to handle a larger than usual number of simultaneous requests. This is best when you need to handle a large number of queries and don't care if the Indexing Service uses more memory and CPU time than usual.

You can optimize the Indexing Service performance by completing the following steps:

1. Start Computer Management and then expand the Services And Applications node by clicking the plus sign (+) next to it.

2. Select the Indexing Service node in the left pane. The right pane displays the status conditions for each individual catalog.

3. Right-click the Indexing Service node in the left pane and then select Stop.

4. Right-click the Indexing Service node again, choose All Tasks, and then select Tune Performance. The Indexing Service Usage dialog box shown in Figure 12-3 is displayed.

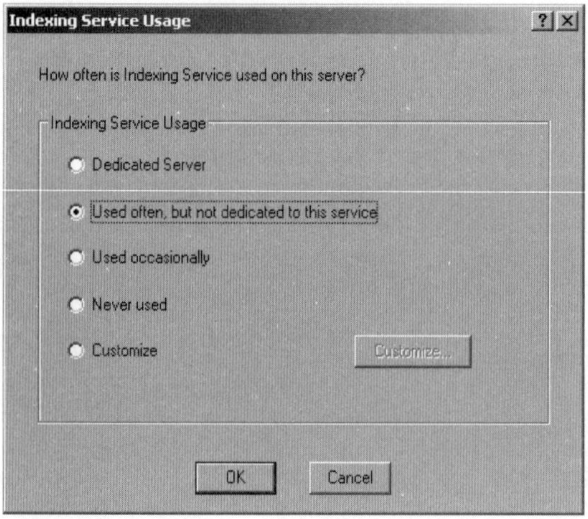

Figure 12-3. *Use the Indexing Service Usage dialog box to optimize indexing and querying.*

5. You can set a fixed or custom optimization value. To set fixed values, select one of the following options in the Indexing Service Usage dialog box:

   - **Dedicated Server** Sets instant indexing and heavy load querying options.

   - **Used Often, But Not Dedicated To This Service** Sets Lazy indexing and Moderate Load querying options.

- **Used Occasionally**   Sets Lazy indexing and Low Load querying options.

- **Never Used**   Disables the Indexing Service (as if you had disabled it from the Services node). Once selected, the Indexing Service stops permanently unless you reenable it manually.

6. To set a custom optimization value, select the Customize option and then click Customize. As shown in Figure 12-4, you can do the following:

- Use the Indexing slider to configure indexing as Lazy, Moderate, or Instant. The Moderate value is the middle option, and it isn't labeled.

- Use the Querying slider to configure querying handling as Low Load, Moderate Load, or High Load. The Moderate Load value is the middle option, and it isn't labeled.

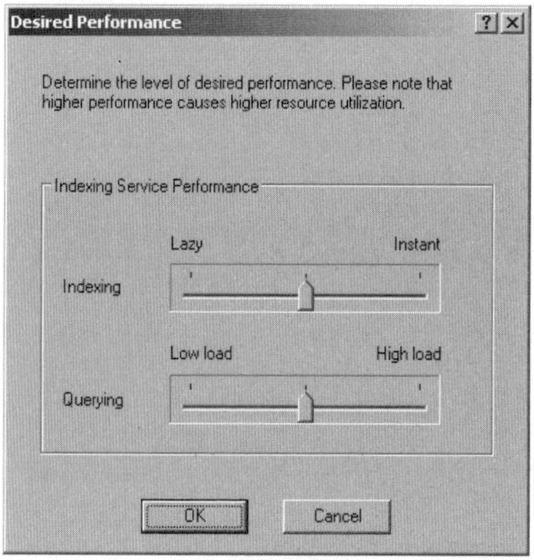

Figure 12-4. *You can customize the way indexing and querying are performed by using the Desired Performance dialog box.*

7. Click OK twice to save your settings and return to the Computer Management console.

Managing Catalogs

The Indexing Service stores all the information you're indexing in catalogs. Catalogs contain the extracted contents from the main body of documents as well as metadata that describes the document and its properties. During the catalog creation process you specify which Web site you want to associate the catalog with. Once you create a catalog for a Web site, users can search it using a Web-based query form.

The Indexing Service automatically maintains catalogs, and they're updated through the scan and merge processes. You can control catalogs manually as well by starting, stopping, or pausing the update monitor for the catalog. You can also force the Indexing Service to merge separate indexes into the master to improve the Indexing Service's overall performance and responsiveness.

Viewing Catalog Properties and Directories Being Indexed

Each catalog configured on the server has a separate set of properties that you can manage. These properties control the tracking of network shares, the generation of document abstracts, and the indexing configuration. You can configure catalogs to have unique property settings or to inherit global properties from the Indexing Service.

Catalogs can be associated with a Web site, an NNTP site, and one or more external directories. External directories can include local and remote resources. When you associate a catalog with a Web or NNTP site, you use the IIS snap-in to specify which resources are indexed as discussed in the section of this chapter entitled "Setting Web Resources to Index." When you associate a catalog with a network share, you can elect to index the directory when you add it to the catalog.

To view the current property settings for a catalog as well as the directories that are currently being indexed, follow these steps:

1. Start Computer Management. Expand the Services And Applications node by clicking the plus sign (+) next to it, and then expand the Indexing Service node.

2. You should see a list of catalogs configured on the server. Expand a catalog node by clicking the plus sign (+) next to it. Select the Directories node in the left pane to display a list of external directories associated with a catalog in the right pane.

3. If you want to view the properties of a catalog, right-click the catalog you want to work with and then select Properties. This displays a Properties dialog box that you can use to view or set properties.

Adding Physical Directories to a Catalog

You can add external directories to a catalog that can be indexed along with the content of a Web or NNTP site. These external directories can be on the local file system or on a remote file system. If you don't select Add Network Share Alias Automatically, you must configure aliases manually for each network share you want to index.

To add an external directory to a catalog, follow these steps:

1. Start the Computer Management console. Expand the Services And Applications node by clicking the plus sign (+) next to it, and then expand the Indexing Service node.

2. You should see a list of catalogs configured on the server. Right-click the catalog you want to work with, choose New, and then select Directory. This
   displays the Add Directory dialog box shown in Figure 12-5.

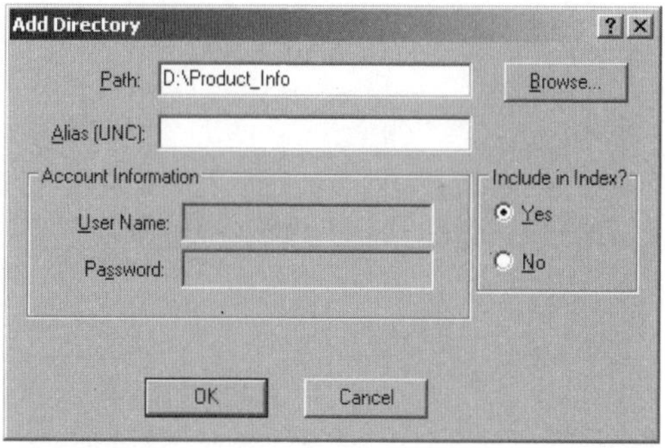

Add Directory	? X
Path: `D:\Product_Info`	Browse...
Alias (UNC):	
Account Information	**Include in Index?**
User Name:	⦿ Yes
Password:	○ No
OK	Cancel

Figure 12-5. *You can add physical directories to a catalog and map them to*
aliases using the Add Directory dialog box.

3. In the Path field, type the complete file path to the directory you want to
   index. If you don't know the directory path, click Browse to search for the
   directory.

4. If you're configuring indexing for a network share, type the network share
   alias that you want to use for this directory in the Alias (UNC) field. This
   alias should be in Universal Naming Convention (UNC) format and is
   returned in the search results sent to clients. For example, you could set
   the alias \\myserver\data to map to the actual network share path
   \\Galileo\reports\fy2001.

Tip   When you work with remote systems, you must allow the Indexing Service to map administrative shares. If it's unable to map administrative shares, the Indexing Service won't be able to index content.

5. If you're configuring indexing for a network share, you can also set the User
   Name and Password that the Indexing Service can use to authenticate on the
   remote system.

6. Select Yes to specify whether the directory should be included in the catalog
   index. Select No to exclude the directory from the index.

7. Click OK.

Forcing Full and Incremental Directory Rescans

The Indexing Service watches for change notification requests from the operating system to determine if files have been added to or changed within directories set for indexing. When a request is received, the Indexing Service schedules
the related directory for an incremental scan. At times the Indexing Service
might lose change notifications. This can happen during periods of high I/O or

CPU processing; the Indexing Service might not be able to keep up with the change notifications. It can also happen when the Indexing Service is unable to receive change notifications for directories on remote systems.

Typically, you can identify a problem with scanning by searching for documents that have been updated recently or added to an indexed directory. If the search results don't contain references to these documents, you might need to force a full or incremental rescan. You can do this only at the external directory level.

To force a directory rescan of an external directory, follow these steps:

1. Start Computer Management. Expand the Services And Applications node by clicking the plus sign (+) next to it, and then expand the Indexing Service node.

2. You should see a list of catalogs configured on the server. Double-click the catalog you want to work with and then select the related Directories node.

3. In the right pane, you should see a list of external directories configured for the catalog. Right-click the directory you want to work with, choose All Tasks, and then select Rescan (Full) or Rescan (Incremental) as appropriate.

4. When prompted, confirm the action by clicking Yes. Keep in mind that rescans of directories with a large number of documents can be resource-intensive. This means you'll use additional CPU, memory, and file I/O resources during the rescan.

Starting, Stopping, and Pausing Individual Catalogs

When you need to perform a large number of updates to directories monitored by a catalog, it's a good idea to pause or stop the catalog temporarily. Pausing or stopping the catalog tells the Indexing Service that it shouldn't handle change notification requests for this catalog. The difference between pausing and stopping a catalog is important. When you stop a catalog, the Indexing Service stops both indexing and querying activities, which means that the related directories are no longer indexed and users can't search the catalog. When you pause a catalog, Indexing Service stops indexing but still allows result sets from queries that are currently being processed to be returned. However, users can't make new queries or attempt to get additional results within a query set.

To start, stop, or pause a catalog, complete the following steps:

1. Start the Computer Management console. Expand the Services And Applications node by clicking the plus sign (+) next to it, and then expand the Indexing Service node.

2. Right-click the catalog you want to work with, choose All Tasks, and then select Start, Pause, or Stop as appropriate.

 Note The Indexing Service automatically performs an incremental scan when you stop and then restart a catalog. This ensures that updated or new documents are indexed as appropriate.

Merging Catalogs

As the Indexing Service updates the catalog, it creates temporary indexes, called *shadow indexes*, which extend the master index. These shadow indexes reflect the changes within catalog directories. Over time, the number of shadow indexes can grow substantially, and this is reflected in the number of saved indexes associated with a catalog. Because shadow indexes contain additional pointers and information, they use more space than a fully merged master index. As the number of shadow indexes grows, the responsiveness of queries against the catalog can slow.

You can improve the Indexing Service's responsiveness and reduce storage space usage by merging the temporary indexes with the master index. To perform this task, complete the following steps:

1. Start Computer Management. Expand the Services And Applications node by clicking the plus sign (+) next to it, and then expand the Indexing Service node.

2. Right-click the catalog you want to work with, choose All Tasks, and then select Merge.

3. When prompted to confirm the action, click Yes. As with rescanning, the merge process can be resource-intensive, and you might temporarily reduce the Indexing Service's responsiveness. The net gain, however, is that once merging is completed, the Indexing Service should be more responsive to user queries.

Specifying Web or NNTP Sites to Include in Catalogs

Each catalog can be associated with one Web site and one NNTP site. After you associate a site with a catalog, you can use the IIS snap-in to specify the resources that should be indexed as discussed in the section of this chapter entitled "Setting Web Resources to Index." You specify the site to include in a catalog by completing these steps:

1. Start the Computer Management console. Expand the Services And Applications node by clicking the plus sign (+) next to it, and then expand the Indexing Service node.

2. Right-click the catalog you want to work with and then select Properties. Select the Tracking tab.

3. As shown in Figure 12-6 on the following page, you can now take one of the following actions:

    • Use the WWW Server drop-down list in the Tracking tab to specify the Web site that you want to associate with a catalog.

    • Use the NNTP Server drop-down list in the Tracking tab to specify an NNTP site that you want to associate with a catalog.

Note   The NNTP Server drop-down list won't be available if the NNTP Service isn't installed on the system.

4. Click OK.

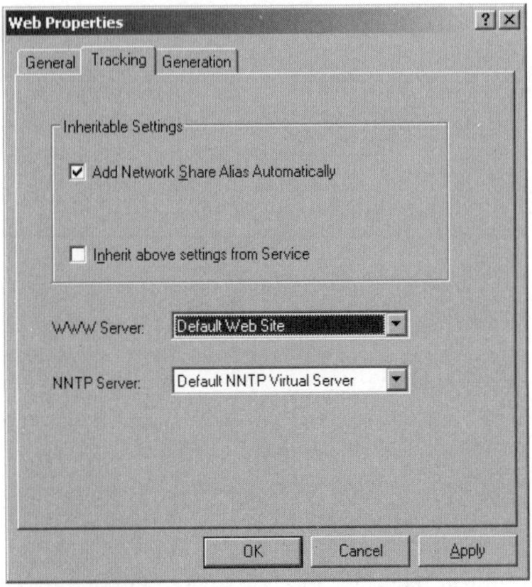

Figure 12-6. *Specify the site to index in the Tracking tab.*

Testing Catalogs with Queries

After you configure a catalog for indexing, you should query the catalog to ensure that you get the expected results. The Indexing Service has a built-in query form to perform this task. To access this form and enter a query, follow these steps:

1. Start the Computer Management console. Expand the Services And Applications node by clicking the plus sign (+) next to it, and then expand the Indexing Service node.

2. You should see a list of catalogs configured on the server. Double-click the catalog you want to work with and then select Query The Catalog in the left pane.

3. As shown in Figure 12-7, type the query you want to use in the field labeled Enter Your Free Text Query Below, and then click Search. If indexing is configured correctly, the Indexing Service should display search results. Then click a document title or path entry to ensure that documents can be accessed from the results page. If you experience problems with either of these procedures, you should check the indexing configuration.

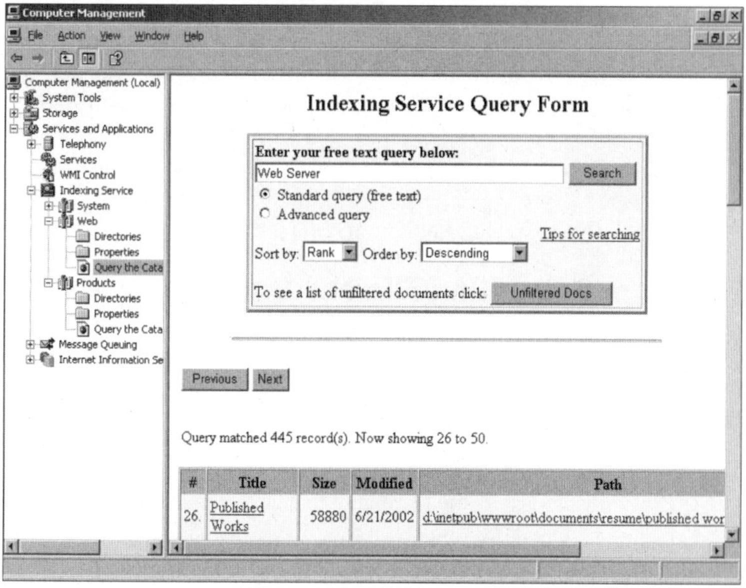

Figure 12-7. *After you configure indexing, check the configuration using the predefined query form.*

Finding and Resolving Catalog Problems

The Indexing Service can't index documents that are corrupt, that are missing data, or that are locked for writing. If a document is repeatedly found in a non-indexable state, the indexing engine marks the document so that it's filtered out of the catalog. Although documents can be filtered out of the catalog for other reasons, periodically searching for unfiltered documents is a good way to uncover potential problems with the catalog.

To find unfiltered documents, follow these steps:

1. Start the Computer Management console. Expand the Services And Applications node by clicking the plus sign (+) next to it, and then expand the Indexing Service node.

2. You should see a list of catalogs configured on the server. Double-click the catalog you want to work with, and then select Query The Catalog in the left pane.

3. Without entering any parameters in the query text field, click Unfiltered Documents.

4. Examine the documents that are listed as unfiltered to determine their potential status as corrupt, missing data, or locked.

If you suspect the catalog is itself corrupt, one way to resolve this is to empty the catalog and then recreate it. To do this, follow these steps:

1. Start the Computer Management console. Expand the Services And Applications node by clicking the plus sign (+) next to it, and then expand the Indexing Service node.

2. Right-click the catalog you want to work with, choose All Tasks, and then select Empty Catalog.

3. Force a full rescan of the catalog to rebuild it.

Limiting or Preventing File and Directory Indexing

You can use security permissions on files and directories to limit indexing. When a catalog is on an NTFS volume, Windows security permissions for documents are maintained. In this case, if the user doesn't have permission to access a document, the document won't be listed when the user queries the catalog. If you index a shared folder from another system, however, documents in the shared folder are listed in result sets regardless of access permissions, and it's only when the user tries to access the document that access permissions are enforced.

If you want to prevent files or directories from being indexed, the technique you use depends on whether the documents are stored on a FAT or NTFS volume. If the documents are on a FAT volume and you don't want them to be indexed, follow these steps:

1. You must add the directory containing the files to exclude from the directory. Follow the procedure detailed in the section of this chapter entitled "Adding Physical Directories to a Catalog."

2. Start the Computer Management console. Expand the Services And Applications node by clicking the plus sign (+) next to it, and then expand the Indexing Service node.

3. You should see a list of catalogs configured on the server. Double-click the catalog you want to work with and then select the Directories node.

4. Right-click the directory you want to configure and select Properties.

5. Clear Include In Catalog and then click OK.

If the documents are on an NTFS volume and you don't want them to be indexed, follow these steps:

1. Start Windows Explorer and then browse to the file or folder you want to exclude from the catalog.

2. Right-click the file or folder and then select Properties.

3. In the General tab, click Advanced.

4. Clear the For Fast Searching, Allow Indexing Service To Index This Folder check box, and then click OK.

Part IV

Performance, Optimization, and Maintenance

Part IV covers administration tasks you'll use to enhance and maintain Internet Information Services (IIS). Chapter 13 provides the essentials for monitoring IIS and solving performance problems related to the operating system and hardware configuration. Chapter 14 provides an essential background on IIS logs and then details how to configure server logs. Chapter 15 explores IIS optimization. You'll learn how to update registry settings for IIS and how to work with the IIS metabase. Chapter 16, the final chapter, discusses procedures for backing up and recovering the IIS configuration. Standard system backup procedures are examined as well.

Chapter 13

Performance Tuning and Monitoring

Monitoring and performance tuning are essential parts of Web administration. You monitor servers to ensure that they're running smoothly and to troubleshoot problems as they occur. You tune the performance of servers to achieve optimal performance based on the current system resources and traffic load. Microsoft Windows Server 2003 includes several tools that you'll use to monitor Internet Information Services (IIS). The key tools are the Performance tool, Windows event logs, and the IIS access logs. You'll often use the results of your monitoring to optimize IIS.

Performance tuning is as much an art as it is a science. You often tune performance based on trial and error. You adjust the server, monitor the server's performance over time, and then gauge the success of the updated settings. If things aren't working as expected, you adjust the settings again. In an ideal world you'd have staging or development servers that are similar in configuration to your production servers to work with while tuning server performance. Then, once you've made adjustments that worked in staging, you could configure these changes on the production servers.

Monitoring IIS Performance and Activity

Monitoring IIS isn't something you should do haphazardly. You need to have a clear plan—a set of goals that you hope to achieve. Let's look at some reasons that you might want to monitor IIS and the tools you can use to do this.

Why Monitor IIS?

Troubleshooting performance problems is a key reason for monitoring. For example, users might be having problems connecting to the server, and you might want to monitor the server to troubleshoot these problems. Here, your goal would be to track down the problem using the available monitoring resources and then to solve it.

Another common reason for wanting to monitor IIS is to use the results to improve server performance. Improving server performance can reduce the need for costly additional servers or additional hardware components, such as CPUs and memory. This allows you to squeeze additional processing power out of the server and budget for when you really need to purchase new servers and components.

To achieve optimal performance, you need to identify performance bottlenecks, maximize throughput, and minimize the time it takes for World Wide Web (WWW) applications to process user requests. You achieve this by doing the following:

- Monitoring memory and CPU usage and taking appropriate steps to reduce the load on the server, as necessary. Other processes running on the server might be using memory and CPU resources needed by IIS. Resolve this issue by stopping nonessential services and moving support applications to a different server.

- Resolving hardware issues that might be causing problems. If slow disk drives are delaying file reads, work on improving disk input/output (I/O). If the network cards are running at full capacity, install additional network cards for performing activities, such as backups or load balancing.

- Optimizing Web pages and applications running on IIS. You should test Web pages and IIS applications to ensure that the source code performs as expected. Eliminate unnecessary procedures and optimize inefficient processes.

Unfortunately, there are often tradeoffs to be made when it comes to resource usage. For example, as the number of users accessing IIS grows, you might not be able to reduce the network traffic load, but you might be able to improve server performance by optimizing Web pages and IIS applications.

Getting Ready to Monitor

Before you start monitoring IIS, you should establish baseline performance metrics for your server. To do this, you measure server performance at various times and under different load conditions. You can then compare the baseline performance with subsequent performance to determine how IIS is performing. Performance metrics that are well above the baseline measurements might indicate areas where the server needs to be optimized or reconfigured.

After you establish the baseline metrics, you should formulate a monitoring plan. A comprehensive monitoring plan involves the following steps:

1. Determine which server resources should be monitored to help you accomplish your goal

2. Set filters to reduce the amount of information collected

3. Configure performance counters to watch the resource usage

4. Log the usage data so that it can be analyzed

5. Analyze the usage data and replay the data as necessary to find a solution

These procedures are examined later in this chapter in the section entitled "Monitoring IIS Performance." Although you should develop a monitoring plan in most cases, there are times when you might not want to go through all these steps to monitor IIS. In this case, use the steps that make sense for your situation.

Monitoring Tools and Resources

The primary tools you'll use to monitor IIS are:

- **Performance tool**   Configure counters to watch resource usage over time. Use the usage information to gauge the performance of IIS and determine areas that can be optimized.

- **Access logs**   Use information in the access logs to find problems with pages, applications, and IIS. Entries logged with a status code beginning with a 4 or 5 indicate a potential problem. Access logs can be written in several different formats, including IIS log file format, National Center for Supercomputing Applications (NCSA) common log file format, and World Wide Web Consortium (W3C) extended log file format.

- **Event logs**   Use information in the event logs to troubleshoot system-wide problems, including IIS and Indexing Service problems. The primary logs you'll want to work with are the System, Security, and Application event logs.

Many other monitoring tools are available in the *Microsoft Windows Server 2003 Resource Kit*. The resource kit tools you'll want to use include:

- **HTTP Monitoring Tool**   Monitors Hypertext Transfer Protocol (HTTP) activity on the server and records the tracking information to a file or to the Windows Event logs. The information tracked can alert you to changes in HTTP activity. You can import the output file generated by the tool directly into Microsoft SQL Server as well.

- **Playback**   Playback is a tool suite that includes two components: Recorder.dll and Playback.exe. Recorder.dll records ongoing activity at a Web site so that it can be played back. Playback.exe plays back the recorded activity on a Web site so that you can simulate real-world traffic on development or testing servers.

- **Web Application Stress Tool**   Simulates Web activity so that you can evaluate server performance. Parameters you can set include the number of users, the frequency of requests, and the type of request. The tool produces a detailed report that tells you the number of requests, number of errors, elapsed time for processing requests, and more.

- **Web Capacity Analysis Tool (WCAT)**   Tests different server and network configurations using workload simulations and content developed specifically for WCAT. When you change your hardware and software configuration and repeat the testing, you can identify how the new configuration affects server response.

Detecting and Resolving IIS Errors

IIS records errors in two locations: the IIS access logs and the Windows event logs. In the access logs, you'll find information related to missing resources, failed authentication, and internal server errors. In the event logs, you'll find IIS errors, failed authentication, IIS application errors, and errors related to other applications running on the server.

Examining the Access Logs

Access logs are created when you enable logging for Web, File Transfer Protocol (FTP), Simple Mail Transfer Protocol (SMTP), and NNTP sites. Every time someone requests a file from a site, an entry goes into the access log, making the access log a running history of resource requests. Because each entry has a status code, you can examine entries to determine the success or failure of a request. Failed requests have a status code beginning with a 4 or 5.

The most common error you'll see is a 404 error, which indicates that a resource wasn't found at the expected location. You can correct this problem by doing the following:

- Placing the file in the expected location
- Renaming the file if the current name is different than expected
- Modifying the linking file to reflect the file's correct name and location

If you want to find the access log for a particular site, follow these steps:

1. Start the IIS snap-in and then, in the left pane (Console Root), click the plus sign (+) next to the computer you want to work with. If the computer isn't shown, connect to it as discussed in the section entitled "Connecting to Other Servers" in Chapter 2, "Core IIS Administration."

2. Right-click the Web, FTP, SMTP, or NNTP site you want to manage and then select Properties.

3. In the Enable Logging frame, click Properties to display a dialog box similar to the one shown in Figure 13-1.

4. The Log File Directory field shows the top-level directory for this site's logs. The default top-level directory is \%WinDir%\System32\LogFiles.

5. The Log File Name field shows the subdirectory and log file naming format. For example, if the name shows \W3SVC1\EXYYMMDD.LOG, you'll find the site's logs in the W3SVC1 subdirectory. The current log is the file in this subdirectory with the most recent date and time stamp. All other logs are archive files that could be moved to a history directory.

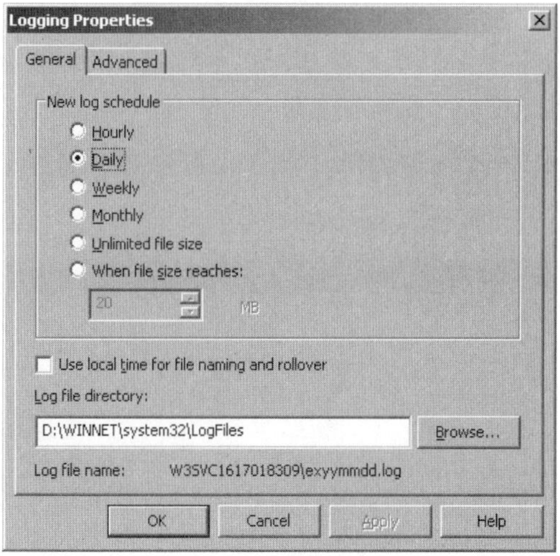

Figure 13-1. *The Logging Properties dialog box tells you where logs are being written.*

Now that you know where the log files are located for the site, you can search for errors in the log file. Because logs are stored as American Standard Code of Information Interchange (ASCII) text, one way to do this would be to open a log in Microsoft Notepad or another text editor and search for error codes, such as 404. Another way to search for errors would be to use the FIND command. At a command prompt, you could search for 404 errors in any log file within the current directory using the following command:

```
find "404" *
```

Once you identify missing files, you can use any of the previously recommended techniques to resolve the problem. You'll learn more about access logs and status codes in Chapter 14, "Tracking User Access and IIS Logging."

Examining the Windows Event Logs

Windows event logs provide historical information that can help you track down problems with services, processes, and applications. The event-logging service controls the events tracked. When this service is started, user actions and system resource usage events can be tracked through the following event logs:

- **Application**   Records events logged by applications, such as IIS. This is a default Windows event log.

- **Directory Service**   Records events logged by the Active Directory service and its related services. This event log is available only when Directory Services is installed.

- **DNS Server** Records Domain Name System (DNS) queries, responses, and other DNS activities. This event log is available only when DNS is installed.
- **File Replication Service** Records file replication activities on the system. This event log is available only when the File Replication Service (FRS) is installed.
- **Security** Records events you've set for auditing with local or global group policies. Note that administrators must be granted access to the security log through user rights assignment. This is a default Windows event log.
- **System** Records events logged by the operating system or its components, such as the failure of a service to start when the system boots up. This is a default Windows event log.

You access the Windows event logs by completing the following steps:

1. Open the Start menu, select All Programs, select Administrative Tools, and then select Event Viewer. This starts Event Viewer.
2. Event Viewer displays logs for the local computer by default. If you want to view logs on a remote computer, right-click the Event Viewer entry in the console tree (left pane), and then select Connect To Another Computer. In the Select Computer dialog box, type the name of the computer you want to access, and then click OK.
3. Select the log you want to view, as shown in Figure 13-2. Use the information in the Source column to determine which service or process logged a particular event.

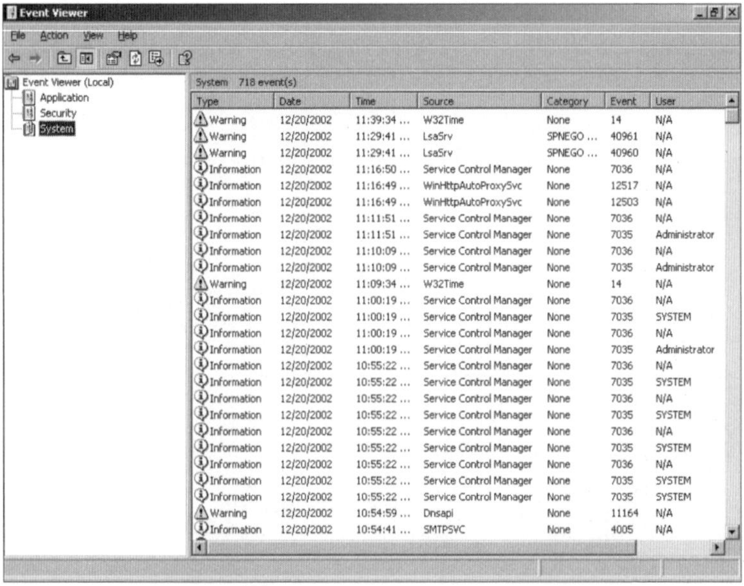

Figure 13-2. *Event Viewer displays events for the selected log.*

Entries in the right-hand pane of Event Viewer provide a quick overview of when, where, and how an event occurred. To obtain detailed information on an event, double-click its entry. The event type precedes the date and time of the event. Event types include:

- **Information**   An informational event, which is generally related to a successful action.
- **Success Audit**   An event related to the successful execution of an action.
- **Failure Audit**   An event related to the failed execution of an action.
- **Warning**   A warning. Details for warnings are often useful in preventing future system problems.
- **Error**   An error, such as the failure of a service to start.

Note   Warnings and errors are the two key types of events that you'll want to examine closely. Whenever these types of events occur and you're unsure of the cause, double-click the entry to view the detailed event description.

In addition to type, date, and time, the summary and detailed event entries provide the following information:

- **Source**   The application, service, or component that logged the event
- **Category**   The category of the event, which is almost always set to None, but is sometimes used to further describe the related action, such as a process or a service
- **Event**   Generally a numeric identifier for the specific event, which could be helpful when searching knowledge bases
- **User**   The user account that was logged on when the event occurred, if applicable
- **Computer**   The name of the computer on which the event occurred
- **Description**   In the detailed entries, a text description of the event
- **Data**   In the detailed entries, any data or error code output by the event

The sources you'll want to look for include:

- **Active Server Pages (ASP)**   Applications and ASP engines
- **CERTSVC**   Certificate services
- **Ci**   The Indexing Service
- **MSDTC**   Microsoft Distributed Transaction Coordinator
- **MSFTPSVC**   The FTP service
- **NNTPSVC**   The Network News Transfer Protocol (NNTP) service
- **SMTPSVC**   The SMTP service
- **W3SVC**   The World Wide Web service

If you want to see only warnings and errors, you can filter the log by completing the following steps:

1. From the View menu, select the Filter option. This opens the dialog box shown in Figure 13-3.

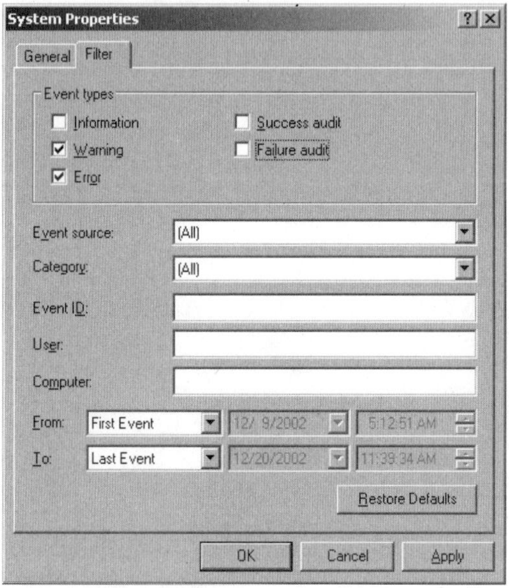

Figure 13-3. *You can filter events so that only warnings and errors are displayed.*

2. Clear the following check boxes: Information, Success Audit, and Failure Audit.

3. Select the Warning and Error check boxes.

4. Click OK. You should now see a list of only warning and error messages. Read these messages carefully and take steps to correct any problems that exist.

Monitoring IIS Performance

The Performance tool is the tool of choice for monitoring IIS performance. The Performance tool graphically displays statistics for the set of performance parameters you've selected for display. These performance parameters are referred to as *counters*. When you install IIS on a system, the Performance tool is updated with a set of counters for tracking IIS performance. You can update these counters when you install additional services and add-ons for IIS as well.

The Performance tool creates a graph depicting the counters you're tracking. The update interval for this graph is configurable but is set to 1 second by default. As you'll see when you work with the Performance tool, the tracking information is most valuable when you record performance information in a log file so that it can be played back. Also, the Performance tool is helpful when you configure alerts to send messages when certain events occur, such as when an automatic IIS restart is triggered.

The sections that follow examine key techniques you'll use to work with the Performance tool. You start the Performance tool by selecting the Performance option from the Administrative Tools menu.

Choosing Counters to Monitor

The Performance tool only displays information for counters you're tracking. More than a hundred IIS counters are available, provided you've installed the related service. Counters are organized into object groupings. For example, all ASP-related counters are associated with the Active Server Pages performance object. You'll find object counters for other services as well. A list of the main IIS-related counter objects follows:

- **ASP.NET** Object counters for general tracking of ASP.NET applications, application requests, and worker processes

- **ASP.NET Applications** Object counters for tracking the ASP.NET application queue and other specific ASP.NET application counters

- **Active Server Pages** Object counters for ASP scripts and applications running on the server

- **FTP Service** Object counters for the FTP service

- **Indexing Service** Object counters for Indexing Service that relate to indexing processes, word lists, and queries

- **Indexing Service Filter** Object counters provide additional performance information related to content filters and indexing speed related to filters

- **Internet Information Services Global** Object counters for all Internet services (WWW, FTP, SMTP, NNTP, and so on) running on the server

- **NNTP Commands** Object counters related to NNTP commands that users are executing on the server

- **NNTP Server** Object counters that track overall NNTP performance, such as the number of articles sent, received, and posted per second

- **SMTP NTFS Store Driver** Object counters for tracking the total number of messages and message streams

- **SMTP Server** Object counters that track overall SMTP performance, such as the number of messages sent and received per second

- **Web Service** Object counters for the World Wide Web Publishing Service

- **Web Service Cache** Object counters that provide detailed information on the cache used by the Web service, including cache for metadata, files, memory, and Uniform Resource Identifiers (URIs)

Counters for monitoring performance are summarized by issue and object in Table 13-1. The easiest way to learn about these counters is to read the explanations available in the Add Counters dialog box. Start the Performance tool, click the Add button on the toolbar, and then select an object in the Performance Object drop-down list. Afterward, click Explain and then scroll through the list of counters for this object.

 Tip Multiple versions of ASP.NET can be installed. As a result, the ASP.NET and ASP Applications counter objects have version-specific instances. Use the counter objects for the specific ASP.NET versions you want to track.

Table 13-1. Key Counters Used to Monitor Web Server Performance

Issue	Counter	Object Available For
Application Status	Application Restarts	ASP.NET
	Applications Running	ASP.NET
ASP sessions	Session Duration	Active Server Pages
	Sessions Current	Active Server Pages
	Sessions Timed Out	Active Server Pages, ASP.NET Applications
	Sessions Total	Active Server Pages, ASP.NET Applications
ASP transactions	Transactions Aborted	Active Server Pages, ASP.NET Applications
	Transactions Committed	Active Server Pages, ASP.NET Applications
	Transactions Pending	Active Server Pages, ASP.NET Applications
	Transactions Total	Active Server Pages, ASP.NET Applications
	Transactions/Sec	Active Server Pages, ASP.NET Applications
Bandwidth usage	Current Blocked Async I/O Requests	Internet Information Services Global, Web Service
	Measured Async I/O Bandwidth usage	Internet Information Services Global, Web Service
	Total Allowed Async I/O Requests	Internet Information Services Global, Web Service
	Total Blocked Async I/O Requests	Internet Information Services Global, Web Service
	Total Rejected Async I/O Requests	Internet Information Services Global, Web Service
Caching and Memory	File Cache Flushes, URI Cache Flushes	Internet Information Services Global
	File Cache Hits, URI Cache Hits	Internet Information Services Global

Table 13-1.   Key Counters Used to Monitor Web Server Performance

Issue	Counter	Object Available For
	File Cache Hits %, URI Cache Hits %	Internet Information Services Global
	File Cache Misses, URI Cache Misses	Internet Information Services Global
	Maximum File Cache Memory Usage	Internet Information Services Global
	Script Engines Cached	Active Server Pages
	Template Cache Hit Rate	Active Server Pages
	Template Notifications	Active Server Pages
	Templates Cached	Active Server Pages
Connections	Connection Attempts/Sec	Web Service
	Current Anonymous Users	Web Service, FTP Service
	Current Connections	Web Service, FTP Service
	Current File Cache Memory Usage	Internet Information Services Global
	Maximum Connections	Web Service, FTP Service
	Current Files Cached	Internet Information Services Global
	Current NonAnonymous Users	Web Service, FTP Service
	Maximum Anonymous Users	Web Service, FTP Service
	Maximum NonAnonymous Users	Web Service, FTP Service
	Total Anonymous Users	Web Service, FTP Service
	Total Connection Attempts (all instances)	Web Service, FTP Service
	Total Logon Attempts	Web Service, FTP Service
	Total NonAnonymous Users	Web Service, FTP Service
Errors	Errors During Script Runtime	Active Server Pages
	Errors From ASP Preprocessor	Active Server Pages
	Errors From Script Compilers	Active Server Pages

(continued)

Table 13-1. Key Counters Used to Monitor Web Server Performance *(continued)*

Issue	Counter	Object Available For
	Errors/Sec	Active Server Pages
	Not Found Errors/Sec	Web Service
	Requests Not Authorized	Active Server Pages, ASP.NET Applications
	Requests Not Found	Active Server Pages, ASP.NET Applications
	Requests Rejected	Active Server Pages, ASP.NET
	Requests Timed Out	Active Server Pages, ASP.NET Applications
	Service Uptime	Web Service
	Total Not Found Errors	Web Service
Indexing	Running Queries	Indexing Service
	Total # of Documents	Indexing Service
	Total # of Queries	Indexing Service
	Total Indexing Speed (MB/hr)	Indexing Service Filter
Requests	Get Requests/Sec	Web Service
	Head Requests/Sec	Web Service
	ISAPI Extension Requests/Sec	Web Service
	Post Requests/Sec	Web Service
	Put Requests/Sec	Web Service
	Request Bytes In Total	Active Server Pages, ASP.NET Applications
	Request Bytes Out Total	Active Server Pages, ASP.NET Applications
	Requests Executing	Active Server Pages, ASP.NET Applications
	Requests Queued	Active Server Pages, ASP.NET
	Requests Rejected	Active Server Pages, ASP.NET
	Requests Succeeded	Active Server Pages, ASP.NET Applications
	Requests Timed Out	Active Server Pages, ASP.NET Applications
	Requests Total	Active Server Pages, ASP.NET Applications
	Requests/Sec	Active Server Pages, ASP.NET Applications
Throughput	Bytes Received/Sec	Web Service, FTP Service
	Bytes Sent/Sec	Web Service, FTP Service
	Bytes Total/Sec	Web Service, FTP Service
	Files Received/Sec	Web Service
	Files Sent/Sec	Web Service
	Files/Sec	Web Service
	Total Files Received	Web Service, FTP Service

Table 13-1.   Key Counters Used to Monitor Web Server Performance

Issue	Counter	Object Available For
	Total Files Sent	Web Service, FTP Service
	Total Files Transferred	Web Service, FTP Service
Worker Process Status	Worker Process Restarts	ASP.NET
	Worker Processes Running	ASP.NET

When the Performance tool is monitoring a particular object, it can track all instances of all counters for that object. Instances are multiple occurrences of a particular counter. For example, when you track counters for the Web Service object, you often have a choice of tracking all Web site instances or specific Web site instances. Following this, if you configured CorpWeb, CorpProducts, and CorpServices sites, you could use Web Service counters to track a specific Web site instance or multiple Web site instances.

To select which counters you want to monitor, complete the following steps:

1. Start the Performance tool by clicking Start and selecting All Programs and then Performance from the Administrative Tools menu.

2. The Performance tool has several views. Click View Graph on the toolbar or press Ctrl + G to ensure that you're in Graph view.

3. To add counters, click Add on the toolbar or press Ctrl + I. This displays the Add Counters dialog box shown in Figure 13-4 on the following page. The key fields are the following:

   - **Use Local Computer Counters**   Configure performance options for the local computer.

   - **Select Counters From Computer**   Enter the Universal Naming Convention (UNC) name of the IIS server you want to work with, such as \\ENGSVR01.

   - **Performance Object**   Select the type of object you want to work with, such as Active Server Pages.

   - **All Counters**   Select all counters for the current performance object.

   - **Select Counters From List**   Select one or more counters for the current performance object. For example, you could select Requests Not Found, Requests Queued, and Requests Total.

   - **All Instances**   Select all counter instances for monitoring.

   - **Select Instances From List**   Select one or more counter instances to monitor. For example, you could select instances of Anonymous Users/Sec for individual Web sites or for all Web sites.

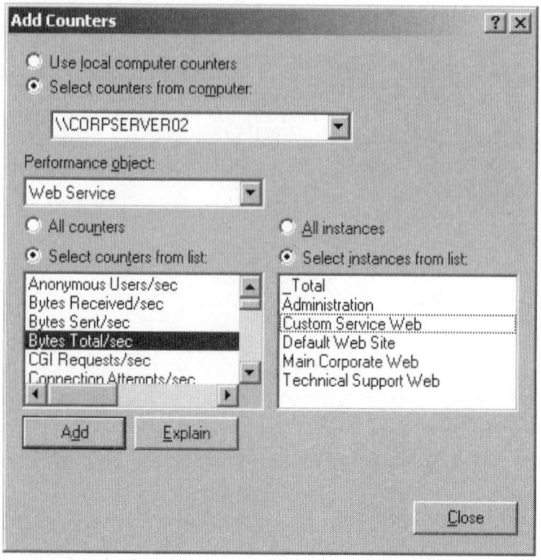

Figure 13-4. *Select the counter you want to monitor.*

Tip Don't try to chart too many counters or counter instances at once. You'll make the display too difficult to read and you'll use system resources—namely, CPU time and memory—that might affect server responsiveness.

4. When you've selected all the necessary options, click Add to add the counters to the graph. Repeat this process as necessary to add other performance parameters.

5. Click Close when you're finished.

Creating and Managing Performance Logs

You can use performance logs to track the performance of IIS, and you can replay them later. As you set out to work with logs, keep in mind that the parameters you track in log files are recorded separately from the parameters you're charting in the Performance console. You can configure log files to update counter data automatically or manually. With automatic logging, a snapshot of key parameters is recorded at specific time intervals, such as every 15 seconds. With manual logging, you determine when snapshots are made. Two types of performance logs are available:

- **Counter logs** These logs record performance data on the selected counters when a predetermined update interval has elapsed.

- **Trace logs** These logs record performance data whenever their related events occur.

Creating and Managing Performance Logging

To create and manage performance logging, complete the following steps:

1. Access the Performance console by selecting the Performance option on the Administrative Tools menu.

2. Expand the Performance Logs And Alerts node by clicking the plus sign (+) next to it. If you want to configure a counter log, select Counter Logs. Otherwise, select Trace Logs.

3. As shown in Figure 13-5, you should see a list of current logs (if any) in the right pane. A green log symbol next to the log name indicates logging is active. A red log symbol indicates logging is stopped.

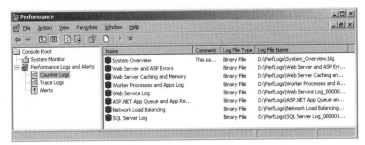

Figure 13-5. *Current performance logs are listed with summary information.*

4. You can create a new log by right-clicking in the right pane and selecting New Log Settings from the shortcut menu. A New Log Settings dialog box appears asking you to give a name to the new log settings. Type a descriptive name here before continuing.

5. To manage an existing log, right-click its entry in the right pane and then select one of the following options:

   - **Start** Activates logging
   - **Stop** Halts logging
   - **Save Settings As** Saves the performance log as a Web page for easy access
   - **Delete** Deletes the log
   - **Properties** Displays the Log Properties dialog box

Creating Counter Logs

Counter logs record performance data on the selected counters at a specific sample interval. For example, you could sample performance data for the Web service every 5 minutes. To create a counter log, complete the following steps:

1. Select Counter Logs in the left pane of the Performance console, and then right-click in the right pane to display the shortcut menu. Select New Log Settings.

2. In the New Log Settings dialog box, type a name for the log, such as HTTP Performance Monitor or Total Request Monitor, and then click OK.

3. In the General tab, click Add Counters to display the Add Counters dialog box. This dialog box is identical to the Add Counters dialog box shown previously in Figure 13-4.

4. Use the Add Counters dialog box to add counters for logging. Click Close when you're finished.

5. In the Interval field, type in a sample interval and select a time unit in seconds, minutes, hours, or days. The sample interval specifies when new data is collected. For example, if you select a sample interval of 15 minutes, the log is updated every 15 minutes.

6. As shown in Figure 13-6, select the Log Files tab and then specify how the log file should be created using the following fields:

- **Log File Type**   Sets the type of log file to create. Use Text File (Comma Delimited) for a log file with comma-separated entries. Use Text File (Tab Delimited) for a log file with tab-separated entries. Use Binary File to create a binary file that only can be read by the Performance console. Use Binary Circular File to create a binary file that overwrites old data with new data when the file reaches a specified size limit.

- **End File Names With**   Sets an automatic suffix for each new file created when you run the counter log. Logs can have a numeric suffix or a suffix in a specific date format.

- **Start Numbering At**   Sets the first serial number for a log that uses an automatic numeric suffix.

- **Comment**   Sets an optional description of the log, which is displayed in the Comment column.

- **Overwrite Existing Log File**   Specifies that any existing log file at the current log file location can be overwritten as necessary.

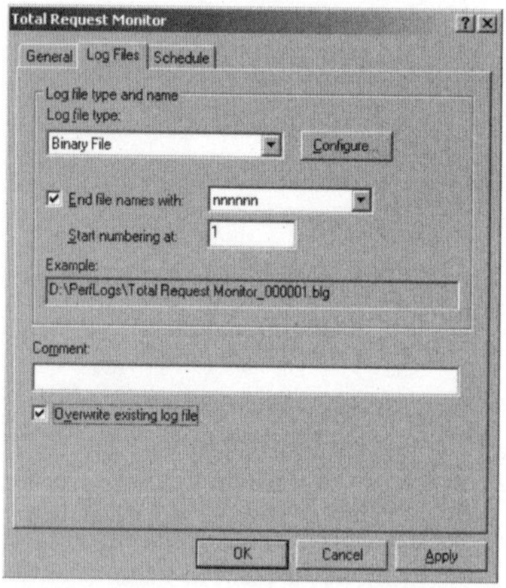

Figure 13-6. *Configure the log file format and usage.*

7. By default, the operating system stores performance logs in the %System-Drive%\PerfLogs folders. The first time you create a counter or trace log, you'll be prompted to create this folder. If you want to configure a unique log location or set size limits for this counter log, click Configure. This displays the Configure Log Files dialog box. You can now specify the following options:

- **Location**   Sets the folder location for the log file
- **File Name**   Sets the name of the log file
- **Maximum Limit**   Sets no predefined limit on the size of the log file
- **Limit Of**   Sets a specific limit in megabytes on the size of the log file

8. As shown in Figure 13-7, select the Schedule tab and then specify when logging should start and stop.

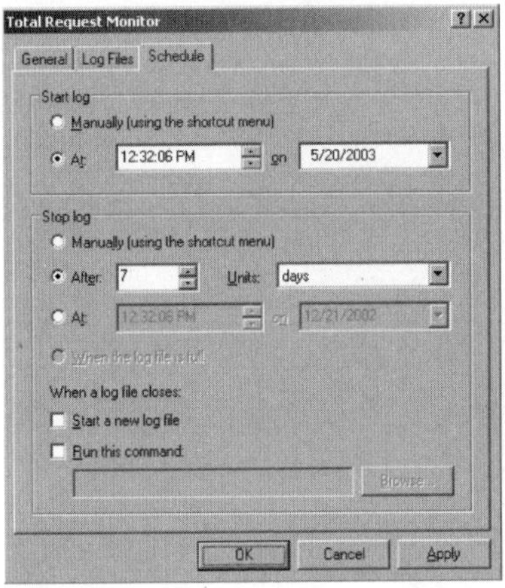

Figure 13-7. *Specify when logging starts and stops.*

9. You can configure the logging to start manually or automatically at a specific date. Select the appropriate option and then specify a start date if necessary.

Tip Log files can grow in size very quickly. If you plan to log data for an extended period, be sure to place the log file on a drive with lots of free space. Remember, the more frequently you update the log file, the higher the drive space and CPU resource usage on the system.

10. You can configure the log file to stop in the following ways:

- Manually
- After a specified period of time, such as 7 days
- At a specific date and time
- When the log file is full (if you've set a specific file size limit)

11. Click OK when you've finished setting the logging schedule. The log is then created, and you can manage it as explained in the "Creating and Managing Performance Logging" section of this chapter.

Creating Trace Logs

Trace logs record performance data whenever events for their source providers occur. A source provider is an application or operating system service that has traceable events. On domain controllers, you'll find System, Local Security Authority, and Active Directory:NetLogon providers. On other servers, the System and Local Security Authority providers probably will be the only providers available.

To create a trace log, complete the following steps:

1. Select Trace Logs in the left pane of the Performance console, and then right-click in the right pane to display the shortcut menu. Select New Log Settings.

2. In the New Log Settings dialog box, type a name for the log, such as Disk I/O Trace or Network TCP/IP Trace, and then click OK. This opens the dialog box shown in Figure 13-8.

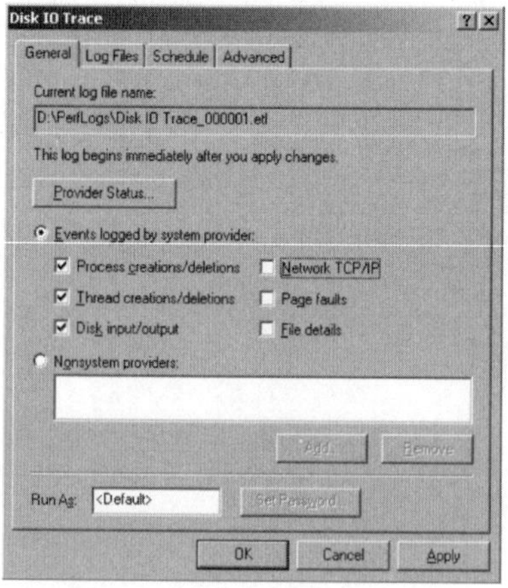

Figure 13-8. *Use the General tab to select the provider to use in the trace.*

3. If you want to trace operating system events, select the Events Logged By System Provider option. You can now select system events to trace.

Caution Collecting page faults and file detail events puts a heavy load on the server and causes the log file to grow rapidly. Because of this, you should collect page faults and file details for only a limited amount of time.

4. If you want to trace another provider, select the Nonsystem Providers option button and then click Add. This displays the Add Nonsystem Providers dialog box, which you'll use to select the provider to trace.

5. When you're finished selecting providers and events to trace, select the Log Files tab. You can now configure the trace file as detailed in steps 6 and 7 of the "Creating Counter Logs" section of this chapter. The only change is that the log file types are different. With trace logs, you have two log types:

   • **Sequential Trace File**   Writes events to the trace log sequentially up to the maximum file size (if any)

   • **Circular Trace File**   Overwrites old data with new data when the file reaches a specified size limit

6. Select the Schedule tab and then specify when tracing starts and stops.

7. You can configure the logging to start manually or automatically at a specific date. Select the appropriate option and then specify a start date if necessary.

8. You can configure the log file to stop manually, after a specified period (such as 7 days), at a specific date and time, or when the log file is full (if you've set a specific file size limit).

9. When you finish setting the logging schedule, click OK. The log is then created and can be managed as explained in the "Creating and Managing Performance Logging" section of this chapter.

Replaying Performance Logs

When you're troubleshooting problems, you'll often want to log performance data over an extended period and analyze the data later. To do this, complete the following steps:

1. Configure automatic logging as described in the "Creating Counter Logs" section of this chapter.

2. Load the log file in the Performance console when you're ready to analyze the data. Select System Monitor in the Performance console and then click View Log Data on the System Monitor toolbar or right-click in the right pane and select Properties. This displays the System Monitor Properties dialog box.

3. In the Source tab, select Log Files and then click Add. Use the Select Log File dialog box to browse to the log you want to use. Remember, log files are stored in %SystemDrive%\PerfLogs by default.

4. After you select the log you want to view, click Open. Repeat this step to add other log files for display. When you're ready to proceed, click OK.

5. Counters you've logged are available for charting. Click Add and then select the counters you want to display.

Tip Unlike previous versions, the current System Monitor can display and play back performance data stored in any of the defined file formats. If you see an error message when trying to play back a log, it might have an erroneous error description that says you can't play back logs of this type. Make sure the log file contains data. There's no data to play back in an empty file.

Configuring Alerts for Performance Counters

You can configure alerts to notify you when certain events occur or when certain performance thresholds are reached. You can send these alerts as network messages and as events that are logged in the application event log. You can also configure alerts to start applications and performance logs.

To add alerts in Performance console, complete the following steps:

1. Select Alerts in the left pane of the Performance console, and then right-click in the right pane to display the shortcut menu. Select New Alert Settings.

2. In the New Alert Settings dialog box, type a name for the alert, such as ASP Error Alert or High User Connection Alert. Then click OK. This opens the dialog box shown in Figure 13-9.

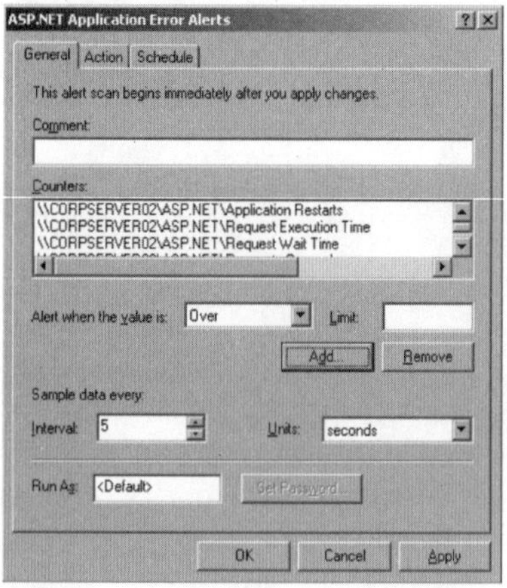

Figure 13-9. *Use the Alert dialog box to configure counters that trigger alerts.*

3. On the General tab, type an optional description of the alert in the Comment field. Then click Add to display the Add Counters dialog box. This dialog box is identical to the Add Counters dialog box shown previously in Figure 13-4.

4. Use the Add Counters dialog box to add counters that trigger the alert. Click Close when you're finished.

5. In the Counters frame, in the General tab of the Add Counters dialog box, select the first counter and then use the Alert When The Value Is field to set the occasion when an alert for this counter is triggered. Alerts can be triggered when the counter is over or under a specific value. Select Over or Under and then set the trigger value in the Limit field. The unit of measurement is whatever makes sense for the currently selected counters. For example, to trigger an alert if processor time is over 95 percent, you would select Over and then type **95**. Repeat this process to configure other counters you've selected.

6. In the Sample Data Every field, type in a sample interval and select a time unit in seconds, minutes, hours, or days. The sample interval specifies when new data is collected. For example, if you set the sample interval to 5 minutes, the log is updated every 5 minutes.

Caution Don't sample too frequently. You'll use system resources and might cause the server to seem unresponsive to user requests.

7. Select the Action tab, as shown in Figure 13-10. You can now specify any of the following actions to take place when an alert is triggered:

- **Log An Entry In The Application Event Log** Creates log entries for alerts
- **Send A Network Message To** Sends a network message to the computer specified
- **Start Performance Data Log** Sets a counter log to start when an alert occurs
- **Run This Program** Sets the complete file path of a program or script to run when the alert occurs

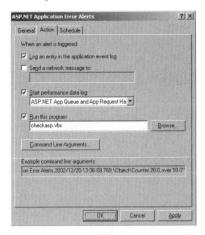

Figure 13-10. *Set actions that are executed when the alert occurs.*

Tip You can run any type of executable file, including batch scripts with the .bat or .cmd extension and Windows scripts with the .vbs, .js, .pl, or .wsc extension. To pass arguments to a script or application, use the options in the Command Line Arguments dialog box. Normally, arguments are passed as individual strings. However, if you select Single Argument String, the arguments are passed in a comma-separated list within a single string. The Example field at the bottom of the dialog box shows how the arguments would be passed.

8. Select the Schedule tab and then specify when alerting starts and stops. For example, you could configure the alerts to start on a Friday evening and stop on Monday morning. Then each time an alert occurs during this period, the specified actions are executed.

9. You can configure alerts to start manually or automatically at a specific date. Select the appropriate option and then specify a start date if necessary.

10. You can configure alerts to stop manually, after a specified period of time, such as 7 days, or at a specific date and time.

11. When you've finished setting the alert schedule, click OK. The alert is then created and you can manage it in much the same way that you manage counter and trace logs.

Tuning Web Server Performance

Now that you know how to monitor your Web servers, let's look at how you can tune the operating system and hardware performance. The areas I'll examine are the following:

- Memory usage and caching
- Processor utilization
- Disk I/O
- Network bandwidth and connectivity

Monitoring and Tuning Memory Usage

Memory is often the source of performance problems, and you should always rule out memory problems before examining other areas of the system. One of the key reasons memory can be such a problem is that the IIS file cache is configured to use up to half of the available system memory by default. This means that on a system with 512 MB of RAM, the IIS file cache could use as much as 256 MB of memory. (Of course, the amount of memory used for caching depends on the number of files and the frequency of requests.) IIS calculates its memory cache requirements every 60 seconds and makes any memory that isn't required available for other applications.

To control the IIS file cache manually, add the Registry entry, MemCacheSize, as a REG_DWORD, and set its decimal value between 0 and 2500 MB at the following location:

```
HKEY_LOCAL_MACHINE
\SYSTEM
\CurrentControlSet
\Services
\InetInfo
\Parameters
```

Caching and virtual memory settings can also present a problem. Adding memory when there's a caching or virtual memory problem on the server won't solve performance problems. Because of this, you should always check for memory, caching, and virtual memory problems at the same time.

To rule out memory, caching, and virtual memory problems with the server, you should do the following:

- Configure application performance
- Configure data throughput

Once you've performed these tasks and rebooted the server, you can monitor the server's memory usage to check for problems.

Setting Application Performance

Application performance determines the responsiveness of foreground and background applications that might be running on the system. In most cases you want a server to be equally responsive to foreground and background applications rather than give precedence to an application the Web administrator might be running on the computer. To ensure that the server is responsive to background applications, follow these steps:

1. Click Start, choose Control Panel, and then click System. This displays the System Properties dialog box.

2. Access the Advanced tab in System Properties and then display the Performance Options dialog box by clicking Settings in the Performance frame.

3. In the Visual Effects tab, you might want to select Adjust For Best Performance. This reduces the load on the system when displaying windows and menus.

4. In the Advanced tab, select Background Services. Ensure that under Adjust For Best Performance Of, System Cache is selected, and then click OK.

Setting Data Throughput

If you use the server primarily as a Web server, you should configure the server as an application server. This setting optimizes the server for networking performance, makes more memory available to Web applications, and enhances the server's multiprocessor capabilities. To configure the server as an application server, complete the following steps:

1. Click Start and choose Control Panel, Network Connections, and finally Local Area Connection. The Local Area Connection Properties dialog box is displayed, as shown in Figure 13-11.

Figure 13-11. *Use the Local Area Connection Properties dialog box to configure file and printer sharing settings for the Web server.*

 Note Servers with multiple network interface cards will have multiple network connections shown in Network And Dial-Up Connections. You should optimize each of these connections appropriately.

2. Select File And Printer Sharing For Microsoft Networks and then click Properties.

3. In the Server Optimization tab, select Maximize Data Throughput For Network Applications. Click OK twice.

4. You will need to reboot the server for these changes to take effect.

Checking Memory, Caching, and Virtual Memory Usage

Now that you've optimized the system, you can determine how the system is using memory and check for problems. Table 13-2 provides an overview of counters that you'll want to track to uncover memory, caching, and virtual memory (paging) bottlenecks. The table is organized by issue category.

Table 13-2. Uncovering Memory-Related Bottlenecks

Issue	Counters to Track	Details
Physical and virtual memory usage	Memory\ Available Kbytes; Memory\ Committed Bytes	Memory\Available Kbytes is the amount of physical memory available to processes running on the server. Memory\Committed Bytes is the amount of committed virtual memory. If the server has very little available memory, you might need to add memory to the system. In general, you want the available memory to be no less than 5 percent of the total physical memory on the server. If the server has a high ratio of committed bytes to total physical memory on the system, you might need to add memory as well. In general, you want the committed bytes value to be no more than 75 percent of the total physical memory.
Memory caching	Memory\Cache Bytes; Internet Information Services Global\ Current File Cache Memory Usage; Internet Information Services; Global\ File Cache Hits %; Internet Information Services Global\ File Cache Flushes	Memory\Cache Bytes represents the total size of the file system cache. Internet Information Services Global\Current File Cache Memory Usage represents the current memory used by the IIS file cache. Internet Information Services Global\File Cache Hits % represents the ratio of cache hits to total cache requests and reflects how well the settings for the IIS file cache are working. A site with mostly static files should have a very high cache hit percentage (70-85 percent). Internet Information Services Global\File Cache Flushes tells you how quickly IIS is flushing files out of cache. If flushes are occurring too quickly, you might need to increase the time-to-live value for cached objects (ObjectCacheTTL). If flushes are occurring too slowly, you might be wasting memory and might need to decrease the time-to-live value for cached objects.

(continued)

Table 13-2. Uncovering Memory-Related Bottlenecks   *(continued)*

Issue	Counters to Track	Details
Memory page faults	Memory\Page Faults/sec; Memory\ Pages Input/ sec; Memory\ Page Reads/sec	A page fault occurs when a process requests a page in memory and the system can't find it at the requested location. If the requested page is elsewhere in memory, the fault is called a soft page fault. If the requested page must be retrieved from disk, the fault is called a hard page fault. Most processors can handle large numbers of soft faults. Hard faults, however, can cause significant delays. Page Faults/sec is the overall rate at which the processor handles all types of page faults. Pages Input/sec is the total number of pages read from disk to resolve hard page faults. Page Reads/sec is the total disk reads needed to resolve hard page faults. Pages Input/sec will be greater than or equal to Page Reads/sec and can give you a good idea of your hard page fault rate. If there are a high number of hard page faults, you might need to increase the amount of memory or reduce the cache size on the server. Memory used by IIS can be controlled by the MemCacheSize and MaxCachedFileSize registry settings. If these entries are not added manually, and their values set in the registry, the default values are used.
Memory paging	Memory\Pool Paged Bytes; Memory\Pool Nonpaged Bytes	These counters track the number of bytes in the paged and nonpaged pool. The paged pool is an area of system memory for objects that can be written to disk when they aren't used. The nonpaged pool is an area of system memory for objects that can't be written to disk. If the paged pool's size is large relative to the total amount of physical memory on the system, you might need to add memory to the system. If the nonpaged pool's size is large relative to the total amount of virtual memory allocated to the server, you might want to increase the virtual memory size.

Monitoring and Tuning Processor Usage

The CPU does the actual processing of information on your server. As you examine a server's performance, you should focus on the CPUs after memory bottlenecks have been eliminated. If the server's processors are the performance bottleneck, adding memory, drives, or network connections won't overcome the problem. Instead, you might need to upgrade the processors to faster clock speeds or add processors to increase the server's upper capacity. You could also move processor-intensive applications, such as SQL Server, to another server. Before you make a decision to upgrade or add CPUs, you should rule out problems with memory and caching. If signs still point to a processor problem, you should monitor the performance counters discussed in Table 13-3. Be sure to monitor these counters for each CPU installed on the server.

Table 13-3. Uncovering Processor-Related Bottlenecks

Issue	Counters to Track	Details
Thread queuing	System\Processor Queue Length	This counter displays the number of threads waiting to be executed. These threads are queued in an area shared by all processors on the system. If this counter has a sustained value of 10 or more threads, you'll need to upgrade or add processors.
CPU usage	Processor\% Processor Time	This counter displays the percentage of time the selected CPU is executing a nonidle thread. You should track this counter separately for all processor instances on the server. If the % Processor Time values are high while the network interface and disk I/O throughput rates are relatively low, you'll need to upgrade or add processors.
ASP performance	Active Server Pages\Request Wait Time; Active Server Pages\Requests Queued; Active Server Pages\Requests Rejected; Active Server Pages\Requests/sec	These counters indicate the relative performance of IIS when working with ASP. Active Server Pages\Request Wait Time is the number of milliseconds the most recent request was waiting in the queue. Active Server Pages\Requests Queued is the number of requests waiting to be processed. Active Server Pages\Requests Rejected is the total number of requests not executed because there weren't resources to process them. Active Server Pages\Requests/sec is the number of requests executed per second. In general, you don't want to see requests waiting in the queue, and, if requests are queuing, the wait time should be very low. You also don't want to see requests rejected because resources aren't available. Keep these problems relative to the number of requests handled per second. You might notice some variance under peak loads. To resolve these issues you might need to upgrade or add processors.

Real World In many cases a single server might not be sufficient to handle the network traffic load. If that happens, you might need to scale your site across multiple servers. For example, you could replicate the site to additional servers and then distribute the traffic across these servers using a load balancer. If you already have a multiple-server Web farm, you could add Web servers.

Monitoring and Tuning Disk I/O

With today's high-speed disks, the disk throughput rate is rarely the cause of a bottleneck. That said, however, accessing memory is much faster than accessing disks. So if the server has to do a lot of disk reads and writes, the server's overall performance can be degraded. To reduce the amount of disk I/O, you want the server to manage memory very efficiently and page to disk only when necessary. You monitor and tune memory usage as discussed previously in the "Monitoring and Tuning Memory Usage" section of this chapter.

Beyond the memory tuning discussion, you can monitor some counters to gauge disk I/O activity. Specifically, you should monitor the counters discussed in Table 13-4.

Table 13-4. Uncovering Drive-Related Bottlenecks

Issue	Counters to Track	Details
Overall drive performance	PhysicalDisk\% Disk Time in conjunction with Processor\% Processor Time and Network Interface \Bytes Total/sec	If the % Disk Time value is high and the processor and network connection values aren't high, the system's hard disk drives might be creating a bottleneck. Be sure to monitor % Disk Time for all hard disk drives on the server.
Disk I/O	PhysicalDisk\Disk Writes/sec; PhysicalDisk\Disk Reads/sec; PhysicalDisk\Avg. Disk Write Queue Length; PhysicalDisk\Avg. Disk Read Queue Length; Physical Disk\Current Disk Queue Length	The number of writes and reads per second tells you how much disk I/O activity there is. The write and read queue lengths tell you how many write or read requests are waiting to be processed. In general, you want there to be very few waiting requests. Keep in mind that the request delays are proportional to the length of the queues minus the number of drives in a redundant array of independent disks (RAID) set.

Note Counters for physical and logical disks might need to be enabled before they're available. To enable these objects, type the following commands at a command prompt:

Diskperf –y for a hard disk drive

Diskperf –yv for a software RAID set

Diskperf -? for a complete list of commands

Monitoring and Tuning Network Bandwidth and Connectivity

No other factor weighs more in a visitor's perceived performance of your Web site than the network that connects your server to the visitor's computer. The delay, or latency, between when a request is made and the time it's received can make all the difference. If there's a high degree of latency, it doesn't matter if you have the fastest server on the planet. The user experiences a delay and perceives that your Web site is slow.

Generally speaking, the latency experienced by the user is beyond your control. It's a function of the type of connection the user has and the route the request takes through the Internet to your server. Your server's total capacity to handle requests and the amount of bandwidth available to your servers are factors under your control, however. Network bandwidth availability is a function of your organization's connection to the Internet. Network capacity is a function of the network cards and interfaces configured on the servers.

A typical network card is equipped to handle a 100-megabit-per-second (Mbps) Fast Ethernet connection with fair efficiency, which is much more traffic than the typical site experiences and much more traffic than the typical server can handle. Because of this, your organization's bandwidth availability is typically the limiting factor. If you have a shared T1 for all Internet activity, your servers are sharing the 1.544 Mbps connection with all other Internet traffic. If you have a dedicated T1 for your Web servers, your servers have 1.544 Mbps of bandwidth availability. If you have multiple T1s or a T3, the bandwidth available to your servers could range from 3 Mbps to 45 Mbps.

To put this in perspective, consider that the number of simultaneous connections your network can handle is relative to the speed of the connection, the average size of the data transferred per connection, and the permitted transfer time. For example, if you have a T1, the typical data transfer per connection (for a dial-up connection) is 50 kilobits per second (Kbps), and transfer time allowable is 15 seconds, your connection could handle this capacity:

- 30 data transfers per second (1544 Kbps / 50 Kbps), or
- 450 simultaneous transfers within 15 seconds (30 data transfers * 15 seconds)

On the other hand, if you have a T3, the typical data transfer per connection is 250 Kbps, and transfer time allowable is 15 seconds, your connection could handle this capacity:

- 180 data transfers per second (45,000 Kbps/ 250 Kbps), or
- 2700 simultaneous transfers within 15 seconds (180 data transfers * 15 seconds)

Tip Your network card's capacity can be a limiting factor in some instances. Most servers use 10/100 network cards, which can be configured in many ways. Someone might have configured a card for 10 Mbps, or the card might be configured for half duplex instead of full duplex. If you suspect a capacity problem with a network card, you should always check the configuration.

 Real World A T1 connection is a useful example for many commercial sites. Larger commercial sites are typically collocated at a hosting service, such as Genuity Managed Services, and might have 100 Mbps or greater connections to the Internet. If this is the case for your site, keep in mind that some devices configured on your network might restrict the permitted bandwidth. For example, your company's firewall might be configured so that it allows only 5 Mbps for Web, 2 Mbps for FTP, and 1 Mbps for SMTP.

To determine the throughput and current activity on a server's network cards, you can check the following counters:

- Network Interface\Bytes Received/sec
- Network Interface\Bytes Sent/sec
- Network Interface\Bytes Total/sec
- Network Interface\Current Bandwidth

If the total bytes-per-second value is more than 50 percent of the total capacity under average load conditions, your server might have problems under peak load conditions. You might want to ensure that operations that take a lot of network bandwidth, such as backups, are performed on a separate interface card. Keep in mind that you should compare these values in conjunction with PhysicalDisk\% Disk Time and Processor\% Processor Time. If the process time and disk time values are low but the network values are very high, there might be a capacity problem.

IIS provides several ways to restrict bandwidth usage and to improve bandwidth-related performance. These features are the following:

- Bandwidth throttling
- Connection limitations
- HTTP compression

Configuring Bandwidth Throttling and Connection Limits

You can restrict bandwidth usage by enabling bandwidth throttling and limiting the maximum number of allowable connections. Bandwidth throttling restricts the total bandwidth available to a service or individual sites. Connection limitations restrict the total number of allowable connections to a service. Because users might be denied service when these values are exceeded, you should enable these features only when you're sure that this setting is acceptable.

Before you restrict bandwidth, you should monitor the network interface object counters discussed earlier in this chapter. If these counters indicate a possible problem, restricting bandwidth is one answer. You can configure bandwidth throttling for all Web sites on a server by completing the following steps:

1. In the IIS Manager snap-in, expand the node for the computer that you want to work with, right-click Web Sites, and then select Properties.

2. In the Performance tab, select the Limit The Total Network Bandwidth check box.

3. In the Maximum Bandwidth field, type the maximum number of kilobytes per second (Kbps) you want IIS to use. Remember, this value is for all Web sites.

4. Click OK.

To configure bandwidth throttling for individual Web sites, complete these steps:

1. In the IIS Manager snap-in, right-click the Web site you want to work with and then select Properties.

2. In the Performance tab, select Limit The Total Network Bandwidth.

3. In the Maximum Bandwidth box, type the maximum number of kilobytes per second you want the site to use.

4. Click OK.

Setting connection limits for Web and FTP sites was covered previously in this book. To learn how to configure limits for Web sites, see the section entitled "Restricting Incoming Connections and Setting Time-Out Values" in Chapter 3, "Configuring Web Sites and Servers." For FTP sites, see the section of the same name in Chapter 9, "Managing FTP Servers."

Configuring HTTP Compression

With HTTP compression enabled, the Web server compresses files before sending them to client browsers. File compression reduces the amount of information transferred between the server and the client, which in turn can reduce network bandwidth usage, network capacity, and transfer time. For HTTP compression to work, the client browser must support HTTP 1.1 and this feature must be enabled. Although most current browsers support HTTP 1.1 and have the feature enabled by default, older browsers might not support HTTP 1.1. Older browsers will still be able to retrieve files from your site, but they won't be taking advantage of HTTP compression.

Before you enable compression, you should monitor the current processor usage on the server. HTTP compression adds to the overhead on the server, which means that it will increase overall processor utilization. If your site uses dynamic content extensively and process utilization (% Processor Time) is already high, you might want to upgrade or add processors before enabling HTTP compression.

Once you've completed your processor evaluation and have decided to use HTTP compression, you can enable this feature by completing the following steps:

1. In the IIS Manager snap-in, expand the node for the computer that you want to work with, right-click Web Sites, and then select Properties.

2. Select the Service tab, as shown in Figure 13-12.

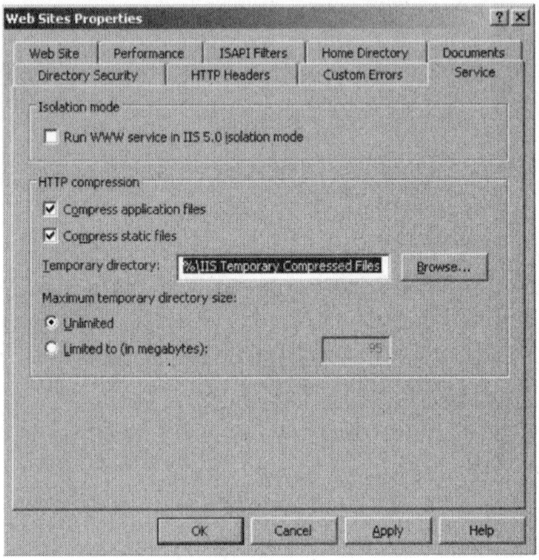

Figure 13-12. *Use the Service tab to configure HTTP compression.*

3. To compress dynamic content, such as ASP, select Compress Application Files. Compressed dynamic files are stored in memory.

4. To compress static files, such as Hypertext Markup Language (HTML) pages, select Compress Static Files. Compressed static files are stored on disk in the directory specified by the Temporary Directory field.

5. You use the Temporary Directory field to specify where compressed static files are stored until the time-to-live period expires. When using compression for static files, type the name and path of the directory you want to use. Or click Browse to locate a directory where compressed files will be stored.

Note The directory must be on a local drive on a NTFS file system (NTFS) partition. In addition, the directory shouldn't be shared and can't be a compressed directory.

6. To limit the size of the static file cache, select Limited To, and then type a limit in megabytes for the directory.

7. Click OK.

Chapter 14

Tracking User Access and Logging

One of your primary responsibilities as a Web administrator might be to log access to your company's Internet servers. As you'll see in this chapter, enabling logging on Hypertext Transfer Protocol (HTTP), File Transfer Protocol (FTP), and Simple Mail Transfer Protocol (SMTP) servers isn't very difficult. What is difficult, however, is gathering the correct access information and recording this information in the proper format so that it can be read and analyzed. Software used to analyze IIS access logs is called *tracking software*. You'll find many types of tracking software. Most commercial tracking software produces detailed reports that include tables and graphs that summarize activity for specific periods. For example, you could compile tracking reports daily, weekly, or monthly.

You can configure logging for HTTP, FTP, and SMTP servers. You can configure the file format for access logs in several ways. You can configure standard logging, Open Database Connectivity (ODBC) logging, and extended logging. With standard logging, you choose a log file format and rely on the format to record the user access information you need. With ODBC logging, you record user access directly to an ODBC-compliant database, such as Microsoft SQL Server 2000. With extended logging, you can customize the logging process and record exactly the information you need to track user access.

Tracking Statistics: The Big Picture

Access logs are created when you enable logging for an HTTP, FTP, or SMTP server. Every time someone requests a file from your Web site, an entry goes into the access log, making the access log a running history of every successful and unsuccessful attempt to retrieve information from your site. Because each entry has its own line, entries in the access log can be easily extracted and compiled into reports. From these reports, you can learn many things about those who visit your site. You can do the following:

- Determine the busiest times of the day and week
- Determine which browsers and platforms are used by people who visit your site
- Discover popular and unpopular resources

- Discover sites that refer users to your site
- Learn more about the effectiveness of your advertising
- Learn more about the people who visit your site
- Obtain information about search engine usage and keywords
- Obtain information about the amount of time users spend at the site

You can configure access logs in several formats. The available formats are:

- **National Center for Supercomputer Applications (NCSA) common log file format (Web and SMTP Only)**   Use the NCSA common log file format when your reporting and tracking needs are basic. With this format, log entries are small, which reduces the amount of storage space required for logging.

- **Microsoft Internet Information Services (IIS) log file format**   Use the IIS log file format when you need a bit more information from the logs but don't need to tailor the entries to get detailed information. With this format, log entries are compact, which reduces the amount of storage space required for logging.

- **World Wide Web Consortium (W3C) extended log file format**   Use the W3C extended log file format when you need to customize the information tracked and obtain detailed information. With this format, log entries can become large, which greatly increases the amount of storage space required. Recording lengthy entries can affect the performance of a busy server as well.

- **ODBC logging**   Use ODBC logging when you want to write access information directly to an ODBC-compliant database. With this format, you'll need tracking software capable of reading from a database. Entries are compact, however, and data can be read much more quickly than from a standard log file. Keep in mind that ODBC logging is more processor-intensive when you log directly to a local database instance.

- **Centralized binary logging**   Use centralized binary logging when you want all Web sites running on a server to write log data to a single log file. With centralized binary logging, the log files contain fixed-length and index records that are written in a raw binary format called the Internet Binary Log (IBL) format, giving the log file an .ibl extension. Professional software applications or tools in the IIS 6.0 Software Development Kit can read this format.

Tip   Microsoft distributes a tool for converting a log file to NCSA common log file format. The tool is called CONVLOG, and it's located in the \%WinDir%\System32 directory. You can use CONVLOG to convert logs formatted using IIS and W3C extended log file formats to NCSA common log file format. The tool also performs reverse Domain Name System (DNS) lookups during the conversion process. This allows you to resolve some Internet Protocol (IP) addresses to domain names.

Because an understanding of what is written to log files is important to understanding logging itself, the sections that follow examine the main file formats. After this discussion, you'll be able to determine what each format has to offer and, hopefully, to better determine when to use each format.

Working with the NCSA Common Log File Format

NCSA common log file format is the most basic of the log file formats. The common log file format is a fixed American Standard Code of Information Interchange (ASCII) format in which each log entry represents a unique file request. You'll use the common log file format when your tracking and reporting needs are basic. More specifically, the common log file format is a good choice when you need to track only certain items, such as:

- Hits (the number of unique file requests)
- Page views (the number of unique page requests)
- Visits (the number of user sessions in a specified period)
- Other basic access information

With this format, log entries are small, which reduces the amount of storage space required for logging. Each entry in the common log file format has only seven fields:

- Host
- Identification
- User Authentication
- Time Stamp
- HTTP Request Type
- Status Code
- Transfer Volume

As you'll see, the common log file format is easy to understand, which makes it a good stepping-stone to more advanced log file formats. The following listing shows entries in a sample access log that are formatted using the NCSA common log file format. As you can see from the sample, log fields are separated by spaces.

```
192.168.11.15 - ENGSVR01\wrstanek [15/Jan/2003:18:44:57 -0800] "GET /
HTTP/1.1" 200 1970
192.168.11.15 - ENGSVR01\wrstanek [15/Jan/2003:18:45:06 -0800] "GET /
home.gif HTTP/1.1" 200 5032
192.168.11.15 - ENGSVR01\wrstanek [15/Jan/2003:18:45:28 -0800] "GET /
main.htm HTTP/1.1" 200 5432
192.168.11.15 - ENGSVR01\wrstanek [15/Jan/2003:18:45:31 -0800] "GET /
details.gif HTTP/1.1" 200 1211
192.168.11.15 - ENGSVR01\wrstanek [15/Jan/2003:18:45:31 -0800] "GET /
menu.gif HTTP/1.1" 200 6075
192.168.11.15 - ENGSVR01\wrstanek [15/Jan/2003:18:45:31 -0800] "GET /
sidebar.gif HTTP/1.1" 200 9023
```

```
192.168.11.15 - ENGSVR01\wrstanek [15/Jan/2003:18:45:31 -0800] "GET /
sun.gif HTTP/1.1" 200 4706
192.168.11.15 - ENGSVR01\wrstanek [15/Jan/2003:18:45:38 -0800] "GET /
moon.gif HTTP/1.1" 200 1984
192.168.11.15 - ENGSVR01\wrstanek [15/Jan/2003:18:45:41 -0800] "GET /
stars.gif HTTP/1.1" 200 2098
```

Since most other log file formats build off the NCSA common log file format, it's useful to examine how these fields are used.

Host Field

Host is the first field in the common log format. This field identifies the host computer requesting a file from your Web server. The value in this field is either the remote host's IP address, such as 192.168.11.15, or the remote host's fully qualified domain name (FQDN), such as *net48.microsoft.com*. The following example shows an HTTP query initiated by a host that was successfully resolved to a domain name (the host field information is bold):

net48.microsoft.com - ENGSVR01\wrstanek [15/Jan/2003:18:44:57 -0800] "GET / HTTP/1.1" 200 1970

IP addresses are the numeric equivalent of FQDNs. You can often use a reverse DNS lookup to determine the actual domain name from the IP address. When you have a domain name or resolve an IP address to an actual name, you can examine the name to learn more about the user accessing your server. Divisions within the domain name are separated by periods. The final division identifies the domain class, which can tell you where the user lives and works.

Domain classes are geographically and demographically organized. Geographically organized domain classes end in a two- or three-letter designator for the state or country in which the user lives. For example, the .ca domain class is for companies in Canada. Demographically organized domain classes tell you the type of company providing network access to the user. Table 14-1 summarizes these domain classes.

Table 14-1.   Basic Domain Classes

Domain Name	Description
.com	Commercial; users from commercial organizations
.edu	Education; users from colleges and universities
.gov	U.S. government; users from U.S. government agencies, except the military
.mil	U.S. military; users who work at military installations
.net	Network; users who work at network service providers and other network-related organizations
.org	Nonprofit organizations; users who work for nonprofit organizations

Identification Field

The Identification field is the second field in the common log file format. This field is meant to identify users by their user name but in practice is rarely used. Because of this, you'll generally see a hyphen (-) in this field, as in the following:

```
net48.microsoft.com - ENGSVR01\wrstanek [15/Jan/2003:18:44:57 -0800]
"GET / HTTP/1.1" 200 1970
```

If you do see a value in this field, keep in mind that the user name isn't validated. This means it could be made up and shouldn't be trusted.

User Authentication Field

The User Authentication field is the third field in the common log format. If you have a password-protected area at your Web site, users must authenticate themselves with a user name and password that's registered for this area. After users validate themselves with their user name and password, their user name is entered in the User Authentication field. In unprotected areas of a site, you'll usually see a hyphen (-) in this field. In protected areas of a site, you'll see the authenticated user's account name. The account name can be preceded by the name of the domain in which the user is authenticated, as shown in this example (the user authentication field information is bold):

```
net48.microsoft.com - ENGSVR01\wrstanek [15/Jan/2003:18:44:57 -0800]
"GET / HTTP/1.1" 200 1970
```

Time Stamp Field

The Time Stamp field is the fourth field in the common log file format. This field tells you exactly when someone accessed a file on the server. The format for the Time Stamp field is as follows:

```
DD/MMM/YYYY:HH:MM:SS OFFSET
```

such as:

```
15/Jan/2003:18:44:57 -0800
```

The only designator that probably doesn't make intuitive sense is the offset, which indicates the difference in the server's time from Greenwich Mean Time (GMT). In the following example, the offset is -8 hours, meaning that the server time is 8 hours behind GMT:

```
net48.microsoft.com - ENGSVR01\wrstanek [15/Jan/2003:18:44:57 -0800]
"GET / HTTP/1.1" 200 1970
```

HTTP Request Field

The HTTP Request field is the fifth field in the common log format. Use this field to determine the method that the remote client used to request the resource, the resource that the remote client requested, and the HTTP version that the client used to retrieve the resource. In the following example, the HTTP Request field information is bold:

```
192.168.11.15 - ENGSVR01\wrstanek [15/Jan/2003:18:45:06 -0800] "GET /
home.gif HTTP/1.1" 200 5032
```

Here, the transfer method is GET, the resource is /Home.gif, and the transfer method is HTTP 1.1. One thing you should note is that resources are specified using relative Uniform Resource Locators (URLs). The server interprets relative URLs. For example, if you request the file *http://www.microsoft.com/home/main.htm*, the server will use the relative URL */home/main.htm* to log where the file is found. When you see an entry that ends in a slash, keep in mind that this refers to the default document for a directory, which is typically called Index.htm, Default.htm, or Default.asp.

Status Code Field

The Status Code field is the sixth field in the common log file format. Status codes indicate whether files were transferred correctly, were loaded from cache, weren't found, and so on. Generally, status codes are three-digit numbers. As shown in Table 14-2, the first digit indicates the status code's class or category.

Table 14-2. Status Code Classes

Code Class	Description
1XX	Continue/protocol change
2XX	Success
3XX	Redirection
4XX	Client error/failure
5XX	Server error

Because you'll rarely see a status code beginning with 1, you need to remember only the other four categories. A status code that begins with 2 indicates that the associated file transferred successfully. A status code that begins with 3 indicates that the server performed a redirect. A status code that begins with 4 indicates some type of client error or failure. Finally, a status code that begins with 5 tells you that a server error occurred.

Transfer Volume Field

The last field in the common log file format is the Transfer Volume field. This field indicates the number of bytes transferred to the client because of the request. In the following example, 4096 bytes were transferred to the client (the transfer volume field information is bold):

```
net48.microsoft.com - ENGSVR01\wrstanek [15/Jan/2003:18:45:06 -0800]
"GET / HTTP/1.1" 200 4096
```

You'll only see a transfer volume when the status code class indicates success. If another status code class is used in field six, the Transfer Volume field will contain a hyphen (-) or a 0 to indicate that no data was transferred.

Working with the Microsoft IIS Log File Format

Like the common log file format, the Microsoft IIS log file format is a fixed ASCII format. This means that the fields in the log are of a fixed type and can't be changed. It also means the log is formatted as standard ASCII text and can be read with any standard text editor or compliant application.

You'll use the IIS log file format when you need a bit more information than the common log file format provides but don't need to tailor the entries to get detailed information. Since the log entries are compact, the amount of storage space required for logging is much less than the expanded or ODBC logging formats.

The following listing shows entries from a sample log using the IIS log file format. The IIS log entries include common log fields such as the client IP address, authenticated user name, request date and time, HTTP status code, and number of bytes received. IIS log entries also include detailed items such as the Web service name, the server IP address, and the elapsed time. Note that commas separate log fields and entries are much longer than those in the common log file format.

```
192.14.16.2, -, 04/15/2003, 15:42:25, W3SVC1, ENGSVR01, 192.15.14.81,
0, 594, 3847, 401, 5, GET, /localstart.asp, -,
192.14.16.2, ENGSVR01\wrstanek, 04/15/2003, 15:42:25, W3SVC1,
ENGSVR01, 192.15.14.81, 10, 412, 3406, 404, 0, GET, /localstart.asp,
|-|0|404_Object_Not_Found,
192.14.16.2, -, 04/15/2003, 15:42:29, W3SVC1, ENGSVR01, 192.15.14.81,
0, 622, 3847, 401, 5, GET, /IISHelp/iis/misc/default.asp, -,
192.14.16.2, ENGSVR01\wrstanek, 04/15/2003, 15:42:29, W3SVC1,
ENGSVR01, 192.15.14.81, 10, 426, 0, 200, 0, GET, /IISHelp/iis/misc/
default.asp, -,
192.14.16.2, ENGSVR01\wrstanek, 04/15/2003, 15:42:29, W3SVC1,
ENGSVR01, 192.15.14.81, 10, 368, 0, 200, 0, GET, /IISHelp/iis/misc/
contents.asp, -,
192.14.16.2, -, 04/15/2003, 15:42:29, W3SVC1, ENGSVR01, 192.15.14.81,
0, 732, 3847, 401, 5, GET, /IISHelp/iis/misc/navbar.asp, -,
192.14.16.2, -, 04/15/2003, 15:42:29, W3SVC1, ENGSVR01, 192.15.14.81,
0, 742, 3847, 401, 5, GET, /IISHelp/iis/htm/core/iiwltop.htm, -,
192.14.16.2, ENGSVR01\wrstanek, 04/15/2003, 15:42:29, W3SVC1,
ENGSVR01, 192.15.14.81, 20, 481, 0, 200, 0, GET, /IISHelp/iis/misc/
navbar.asp, -,
192.14.16.2, ENGSVR01\wrstanek, 04/15/2003, 15:42:29, W3SVC1,
ENGSVR01, 192.15.14.81, 91, 486, 6520, 200, 0, GET, /IISHelp/iis/htm/
core/iiwltop.htm, -,
```

The fields supported by IIS are summarized in Table 14-3 on the following page. Note that the listed field order is the general order used by IIS to record fields.

Table 14-3.   Fields for the IIS Log File Format

Field Name	Description	Example
Client IP	IP address of the client	192.14.16.2
Username	Authenticated name of the user	ENGSVR01\wrstanek
Date	Date at which the transaction was completed	04/15/2003
Time	Time at which the transaction was completed	15:42:29
Service	Name of the Web service logging the transaction	W3SVC1
Computer Name	Name of the computer that made the request	ENGSVR01
Server IP	IP address of the Web server	192.15.14.81
Elapsed Time	Time taken (in milliseconds) for the transaction to be completed	40
Bytes Received	Number of bytes received by the server in client request	486
Bytes Sent	Number of bytes sent to the client	6520
Status Code	HTTP status code	200
Windows Status Code	Error status code from Windows	0
Method Used	HTTP request method	GET
File URI	The requested file	/localstart.asp
Referrer	The referrer—the location the user came from	http: // www.microsoft.com/

Working with the W3C Extended Log File Format

The W3C extended log file format is very different from either of the previously discussed formats. With this format you can customize the information tracked and obtain detailed information. When you customize an extended log file, you select the fields you want the server to log, and the server handles the logging for you. Keep in mind that each additional field you track increases the size of entries recorded in the access logs, which can greatly increase the amount of storage space required.

The following listing shows sample entries from an extended log. Note that, as with the common log file format, extended log fields are separated with spaces.

```
#Software: Microsoft Internet Information Services 6.0
#Version: 1.0
#Date: 2003-04-05 06:27:58
#Fields: date time c-ip cs-username s-ip s-port cs-method cs-uri-stem
cs-uri-query sc-status cs(User-Agent)
```

```
2003-04-05 06:27:58 192.14.16.2 ENGSVR01\wrstanek 192.14.15.81 80 GET
/iishelp/iis/htm/core/iierrcst.htm - 304 Mozilla/
4.0+(compatible;+MSIE+6.01;+Windows+NT+5.2;+.NET+CLR+1.1.4322)
2003-04-05 06:28:00 192.14.16.2 ENGSVR01\wrstanek 192.14.15.81 80 GET
/iishelp/iis/htm/core/iierrdtl.htm - 304 Mozilla/
4.0+(compatible;+MSIE+6.01;+Windows+NT+5.2;+.NET+CLR+1.1.4322)
2003-04-05 06:28:02 192.14.16.2 ENGSVR01\wrstanek 192.14.15.81 80 GET
/iishelp/iis/htm/core/iierrabt.htm - 200 Mozilla/
4.0+(compatible;+MSIE+6.01;+Windows+NT+5.2;+.NET+CLR+1.1.4322)
2003-04-05 06:28:02 192.14.16.2 ENGSVR01\wrstanek 192.14.15.81 80 GET
/iishelp/iis/htm/core/iierradd.htm - 200 Mozilla/
4.0+(compatible;+MSIE+6.01;+Windows+NT+5.2;+.NET+CLR+1.1.4322)
2003-04-05 06:28:05 192.14.16.2 ENGSVR01\wrstanek 192.14.15.81 80 GET
/iishelp/iis/htm/core/iiprstop.htm - 200 Mozilla/
4.0+(compatible;+MSIE+6.01;+Windows+NT+5.2;+.NET+CLR+1.1.4322)
```

The first time you look at log entries that use the extended log file format, you might be a bit confused because the extended logs are written with server directives as well as file requests. The good news is that server directives are always preceded by the hash symbol (#), which easily allows you to distinguish them from actual file requests. The key directives you'll see are those that identify the server software and the fields being recorded. These directives are summarized in Table 14-4.

Table 14-4.   Directives Used with the Extended Log File Format

Directive	Name Description
Date	Identifies the date and time the entries were made in the log
End-Date	Identifies the date and time the log was finished and then archived
Fields	Specifies the fields and the field order used in the log file
Remark	Specifies comments
Software	Identifies the server software that created the log entries
Start-Date	Identifies the date and time the log was started
Version	Identifies the version of the extended log file format used

Most extended log fields have a prefix. The prefix tells you how a particular field is used or how the field was obtained. For example, the *cs* prefix tells you the field was obtained from a request sent by the client to the server. Field prefixes are summarized in Table 14-5.

Table 14-5.   Prefixes Used with the Extended Log Fields

Prefix	Description
c	Identifies a client-related field
s	Identifies a server-related field
r	Identifies a remote server field

(continued)

Table 14-5.   Prefixes Used with the Extended Log Fields   *(continued)*

Prefix	Description
cs	Identifies information obtained from a request sent by the client to the server
sc	Identifies information obtained from a request sent by the IIS server to the client
sr	Identifies information obtained from a request sent by the Web server to a remote server (used by proxies)
rs	Identifies information obtained from a request sent by a remote server to the IIS server (used by proxies)
x	Application-specific prefix

All fields recorded in an extended log have a field identifier. This identifier details the type of information a particular field records. To create a named field, the IIS server can combine a field prefix with a field identifier, or it can simply use a field identifier. The most commonly used field names are summarized in Table 14-6. As you examine the table, keep in mind that most of these fields relate directly to the fields we've already discussed for the common and extended log file formats. Again, the key difference is that the extended format can give you information that's much more detailed.

Table 14-6.   Field Identifiers Used with the Extended Log File Format

Field Type	Actual Field Name	Description
Bytes Received	cs-bytes	Number of bytes received by the server
Bytes Sent	sc-bytes	Number of bytes sent by the server
Client IP Address	c-ip	IP address of the client that accessed the server
Cookie	cs(Cookie)	Content of the cookie sent or received (if any)
Date	Date	Date on which the activity occurred
Method Used	cs-method	HTTP request method
Protocol Status	sc-status	HTTP status code, such as 404
Protocol Substatus	sc-status	HTTP substatus code, such as 2
Protocol Version	cs-protocol	Protocol version used by the client
Referrer	cs(Referrer)	Previous site visited by the user, which provided a link to the current site
Server IP	s-ip	IP address of the IIS server
Server Name	s-computername	Name of the IIS server
Server Port	s-port	Port number to which client is connected
Service Name and Instance Number	s-sitename	Internet service and instance number that was running on the server
Time	Time	Time the activity occurred

Table 14-6. Field Identifiers Used with the Extended Log File Format

Field Type	Actual Field Name	Description
Time Taken	time-taken	Time taken (in milliseconds) for the transaction to be completed
URI Query	cs-uri-query	Query parameters passed in request (if any)
URI Stem	cs-uri-stem	Requested resource
User Agent	cs(User-Agent)	Browser type and version used on the client
User Name	c-username	Name of an authenticated user (if available)
Win32 Status	sc-win32-status	Error status code from Windows

Real World   In IIS 6, the HTTP Status option is renamed Protocol Status and you have the additional option of being able to log Protocol Substatus. Protocol Status logs the request's HTTP status code, such as 404. Protocol Substatus logs the request's HTTP substatus code, such as 2. When used together, the fields provide the request's complete status, such as 404.2. This is important, because in IIS 6, the server no longer reports complete status and substatus codes to clients. To increase security and reduce the possibility of an attack, clients see only the HTTP status code.

Working with ODBC Logging

You can use the ODBC logging format when you want to write access information directly to an ODBC-compliant database, such as Microsoft Access or SQL Server 2000. The key advantage of ODBC logging is that access entries are written directly to a database in a format that ODBC-compliant tracking software can quickly read and interpret. The major disadvantage of ODBC logging is that it requires basic database administration skills to configure and maintain.

With ODBC logging, you must configure a Data Source Name (DSN) that allows IIS to connect to your ODBC database. You must also create a database that can be used for logging. This database must have a table with the appropriate fields for the logging data.

Typically, you'll use the same database for logging information from multiple sites, with each site writing to a separate table in the database. For example, if you wanted to log HTTP, FTP, and SMTP access information in your database, and these services were running on separate sites, you'd create three tables in your database:

- HTTPLog
- FTPLog
- SMTPLog

These tables would have the columns and data types for field values summarized in Table 14-7. The columns must be configured exactly as shown in the table. Don't worry; IIS includes a SQL script that you can use to create the necessary table structures. This script, named Logtemp.sql, is located in the \%WinDir%\System32\Inetsrv directory.

> **Note** If you use the Logtemp.sql script, be sure to edit the table name set in the CREATE TABLE statement. The default table name is Inetlog. For more information about working with SQL scripts, see *Microsoft SQL Server 2000 Administrator's Pocket Consultant* (Microsoft Press, 2000).

Table 14-7.   Table Fields for ODBC Logging

Field Name	Field Type	Description
ClientHost	varchar(255)	IP address of the client that accessed the server
Username	varchar(255)	Name of an authenticated user (if available)
LogTime	datetime	Date and time on which the activity occurred
Service	varchar(255)	Internet service and instance number that was running on the server
Machine	varchar(255)	Name of the computer that made the request
ServerIP	varchar(50)	IP address of the IIS server
Processing-Time	int	Time taken (in milliseconds) for the transaction to be completed
BytesRecvd	int	Number of bytes received by the server
BytesSent	int	Number of bytes sent by the server
ServiceStatus	int	HTTP status code
Win32Status	int	Error status code from Windows
Operation	varchar(255)	HTTP request method
Target	varchar(255)	Requested resource
Parameters	varchar(255)	Query parameters passed in request (if any)

Working with Centralized Binary Logging

You can use centralized binary logging when you want all Web sites running on a server to write log data to a single log file. With centralized binary logging, the log files are written in IBL format, which can be read by many professional software applications, or you can read it using tools in the IIS 6 Resource Kit.

On a large IIS installation where the server is running hundreds or thousands of sites, centralized binary logging can dramatically reduce the overhead associated with logging activities. Two types of records are written to the binary log files:

- **Index records**   Act as record headers, similar to the W3C extended log file format where software, version, date, and field information is provided.

- **Fixed-length records** Provide the detailed information about requests. Each value in each field in the entry is stored with a fixed length.

For information on configuring centralized binary logging, see the section of this chapter entitled "Configuring Centralized Binary Logging."

Understanding Logging

When IIS logging is enabled, new log entries are generated whenever users access the server. This causes a steady increase in log file size and, eventually, in the number of log files. On a busy server, log files can quickly grow to several gigabytes and, therefore, you might need to balance the need to gather information against the need to limit log files to a manageable size.

Tip Keep in mind that log files are stored as ASCII or Unicode Transformation Format 8 (UTF-8) text files, and, if you need to, you can split or combine log files as you would with any text file. If your server runs out of disk space when IIS is attempting to add a log entry to a file, IIS logging shuts down and logs a logging error event in the Application log. When disk space is available again, IIS resumes logging file access and writes a start-logging event in the Application log.

When you configure logging, you specify how log files are created and saved. Logs can be created according to a time schedule, such as hourly, daily, weekly, and monthly. Logs can also be set to a fixed file size, such as 100 MB, or they can be allowed to grow to an unlimited file size. A log file's name indicates its log file format as well as the log's time frame or sequence. The various naming formats are summarized in Table 14-8.

Table 14-8. Conventions for Log File Names by Log File Format

Format	Log Period	File Name
IIS log file format	By file size	INETSV*NN*.LOG
	Unlimited	INETSV*NN*.LOG
	Hourly	IN*YYMMDDHH*.LOG
	Daily	IN*YYMMDD*.LOG
	Weekly	IN*YYMMWW*.LOG
	Monthly	IN*YYMM*.LOG
NCSA common log file format	By file size	NCSA*NN*.LOG
	Unlimited	NCSA*NN*.LOG
	Hourly	NC*YYMMDDHH*.LOG
	Daily	NC*YYMMDD*.LOG
	Weekly	NC*YYMMWW*.LOG
	Monthly	NC*YYMM*.LOG

(continued)

Table 14-8. **Conventions for Log File Names by Log File Format** *(continued)*

Format	Log Period	File Name
W3C extended log file format	By file size	EXTEND*NN*.LOG
	Unlimited	EXTEND*NN*.LOG
	Hourly	EX*YYMMDDHH*.LOG
	Daily	EX*YYMMDD*.LOG
	Weekly	EX*YYMMWW*.LOG
	Monthly	EX*YYMM*.LOG
Centralized binary logging	Hourly	RA*YYMMDDHH*.IBL
	Daily	RA*YYMMDD*.IBL
	Weekly	RA*YYMMWW*.IBL
	Monthly	RA*YYMM*.IBL

By default, log files are written to the \%WinDir%\System32\LogFiles directory. You can configure logging to a different directory, such as D:\LogFiles. Regardless of whether you use the default directory location or assign a new directory location for logs, you'll find separate subdirectories for each service that's enabled for logging under the primary directory.

Subdirectories for sites are named using the following syntax:

- MSFTPSVC*N*
- W3SVC*N*
- SMTPSVC*N*

where *N* is the index number of the service or a random tracking value. The only exception is when you use centralized binary logging. Here, Web site logs are stored in the %WinDir%\System32\LogFiles\W3SVC directory.

The default server created is number 1. Following this, you could have site directories named W3SVC1, MSFTPSVC1, and SMTPSVC1. If you create additional sites, a random 5- to 10-digit identifier is used. To correlate the identifier value to specific Web sites, select the Web Sites node in Internet Information Services (IIS) Manager and then look in the Description and Identifier columns in the right-hand pane to determine which identifier belongs to which site.

 Note As with many IIS 6 improvements, the reason identifiers are used is to enhance security by making it more difficult to determine where IIS data is being logged.

HTTP requests that return a status code indicating an internal server error are written to a central error log, which is stored in the %WinDir%\System32\LogFiles\Httperr directory. This error log file is named Httperr*N*.log, where *N* is the tracking number of the Web site experiencing the internal server errors.

Configuring Logging for HTTP, SMTP, and FTP

Now that you know how log files are used and created, let's look at how you can enable and configure logging. The following sections examine each of the available logging formats.

Configuring NCSA Common Log File Format

The NCSA common log file format is used with HTTP and SMTP sites only. Use the common log file format when your reporting and tracking needs are basic. With this format, log entries are small, which reduces the amount of storage space required for logging.

You enable logging and configure the common log file format by completing the following steps:

1. Start the IIS snap-in and then, in the left pane (Console Root), click the plus sign (+) next to the computer you want to work with. If the computer isn't shown, connect to it as discussed in the section entitled "Connecting to Other Servers" in Chapter 2, "Core IIS Administration."

2. Right-click the HTTP or SMTP site you want to manage and then select Properties.

3. Select Enable Logging to start logging, and then set the Active Log Format to NCSA Common Log File Format.

4. Click Properties to display the NCSA Logging Properties dialog box shown in Figure 14-1.

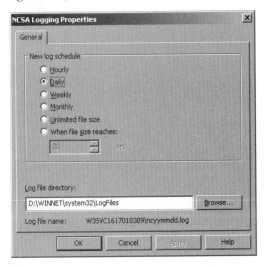

Figure 14-1. *Use the common log format when you have basic logging requirements.*

5. In the New Log Schedule frame, select one of the following time period options:

   - **Hourly** IIS creates a new log each hour.
   - **Daily** IIS creates a new log daily at midnight.
   - **Weekly** IIS creates a new log file each Saturday at midnight.
   - **Monthly** IIS creates a new log file at midnight on the last day of the month.
   - **Unlimited File Size** IIS doesn't end the log file automatically. You must manage the log file.
   - **When File Size Reaches** If you select this option, you must set a maximum log file size in megabytes. When the log file reaches this size, a new log file is created.

6. By default, log files are located in a subdirectory under \%WinDir%\System32\Logfiles. If you want to change the default logging directory, type the directory path in the Log File Directory field or click Browse to look for a directory that you want to use.

7. Click OK twice. The service directory and log file are created automatically, if necessary. If IIS doesn't have Read/Write permission on the logging directory, an error is generated.

Configuring Microsoft IIS Log File Format

You can use the Microsoft IIS log file format with HTTP, SMTP, and FTP sites. Use the IIS format when you need a bit more information from the logs but don't need to tailor the entries to get detailed information. With this format, log entries are compact, and this reduces the amount of storage space required for logging.

You enable logging and configure the IIS log file format by completing the following steps:

1. Start the IIS snap-in and then, in the left pane (Console Root), click the plus sign (+) next to the computer you want to work with. If the computer isn't shown, connect to it as discussed in the "Connecting to Other Servers" section of Chapter 2.

2. Right-click the HTTP, FTP, or SMTP site you want to manage and then select Properties.

3. Select Enable Logging to start logging, and then set the Active Log Format to Microsoft IIS Log File Format.

4. Click Properties to display the Microsoft Logging Properties dialog box shown in Figure 14-2.

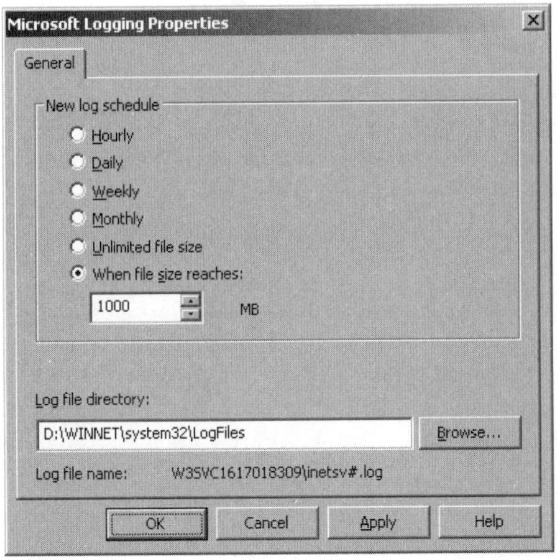

Figure 14-2. *Use the IIS log format when you have additional logging requirements but don't need to customize settings.*

5. In the New Log Schedule frame, select one of the following time period options:

   - **Hourly** IIS creates a new log each hour.
   - **Daily** IIS creates a new log daily at midnight.
   - **Weekly** IIS creates a new log file each Saturday at midnight.
   - **Monthly** IIS creates a new log file at midnight on the last day of the month.
   - **Unlimited File Size** IIS doesn't end the log file automatically. You must manage the log file.
   - **When File Size Reaches** If you select this option, you must set a maximum log file size in megabytes. When the log file reaches this size, a new log file is created.

6. By default, log files are located in a subdirectory under \%WinDir%\ System32\Logfiles. If you want to change the default logging directory, type the directory path in the Log File Directory field or click Browse to look for the directory that you want to use.

7. Click OK twice. The service directory and log file are created automatically, if necessary. If IIS doesn't have Read/Write permission on the logging directory, an error might be generated.

Configuring W3C Extended Log File Format

You can use the W3C extended log file format with HTTP, FTP, and SMTP sites. Use the extended format when you need to customize the information tracked and obtain detailed information. With this format, log entries can become large, which greatly increases the amount of storage space required. Recording lengthy entries can affect the performance of a busy server as well.

You enable logging and configure the W3C extended log file format by completing the following steps:

1. Start the IIS snap-in and then, in the left pane (Console Root), click the plus sign (+) next to the computer you want to work with. If the computer isn't shown, connect to it as discussed in the "Connecting to Other Servers" section of Chapter 2.

2. Right-click the HTTP, FTP, or SMTP site you want to manage and then select Properties.

3. Select Enable Logging to start logging, and then set the Active Log Format to W3C Extended Log File Format.

4. Click Properties to display the Logging Properties dialog box shown in Figure 14-3.

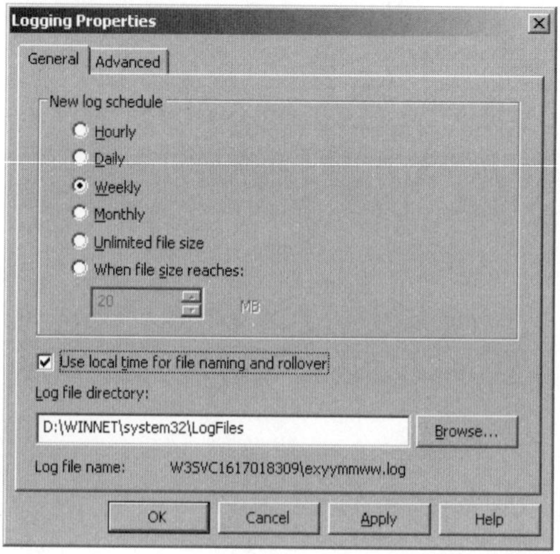

Figure 14-3. *Use the extended log file format when you need to customize the logging process.*

5. In the New Log Schedule frame, select one of the following time period options:

- **Hourly** IIS creates a new log each hour.
- **Daily** IIS creates a new log daily at midnight.

- **Weekly**   IIS creates a new log file each Saturday at midnight.
- **Monthly**   IIS creates a new log file at midnight on the last day of the month.
- **Unlimited File Size**   IIS doesn't end the log file automatically. You must manage the log file.
- **When File Size Reaches**   If you select this option, you must set a maximum log file size in megabytes. When the log file reaches this size, a new log file is created.

6. By default, the extended format uses GMT to determine when to create new log files. This means daily, weekly, and monthly logs are generated at midnight GMT unless you specify otherwise. To use local time for determining when to create new logs, select Use Local Time For File Naming And Rollover.

7. By default, log files are located in a subdirectory under \%WinDir%\ System32\Logfiles. If you want to change the default logging directory, type the directory path in the Log File Directory field, or click Browse to look for a directory that you want to use.

8. Select the Advanced Properties tab and then select the properties that you want to log. The fields you'll want to track in most cases are

- Date
- Time
- Client IP Address
- Server IP Address
- Method
- URI Stem
- URI Query
- Protocol Status
- Protocol Substatus
- Bytes Sent
- Bytes Received
- User Agent
- Cookie
- Referrer

Note   The more fields you track, the larger the log entries.

9. Click OK twice. The service directory and log file are created automatically, if necessary. If IIS doesn't have Read/Write permission on the logging directory, an error might be generated.

Configuring ODBC Logging

You can configure ODBC Logging for HTTP, FTP, and SMTP sites. Use the ODBC format when you want to write access information directly to an ODBC-compliant database. With ODBC logging, you'll need tracking software capable of reading from a database. Entries are compact, however, and data can be read much more quickly than from a standard log file.

To use ODBC logging, perform the following tasks:

1. Create a database using ODBC-compliant database software. As long as IIS can connect to the database using an ODBC connection, the database doesn't have to reside on the IIS server. Access can be used for small to medium-sized sites with moderate traffic. For large or busy sites, use a more robust solution, such as SQL Server 2000.

2. Within the database, create a table for logging access entries. This table must have the field names and data types listed in Table 14-8. You can use the Logtemp.sql script to create this table.

3. Create a DSN that IIS can use to connect to the database. You'll probably want to use a system DSN to establish the database connection. With SQL Server, you must specify the technique that should be used to verify the authenticity of the logon identification (ID). With Microsoft Windows NT authentication, the account you specify when configuring IIS must have permission to write to the database. With SQL Server authentication, you can specify a SQL Server logon ID and password to use.

4. Complete the process by enabling logging for the site and setting the active log format to ODBC logging. When you configure logging, you'll need to specify the DSN name, the table name, and the logon information.

The following sections describe how you can use SQL Server 2000 and IIS to configure ODBC logging. These sections assume that you have a fair amount of knowledge of SQL Server 2000 and database administration. If you need more assistance, refer to the *Microsoft SQL Server 2000 Administrator's Pocket Consultant*.

Creating a Logging Database and Table in SQL Server 2000

You can use SQL Server 2000 as your logging server. To do this, you must create a database and configure a logging table. To create a database, complete the following steps:

1. Start Enterprise Manager and then, in the left pane (Console Root), click the plus sign (+) next to Microsoft SQL Servers, and then the one next to the server group you want to work with.

2. Click the plus sign (+) next to the server you want to work with again, and then, if necessary, authenticate yourself, establish a connection, or both.

3. Right-click the Databases folder and then select New Database from the shortcut menu. This opens the Database Properties dialog box.

4. Select the General tab and type **LoggingDB** as the database name in the Name field.

5. Click OK, and SQL Server creates the database.

Next, locate the Logtemp.sql script, which is located in the \%WinDir%\ System32\Inetsrv directory on the IIS server. Edit the script so that it sets the table name you want to use for the site's log entries. For example, if you wanted to name the table HTTPLog, you'd update the script as shown in the following listing:

```
use LoggingDB

create table HTTPLog (
ClientHost varchar(255),
username varchar(255),
LogTime datetime,
service varchar(255),
machine varchar(255),
serverip varchar(50),
processingtime int,
bytesrecvd int,
bytessent int,
servicestatus int,
win32status int,
operation varchar(255),
target varchar(255),
parameters varchar(255)
)
```

After you update the script, start Query Analyzer. In Query Analyzer you can access scripts by clicking the Load SQL Script button on the toolbar and then entering the script's location. Run the script by clicking Execute Query. When the script completes, a new table should be created in the LoggingDB database. If necessary, make sure you connect to the SQL server using an account with database administrator privileges.

Creating a DSN for SQL Server 2000

Once you create the logging database and the input table, you can configure IIS to connect to the database. IIS connects to the database using a DSN. You must create the DSN on the IIS server. To do this, complete the following steps:

1. Start Data Sources (ODBC) from the Administrative Tools menu.

2. On the System DSN tab, click Add. This displays the Create New Data Source dialog box.

3. Select SQL Server on the Driver selection list and then click Finish. As shown in Figure 14-4 on the following page, you should now see the Create A New Data Source To SQL Server dialog box.

4. In the Name field, type the name of the DSN, such as **IISDB**.

5. In the Description field, type a descriptive name for the DSN.

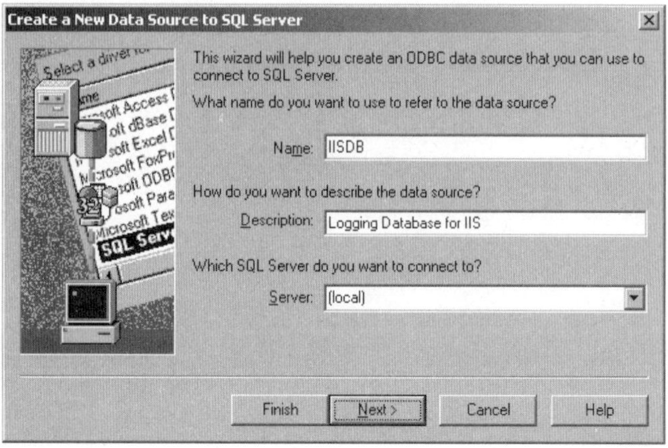

Figure 14-4. *Use the Create A New Data Source To SQL Server dialog box to configure the data source.*

6. In the Server field, type the name of the SQL Server to which you want to connect, or select (Local) if SQL Server is running on the same hardware as IIS. Click Next.

7. As shown in Figure 14-5, specify the technique that should be used to verify the logon ID's authenticity. If you use Windows NT authentication, the account you specify when configuring IIS must have permission to write to the logging database. If you use SQL Server authentication, you can specify a SQL Server logon ID and password to use.

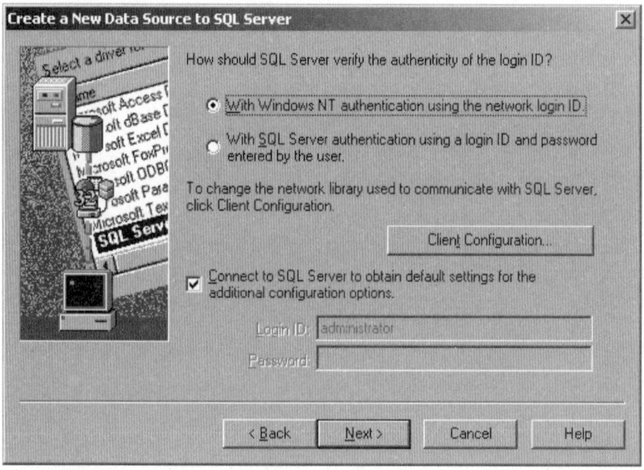

Figure 14-5. *Set the authentication method for the DSN connection.*

8. Click Next, and then select the Change The Default Database To check box. From the enabled drop-down list, select the database you created using the Logtemp.sql script.

9. Click Finish to complete the process. If Windows is unable to establish a connection to the database, you might need to recheck the information you've entered to ensure that it's correct. You also might need to confirm that the account you're using has the appropriate permissions in the database.

Enabling and Configuring ODBC Logging in IIS

To complete the configuration process, you must enable and configure ODBC logging in IIS. Complete the following steps:

1. Start the IIS snap-in and then, in the left pane (Console Root), click the plus sign (+) next to the computer you want to work with. If the computer isn't shown, connect to it as discussed in the "Connecting to Other Servers" section of Chapter 2.

2. Right-click the HTTP, FTP, or SMTP site you want to manage and then select Properties.

3. Select Enable Logging to start logging and then set the Active Log Format to ODBC Logging.

4. Click Properties to display the ODBC Logging Properties dialog box shown in Figure 14-6.

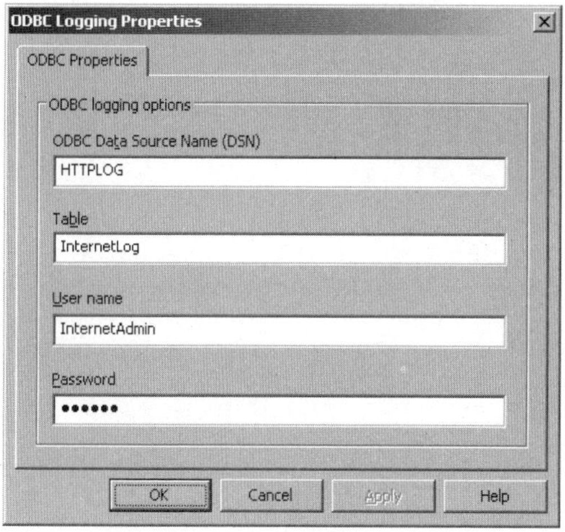

Figure 14-6. *Use ODBC logging when you need to write to a database.*

5. Type the name of the DSN in the ODBC Data Source Name (DSN) field. The DSN name must be exactly as you defined it.

6. Type the name of the logging table in the Table field.

7. If you're using Windows authentication, set the User Name and Password fields to the appropriate values for the account you want to use to log on to the database.

8. Click OK. If prompted, confirm the password you just entered, click OK, and then click OK again to save your settings.

Configuring Centralized Binary Logging

Before you implement centralized binary logging, you should consider many issues, including how using this format will affect the server and what tools you'll use to read the raw binary logs. After planning, you should set up a test installation and determine if it's feasible to switch to centralized binary logging and obtain the information your organization needs from the raw binary log files. You should enable binary logging only when you're certain that this format will work for you.

When you're ready to implement centralized binary logging, complete the following steps:

1. Start a command prompt, navigate to the %SystemDrive%\InetPub\Admin-Scripts folder, and then type the following command:

   `cscript adsutil.vbs SET W3SVC/CentralBinaryLoggingEnabled 1`

2. If you typed the command correctly, you should see the following:

   `CentralBinaryLoggingEnabled    : (BOOLEAN) True`

3. Now you need to stop and then start the WWW Service, so type the following at the command prompt:

   `net stop w3svc`

   `net start w3svc`

4. The first time a site on the Web server is accessed, a raw binary log is created in the %WinDir%\System32\LogFiles\W3SVC directory.

If you decide that you no longer want to use centralized binary logging, you can disable this feature by typing the previous command, replacing the "1" with a "0," as follows:

`cscript adsutil.vbs SET W3SVC/CentralBinaryLoggingEnabled 0`

This will produce the following text:

`CentralBinaryLoggingEnabled    : (BOOLEAN) False`

Disabling Logging

If you don't plan to generate reports from access logs for a particular site, you might not want to log user access to the site. In this case you can disable logging for the site by completing the following steps:

1. Start the IIS snap-in and then, in the left pane (Console Root), click the plus sign (+) next to the computer you want to work with. If the computer isn't shown, connect to it as discussed in the "Connecting to Other Servers" section of Chapter 2.

2. Right-click the HTTP, FTP, or SMTP site you want to manage, and then select Properties.

3. Clear Enable Logging and then click OK.

Chapter 15

IIS Optimization and the Metabase

Previous chapters in this part of the book focused on techniques you can use to monitor Internet Information Services (IIS) and to optimize server hardware. In this chapter you'll learn how to optimize IIS and its related services. You'll learn techniques for improving IIS performance, configuring automatic restarts of IIS, and getting the most from IIS applications. You'll also learn advanced techniques for managing IIS through the Microsoft Windows Registry and the IIS metabase.

The Windows Registry contains configuration settings for the operating system, the server hardware, and all applications installed on the server, including IIS. The metabase contains configuration settings that are specific to the sites and virtual servers you've implemented on a particular server. Although you can manage most configuration settings through the IIS properties dialog boxes, you can change some properties only through editing the registry or the metabase directly. These settings typically are advanced values that you should change only when you have unique needs.

Strategies for Improving IIS Performance

In this section I examine strategies you can use to improve the performance of IIS. The focus of this section is on improving the overall responsiveness of IIS and not the underlying server hardware.

Removing Unnecessary Applications and Services

One of the most obvious ways to improve IIS performance is to remove resource drains on the server. Start by removing applications that might be affecting the performance of IIS, including:

- Microsoft SQL Server
- Microsoft Exchange Server
- File and print services
- UNIX services

If necessary, move these applications and services to a separate server. This will give IIS more resources to work with. For applications that you can't move, see if there's a way to run the applications only during periods of relatively low activity. For example, if you're running server backups daily, see if you can schedule backups to run late at night when user activity is low.

System services are another area you can examine to see if there are unnecessary resource drains. Every service running on the server uses resources that can be used in other ways. You should stop services that aren't necessary and set them to start manually. Before you stop any service, you should check for dependencies to ensure that your server isn't adversely affected.

If you have a dedicated IIS server, the following services aren't required in most instances:

- Alerter
- Automatic Updates
- ClipBook
- Computer Browser
- DHCP Client
- DHCP Server
- Fax Service
- File Replication
- Infrared Monitor
- Internet Connection Firewall (ICF) / Internet Connection Sharing (ICS)
- Messenger
- NetMeeting Remote Desktop Sharing
- Network DDE
- Network DDE DSDM
- Print Spooler
- TCP/IP NetBIOS Helper
- Telephony
- Telnet
- Themes
- Uninterruptible Power Supply
- Wireless Configuration

Optimizing Content Usage

Your server's responsiveness is tied directly to the content you're publishing. You can often realize substantial performance benefits by optimizing the way content is used. IIS can handle both static and dynamic content. Although static content is passed directly to the requesting client, dynamic content must be processed before it can be passed to the client. This places a resource burden on the server that you can reduce by using static content.

Note I'm not advocating replacing all dynamic content with static content. Dynamically generated content is a powerful tool for building highly customized and full-featured sites. However, if there are places where you're using dynamic content for no specific reason, you might want to rethink this strategy.

When you use static content, keep in mind that you should set expire headers whenever possible. Expire headers allow the related files to be stored in the client's cache, and this can greatly improve performance on repeat visits when the original content hasn't changed. For details on setting expire headers, see the section entitled "Customizing Web Site Content and HTTP Headers" in Chapter 4, "Customizing Web Server Content."

With dynamic content, you should limit your use of Common Gateway Interface (CGI) applications. CGI applications require more processor and memory resources than their Internet Server Application Programming Interface (ISAPI), Active Server Pages (ASP), and ASP.NET counterparts. Because of this, you should replace or convert CGI applications to ISAPI, ASP, or ASP.NET.

Whenever you work with ISAPI, ASP, or ASP.NET applications, try to push as much of the processing load onto the client as possible. This reduces the server resource requirements and greatly improves application responsiveness. One example of pushing processing to the client is to use client-side scripting to evaluate form submissions before data is sent to the server. This technique reduces the number of times information is sent between the client and the server; therefore, it can greatly improve the application's overall performance.

To improve content-related performance, you might also want to do the following:

- **Analyze the way content is organized on your hard disk drives** In most cases you should keep related content files on the same logical partitions of a disk. Keeping related files together improves IIS file caching.

- **Defragment your drives periodically** Over time, drives can become fragmented, and this decreases read/write performance. To correct this, defragment your server's drives periodically. Many defragmentation tools allow you to automate this process so that you can configure a scheduled job to automatically defragment drives without needing administrator intervention.

- **Reduce the size of content files** The larger the file size, the more time it takes to send the file to a client. If you can optimize your source Hypertext Markup Language (HTML) or ASP code and reduce the file size, you can increase your Web server's performance and responsiveness. Some of the biggest bandwidth users are multimedia files. Compress image, video, or audio files using an appropriate compression format whenever possible.

- **Store log files on separate disks from content files** Logging activity can reduce the responsiveness of a busy server. One way to correct this is to store access logs on a different physical drive from the one storing your site's content files. In this way, disk writes for logging are separate from the disk reads or writes for working with content files, which can greatly improve the overall server responsiveness.

- **Log only essential information** Trying to log too much information can also slow down a busy server. With the World Wide Web Consortium (W3C) extended logging format, you can reduce logging overhead by logging only the information that you need to generate reports and by removing logging for nonessential information. With any type of logging, you can reduce logging overhead by organizing different types of content appropriately and then disabling logging on directories containing content whose access doesn't need to be logged. For example, you could place all your image files in a directory called Images and then disable logging on this directory.

> **More Info** Techniques for configuring logging are discussed in Chapter 14, "Tracking User Access and IIS Logging." If your organization has large IIS installations running dozens or hundreds of IIS sites per server, you should consider using centralized binary logging, which is also discussed in Chapter 14.

Optimizing ISAPI, ASP, and ASP.NET Applications

Improperly configured and poorly optimized applications can be major resource drains on an IIS server. To get the most from the server, you need to optimize the way applications are configured. Do the following to optimize applications:

- **Enable ISAPI application caching** IIS can cache ISAPI applications in memory. This allows frequently used applications to be accessed quickly. You can control caching with the metabase property CacheISAPI.

- **Manage application buffering and flushes appropriately** Application buffering allows all output from an application to be collected in the buffer before being sent to the client. This cuts down on network traffic and response times. However, users don't receive data until the page is finished executing, which can give the perception that a site isn't very responsive. You can control application buffering with the metabase property AspBufferingOn.

- **Disable application debugging** Application debugging slows IIS performance considerably. You should use debugging only for troubleshooting. Otherwise, you should disable debugging. You can control debugging with the metabase property AppAllowDebugging.

- **Optimize application performance** You can configure ASP and ASP.NET applications to shut down idle processes, limit memory leaks and outages, and rapidly detect failures. For more information, see Chapter 6, "Managing ASP.NET, Application Pools, and Worker Processes."

- **Manage session configuration appropriately** As the usage of your server changes, so should the session management configuration. By default, session management is enabled for all applications. If your applications don't use sessions, however, you're wasting system resources. Instead of enabling sessions by default, you should disable sessions by default and then enable sessions for individual applications. You can control sessions with the metabase properties AspAllowSessionState, AspSessionMax, and AspSessionTimeout.

- **Set a meaningful session time-out**   The session time-out value is extremely important in determining the amount of resources used in session management. Set this value accurately. Sessions should time out after an appropriate period. Configure session time-out with the metabase property AspSessionTimeout.

- **Set appropriate script and connection time-out values**   ASP scripts and user connections should time out at an appropriate interval. By default, ASP scripts time out after 90 seconds and user connections time out after 2 minutes. Zombie scripts and open connections use resources and can reduce the server's responsiveness. To reduce this drain, set appropriate time-outs based on the way your site is used. You can control script and connection time-outs with the metabase properties AspScriptTimeout and Connection-Timeout, respectively.

Optimizing IIS Caching, Queuing, and Pooling

IIS uses many memory-resident caches and queues to manage resources. If you make extensive use of dynamic content or have a heavily trafficked site, you should optimize the way these caches and queues work for your environment. You might want to do the following:

- **Consider changing application pool queue length**   Whenever requests for applications come in, the HTTP listener (Http.sys) picks them up and passes them to an application request queue. To prevent large numbers of requests from queuing up and flooding the server, each application request queue has a default maximum on the amount of concurrent requests. If this value doesn't meet your needs, you can modify it using the metabase property AspRequestQueueMax. In most cases you'll want to set this value to the maximum number of connection requests you want the server to maintain.

- **Consider changing the maximum entity size**   By default, IIS limits the maximum number of bytes allowed in the entity body of an ASP request but doesn't limit the size of other types of requests. To control the maximum entity size, you use the metabase properties AspMaxRequestEntityAllowed and MaxRequestEntityAllowed.

- **Consider disabling thread pooling for CGI**   By default, long-running CGI requests can use a server pool thread. If you make extensive use of CGI applications, you might want to examine performance with and without thread pooling, and then determine which method works best for your server.

- **Consider changing connection queue length**   When you use HTTP keep-alives, IIS maintains connections for a user's HTTP session in a connection queue. By default, this queue can hold a maximum of 25 connections at any one time. With application pools and queuing, the need for the connection queue is reduced. Still, on a server with a very heavy load and high traffic you might want to increase the connection queue's size. To do this, set the Windows Registry value ServerListenBackLog.

- **Consider changing the IIS File Cache settings** By default, IIS uses up to 50 percent of the server's available physical memory. This value ensures that IIS works well with other applications that might be running on the server. If the server is dedicated to IIS or has additional memory available, you might want to increase this setting to allow IIS to use more memory. To control IIS file caching, you create and then set the Windows Registry value MemCacheSize.

- **Consider changing the maximum cached file size** By default, IIS caches only files that are 256 KB or less in size. If you have large data or multimedia files that are accessed frequently, you might want to increase this value to allow IIS to cache larger files. Keep in mind that with file sizes over 256 KB you'll reach a point at which caching won't significantly improve performance. The reason for this is that with small files the overhead of reading from disk rather than the file cache is significant, but with large files the disk read might not be the key factor in determining overall performance. To control the maximum cached file size, you create and then set the Windows Registry value MaxCachedFileSize.

- **Consider adjusting the Time to Live (TTL) value for cached resources** By default, IIS purges from cache any resources that haven't been requested within the last 30 seconds. If you have additional memory on the server, you might want to increase this value so that files aren't removed from cache as quickly. To control the TTL value for cached resources, you create and then set the Windows Registry value ObjectCacheTTL.

Tip If you have a dedicated server running only IIS, you might want to consider allowing resources to remain in cache until they are overwritten (due to MemCacheSize limits). In this case, you would set Object-CacheTTL to Unlimited (0xFFFFFFFF).

- **Consider modifying the ASP template cache** The ASP template cache controls the number of ASP pages that are cached in memory. By default, IIS will cache up to 500 files. This might not be enough on a site with lots of ASP content. Template cache entries can reference one or more entries in the ASP Script Engine Cache. To control template caching, you set the metabase property AspScriptFileCacheSize.

- **Consider modifying the script engine cache** The ASP Script Engine Cache is an area of memory directly accessible to the scripting engines used by IIS. As such, the preferred area for IIS to retrieve information from is the script engine cache. By default, the script engine cache can hold up to 250 entries. To control script engine caching, you set the metabase property AspScriptEngineCacheMax.

More Info   To learn more about editing the cache settings in the Windows Registry, see Chapter 13, "Performance Tuning and Monitoring."

Configuring Automatic Restarts of IIS

Chapter 2, "Core IIS Administration," focused on core administration tasks for IIS. In that chapter you learned how to manage services and how to use the IIS Reset utility. To get the best performance from IIS, configure the IIS Admin Service to run the IIS Reset utility automatically if a problem occurs with the service. This allows IIS to recover automatically from most situations that otherwise would have stopped IIS from handling user requests altogether.

You can configure automatic restart of IIS by completing the following steps:

1. From Administrative Tools, start the Computer Management console, and then connect to the computer whose services you want to manage.

2. Expand the Services And Applications node by clicking the plus sign (+) next to it and then select Services.

3. Right-click IIS Admin Service and then select Properties.

4. Select the Recovery tab. Set the First Failure, Second Failure, and Subsequent Failures fields to Run A Program, as shown in Figure 15-1.

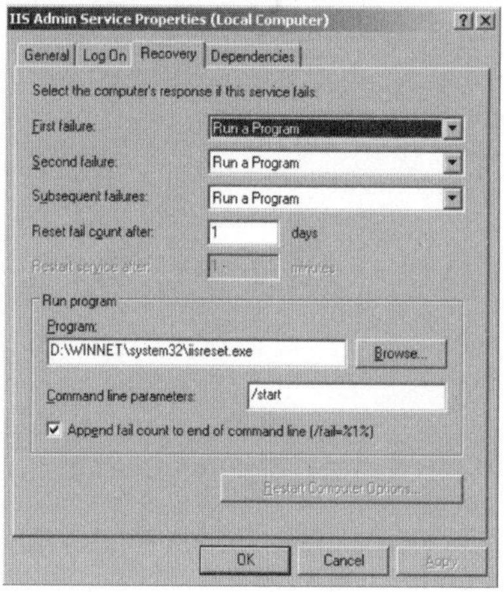

Figure 15-1.   *Configure the IIS Admin Service to run the IIS Reset utility.*

5. In the Program field of the Run Program frame, type **\%SystemRoot%\ System32\ Iisreset.exe**.

6. Click OK.

Managing IIS Registry Settings

The Windows Registry stores configuration settings for the operating system, the server hardware, and all installed applications. The registry is essential to the proper operation of the operating system. You should make changes to the registry only when you know how these changes will affect the system.

Working with the Registry

Registry settings are stored as keys and values. These keys and values are placed under a specific root key. The root key controls when and how other keys and values are used. The root keys are:

- **HKEY_CLASSES_ROOT** Configuration settings for applications and files. Ensures that the correct application is opened when a file is started through Microsoft Windows Explorer or object linking and embedding (OLE).
- **HKEY_CURRENT_USER** Controls configuration settings for the current user.
- **HKEY_LOCAL_MACHINE** Controls system-level configuration settings.
- **HKEY_USERS** Stores default user and other user settings by profile.
- **HKEY_CURRENT_CONFIG** Contains information about the hardware profile being used.

Under the root keys, you'll find the main keys that control various facets of the system, user, and application environments. These keys are organized into a tree structure in which folders represent keys. Settings that control the IIS Admin Service are stored under the following registry path:

```
HKEY_LOCAL_MACHINE
 \SYSTEM
 \CurrentControlSet
 \Services
 \InetInfo
 \Parameters
```

Here, the key is Parameters. The values associated with this or any other keys have three components: a value name, a value type, and an actual value. Numeric values are often expressed in hexadecimal format. Hexadecimal values use the prefix 0x, such as 0x19 for the decimal value 25. In the following example the ListenBackLog value has a type of REG_DWORD and a value of 0x19:

```
ListenBackLog : REG_DWORD : 0x19
```

REG_DWORD is one of several possible value types. The complete list of value types follows:

- **REG_BINARY** Sets a binary value. Binary values must be entered using base-2 (0 or 1).
- **REG_DWORD** Sets a DWORD value, which is composed of hexadecimal data with a maximum length of 4 bytes.
- **REG_SZ** Sets a string value containing a sequence of characters.

- **REG_EXPAND_SZ** Sets an expandable string value, which is usually used with directory paths.
- **REG_MULTI_SZ** Sets a multiple string value.

The main tool that you'll use to work with the Windows Registry is the Registry Editor (Regedt32.exe). You can start the Registry Editor by clicking Start and then selecting Run. Then type **REGEDT32** in the Open field and click OK.

If you're an experienced administrator, you might want to use a Windows script to manage the registry. With scripts you can create, update, and delete registry settings. Here is a Microsoft Visual Basic, Scripting Edition (VBScript) script example that updates the ListenBackLog value:

```
'Initialize variables and objects
Dim Path
Path = "HKLM\SYSTEM\CurrentControlSet\Services\Inetinfo\Parameters\"
Set ws = WScript.CreateObject("WScript.Shell")

'Read and display key value
val = ws.RegRead(Path & "ListenBackLog")
WScript.Echo "Orginal ListenBackLog value: " & val

'Write new key value and then display new value
retVal = ws.RegWrite(Path & "ListenBackLog", 50, "REG_DWORD")
val = ws.RegRead(Path & "ListenBackLog")
WScript.Echo "Updated ListenBackLog value: " & val
```

Controlling IIS Through the Registry

Settings that control IIS are stored in the registry under:

```
HKEY_LOCAL_MACHINE\SYSTEM
 \CurrentControlSet
 \Services
 \Inetinfo
 \Parameters
```

With the changes to the IIS architecture for application pools and queues, many of the previously used registry keys aren't created automatically. You can still create these keys, however, if you'd like to use them.

The key values you might want to work with are the following:

- **CacheSecurityDescriptor** Indicates whether security descriptors are cached for file objects. A value of 1 enables this feature. A value of 0 disables this feature. When enabled (the default setting), security descriptors for files are saved when caching a file object. As long as the file is cached, IIS won't need to reaccess the file to determine access rights for new users. This value is most useful for sites that authenticate users and isn't useful for sites that allow anonymous access.

- **CheckCertRevocation** Indicates whether IIS checks to see if a client certificate is revoked. If you issue your own certificates and make local certificate checks, you might want to enable this feature (setting the value to 1). Otherwise, the feature should be disabled (with a value of 0), which is the default.

- **DisableMemoryCache** Indicates whether IIS memory caching is enabled or disabled. By default, this value is set to 0 (meaning that memory caching is not disabled). Disable memory caching only for testing or development purposes.

- **ListenBackLog** Specifies the maximum number of active connections that IIS maintains in the connection queue. The default value is 15 and the range of acceptable values is from 1 to 250.

- **MaxCachedFileSize** Determines the maximum size of a file that can be placed in the file cache. IIS won't cache files that are larger than this value. The default value is 262,144 bytes (256 KB).

- **MaxConcurrency** Specifies how many threads per processor should be allowed to run simultaneously if there's a pending input/output (I/O) operation. The default value (0) allows IIS to control the number of threads per processor. You can also set a specific value.

- **MaxPoolThreads** Sets the number of pool threads to create per processor. Each pool thread watches for a network request for a CGI application and processes it. This value doesn't control threads that are used by ISAPI applications. By default, the value is set to 4. On a single processor system, this means that only four CGI applications could run simultaneously.

- **MemCacheSize** Sets the maximum amount of memory that IIS will use for its file cache. If IIS doesn't need this much memory, it'll be left for other applications to use. By default, IIS uses 50 percent of the available memory. The valid range is from 0 MB to 2,500 MB (2.5 GB).

- **ObjectCacheTTL** Sets the length of time (in milliseconds) that objects are held in memory. If the object hasn't been used in this interval, it's removed from memory. The default value is 30 seconds (300,000 milliseconds).

- **PoolThreadLimit** Sets the maximum number of pool threads that can be created on the server. This limit is for all IIS threads. The default value is twice the size of physical memory in megabytes.

Controlling the Indexing Service Through the Registry

Settings that control the Indexing Service are stored in the registry under:

```
HKEY_LOCAL_MACHINE
  \SYSTEM
  \CurrentControlSet
  \Control
  \ContentIndex
```

You'll find a detailed discussion of related settings and keys in the section entitled "Indexing Service Essentials" in Chapter 12, "Administering the Indexing Service."

Settings for the World Wide Web Publishing, File Transfer Protocol (FTP), and Simple Mail Transfer Protocol (SMTP) Services are stored in separate registry keys. The path to these keys is:

```
HKEY_LOCAL_MACHINE
  \SYSTEM
  \CurrentControlSet
  \Services
  \ServiceName
  \Parameters
```

ServiceName is the name of the service you want to work with. Services you might work with are:

- MSFTPSVC for the FTP Service
- W3SVC for the World Wide Web Publishing Service
- SMTPSVC for the SMTP Service

Although most of the keys under this path are used only by IIS, you might want to set the AllowGuestAccess key value. This key value determines whether Guest logons are allowed for Internet services. By default, Guest logons are permitted, but you can disable this feature by creating the key and setting its value to 0.

For the World Wide Web Publishing Service, you might also want to work with the following key values:

- **SSIEnableCmdDirective**   Determines whether Web pages can issue server-side include statements that execute shell commands. By default, the ability to execute shell commands is disabled (set to 0), and this is the value you should use in most cases. If you allow the direct execution of shell commands from Web pages, you might inadvertently open up the server to attack from malicious coders.

- **TryExceptDisable**   Determines whether exception caching is enabled for debugging. The value is disabled by default (set to 0). If enabled (set to 1), the server stops when any exception is thrown and allows a developer to debug the application that threw the exception.

- **UploadReadAhead**   When a client posts data to the server, this value determines the amount of data the server reads before passing control to the application responsible for handling the data. The default value is 48 KB.

- **UsePoolThreadForCGI**   Determines whether CGI requests can use pooled threads. By default, this value is enabled (set to 1). If disabled, CGI requests don't use pooling and the Inetinfo value MaxPoolThreads doesn't apply.

Controlling Secure Sockets Layer Through the Registry

Settings that control Secure Sockets Layer (SSL) are stored in the registry under

```
HKEY_LOCAL_MACHINE
  \SYSTEM \CurrentControlSet \Control \SecurityProviders \SCHANNEL
```

After you've started the Registry Editor and accessed this location, the key values you might want to work with are:

- **EventLogging** Determines whether SSL connections are logged for Web sites configured on the server. By default, this value is enabled (set to 1). To disable this feature, set the value to 0.

- **ServerCacheTime** Determines the amount of time (in milliseconds) that an SSL session lasts. Establishing an SSL session is a time-intensive and resource-intensive process. If you expect SSL sessions to last, on average, longer than the default value, you might want to modify this value. By default, an SSL session lasts 5 minutes (300,000 milliseconds). When the session expires, a new SSL session must be established.

Managing IIS Metabase Settings

The metabase is one of the most important components in an IIS installation. The metabase is where IIS stores configuration settings for sites and virtual servers. The metabase also contains default settings for sites and virtual servers, such as the global Web Sites properties.

 Tip When you work with the metabase files, it's important to note that you shouldn't use the Encrypting File System (EFS) to encrypt them. Sensitive values in the metabase are already encrypted, and if you encrypt the metabase files themselves, you'll unnecessarily slow down IIS.

Examining and Editing the Metabase

In IIS 6.0, IIS stores the metabase configuration in structured Extensible Markup Language (XML) files. The main configuration information is in a file that's located in the %SystemRoot%\system32\Inetsrv directory and is named Meta-Base.xml. You'll also find a related file called MBSchema.xml, shown in Figure 15-2. MBSchema.xml is an XML Schema file, which tells IIS about the structure of the MetaBase.xml file.

```
MetaBase.xml - Notepad                                          _|□|×|
File  Edit  Format  View  Help
<IISWebService  Location ="/LM/W3SVC"
                AllowKeepAlive="TRUE"
                AnonymousUserName="IUSR_CORPSERVER03"
                AnonymousUserPass="4963446270000000220000004000000f631
                AppAllowClientDebug="FALSE"
                AppAllowDebugging="FALSE"
                AppPoolId="DefaultAppPool"
                ApplicationDependencies="Active Server Pages;ASP
                        Internet Data Connector;HTTPODBC
                        Server Side Includes;SSINC
                        WebDAV;WEBDAV
                        Internet Printing;ASP"
                AspAllowOutOfProcComponents="TRUE"
                AspAllowSessionState="TRUE"
                AspAppServiceFlags="0"
                AspBufferingLimit="4194304"
                AspBufferingOn="TRUE"
                AspCalcLineNumber="TRUE"
                AspCodepage="0"
                AspDiskTemplateCacheDirectory="%windir%\system32\inetsr
                AspEnableApplicationRestart="TRUE"
                AspEnableAspHtmlFallback="FALSE"
                AspEnableChunkedEncoding="TRUE"
                AspEnableParentPaths="FALSE"
                AspEnableTypelibCache="TRUE"
                AspErrorsToNTLog="FALSE"
```

Figure 15-2. *MetaBase.xml is a structured XML file that can be viewed in any standard text editor.*

You can examine and work with the Metabase files in any standard text editor. However, you should know several things before you do this:

- Each time IIS is started, the server reads the MBSchema.xml file and then uses this file to read and interpret the MetaBase.xml file. IIS must be able to read and store both files in memory in order for IIS to start up properly. If the read fails, IIS won't start up.

- Although the metabase schema can be extended, you don't want to edit the MBSchema.xml file directly. Instead, you extend the schema by creating custom properties that are stored in the MetaBase.xml file. Any mistake, though, in creating custom properties could introduce errors that prevent IIS from reading the file and starting.

- You can edit the MetaBase.xml file directly in any standard text editor. If you plan to do this while IIS is running, you must enable the metabase edit-while-running feature. In the IIS snap-in, right-click the computer node and then select Properties. In the Properties dialog box, select Enable Direct Metabase Edit and then click OK. If you don't enable this feature, you must stop IIS before making changes to the metabase.

- Rather than directly editing MetaBase.xml, you might want to use the IIS administration scripts or Windows scripts to perform editing tasks for you. That way, you reduce the possibility that you'll introduce errors that prevent IIS from reading the metabase file. Remember, if IIS can't read this file, the related services won't start.

- IIS maintains a change history for the metabase that allows you to roll back changes in some instances. To learn more about this important feature, see the section entitled "Understanding IIS Metabase History" in Chapter 16, "IIS Backup & Recovery."

If you plan to use scripts to work with the metabase, you need to understand the metabase's structure and know how to locate properties. Every XML element that corresponds to a metabase property has a Location property that specifies the element's path in the metabase hierarchy. The hierarchy follows this convention:

/LM/Service/Website

where LM is a key that represents the local machine; *Service* is a placeholder that represents an Internet service, such as W3SVC or MSFTPSVC; and *Website* is a placeholder that represents the site or virtual server instance.

To see how metabase paths are used, consider the following example. The metabase path /LM/W3SVC/1 is the path to the Web site instance installed on the local machine with the tracking ID of 1. In the MetaBase.xml file, you could locate the entries related to this path, and they might look like this:

```
<IIsWebServerLocation ="/LM/W3SVC/1"

    AppPoolId="DefaultAppPool"

    DefaultDoc="Default.htm,Default.asp,index.htm,iisstart.htm,Default
    .aspx"

    ServerBindings=":80:"

    ServerComment="Default Web Site"

    ServerSize="1"

>

</IIsWebServer>
```

If you're familiar with HTML or XML, you'll know that IISWebServer is an XML element. Each property of this XML element corresponds to a specific metabase property. The value assigned to the property is the current value of the related metabase property. For example, according to the previous code sample, the metabase property ServerSize is set to 1 and the complete metabase path to this property is:

```
/LM/W3SVC/1/ServerSize
```

The hierarchy can extend downward as well. For example, the metabase path to the root directory or a Web site follows this convention:

```
/LM/Service/Website/Root ,
```

where LM is a key that represents the local machine; *Service* is a placeholder that represents an Internet service, such as W3SVC or MSFTPSVC; *Website* is a placeholder that represents the site or virtual server instance; and Root is the virtual directory root of the server instance.

If you examine the MetaBase.xml file, you'd find an IIsWebVirtualDir element for the root directory of the first Web server instance. The stored values might look like this:

```
<IIsWebVirtualDirLocation ="/LM/W3SVC/1/ROOT"

    AccessFlags="AccessRead | AccessScript"

    AppFriendlyName="Default Application"

    AppIsolated="2"

    AppPoolId="DefaultAppPool"

    AppRoot="/LM/W3SVC/1/ROOT"

    Path="d:\inetpub\wwwroot"

>

</IIsWebVirtualDir>
```

Here, the path to any property is the Location value plus the property name, such as:

```
/LM/W3SVC/1/ROOT/AppIsolated
```

When you work with metabase properties, the inheritance rules discussed in previous chapters still apply. Properties that you set at the Server level can apply to sites, directories within a site, and subdirectories within a directory. Similarly, child nodes could inherit properties that you set for a site or a directory. Inheritance is automatic and works just as discussed in previous chapters.

Modifying Metabase Properties

As you can probably imagine, you can set hundreds of metabase properties. The ones you'll work with the most relate to global settings for Web servers. You'll set these properties in the metabase location /LM/W3SVC.

Global values for the Web Service are set using the IIsWebService element in the MetaBase.xml file. The Location attribute of this element corresponds to the metabase location (/LM/W3SVC). Values for individual Web sites and virtual directories are set using the IIsWebServer and IIsWebVirtualDir elements respectively. The Location attribute of these elements is set according to the specific element's location in the metabase hierarchy.

The properties you'll want to work with include the following:

- **AppAllowDebugging** Specifies whether ASP debugging is enabled on the server. When you enable this property, only one thread of execution is allowed for each IIS application you've configured on the server. This allows you to debug applications individually. By default, this value is set to FALSE. Set this value to TRUE only for debugging purposes.

- **AspAllowSessionState** Specifies whether sessions are enabled for applications. When you enable this property, IIS tracks information for user sessions. By default, this value is set to TRUE (enabling sessions). If sessions aren't used, however, you can achieve better performance by setting this value to FALSE and then enabling sessions within the individual applications as needed using <% @ENABLESESSIONSTATE=TRUE %>.

- **AspBufferingOn** Specifies whether ASP buffering is enabled. With buffering, output is collected in a buffer before it's sent to the client. By default, this value is set to TRUE (enabling buffering). If you set this property to FALSE, output from ASP scripts is sent to the client browser as it becomes available.

- **AspQueueConnectionTestTime** Sets the interval used to determine if a client is still connected to the server. If a request has been in the queue longer than the test time, the server checks to see if the client is still connected before beginning execution. The default value is 3 seconds. This feature is designed to handle the problem of impatient users filling the request queue with numerous requests for the same page. ASP pages can also use the Response.IsClientConnected method to see if the client is still connected.

- **AspRequestQueueMax** Specifies the default limit for ASP requests in the connection queue. The default value is 3000. The way you set this value depends on your applications. If the average request has a very short execution time and the time in the queue is short, you might want to increase this limit (particularly if you have a very busy server).

- **AspScriptEngineCacheMax** Specifies the maximum number of scripts to cache in memory. A hit in the script engine cache means that you can avoid recompiling a template into byte code. The default value is 250.

- **AspScriptFileCacheSize** Specifies the number of precompiled script files to store in the ASP Template Cache. The default value is 500. If you set this property to –1, all script files requested are cached. If you set this property to 0, no script files are cached.

- **AspSessionMax** Sets the maximum number of concurrent user sessions for ASP applications. By default, the total number of connections isn't limited.

- **AspSessionTimeout** Determines when ASP sessions time out and have to be refreshed. By default, sessions time out after 10 minutes.

- **CacheISAPI** Specifies whether ISAPI dynamic-link libraries (DLLs) are cached in memory after use. By default, this property is set to TRUE and ISAPI DLLs remain in the cache until the server is stopped. If the property is FALSE, DLLs are unloaded from memory after use.

- **ConnectionTimeout** Specifies the time in seconds that the server will wait before disconnecting an inactive connection. The default value is 120 seconds (2 minutes).

- **ServerListenBackLog** Sets the request queue size. The default value is based on the AcceptEx operating system parameter and on the value of the ServerSize metabase property. If ServerSize is set to 1, the default for this property is 40. If ServerSize is set to 2, the default is 100. Valid values for this property range from 5 to 500.

- **ServerSize** Specifies the server's general size in terms of the number of client requests processed per day. A value of 0 indicates fewer than 10,000 requests per day, a value of 1 indicates between 10,000 and 100,000 requests per day, and a value of 2 indicates more than 100,000 requests per day.

Scripting the Metabase

Windows scripts provide another technique you can use to work with the metabase. To access metabase properties in a Windows script, you use the Active Directory Services Interface (ADSI) provider for IIS. This provider allows you to manipulate the IIS administrative objects. Key administrative objects that you'll work with include IIsComputer, IIsWebServer, and IIsFtpServer. These objects correspond to the like-named elements in the MetaBase.xml file.

You can use the IIsComputer object to set global IIS properties and to manage metabase backups. Keep in mind that all child nodes (sites, directories, and others) can inherit global properties. The IIsComputer object is an ADSI container object that has this AdsPath:

`IIS://MachineName`

where *MachineName* can be any computer name or LocalHost, such as

`IIS://engsvr01`

In VBScript, you could get the IIsComputer object for ENGSVR01 using the following code:

```
'Initialize variables
Dim compObject, serverName
serverName = "engsvr01"
'Get IIsWebServer object
Set compObject = GetObject("IIS://" & serverName)
```

Note A detailed discussion of scripting the metabase is beyond the scope of this book. If you want to learn Windows scripting, a good resource is the *Windows 2000 Scripting Bible* (John Wiley & Sons, 2000). Once you know how to program Windows scripts, use the IIS online help documentation to get a better understanding of what objects are available and how you can use them.

You can then work with any of the IIsComputer object's methods and properties, such as these:

```
'Initialize variables
Dim compObject, serverName
serverName = "engsvr01"

'Get IIsWebServer object
Set compObject = GetObject("IIS://" & serverName)

'Restore metabase config from last backup
'backup is stored in the default location

compObject.Restore "MyBackup", MD_BACKUP_HIGHEST_VERSION, 0
```

You use the IIsWebServer object to set metabase properties that apply to a specific Web site and to set inheritable properties for directories and files. Methods are also available to control server operation. For example, you can use the Stop method to stop a site and then use the Start method to start the site.

Web sites are identified according to their index number in the metabase. The first Web site instance created on the server has an index number of 1, the second has an index of 2, and so on. The IIsWebServer object is an ADSI container object that has this AdsPath:

IIS://MachineName/W3SVC/N

where *MachineName* can be any computer name or LocalHost, W3SVC identifies the Web service, and *N* is the site's index number. In the following example the AdsPath string specifies the first Web site instance on the server named ENGSVR01:

```
IIS://engsvr01/W3SVC/1
```

In VBScript, you can get the IIsWebServer object for the first Web site instance using the following code:

```
'Initialize variables
Dim webObject, serverName, webN
serverName = "engsvr01"
webN = "1"

'Get IIsWebServer object
Set webObject = GetObject("IIS://" & serverName & "/W3SVC/" & webN)
```

You can then work with any of the IIsWebServer object's methods and properties, such as these:

```
'Initialize variables
Dim webObject, serverName, webN
serverName = "engsvr01"
webN = "1"

'Get IIsWebServer object
Set webObject = GetObject("IIS://" & serverName & "/W3SVC/"& webN)
```

```
'Stop Web site
webObject.Stop

'Turn on ASP Buffering
webObject.AspBufferingOn = True

'Save the changed value to the metabase
webObject.SetInfo

'Start the Web server
webObject.Start
```

You can use the IIsFtpServer object to set metabase properties that apply to a specific FTP server and to set inheritable metabase properties for directories. As with the IIsWebServer object, methods are also available to control server operation. You can, for example, call the Pause method to pause the FTP server and then call the Continue method to resume operation.

FTP servers are identified according to their index number in the metabase. The first server has an index number of 1, the second has an index of 2, and so on. The IIsFTPServer object is an ADSI container object that has this AdsPath:

IIS://MachineName/MSFTPSVC/N

where *MachineName* can be any computer name or LocalHost, MSFTPSVC identifies the FTP Service, and *N* is the server's index number. In the following example the AdsPath string specifies the first FTP server on ENGSVR01:

```
IIS://engsvr01/MSFTPSVC/1
```

In VBScript you can get the IIsFtpServer object for the first FTP server instance using the following code:

```
'Initialize variables
Dim ftpObj, serverName, ftpN
serverName = "engsvr01"
ftpN = "1"

'Get IIsFtpServer object
Set ftpObj = GetObject("IIS://" & serverName & "/MSFTPSVC/" & ftpN)
```

You can then work with any of the IIsFtpServer object's methods and properties, such as in the following:

```
'Initialize variables
Dim ftpObj, serverName, ftpN
serverName = "engsvr01"
ftpN = "1"

'Get IIsFtpServer object
Set ftpObj = GetObject("IIS://" & serverName & "/MSFTPSVC/"& ftpN)

'Stop FTP Server
ftpObj.Stop
```

```
'Enable anonymous access
ftpObj.AllowAnonymous = True

'Save the changed value to the metabase
ftpObj.SetInfo
'Start FTP Server
ftpObj.Start
```

Chapter 16
IIS Backup & Recovery

When you back up an Internet Information Services (IIS) server, you need to look at the IIS configuration as well as the system configuration. This means you must do the following:

- Save the IIS configuration whenever you change the properties of the IIS installation
- Maintain several configuration backups as an extra precaution
- Periodically back up the server using a comprehensive backup procedure, such as the one outlined in this chapter

Backing up an IIS server using this technique gives you several recovery options. You can:

- Recover the IIS configuration settings for sites and virtual servers using the IIS configuration backup you've created
- Recover a corrupted IIS installation by reinstalling IIS and then recovering the last working IIS configuration
- Restore the server, its data files, and its IIS configuration by recovering the system from archives
- Perform a partial server restore to retrieve missing or corrupted files from archives

The sections that follow examine backing up and recovering IIS server configurations and data files.

Backing Up the IIS Configuration

Backing up the IIS configuration is an important part of any Web administrator's job. Before you get started, take a moment to learn the key concepts that'll help you every step of the way.

Understanding IIS Configuration Backups

IIS configuration backups contain metadata that describes the configuration settings used by Web sites and virtual servers. IIS uses the metadata to restore values for all resource properties, including security settings, virtual directory options, application pools, and Web service extensions. IIS also uses this information to maintain the run state of sites and virtual servers. So if you save the IIS configuration and then restore the configuration later, the IIS configuration settings are restored and the IIS resources are returned to their original state (running, paused, stopped, and so on) as well.

I recommend that you create an IIS configuration backup every time you make IIS configuration changes and before you make major changes that affect the availability of resources. Unlike previous versions of IIS, IIS 6.0 provides very granular control over the save and restore configuration feature. You can save configurations for:

- An entire server
- A set of related resources, such as all Web sites
- An individual resource, such as a single File Transfer Protocol (FTP) site
- An individual directory

Because IIS 6 uses Extensible Markup Language (XML) to format the metabase, all IIS configuration files are saved in XML format. With server, resource, and directory configuration files, you specify the name and save location. The default directory is %SystemRoot%\System32\Inetsrv. Files are saved with the .xml file extension. If you save the configuration of a server, the configuration is saved in the server's %SystemRoot%\System32\Inetsrv as MetaBase.xml.

IIS configuration backups can help you in many situations. You can:

- **Recover deleted resources**   References to all site, application pool and virtual server instances running on the server are stored with the configuration backup. If you delete a site, application pool or virtual server, you can restore the necessary resource references.

- **Restore resource properties**   All configuration settings of sites, application pools and virtual servers are stored in the configuration backup. If you change properties, you can recover the previous IIS settings from backup.

- **Recover Internet Server Application Programming Interface (ISAPI) application configuration**   ISAPI application settings, including Application Mappings, Application Options, Process Options, and Application Debugging, are stored with the configuration backup. If you change the ISAPI application settings, you can recover the ISAPI application configuration.

- **Recover global service properties**   Global service properties and other top-level IIS settings are stored in configuration backups. This means you can recover default settings for new Web and FTP sites, bandwidth throttling settings, and Multipurpose Internet Mail Extensions (MIME) type mappings. You can't, however, recover global properties for Web Service extensions.

- **Rebuild a damaged IIS installation**   If the IIS installation gets corrupted and you can't repair it through normal means, you can rebuild the IIS installation. You do this by uninstalling IIS, reinstalling IIS, and then using the configuration backup to restore the IIS settings. See the section of this chapter entitled "Rebuilding Corrupted IIS Installations" for details.

If you were to open a backup file in a text editor, you'd find that it contains metabase keys and paths that are specific to the current server installation. The significance of this is that the metabase keys and paths allow you to restore IIS settings.

Understanding IIS Metabase History

IIS automatically maintains a change history for the metabase. The history feature works in the following manner: When IIS starts up, the MetaBase.xml and MBSchema.xml files are read into memory and each is assigned a unique version number. If the metabase is changed and those changes are saved to disk, the current metabase file's version number is incremented and a copy of the old file is archived in the metabase history folder. Each archived file is then available for restoring the metabase from history.

Several metabase parameters control the history feature. These include:

- **EnableHistory**   Specifies whether the history featured is enabled. By default, the history feature is enabled. If you set the parameter to 0, the metabase history feature is disabled.

- **MaxHistoryFiles**   Specifies the maximum number of metabase history files to maintain. The default maximum is 10.

- **EnableEditWhileRunning**   Specifies whether the metabase can be updated directly while IIS is running. If you set the parameter to 1, the metabase can be updated directly based on changes to the in-memory metabase.

The Edit-While-Running feature is important because it allows you to quickly write to disk changes that you've made to the in-memory MetaBase.xml file. Here, any changes you make to the MetaBase.xml file are generally written to disk 60 seconds after the change is made. If Edit-While-Running isn't enabled, changes you make to the MetaBase.xml file are written only when the IIS service is stopped or if you use an IIS administrative script or Windows script to make the changes to the MetaBase.xml file.

You can enable Edit-While-Running using the IIS snap-in as well. To do this, follow these steps:

1. In the IIS snap-in, right-click the computer node and then select Properties.

2. In the *Server* Properties dialog box, select Enable Direct Metabase Edit and then click OK.

Metabase history files are in the %SystemRoot%\System32\Inetsrv\History folder. Because errors and changes to metabase schema are tracked separately from changes to the metabase parameters and values, you'll find three types of files:

- **Metabase History** Metabase_*MajorVersion_MinorVersion*.xml, such as Metabase_0000000375_0000000000.xml

- **Metabase Schema History** MBSchema_*MajorVersion_MinorVersion*.xml, such as MBSchema_0000000112_0000000000.xml

- **Metabase Error** MetabaseError_*Version*.xml, such as MetabaseError_-0000000000.xml

 Note When you work with the metabase files, it's important to note that you shouldn't use the Encrypting File System (EFS) to encrypt them. Sensitive values in the metabase are already encrypted, and if you encrypt the metabase files themselves, you'll slow down IIS unnecessarily.

Creating IIS Configuration Backups

Each IIS server has a configuration that must be backed up to ensure that IIS can be recovered in case of problems. You can create backups at the server, site, or virtual directory level.

At the server level, you create a configuration backup of all sites and virtual servers on the server. To back up the IIS server configuration, follow these steps:

1. In the IIS snap-in, right-click the icon for the computer you want to work with. If the computer isn't shown, connect to it as discussed in the section entitled "Connecting to Other Servers" in Chapter 2, "Core IIS Administration," and then right-click it.

2. On the shortcut menu, choose All Tasks and then select Backup/Restore Configuration. This displays the Configuration Backup/Restore dialog box shown in Figure 16-1.

3. Click Create Backup, type a name for your backup file, and then click OK. IIS creates the backup file. By default, this file is stored in the %SystemRoot%\System32\Inetsrv\MetaBack directory.

Tip Do not enter the file extension. Enter the file name only, such as Config05-03-03. IIS will create two files using this name: a metabase schema file with the .SCO extension and a metabase configuration file with the .MDO extension, such as Config05-03-03.SCO and Config05-03-03.MDO respectively.

4. Click Close.

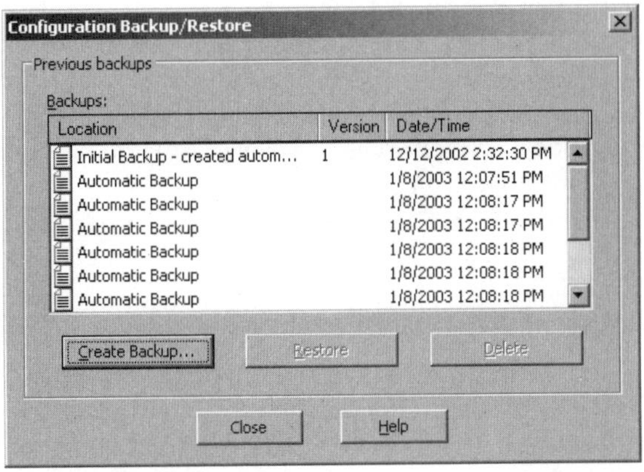

Figure 16-1. *Use Configuration Backup/Restore to create, restore, and delete IIS configuration backups.*

You can also create configuration backups at the Web sites, FTP sites, and Application Pools level. Here the backup contains configuation settings only for the type of resource you choose. To back up the configuration of sites, application pools or virtual directories, follow these steps:

1. In the IIS snap-in, select the Web Sites, FTP Sites or Application Pools mode (as appropriate for the type of configuration backup you want to create).

2. On the Action menu, choose All Tasks and then select Save Configuration To A File.

3. In the Save Configuration To A File dialog box, select a name for your backup file and then click OK. IIS creates the backup file. By default, this file is stored in the %SystemRoot%\System32\Inetsrv directory.

Restoring IIS Server Configurations

You can restore IIS from backup configuration files. When you do this, the previous property settings and state are restored. Recovering the configuration won't repair a corrupted IIS installation. To repair a corrupted installation, follow the technique outlined in the section of this chapter entitled "Rebuilding Corrupted IIS Installations."

Restoring IIS from a backup configuration causes Microsoft Windows Server 2003 to stop and then restart IIS services. Once you've notified users that IIS resources will be unavailable for several minutes, you can restore the IIS configuration by completing the following steps:

1. In the IIS snap-in, right-click the node for the computer you want to work with. If the computer isn't shown, connect to it as discussed in the section entitled "Connecting to Other Servers" in Chapter 2, "Core IIS Administration," and then right-click it.

2. On the shortcut menu, choose All Tasks and then select Backup/Restore Configuration. This displays the Configuration Backup/Restore dialog box shown previously in Figure 16-1.

3. The Backups panel shows the configuration backups that are available for the computer. The Location field provides the name of the file. The Date/Time field provides a date/time stamp.

4. Select a backup file and then click Restore. When asked whether to restore your configuration settings, click Yes. When the restore is complete, click Close.

Rebuilding Corrupted IIS Installations

A corrupt IIS installation can cause problems with your IIS sites and virtual servers. Resources might not run. IIS might not respond to commands. IIS might freeze intermittently. To correct these problems, you might need to rebuild the IIS installation. Rebuilding the IIS installation is a lengthy process that requires a complete outage of IIS sites and virtual servers. The outage can last from 5 to 15 minutes or more.

Caution IIS configuration backups are machine-specific and instance-specific. You can't restore a backup of an entire IIS server configuration on other machines, and you can't restore these configuration settings after reinstalling the operating system. You can however, use configuration backups created at the Web sites, FTP sites, or Application Pools level or below as the basis of new sites or application pools on other servers. To do this, copy the necessary configuration backup file to the desired server and then restore the resource as discussed in this chapter.

You rebuild a corrupt IIS installation by completing the following steps:

1. Log on locally to the computer on which you want to rebuild IIS. Make sure you use an account with Administrator privileges.

2. Click Start, choose Control Panel and then Add Or Remove Programs. This displays the Add Or Remove Programs dialog box.

3. Start the Windows Components Wizard by clicking Add/Remove Windows Components.

4. In the Components list, select Application Server and then click Details.

Caution Be careful not to clear the check box for Application Server when selecting it, which is easy to do accidentally.

5. In the Sub Components Of Application Server list, clear the Internet Information Services (IIS) check box, click OK, and then click Next. After Setup makes the configuration changes you requested, click Finish. If you have services that are dependent on IIS, such as POP3 or ASP.NET, you will be prompted to remove these services as well. You must remove these services and then reinstall them, as described below.

6. In the Add Or Remove Programs dialog box, click Add/Remove Windows Components. This restarts the Windows Component Wizard.

7. Reinstall IIS by selecting the Application Server check box, clicking Details, and then selecting the Internet Information Services check box. If necessary, click Details and then select IIS subcomponents. You can also reinstall any additional components that you previously had to uninstall by selecting them. For example, if you had to uninstall the POP3 Service, you can reinstall it now by selecting the E-Mail Services checkbox.

8. When you're ready to continue, click OK, then Next. After Setup reinstalls IIS, click Finish.

9. Click Close to close the Add Or Remove Programs dialog box and then start the IIS snap-in.

10. In the Services snap-in, right-click the local computer entry in the left pane and then select Backup/Restore Configuration.

11. In the Configuration Backup dialog box, select the backup file that contains the correct IIS settings and then click Restore. When asked whether to restore your configuration settings, click Yes. When the restore is complete, click Close.

Restoring Site Configurations

You restore individual sites using the backup of the Web Sites or FTP Sites node. You can also use this feature to create new instances of a site on the current server or another server.

You can restore individual sites by completing the following steps:

1. In the IIS snap-in, right-click the Web Sites or FTP Sites node, choose New, and then select Web Site (From File) or FTP Site (From File). This displays the Import Configuration dialog box shown in Figure 16-2.

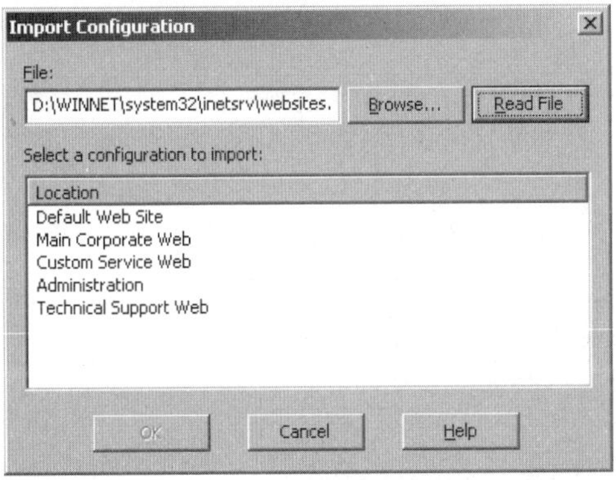

Figure 16-2. *Use the Import Configuration dialog box to create and restore sites from backups.*

2. In the File field, enter the file path to the Web Sites or FTP Sites configuration backup you previously created, or click Browse to search for the backup.

3. Click Read File to display a list of sites that are stored in the configuration backup.

4. Select the site you want to create or restore in the Location list and then click OK.

5. You can now select Create A New Site or Replace The Existing Site. Click OK to complete the operation.

Restoring Virtual Directory Configurations

You restore virtual directories using the backup of the Web Sites or FTP Sites node. You can also use this feature to create new instances of a virtual directory.

You can restore virtual directories by completing the following steps:

1. In the IIS snap-in, right-click the site on which you wish to restore a virtual directory, choose New, and then select Virtual Directory (From File). This displays the Import Configuration dialog box shown previously in Figure 16-2.

2. In the File field, enter the file path to the Web Sites or FTP Sites configuration backup you previously created, or click Browse to search for the backup.

3. Click Read File to display a list of virtual directories that are stored in the configuration backup of the site selected in Step 1.

4. Select the virtual directory you want to create or restore in the Location list and then click OK.

5. You can now select Create A New Virtual Directory or Replace The Existing Virtual Directory. If you choose to create a new virtual directory, you can provide a new name for the directory by entering it in the Alias field.

6. Click OK to complete the operation.

Restoring Application Pool Configurations

You restore application pools using the backup of the Application Pools node. You can also use this feature to create new instances of an application pool.

You can restore application pools by completing the following steps:

1. In the IIS snap-in, right-click Application Pools, choose New, and then select Application Pool (From File). This displays the Import Configuration dialog box shown previously in Figure 16-2.

2. In the File field, enter the file path to the Application Pools configuration backup you previously created, or click Browse to search for the backup.

3. Click Read File to display a list of application pools that are stored in the configuration backup of the site selected in Step 1.

4. Select the application pool you want to create or restore in the Location list and then click OK.

5. You can now select Create A New Application Pool or Replace The Existing Application Pool. If you choose to create a new application pool, you must provide a new name for the application pool by entering it in the Application Pool ID field.

6. Click OK to complete the operation.

Deleting Server Backup Configurations

Over time, you'll gather quite a collection of IIS configuration backups. If you find that you don't need old backups anymore, you can delete them using the Configuration Backup dialog box. To do this, complete the following steps:

1. In the IIS snap-in, select the icon for the computer you want to work with. If the computer isn't shown, connect to it as discussed in the section entitled "Connecting to Other Servers" in Chapter 2, "Core IIS Administration," and then select it.

2. On the Action menu, select Backup/Restore Configuration.

3. The Backups panel shows the configuration backups that are available for the computer. The Location field provides the name of the file. The Date/Time field provides a date/time stamp.

4. Select the backup file or files you want to delete and then click the Delete button. When asked whether to delete the files, click Yes.

Caution The backup files are permanently deleted at this point. You can't recover the files from the Recycle Bin.

Backing Up and Recovering Server Files

Windows Server 2003 provides a utility called Backup for creating server backups. You use Backup to perform common backup and recovery tasks. You can access Backup in several ways, including:

- Click Start and then click Run. In the Run dialog box, type **ntbackup** and then click OK.

- Click Start, choose All Programs, then Accessories, System Tools, and finally Backup.

The first time you use the Backup utility, it starts in basic Wizard mode. As an administrator, you'll want to use advanced mode because it gives you more options. Clear Always Start In Wizard Mode and then click Advanced Mode. You should now see the main Backup Utility interface. As shown in Figure 16-3 on the following page, the standard interface has four tabs that provide easy access to key features. These tabs are:

- **Welcome** Introduces Backup and provides buttons for starting the Backup Wizard, the Restore Wizard, and the Automated System Recovery Wizard.

- **Backup** Provides the main interface for selecting data to back up. You can back up data on local drives and mapped network drives.

- **Restore And Manage Media** Provides the main interface for restoring archived data. You can restore data to the original location or to an alternate location anywhere on the network.

- **Schedule Jobs** Provides a month-by-month job schedule for backups. You can view executed jobs as well as jobs scheduled for future dates.

To perform backup and recovery operations, you must have certain permissions and user rights. Members of the Administrators and the Backup Operators groups have full authority to back up and restore any type of file, regardless of who owns the file and the permissions set on it. File owners and those that have been given control over files can also back up files, but only those that they own or those for which they have Read, Read & Execute, Modify, or Full Control permissions.

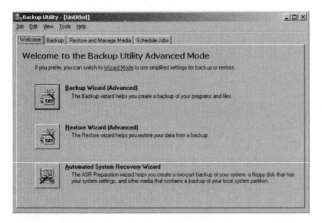

Figure 16-3. *The Windows Backup utility provides a user-friendly interface for backup and restore operations.*

 Note Keep in mind that although local accounts can work only with local systems, domain accounts have domain-wide privileges. Therefore, a member of the local administrators group can work with files only on the local system, but a member of the domain administrators group can work with files throughout the domain.

Setting Default Options for Backup

You create backups using the Backup utility's Backup tab or the Backup Wizards, on the Welcome tab. Both techniques make use of default options set for the Backup Utility. You can view or change the default options by completing the following steps:

1. Click the Advanced Mode button in the initial Backup Utility Wizard page or start the utility with the Wizard mode disabled (by clearing Always Start In Wizard Mode).
2. Click Tools and then select Options.
3. You can now change any of the available default options.

Viewing and Setting Backup Exclusions

Many types of system files are excluded from backups by default. You manage exclusions in the Options dialog box, which you access by selecting Options from the Tools menu in the Backup Utility.

In the Backup Utility you can view file exclusions by selecting the Exclude Files tab in the Options dialog box. File exclusions are based on file ownership and can be set for all users as well as the user currently logged on to the system (as shown in Figure 16-4).

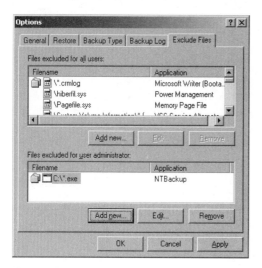

Figure 16-4. *You can view existing file exclusions for users in the Exclude Files tab.*

To exclude additional files, follow these steps:

1. In the Options dialog box, choose the Exclude Files tab.

2. If you want to exclude files that are owned by any user, click Add New under the Files Excluded For All Users list. This displays the Add Excluded Files dialog box shown in Figure 16-5.

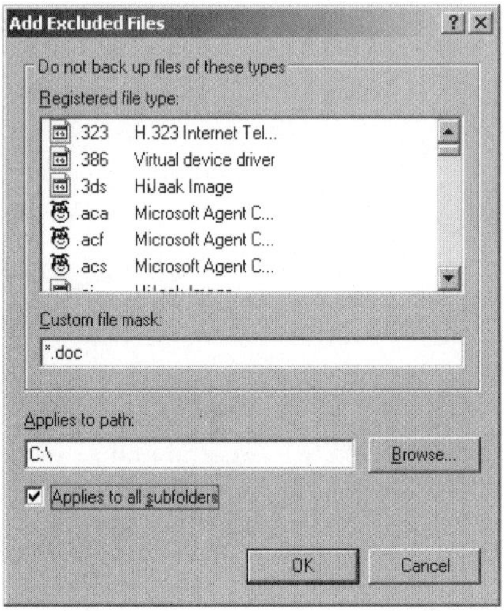

Figure 16-5. *Use the Add Excluded Files dialog box to set file exclusions for users.*

3. If you want to exclude only files that you own, click Add New under the Files Excluded For User... list. This displays the Add Excluded Files dialog box.

4. You can exclude files by registered file type by clicking a file type in the Registered File Type list box. Or you can exclude files by custom file type by typing a period and then the file extension in the Custom File Mask field. For example, you could choose .doc or enter the custom type .wbk.

5. Enter a drive or file path in Applies To Path field. Files are then restricted from all subfolders of that path unless you clear the Applies To All Subfolders check box. For example, if you use C:\ and select Applies To All Subfolders, all files ending with the designated file extension are excluded wherever they occur on the C drive. Click OK.

> **Tip** Enter \ as the path to specify matching files on any file system. For example, if the system had C, D, and E hard disk drives and you wanted to exclude all files of a certain type on all three drives, you'd enter \ in the Applies To Path field.

To change existing exclusions, follow these steps:

1. In the Options dialog box, choose the Exclude Files tab.

2. Select an existing exclusion you want to edit and then click Edit. You can now edit the file exclusion.

3. Select an existing exclusion you want to remove and then click Remove. The exclusion is removed. Click Apply or OK when you're finished.

Backing Up Server Files

You can back up files by completing the following steps:

1. Start the Backup utility. If Wizard mode is enabled, click Advanced Mode and then select the Backup tab as shown in Figure 16-6. Otherwise, just select the Backup tab.

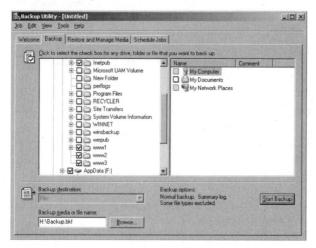

Figure 16-6. *Use the Backup tab to configure backups and then click Start Backup.*

2. Clear any existing selections in the Backup tab by selecting New from the Job menu and clicking Yes when prompted.

3. Choose the data you want to back up as follows:

   • You make selections by selecting or clearing the check boxes associated with a particular drive or folder. When you select a drive's check box, all files and folders on the drive are selected. When you clear a drive's check box, all files and folders on the drive are cleared.

   • If you want to work with individual files and folders on a drive, click the plus sign (+) to the left of the drive icon. You can now select and clear individual directories and files by clicking their associated check boxes. When you do this, the drive's check box shows a shaded checkmark. This indicates that you haven't selected all the files on the drive.

● If you want to back up system state data, select System State below the My Computer node. For servers that aren't domain controllers, system state data includes essential boot and system files, the Windows registry, and the COM+ class registration database. For domain controllers, system state data includes Active Directory data and Sysvol files as well.

4. Use the Backup Destination drop-down list to choose the media type for the backup. Choose File if you want to back up to a file. Choose a storage device if you want to back up files and folders to a tape or removable disk.

5. In Backup Media Or File Name, select the backup file or media you want to use. If you're backing up to a file, type a path and file name for the backup file, or click Browse to find a file. If you're backing up to a tape or removable disk, choose the tape or disk you want to use.

6. Click Start Backup. This displays the Backup Job Information dialog box. You use the options in this dialog box as follows:

● **Backup Description**   Sets the backup label, which applies to the current backup only.

● **Append This Backup To The Media**   Adds the backup after existing data.

● **Replace The Data On The Media With This Backup**   Overwrites existing data.

● **If The Media Is Overwritten, Use This Label To Identify The Media**   Sets the media label, which is changed only when you're writing to a blank tape or overwriting existing data.

● **Allow Only The Owner And Administrator Access To The Backup Data**   If you're overwriting data, you can specify that only the owner and an administrator can access the archive file by selecting this option.

7. Click Advanced if you want to override the default options. The advanced options are:

● **Back Up Data That Is In Remote Storage**   Archives placeholder files for Remote Storage with the backup. This ensures that you can recover an entire file system with necessary Remote Storage references intact.

● **Verify Data After Backup**   Instructs Backup to verify data after the backup procedure is completed. If selected, every file on the backup tape is compared to the original file. Verifying data can protect against write errors or failures.

Caution Backing up system-protected files can substantially increase the backup's size. Often this can add 700–1000 MB to the backup's size.

- **If Possible, Compress Backup Data To Save Space** Allows Backup to compress data as it's written to the storage device. This option is available only if the device supports hardware compression, and only compatible drives can read the compressed information, which might mean that only a drive from the same manufacturer can recover the data.

- **Automatically Back Up System Protected Files With The System State** Backs up all the system files in the %SystemRoot% folder, in addition to the boot files that are included with the system state data.

- **Disable Volume Shadow Copy** Tells the Backup Utility not to perform volume shadow copies. Volume shadow copies are used to back up files that are being written to. Thus, if you disable this feature, the Backup Utility skips files that are locked for writing.

- **Backup Type** Indicates the type of backup to perform. The available types are Normal, Copy, Incremental, Differential, and Daily.

8. At this point, you have two options:

    - If you want to schedule the backup for a later date, click Schedule. When prompted to save the backup settings, click Yes. Next, type a name for the backup selection script and then click Save. Afterward, set the user name and password under which the scheduled job should run and then click OK. In the Scheduled Job Options dialog box, type a job name, click Properties, set a run schedule, and then click OK.

Note Backup selection scripts and backup logs are stored in %UserProfile%\Local Settings\Application Data\Microsoft\Windows NT\ NTBackup\Data. Backup selection scripts are saved with the .bks extension. Backup logs are saved with the .log extension. You can view these files with any standard text editor.

    - If you want to start the backup immediately, click Finish. Later, if you need to, you can cancel the backup by clicking Cancel in the Selection Information and Backup Progress dialog boxes.

9. When the backup is completed, click Close to complete the process or click Report to view the backup log.

Recovering Server Files

You can recover archives by completing the following steps:

1. As necessary, load the backup set you want to work with in the library system.

2. Start the Backup utility. If Wizard mode is enabled, click Advanced Mode and then select the Restore And Manage Media tab as shown in Figure 16-7. Otherwise, just select the Backup And Manage Media tab.

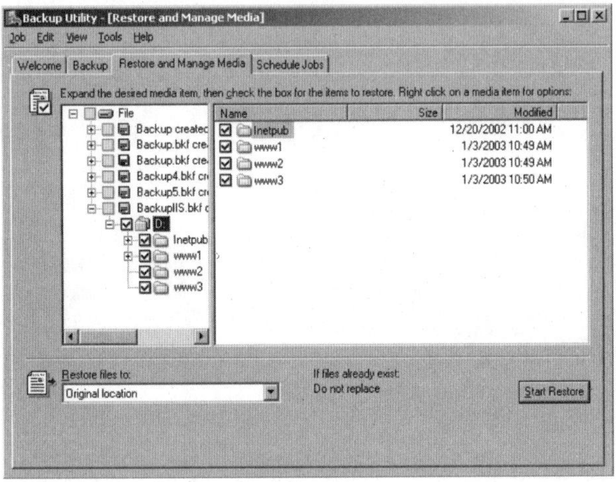

Figure 16-7. *Specify the files and folders to restore.*

3. Choose the data you want to restore. The left view displays files organized by volume. The right view displays media sets.

   - Select the check box next to any drive, folder, or file that you want to restore. If the media set you want to work with isn't shown, right-click File in the left view, select Catalog File, then type the name and path of the catalog you want to use.

   - To restore system state data that was previously backed up, select the check box for System State as well as other data you want to restore. If you're restoring to the original location, the current system state is replaced by the system state data you're restoring. If you restore to an alternate location, only the registry, Sysvol, and system boot files are restored. You can restore system state data only on a local system.

4. Use the Restore Files To drop-down list to choose the restore location. The options are:

   - **Original Location** Restores data to the folder or files it was in when it was backed up.

- **Alternate Location** Restores data to a folder that you designate, preserving the directory structure. After you select this option, enter the folder path to use or click Browse to select the folder path.

- **Single Folder** Restores all files to a single folder without preserving the directory structure. After you select this option, enter the folder path to use or click Browse to select the folder path.

5. Specify how you want to restore files. Click Tools and then select Options. In the Options dialog box, select the Restore tab. Select one of the following options and then click OK:

   - **Do Not Replace The Files On My Computer (Recommended)** Select this option if you don't want to copy over existing files.

   - **Replace The File On Disk Only If The File On Disk Is Older** Select this option to replace older files on disk with newer files from the backup.

   - **Always Replace The File On My Computer** Select this option to replace all files on disk with files from the backup.

6. In the Restore And Manage Media tab, click Start Restore. This displays the Confirm Restore dialog box.

7. If you want to set advanced restore options, click Advanced and then set any of the following options:

   - **Restore Security** Select this option to restore security settings for files and folders on NTFS file system (NTFS) volumes.

   - **Restore Junction Points, And Restore File And Folder Data Under Junction Points To The Original Location** Select this option to restore network drive mappings and the actual data to mapped network drives. Choose this option only if you're trying to recover a drive on a remote system. Otherwise, clear this option to restore folder references to network drives only.

   - **When Restoring Replicated Data Sets, Mark The Restored Data As The Primary Data For All Replicas** Select this option if you're restoring replicated data and want the restored data to be published to subscribers. If you don't choose this option, the data might not be replicated because it will appear older than existing data on the subscribers.

   - **Restore The Cluster Registry To The Quorum Disk And All Other Nodes** Restores the cluster registry, which contains cluster configuration and state information, to the quorum disk and other nodes in a cluster.

   - **Preserve Existing Volume Mount Points** Select this option if you're restoring an entire file system (which includes the volume mount points) and want to retain the current mount points rather than those in the archive. This option is useful if you've remapped a drive and created additional volumes and want to keep the current volume mappings.

8. In the Confirm Restore dialog box, click OK to start the restore operation. If prompted, enter the path and name of the backup set to use. You can cancel the backup by clicking Cancel in the Operation Status and Restore Progress dialog boxes.

9. When the restore is completed, you can click Close to complete the process or click Report to view a backup log containing information about the restore operation.

Index

About the Author

William R. Stanek has 20 years of hands-on experience with advanced programming and development. He is a leading technology expert and an award-winning author. Over the years, his practical advice has helped millions of programmers, developers, and network engineers all over the world. He has written over two dozen computer books. Current or forthcoming books include *Microsoft Windows XP Professional Administrator's Pocket Consultant*, *Microsoft Windows 2000 Administrator's Pocket Consultant 2nd Edition*, and *Microsoft Windows .NET Server and IIS 6.0 Administrator's Pocket Consultant*.

Mr. Stanek has been involved in the commercial Internet community since 1991. His core business and technology experience comes from over 11 years of military service. He has substantial experience in developing server technology, encryption, and Internet solutions. He has written many technical white papers and training courses on a wide variety of topics. He is widely sought after as a subject matter expert.

Mr. Stanek has an MS in Information Systems degree with distinction and a BS Computer Science degree magna cum laude. He is proud to have served in the Persian Gulf War as a combat crew member on an electronic warfare aircraft. He flew on numerous combat missions into Iraq and was awarded nine medals for his wartime service, including one of the United States of America's highest flying honors, the Air Force Distinguished Flying Cross. Currently, he resides in the Pacific Northwest with his wife and children.

At Microsoft Press, we use tools to illustrate our books for software developers and IT professionals. Tools very simply and powerfully symbolize human inventiveness. They're a metaphor for people extending their capabilities, precision, and reach. From simple calipers and pliers to digital micrometers and lasers, these stylized illustrations give each book a visual identity, and a personality to the series. With tools and knowledge, there's no limit to creativity and innovation. Our tagline says it all: *the tools you need to put technology to work.*

The manuscript for this book was prepared and submitted to Microsoft Press in electronic format. Text files were prepared using Microsoft Word 2000 for Windows. Pages were composed by nSight, Inc., using Adobe FrameMaker 6.5 for Windows, with text in Garamond and display type in ITC Franklin Gothic. Composed pages were delivered to the printer as electronic prepress files.

Cover Designer:	Methodologie, Inc.
Interior Graphic Designer:	James D. Kramer
Layout Artist:	Patty Fagan
Project Manager:	Susan McClung
Tech Editor:	Bob Hogan
Copy Editor:	Joseph Gustaitis
Proofreaders:	Charlotte Maurer, Robert Saley, Katie O'Connell
Indexer:	Jack Lewis

For *Windows Server 2003* administrators

Microsoft® Windows® Server 2003 Administrator's Companion
ISBN 0-7356-1367-2

The comprehensive, daily operations guide to planning, deployment, and maintenance. Here's the ideal one-volume guide for anyone who administers Windows Server 2003. It offers up-to-date information on core system-administration topics for Windows, including Active Directory® services, security, disaster planning and recovery, interoperability with NetWare and UNIX, plus all-new sections about Microsoft Internet Security and Acceleration (ISA) Server and scripting. Featuring easy-to-use procedures and handy workarounds, it provides ready answers for on-the-job results.

Microsoft Windows Server 2003 Security Administrator's Companion
ISBN 0-7356-1574-8

The in-depth, practical guide to deployment and maintenance in a secure environment. With this authoritative ADMINISTRATOR'S COMPANION—written by an expert on the Windows Server 2003 security team—you'll learn how to use the powerful security features in the network server operating system. The guide describes best practices and technical details for enhancing security with Windows Server 2003, using a holistic approach to security enhancement.

Microsoft Windows Server 2003 Administrator's Pocket Consultant
ISBN 0-7356-1354-0

The practical, portable guide to Windows Server 2003. Here's the practical, pocket-sized reference for IT professionals who support Windows Server 2003. Designed for quick referencing, it covers all the essentials for performing everyday system-administration tasks. Topics covered include managing workstations and servers, using Active Directory services, creating and administering user and group accounts, managing files and directories, data security and auditing, data back-up and recovery, administration with TCP/IP, WINS, and DNS, and more.

Microsoft IIS 6.0 Administrator's Pocket Consultant
ISBN 0-7356-1560-8

The practical, portable guide to IIS 6.0. Here's the eminently practical, pocket-sized reference for IT and Web professionals who work with Internet Information Services (IIS) 6.0. Designed for quick referencing and compulsively readable, this portable guide covers all the basics needed for everyday tasks. Topics include Web administration fundamentals, Web server administration, essential services administration, and performance, optimization, and maintenance. It's the fast-answers guide that helps users consistently save time and energy as they administer IIS 6.0.

To learn more about the full line of Microsoft Press® products for IT professionals, please visit:

microsoft.com/mspress/IT

Microsoft Press

Complete planning and migration information for Microsoft Windows Server 2003

Introducing Microsoft® Windows® Server 2003
ISBN 0-7356-1570-5

Plan your deployment with this first look at Windows Server 2003, the successor to the Wind 2000 Server network operating system. A first look at the Windows Server 2003 network opera system, this book is ideal for IT professionals engaged in planning and deployment. It provides a comprehensive overview of the powerful new operating system and what's different about it—incl new XML Web services and components, security, networking, Active Directory® directory service, Microsoft Internet Information Services, Microsoft SharePoint™ Team Services, support for IPv6, a more. This book has all the initial planning information and tools IT professionals need, whether t upgrading from Microsoft Windows NT® or Windows 2000.

Migrating from Microsoft Windows NT Server 4.0 to Microsoft Windows Server 2003
ISBN 0-7356-1940-9

In-depth technical information for upgrading Windows NT 4.0–based systems to Windows S 2003 from those who know the technology best. Get essential information for upgrading and migrating Windows-based servers, direct from the experts who know the technology best—the Mi Windows Server product team. This book gives IT professionals the information and resources the need to effectively migrate file servers, print servers, domain controllers, network infrastructure s Web servers, database servers, and other application servers. The book includes practical inform and tips for planning server migrations; consolidating servers; resolving hardware, network, and application compatibility issues; configuring servers for high availability and security; migrating de and domain accounts; transferring and updating account settings and policies; piloting, testing, a rolling out servers; and preparing to automate server administration.

To learn more about the full line of Microsoft Press® products for IT professionals, please vis

microsoft.com/mspress/IT

Get a **Free**
e-mail newsletter, updates,
special offers, links to related books,
and more when you

register on line!

Register your Microsoft Press® title on our Web site and you'll get
a FREE subscription to our e-mail newsletter, *Microsoft Press Book
Connections.* You'll find out about newly released and upcoming books
and learning tools, online events, software downloads, special offers
and coupons for Microsoft Press customers, and information about
major Microsoft® product releases. You can also read useful additional
information about all the titles we publish, such as detailed book descriptions, tables of contents and indexes, sample chapters, links to
related books and book series, author biographies, and reviews by
other customers.

Registration is easy. Just visit this Web pag
and fill in your information:

http://www.microsoft.com/mspress/register

Microsoft®

- -

Proof of Purchase

Use this page as proof of purchase if participating in a promotion or rebate offer
this title. Proof of purchase must be used in conjunction with other proof(s) o
payment such as your dated sales receipt—see offer details.

Microsoft® IIS 6.0 Administrator's Pocket Consultant
0-7356-1560-8

CUSTOMER NAME

Microsoft Press, PO Box 97017, Redmond, WA 98073-9830